T0365398

PRESIDIO OF SAN FRANCISCO

PRESIDIO OF SAN FRANCISCO

POST CLOSURE

BOBBY BILL

authorHOUSE®

AuthorHouse™ LLC
1663 Liberty Drive
Bloomington, IN 47403
www.authorhouse.com
Phone: 1-800-839-8640

© 2014 Bobby Bill. All rights reserved.

No part of this book may be reproduced, stored in a retrieval system, or transmitted
by any means without the written permission of the author.

Published by AuthorHouse   03/24/2014

ISBN: 978-1-4918-9941-0 (sc)
ISBN: 978-1-4918-9940-3 (e)

Any people depicted in stock imagery provided by Thinkstock are models,
and such images are being used for illustrative purposes only.
Certain stock imagery © Thinkstock.

This book is printed on acid-free paper.

Because of the dynamic nature of the Internet, any web addresses or links contained in
this book may have changed since publication and may no longer be valid. The views
expressed in this work are solely those of the author and do not necessarily reflect the views
of the publisher, and the publisher hereby disclaims any responsibility for them.

Approved by the Department of the Army (DA) for public release. The opinions
expressed are those of the author and do not necessarily reflect the views of the
United States Army, Department of Defense, or United States government.

PRESIDIO OF SAN FRANCISCO
POST CLOSURE

by

Dr Robert William Curtis, DBA in Management
Chief Master Sergeant, USAF Ret

The Presidio of San Francisco Closure Study began after the controversial Base Closure and Realignment Act of 1988 (BRAC 88) was enacted and placed the Presidio of San Francisco on the BRAC 88 Base Closure list. The required Presidio of San Francisco Closure Study, prepared by the Headquarters, Sixth US Army staff, tried to justify the continuance of the Presidio Post. This study continued for several years but eventually was ineffective bowing to political and military pressure and interference.

This Case Study complements the Presidio of San Francisco Closure Study that overlaps the same time period that planned and programmed a systematic process where both management theory and assumptions could be applied to justify improvements in management competence, organizational improvements, and cost effectiveness. This caused an administrative dilemma while concurrently, trying to plan the realignment of the Headquarters, Sixth US Army staff; discontinuance of the Presidio Garrison; closing the Presidio of San Francisco as a US Army military Installation; and transferring the Presidio Post operations, repair, and maintenance activities to the US National Park Service. Chapter II and Chapters IX through XIII of this Case Study address the goal and objectives that may have justified the prevention of the Presidio of San Francisco closure.

This Case Study contains a chronological history of events at the Presidio of San Francisco, and reviews a crisis precipitated by the Department of Defense (DOD) action under a Congressional mandate for Post and Base closures. The Presidio Post fell under this mandate when it was ordered to realign the Headquarters, Sixth US Army; discontinue the Presidio Garrison; close the Presidio Post as a historic US Army military Installation; and transfer the Presidio of San Francisco to the US National Park Service. Six other California military Post and Base closures are included in Chapters III through VIII of this Case Study for cross-comparison with the Presidio of San Francisco closure, and the validity of Congressional Post and Base closure criteria.

This Case Study analyzes and reviews political pressures where administrative decisions were made to discontinue the Presidio of San Francisco, and try to determine whether the Presidio Post closure was successful in realizing the goal and objectives of the Congressional Act. That is, was the actual Presidio Post closure based on political decisions regardless of the input of, or socioeconomic impact on local military and civil authorities?

This Case Study addresses socioeconomic and political implications associated with the Base Closure and Realignment Act of 1988. The main thrust of this Act was to test the efficacy of the DOD and its ability to manage sweeping changes after 1988. That is, the degree that the DOD could implement efficiency and effectiveness in realigning single-mission operations at a Post or Base to a multiple-use Post or Base.

This Case Study examines the policy innovations that were implemented to enhance clean-up while closing Posts and Bases in California, and considers their application to other aspects of the DOD's programs and the National discussion regarding hazardous waste removal policy.

Finally, this Case Study endeavors to identify the results that the DOD and the DA eventually accomplished, and analyzes the outcome in terms of socioeconomic and functional reality that affected State and City economies in California. That is, the significance of a major crisis frequently precipitated by decisions based on socioeconomic and political pressure that may have resulted in some dysfunctional administrative choices. To understand the differences in terminology, the Presidio of San Francisco is a "Post" and not a "Base" as referred to in Base Closure legislation that includes all military Installations:

- The word "Base" succeeds the name of an Air Force Installation such as Mather Air Force Base in California, and precedes Base support facilities such as Base Exchange;

- The word "Fort" precedes the name of a US Army Installation such as the Fort Ord in California, and precedes Post support facilities such as Post Exchange;

- The military Installation includes all of the military organizations stationed at the Presidio of San Francisco such as the Headquarters, Sixth US Army staff, Presidio Garrison, tenant units, and support facilities such as the Post Exchange;

- The Spanish word "Presidio" is synonymous to a Garrison. Therefore, the original name "Presidio of San Francisco" remained the name of the Presidio Post rather than being renamed after some retired, distinguished US Army General Officer.

The differences in organizations and missions at two different US Army and five US Air Force Installations; and the distinguishing usage of "Fort," "Post," and "Base" are consistently differentiated within this Case Study. The differences in terminology occurred when the US Army Air Corps became the US Air Force during 1947, and the US Air Force desired to use their own identity apart from the US Army. For example, the US Army has Soldiers and the US Air Force now has Airmen regardless of identical Military Occupation Specialties (MOS).

Chapter XI

Chapter XII

Chapter XIII

Appendixes

ACKNOWLEDGEMENTS

I am deeply indebted to Dr Otto Butz, Dean, Golden Gate University, San Francisco, California, for his inspiration and encouragement to publish this book while a doctoral student at San Francisco in the subject area, and for his friendship and intellectual support. Personnel of the Office of Deputy Chief of Staff Personnel, Headquarters, Sixth US Army provided substantial encouragement and assistance, and significant contributions to the development of the material on the interpretation of Congressional, Department of Defense (DOD), and Department of the Army (DA) organizational goals, objectives, management practices and policies. A specific note of appreciation to my wife, Donna J. Curtis, who proofread and commented on innumerable drafts. Finally, this book is dedicated to my mother, Mrs. Wilhelmina Marie (Serrie) Curtis, born in Amsterdam, Netherlands, 11 January 1898, who was always my life's inspiration.

ABBREVIATIONS

Airport Improvement Program (AIP)
Armed Forces Reserve Center (AFAC)
Army Aviation Support Facility (AASF)
Base Closure and Realignment Act (BRAC)
BRAC Cleanup Team (BCT)
California Army National Guard (CAARNG)
California Aviation Classification Repair Depot (AVCRAD)
California State University (CSU)
California Economic Diversification and Revitalization (CEDAR)
Department of the Army (DA)
Department of Defense (DOD)
Environmental Protection Agency (EPA)
Economic Development Conveyance (EDC)
Explanation of Significant Difference (ESD)
Federal Aviation Administration (FAA)
Federal Facilities Site Remediation Agreement (FFSRA)
Federal Personnel Manual (FPM)
General Services Administration (GSA)
Gross National Product (GNP)
Installation Restoration Program (IRP)
Management by Objectives (MBO)
Major United States Army Reserve Command (MUSARC)
Military Airport Program (MAP)
National Aeronautics and Space Administration (NASA)
National Association of Government Employees (NAGE)
National Council of Technical Service Industries (NCTSI)
National Priorities List (NPL)
Office of Management and Budget (OMB)
Operable Unit (OU)
Office of Military Base Retention and Reuse (OMBARR)
Office of Personnel Management (OPM)
Operations Research (OR)
Organizational Development (OD)
Planning-Programming-Budgeting (PPB)
Presidio of San Francisco (Presidio)
Presidio Yacht Club (PYC)
Priority Placement Program (PPP)
Program Requirement Document (PRD)
Record of Decisions (ROD)
Reduction-in-Force (RIF)
Regional Technology Alliances (RTA)

Remedial Investigation and Feasibility Study (RI/FS)
Request for Proposal (RFP)
Restoration Advisory Board (RAB)
Sacramento Area Commission on Mather Conversion (SACOM-C)
Unexploded Ordnance (UXO)
United States (US)
Volatile Organic Compound (VOC)
Voluntary Early Retirement Authority (VERA)

CHAPTER I

Introduction

The Presidio of San Francisco was the oldest and continuously occupied military Post in the US. The Presidio Post had been dedicated to, and served as an integral part of, the military service and cultural history of three Nations; Spain, Mexico, and the US. The Presidio Post had long been looked upon with pride by military personnel and the City of San Francisco for its beauty and military tradition. The Presidio Post stood as an example of how a military Post could exist in harmony with a civilian community within a major metropolitan area. The citizens of San Francisco, while respecting the military mission at the Presidio Post, looked upon it as their Post and one of the most beautiful Sites in the City of San Francisco, and treasured its tree covered hills and scenic beauty. While it's true that the Presidio Post would continue as part of the Golden Gate National Recreational Area after the Headquarters, Sixth US Army staff and the Presidio Garrison discontinuance, the relationship between the City of San Francisco and the US Army that had developed over many years would be lost. During those times when the US Army and the civilian population seemed to have less and less directed contact with and understanding of each other, they could ill afford to lose this close relationship.

The Presidio of San Francisco closure was predictable when the Congressional Base Closure and Realignment Act (BRAC 88) was enacted. Implementation promulgated the preparation of a highly controversial Presidio of San Francisco Closure and Realignment Study that continued for several years. The Study was conducted by the Headquarters, Sixth US Army staff to determine whether the Presidio Post was cost effective or even required as a US Army Installation according to closure criteria.

During May 1988, the US Congress and the Department of Defense (DOD) had initiated a major attempt to reduce defense spending efforts by closing and realigning military Posts and Bases. The Secretary of Defense chartered a Commission to recommend military Posts and Bases that could be closed or realigned; and the US Congress established legislation requirements for the Commission. The DOD Commission recommended the closure of 86 military Posts and Bases, partial closure of five military Posts and Bases, and the realignment of 54 military Posts and Bases.

The mandate to discontinue the Headquarters, Sixth US Army staff and the Presidio Garrison; reassign military personnel and Civil Service employees to other military Installations; and transfer the Presidio of San Francisco to the US National Park Service (NPS), was one of the first military Installations to be tested and implemented under the purview of this Congressional Act. The closure of the Presidio of San Francisco was finally realized as a result of a Department of Defense (DOD) directive, under a Congressional mandate, that initiated the transfer of the Presidio of San Francisco repair and maintenance mission to the US National Park Service.

During January 1990, the Office of the Secretary of Defense (OSD) and the US Congress accepted all of the Commission's recommendations. The Secretary unilaterally proposed the closure of 35 military Posts and Bases, and the realignment or reduction of military personnel at more than 20 military Posts and Bases as a result of the shrinking Defense budget. However, the OSD did not provide specific written guidance to DOD and military Installations on how to evaluate military Posts and Bases for possible closure or realignment. The military Installations consequently used different processes, none that were as well documented and comprehensive following the 1988 DOD Commission.

During 1990, lesser known but probably the most direct adverse impact of the Presidio of San Francisco closure was the realignment of the Letterman Army Medical Center and the Oakland Naval Medical Center at Oak Knoll. During 1995, the US Army Reserve mission was realigned to Atlanta in Georgia, and the Letterman US Army Institute of Research was realigned to other US Army Medical Research Centers at Fort Sam Houston and Brooks AFB both in Texas, and Bethesda in Maryland.

Disabled veterans from the North and South of the City of San Francisco and Bay Area who had been transported by Veterans Services Officers to Letterman Army Medical Center for basic medical care received very little notice and no alternative means of medical support. The disabled veterans were in fact suddenly left without medical benefits. Initially, it was thought that Federal, State, and City Government agencies would be given use of the Presidio of San Francisco facilities. During 1994, a Federal Government takeover was also possible. However the Presidio of San Francisco was mandated to transfer to the US National Park Service. Unlike the complete takeover of the Presidio of San Francisco property by the US National Park Service, the State of California and some City Governments took accepted military Installation property, as was the case at the Fort Ord Post, George AFB, Norton AFB, Beale AFB, Castle AFB, and Mather AFB all in California.

During 1994, after several years of exhaustive organization and manpower planning and programming, the Presidio of San Francisco Realignment and Closure Study was discarded, and finally resulted in the title transfer of the Presidio of San Francisco to the Department of the Interior's US National Park Service. The contents of this Case Study; therefore, attempts to determine whether the Headquarters, Sixth US Army's goal and objectives to fulfill planned management actions, that could have transferred a dozen Federal Government agencies from the high rent San Francisco and Bay Area to the Presidio Post, were seriously considered or realized that could have deferred the Presidio Post closure.

The Presidio of San Francisco Closure and Realignment Study could have been considered the reverse side of National Defense issues that test military Post and Base closure or realignment possibilities. The Study became a systematic process where management theory and assumptions were applied to a military Installation that tried to fulfill the goal and objectives to justify organizational improvement, competence, and effectiveness. Sorrowfully, the Presidio of San Francisco Closure and Realignment Study fell into disuse and became an administrative expedient for the US Army to show monetary savings above all other tangible results. In essence, the actual outcome appeared to be based on high-level military and civilian political decisions that disregarded most of the rational anti-closure discussions.

Concerned over the Secretary's 1988 proposals, the US Congress passed the Defense Base Closure and Realignment Act of 1990 (PL 101-510) halting military Post and Base closures based on the January list, and required new procedures for closing or realigning military Posts and Bases. The Act created the independent Defense Base Closure and Realignment Commission, and established procedures for the President, the DOD, and the General Accounting Office (GAO) to implement, and required that military Posts and Bases be compared equally against selection criteria developed by the DOD and a Force Structure Plan for the following six-years.[1]

The Federal Government was going to close and realign military Posts and Bases in an effort to downsize and restructure its Force Structure to reduce Defense spending. On March 12, 1992, the DOD recommended 165 military Post and Base closures, realignments, and other actions that would affect military Posts and Bases within the US. Recommendations were submitted to the Defense Base Closure and Realignment Commission who considered them as they developed its list of proposed military Post and Base closures and realignments for Presidential and Congressional approval. As for the Presidio of San Francisco closure, a determination was made that a savings of $2.5 million could be realized in lease costs annually, assuming a dozen nearby Federal Government agencies in the City of San Francisco and Bay Area would be realigned to the Presidio Post. Concurrently, different State agencies and the City of San Francisco were demanding that the DOD continue to maintain military organizations at the Presidio Post for socioeconomic reasons. At the very least, the City of San Francisco wanted to have Presidio Post property for its own use but neither occurred. Instead the Presidio Post property was transferred to the US National Park Service.

---

[1] Charles A. Bowsher, Comptroller General of the US, "Military Bases, Analysis of DOD's Recommendations and Selection Process for Closures and Realignments." (GAO, Washington, DC, April 15, 1993), p. 10.

During 1995, following the rejected results of the Presidio of San Francisco Closure and Realignment Study, this author started to prepare a Case Study summarizing the events that underlined the Presidio of San Francisco closure by researching, investigating, and documenting historical events concentrating on the political and human interventions of the Presidio Post closure. The initial goal to realign the Headquarters, Sixth US Army staff to Treasure Island in California was later changed to Fort Carson in Colorado.

However, instead of the possible realignment of the Headquarters Sixth US Army staff to Fort Carson in Colorado, the discontinuance of the Headquarters, Sixth US Army staff and the Presidio Garrison; reassignment of military personnel and Civil Service employees to other military Installations; and the transfer of the Presidio of San Francisco to the US National Park Service was becoming a reality and on the horizon.

The estimated BRAC 88 savings were more than $700 million yearly. The Presidio of San Francisco; however, got a reprieve until 1993. The Post and Base closure process for 1991 added new checkpoints from previous iterations to further distance politics. The City of San Francisco officials were allowed a chance to defend the Presidio of San Francisco closure, and argue BRAC intervention from a socioeconomic position. BRAC Chair James Courter expanded the on-Site part of the BRAC process.[2]

For comparison with the Presidio of San Francisco closure decision, and for Congressional comprehension and validity of Post and Base criteria, this Case Study includes the Fort Ord Post closure in California; George AFB and Norton AFB both located at Riverside County inland of Los Angles; Beale AFB located eight miles East of Marysville in California; Castle AFB and Mather AFB near Sacramento in California. All of these six closed military Installations that are investigated in this Case Study did compare with the similarities of the Presidio of San Francisco closure decision, and explains that conclusions did agree with, and emphasizes that the political and socioeconomic principles involved in the closure process were identical with the Presidio of San Francisco closure. Chapters III through VIII also include civilian re-use options that were considered after the six California military Posts and Bases were closed by BRAC intervention. All of these six "training" Post and Base closures include examples of re-use policy and procedures used by communities after Post and Base closures, and give a review of their community involvement in civilian re-use policies, procedures, and socioeconomic results after Post and Base closures.

This Case Study investigation reviews and analyzes political pressures where management decisions were made and implemented; and endeavors to determine whether the Presidio of San Francisco closure was successful in accomplishing

---

[2]   David S. Sorenson, "Shutting Down The Cold War: The Politics of Military Base Closure." (St. Martin's PR, New York, July 1998), pp. 92-97.

the goal and objectives of the Congressional Act. The conclusions portray a new thrust in DOD management practices that would affect future military Post and Base closures. The conclusions document a major crisis that occurred during the operation, repair, and maintenance facilities of the Presidio of San Francisco while concurrently, planning and programming the possibilities of consolidation, realignment, or discontinuance of the Headquarters, Sixth US Army staff and the Presidio Garrison; the reassignment of military personnel and Civil Service employees to other military Installations; and the transfer of the Presidio of San Francisco to the US National Park Service.

This Case Study addresses the socioeconomic and political implications associated with the Base Closure and Realignment Act of 1988. The problems that faced the DOD would determine whether or not they could accomplish management actions to achieve the goal and objectives of military personnel and Civil Service employee reassignments, while attrition of military personnel and Civil Service employees were being realized. Also, management decisions influenced by the Act would have to be seriously considered in light of their socioeconomic impact on local communities. After 1988, the primary thrust of this Act was to test the efficacy of the DOD and its ability to manage sweeping changes. That is, the degree that the DOD could implement efficiency and effectiveness by realigning single-mission administrative operations or training of an active military Installation to a multiple-use Post or Base was going to be seriously tested.

This Case Study examines policy innovations that were implemented to enhance clean-up while closing military Posts and Bases in California, and considered their application to other aspects of DOD programs and National discussions regarding hazardous waste policies. The findings identify specific problems relating to this Act, and try to explain why the DOD adopted a change in strategy. In the final analysis, this Case Study identifies results that the DOD discovered, and analyzes the outcome in terms of socioeconomic and functional reality. That is, the significance of a major crisis, precipitated by decisions based on socioeconomic and political pressures that could have resulted in dysfunctional administrative choices affecting the Presidio of San Francisco closure.

This Case Study provides a framework where all parties involved would examine comparable actions with full participation. During 1988, the framework ensured that full disclosure of the facts and intentions of the Presidio of San Francisco closure were important and disclosed after the Presidio Post had received a political reprieve after the announced Presidio Post closure. The rationale for the comparison of closure validity for the six Post and Base closures at the Fort Ord Post, George AFB, Norton AFB, Beale AFB, Castle AFB, and Mather AFB are intensely discussed in Chapters III through VIII.

Presidio of San Francisco Closure Rational

The Base Closure and Realignment Act of 1988 had a detrimental impact on California Posts and Bases with single mission training operations or administrative missions such as the Presidio of San Francisco. Upon notification of the possible Presidio of San Francisco closure and realignment of all military tenant organizations stationed at the Presidio of San Francisco, the Headquarters, Sixth US Army staff and the "Save the Presidio" Committee sponsored by the City of San Francisco formed a coalition vowed to oppose the Headquarters, Sixth US Army staff realignment to Treasure Island; the Presidio Garrison discontinuance; and the transfer of the Presidio Post facilities to the US National Park Service. The Office of Manpower and Budget (OMB) had planned to turn over repair and maintenance support performed by Civil Service employees at the Presidio Post to private contractor operations. Likewise, the Headquarters, Sixth US Army staff and the "Save the Presidio" Committee had proposed to realign Federal agencies located in the City of San Francisco and Bay Area to the Presidio Post rather than realign the Headquarters, Sixth US Army to Treasure Island and discontinue the Presidio Garrison. Both sides of the coalition were organized to resist the DOD plan represented by the Base Closure and Realignment Study of 1988, and OMB's desire to convert all Civil Service positions at the Presidio Post to private contractor operations. In addition, military personnel and Civil Service employees stationed at the Presidio Post were staunchly opposed to any action that would terminate their positions.

The Headquarters, Sixth US Army staff and the Presidio Garrison were proud military organizations that had a long history in an area steeped in military tradition in concert with the public population. However, the original consolidated reorganization of the Headquarters, Sixth US Army staff with the Presidio Garrison was not approved. The remains of the 200-year old historic Presidio of San Francisco would be preserved and still accessible to the public. This at least was an important and viable result of the political process that took place after the discontinuance of the Headquarters, Sixth US Army staff and the Presidio Garrison. The component question in presenting the arguments for the possible prevention of the Presidio Post closure was at issue. However, due to misleading publicity at the beginning of the Presidio Post closure process, the full impact of an aroused public had not begun to surface. The Electorates of the City of San Francisco did not understand that consideration was being given to the removal of a 200-year old military Installation for the sake of what San Francisco's late Mayor Moscone termed "false economy."

The Headquarters, Sixth US Army Executive Board examined the effects of those actions that embodied total system changes. In the political arena, more problems compounded the issues because BRAC legislation was eroded with the purpose to find economies in the military budget by closing military Installations in California; and reassigning military personnel and Civil Service employees; and equipment resources to the US National Park Service. During 1994, one of the first military Installations considered for Post closure was the Presidio of San Francisco, with the concurrent Headquarters, Sixth US Army realignment to Treasure Island in California that was later reprogrammed to Fort Carson in Colorado. Along the same lines, the US Army Reserve mission and functions were being transferred from the Headquarters, Sixth US Army at the Presidio Post to the newly established US Army Reserve Command at Atlanta in Georgia. During 1995, the repair and maintenance mission was transferred from the Presidio Post to the US National Park Service, with the concurrent discontinuance of the Headquarters, Sixth US Army staff and the Presidio Garrison. These actions to include the closing of the Fort Ord Post, George AFB, Norton AFB, Beale AFB, Castle AFB, and Mather AFB would have a far-reaching impact on a number of critical socioeconomic functions in California communities.

Although the DOD had planned to convert repair and maintenance activities of the Presidio Garrison to private contractor usage to increase revenues, the Presidio of San Francisco would eventually by law, would be transferred to the US National Park Service. Even though there was a local outcry against the conversion, in the final analysis, the goal and objectives of BRAC were obviously not accomplished as intended. The importance of this analysis had its greatest significance that many other California Post and Base closures were to follow with essentially the same political problems. Retrospectively, much can be learned by considering what might have been the final outcome if additional management approaches had been fully investigated or implemented such as the transfer of Federal agencies in the City of San Francisco and Bay Area to the Presidio Post.

Presidio of San Francisco Goal and Objectives

The Headquarters, Sixth US Army's final goal and objective was to achieve economy of operations through the possible realignment of Federal agencies in the City of San Francisco and Bay Area geographic area to the Presidio of San Francisco as a planned management action. This could have occurred with little or no further consideration if there had been no strong local objections to the Presidio of San Francisco closure. The problem of presenting valid arguments against the Presidio Post closure had been a concern to the Headquarters, Sixth US Army staff and the City of San Francisco for a number of years. In terms of delaying the Presidio Post closure and preventing a logical and smooth transition of the mission and functions of military personnel and Civil Service employees, they were successful.

How could resistance to change at the Presidio of San Francisco be replaced with the cooperation by managers, supervisors, military personnel, Civil Service employees, and employee Unions and still comply with the Presidio of San Francisco Closure and Realignment Study? Therefore, the goal of this Case Study was not to postulate that a specific, more desirable solution should have been implemented to what proved to be a multi-faceted problem, but rather to identify valid arguments and concerns that were made on both sides. The analysis may be useful as an object lesson to guide future policy decisions relating to similar consolidations, realignments, or closure efforts.

The underlying theme of this Case Study was that rational thought and behavior on both sides may have contributed to a successful solution more than any other specific method for bringing about the desired results as the case with any controversy of this magnitude. Therefore, there seemingly never was a meeting of the minds or attempts to come to a compromise. As a result, management decisions were apparently made more as a natural outcome of the political process rather than from any objective analysis of the final effects of closing the Presidio of San Francisco.

Was it possible for the DOD to implement the basic principles of BRAC? For example, to bring about efficiency and effectiveness by realigning single mission administrative or training operations at a military Installation? That question actually remains unanswered because the original Presidio of San Francisco Closure and Realignment Study was never fully implemented. The goal and objectives of the legislation was to implement a course of action in such a way as to reach the goal and objectives of sound socioeconomic and personnel management and at the same time soften the blow of the Presidio of San Francisco closure by allowing for attrition and reassignment of military personnel and Civil Service employees.

The City of San Francisco's Mayor Moscone lobbied with Federal Government agencies in Washington, DC to maintain the Presidio of San Francisco as a military Installation based on sound socioeconomic justification. Arguments by the Headquarters, Sixth US Army staff and the City of San Francisco officials were driven by possible improved utilization of the Presidio Post by enhancing operating functions. It was argued that this would be more efficient and cost effective than the Presidio of San Francisco closure. Was the US Congress justified in seemingly creating better economies of operation by closing the Presidio Post and transferring the Headquarters, Sixth US Army staff to another military Post? Were the plans first offered by the OMB, the DOD, and the City of San Francisco feasible, and would they ever have met the original goal and objectives of the US Congress? By turning the Presidio Post over to the US National Park Service, would the actions achieve the same budgetary and program efficiency outcome as compared to earlier proposals to allow private contractors to use the facility? Finally, was the actual outcome in reality the only feasible solution at that time?

Mayor Moscone requested public support to create the "Save the Presidio" Committee during this historic time period. When the Committee was established, the Committee engaged Economics Research Associates to prepare a proposal for consulting services related to the socioeconomic impact and implications of the proposed Headquarters, Sixth US Army realignment to Treasure Island in California during 1994; the discontinuance of the Presidio Garrison; the transfer of Presidio of San Francisco mission and functions to the US National Park Service during 1995; the Letterman Army Medical Center realignment; and the Letterman Army Institute of Research realignment. The Committee further engaged Touche Ross & Company to assist the City of San Francisco officials in its negotiations with the DOD.

To further add to the political confusion and controversy, Lieutenant General Eugene P. Forrester, Commanding General, Sixth US Army, was against the Presidio of San Francisco closure by arguing through military channels that the Presidio of San Francisco should remain a US Army Installation; and that it would be more efficient to transfer Federal Government agencies in the San Francisco and Bay Area to the Presidio Post where more than ample building space and support facilities were readily available for use. Due to the unforeseen controversial effect of trying to reach this goal and objectives, a decidedly different outcome resulted. That was the profound and organized local community effort to also defeat the Presidio of San Francisco closure.

By examining the account of a major crisis precipitated by the initial DOD decision to realign the Headquarters, Sixth US Army staff, it was hoped that other approaches would be considered in assembling a change model for future initiatives. Therefore, this Case Study has endeavored to review the political pressures where bureaucratic administrative decisions were in fact made to originally realign the Headquarters, Sixth US Army staff contingent to Fort Carson in Colorado instead of Treasure Island in California, and eventually to its discontinuance. During the data acquisition phase for preparing this Case Study, many organizational methods were investigated.

A review of all pertinent correspondence, newspaper articles, literature, and a behavioral questionnaire were examined and prepared in a logical sequence. A review and analysis of management principles, practices, and procedures were made where appropriate. In particular, the OMB's proposed multi-functional management approach and the opposition to it, along with various counter proposals were analyzed. The basic importance to the eventual outcome of the Presidio of San Francisco closure was that the management proposals were never evaluated for effectiveness, nor analyzed to ascertain if the cost benefit assumptions were accurate. Instead, because of the political impact on military personnel and Civil Service employees, the debate centered on this aspect of Post or Base closure, and whether or not military personnel would be transferred to other military Installations, and Civil Service positions transferred from the public to the private sector. The emphasis became prevalent rather than there being an assessment of whether or not the positions themselves or even the overall mission and functions, and performed tasks were necessary This Case Study was bounded by the military personnel and Civil Service employee interface with the problems associated with the Presidio of San Francisco Closure and Realignment Study. The boundaries of this Case Study provided questions and answers as to why the Presidio Post was finally closed after many-years of opposition. As this

Case Study was written many years after the Presidio of San Francisco closure was initiated, the author has not had access to all the subsequent events and contributions since the actual Presidio Post closure. This Case Study is limited, therefore, to documenting the central theme of that history and an analysis of how different approaches could be utilized in future such actions. The challenge of writing a Case Study such as the Presidio Post closure was to present analytical research while continuing to keep the central theme of chronologically organizing historical events as an example of following the Base Closure and Realignment Act of 1988. The organization of this Case Study was developed largely on the amount of public and official information available under the Freedom of Information Act.

The thrust of this Case Study was devoted to the findings in a manner to maintain objectivity. However, it should be noted that the author is a retired US Air Force Chief Master Sergeant and served for many years as a Civil Service Human Resource Officer, advisor and consultant, serving in this capacity at the Presidio of San Francisco to General Forrester at the time of the Presidio Post closure. Nevertheless, because of the author's history of serving dual roles as both a member of the military service and as a manager in the Federal Government, the experience has actually facilitated an ability to maintain objectivity in analyzing the sequence of events. As a doctoral student of political science and business management, this author was taught that the desire and necessity of seeking methods to curtail excessive expenditures in military organizations was fundamental under current enlightened management theory. In other words, during an era where excessive military expenditures were under a microscope and making political headlines, some form of management action either by the US Congress or by the Federal Government was inevitable.

The immediate and adverse reaction by an effected local economy and the self-Preservationist military was also inevitable. What was singularly important to this author while writing this Case Study was to objectively portray those reactions to show that the initial planned management on the part of the Federal Government oversight institution (OMB) was obviously impractical and shortsighted in terms of meeting the goal and objectives of the BRAC legislation. However, the often passionate and somewhat short-sighted reaction of the political and military officials was also evidently ineffective as the Presidio of San Francisco was transferred to the US National Park Service anyway. Furthermore, as both sides of the political and military officials somewhat refused to work together in an attempt to compromise, there were no other solutions offered to propose or support. Therefore, this author need not nor did not take sides regarding either the wisdom of the Presidio of San Francisco Closure and Realignment Study or its impact on the local economy as in reality neither side won or lost. The process information has been included where it assists the reader to understand the most important part of the Presidio Post transfer to the US National Park Service. The political and military officials made an effort to take politics out of the Presidio Post closure, and then turned around and made that reality impossible.

Even if this author would have had access to other correspondence, telephone calls, or other unpublished information that might have added to the significant events and contributions, this author believes such information would not add or change significantly to the summary of the Presidio of San Francisco closure. Therefore, the history that has been documented in the hope that the many significant events and persons involved who were not mentioned would not be offended by its incompleteness. To quote another author: "I detail what I consider a fascinating effort on the part of a myriad of political actors to fight the battles over Post and Base closures, with all the heat and passion that normally accompanies a high-stakes political alleged wrong doing, but to analyze what happened and try to explain why."[3] Finally, this Case Study provides the precise meaning of significance as to the issue. The purpose of this therefore was not to look under rocks for scandal or to point a finger at political reasons why the Presidio of San Francisco was finally closed. The definitions include the intentions of this author as determined by the outline, extent, and delimitations.

Overview of Remaining Chapters

Chapter II: This chapter introduces the Presidio San Francisco closure and compares the Presidio Post closure issues for validity with the Fort Ord Post, George AFB, Norton AFB, Beale AFB, Castle AFB, and Mather AFB Installations. It analyzes theories underlying the purpose of military Post and Base closures. For example, assuming cost savings could have been realized with changes in Personnel Management, and if these changes could have yielded an increase in productivity. In the case of the Presidio of San Francisco closure, the proposed realignment from public to private contract employment is discussed as were attempts to define other inherent problems and cost saving measures. Alternative realignment proposals and the effect on other military and Federal agencies, and other military Installations in the City of San Francisco and Bay Area, as well as potential realignment areas are portrayed along with the impact of public discussions in the thinking of the citizenry at large.

This investigation concludes with an analysis of the effects of the Presidio San Francisco closure in ancillary health services and the involvement of local citizen groups, officials, and consultants from a business standpoint. This author's conclusions summarize these events. They review the historical events and related literature offered as historical perspective of the problems, and current knowledge related to the problem and information that relate specifically to each of the questions posed. Direct quotes are used concerning the Presidio of San Francisco closure to support the credibility that further investigation would yield information of value to the area of interest.

---

[3]   David S. Sorenson, "Shutting Down The Cold War: The Politics of Military Base Closure." (St. Martin's Press, New York, July 1998), p. 5.

Chapter III: This chapter introduces the Fort Ord Post closure and compares Post closure issues with the Presidio of San Francisco closure. Direct quotes are used in this Chapter concerning the Fort Ord Post closure to support the credibility that further investigation would yield information of value to the area of interest.

Chapter IV: This chapter introduces the George AFB closure and compares Base closure issues with the Presidio of San Francisco and the Fort Ord Post closures. Direct quotes are used in Chapter IV concerning the George AFB closure to support the credibility that further investigation would yield information of value to the area of interest.

Chapter V: This chapter introduces the Norton AFB closure and compares Base closure issues with the Presidio of San Francisco, the Fort Ord Post, and George AFB closures. Direct quotes are used in Chapter V concerning the Norton AFB closure to support the credibility that further investigation would yield information of value to the area of interest.

Chapter VI: This chapter introduces the Beale AFB closure and compares Base closure issues with the Presidio of San Francisco, the Fort Ord Post, George AFB, and Norton AFB closures. Direct quotes are used in Chapter VII concerning the Beale AFB closure to support the credibility that further investigation would yield information of value to the area of interest.

Chapter VII: This chapter introduces the Castle AFB closure and compares Base closure issues with the Presidio of San Francisco, the Fort Ord Post, George AFB, Norton AFB, and Beale AFB closures. Direct quotes are used in Chapter VII concerning the Castle AFB closure to support the credibility that further investigation would yield information of value to the area of interest.

Chapter VIII: This chapter introduces the Mather AFB closure and compares Base closure issues with the Presidio of San Francisco, the Fort Ord Post, George AFB, Norton AFB, Beale AFB, and Castle AFB closures. Direct quotes are used in Chapter VIII concerning the Mather AFB closure to support the credibility that further investigation would yield information of value to the area of interest.

Chapter IX: This chapter assesses the impact on the proposal to close the Presidio of San Francisco. The vulnerability of an alternative realignment of the Headquarters, Sixth US Army staff to Treasure Island in California is described. Research into Federal Personnel Management policies developed a behavioral questionnaire; it was given to a group of selected personnel in the Headquarters, Sixth US Army staff to analyze management policies in effect during the Presidio Post closure. This author's concluding remarks in this investigation involve a discussion of legal decisions regarding the use of contract employees to replace and perform similar work of Civil Service employees.

Chapter X: This chapter discusses and summarizes conclusions of the basic components in this investigation to include the thoughts of those responding to the Personnel and Behavioral Study. It discusses earthquake survivability with the Presidio Post and Treasure Island conclusions and recommendations.

Chapter XI: This chapter outlines several findings in connection with the research investigation, and presents arguments both for and against the Presidio of San Francisco closure.

Chapter XII: This chapter outlines the Personnel Management impact on military personnel and Civil Service employees, and the socioeconomic impact of the San Francisco and Bay Area community after the Presidio of San Francisco closure.

Chapter XII: This chapter presents conclusions of the Presidio of San Francisco closure based on findings, and provides recommendations for further research study. This investigation summarizes what happened and what could have happened to economically prevent the Presidio Post closure. Finally, this investigation summarizing the socioeconomic events that have happened after the discontinuance of the Headquarters, Sixth US Army staff and the Presidio Garrison.

CHAPTER II

History of the Presidio of San Francisco

The Presidio of San Francisco was originally named El Presidio Real de San Francisco; that translates: "The Royal Fortress of Saint Francis." The Presidio Post was located on the Northern most tip of the San Francisco Peninsula at the City of San Francisco in California. The Presidio Post is now a National Park and a part of the Golden Gate National Recreation Area. The Presidio Post was recognized as a California Historical Landmark during 1933 and as a National Historic Landmark during 1962.

The Presidio of San Francisco's coat of arms has an interesting origin. The two Castles derived from the old Spanish kingdom of Castile, so-called from its number of frontier Castles. The rampant lions were derived from the symbol of the ancient Christian kingdom of Leon; that is. West of Old Castile on the peninsula. During various periods of Spanish history, these two kingdoms were separated and reunited, finally joining together during the time of Ferdinand III and Isabella in the late 15th Century. The so-called "supporter" of the shield is the double headed eagle of the Hapsburg, the royal house of Austria that for many years also ruled the Spanish throne. The order suspended from the shield is the collar of the Order of the Golden Fleece. The Grand Master group was the Chief of the House of Hapsburg; that is, the King. The crown was of two arches until 1554, when King Charles I of Spain was on the throne. During this period, his son married Mary, Queen of England and as a result, two more arches were added. The Spanish Crown was then four arches surmounted by the royal orb and cross of the Christian King with eight strawberry leaves. During 1822, these were the royal arms that appeared on the Spanish National flag with minor variations from 1554 to the end of the Spanish occupation of California.

The 200-year old history of the Presidio of San Francisco outlined a chronicle record of historical events of the life and development of a people and of a Country. During 1776, while American colonies on the Atlantic Coast were putting into effect the Declaration of Independence, the Spanish rulers of Mexico sent exploring parties Northward along the California Coast to establish missions and military Posts, and settling land for Spain. The Northern most of these military Posts was the Presidio of San Francisco. At a point that is now the center of the main Presidio Post, the Spaniards laid out their "Presidio;" that translates: "Garrison" or "Fortified Camp." The original Presidio of San Francisco was a fortified Camp previously claimed in the name of the King that is approximately 100-yards square surrounded by a palisade type wall. During 2004, the old quadrangle was marked by bronze plaques placed there by the Daughters of the American Revolution. During 1822, the Presidio Post continued to be used by the

Spanish military until it was taken over by the Mexicans when they gained their independence, and was garrisoned by the Mexican military until the US Army took forcible possession during 1846.

The San Francisco National Cemetery at the Presidio of San Francisco is one of only two cemeteries remaining within the City of San Francisco limits of San Francisco (the other one being at Mission Dolores). Among the military personnel interred are: General Frederick Funston, hero of the Spanish-American War, Philippine-American War, and Commanding Officer of the Presidio Post at the time of the 1906 earthquake; and General Irvin McDowell, Union Army Commander who was defeated by the Confederates in the first Battle of Bull Run (or Manassas).

The Presidio of San Francisco looks over the San Francisco Bay and had served three Countries militarily for more than 200-years notably as the Headquarters for the Western Defense Command during World War II; and later as the Headquarters, Sixth US Army. Its lush environment, expansive views, and proximity to the City of San Francisco made the Presidio Post one of the most desirable military Posts in the Nation. A unique public-private partnership, the Presidio Trust had managed the area and its 500 historic buildings since the military Installation was transferred to the US National Park Service.

During 1870 through 1880s, the US Army trained Union regiments at the Presidio of San Francisco during the Civil War, and maintained the defense for the Western frontiers during the Indian Campaigns. During the Spanish-American War, volunteer trained for service overseas on what is now known as Infantry Terrace.

On March 28, 1776, Spanish Captain Juan Bautista de Anza led 193 military personnel, women and children on a trek from present day Tubac in Arizona, to the San Francisco Bay. The Spanish Fort was built by a party led by José Joaquín Moraga later that year. During 1783, the Presidio Garrison numbered only 33 military personnel. The Presidio of San Francisco is characterized by many wooded areas, hills, and scenic vistas overlooking the Golden Gate Bridge, the San Francisco Bay, and the Pacific Ocean.

On September 17, 1776, the Presidio of San Francisco began as a Spanish Garrison to defend Spain's claim to the San Francisco Bay, and to support Mission Dolores. The Presidio Post was the Northern most outpost of New Spain in the declining Spanish Empire. Since this period, New Spain established the outpost as a fortified location to gain a foothold on Alta California and the San Francisco Bay. The Presidio of San Francisco was passed to Mexico, which in turn passed it to the US during 1848. As part of a 1989 military reduction program, the US Congress voted to end the Presidio of San Francisco's status as an active military Installation.

During 1776 through1821, the Presidio of San Francisco was a simple Fort made up of adobe, brush, and wood. It was often damaged by earthquakes or heavy rains. The Presidio's military personnel duties were to support Mission Dolores by controlling Indian workers at the Mission, and also to farm, ranch, and hunt in order to supply themselves and their families. Socioeconomic support from Spanish authorities in Mexico was very limited.

During 1794, Castillo de San Joaquin, an artillery emplacement was built above present-day Fort Point at San Francisco, complete with iron and bronze cannon. A total of six cannons may be seen at the Presidio of San Francisco today.

During 1821, Mexico became independent of Spain. The Presidio of San Francisco received even less socioeconomic support from Mexico. Residents of Alta California, to include the Presidio of San Francisco, debated separating entirely from Mexico.

During January, 1827, minor earthquakes occurred in the City of San Francisco; some buildings were extensively damaged.

During 1835, the Presidio of San Francisco Garrison, led by Mariano Vallejo, relocated military personnel and civilians to Sonoma. A small detachment remained at the Presidio Post that was in decline.

During 1846, American settlers and adventurers in Sonoma staged the Bear Flag Revolt against Mexican rule. Mariano Vallejo was imprisoned for a brief time. Lieutenant John C. Fremont, a US Army officer, with a small detachment of soldiers and frontiersmen, crossed the Golden Gate in a boat to "capture" the Presidio of San Francisco that was un-resisted. Cannon that was spiked by Lieutenant Fremont remains on the Presidio Post today. The Presidio of San Francisco was seized by the US military at the start of the Mexican-American war. It officially opened as a US Army military Installation during 1848, and became home to several US Army headquarters and military tenant organizations, the last being the US Sixth US Army. Several famous US generals such as William Sherman, George Henry Thomas, and John Pershing made their homes here.

During 1846 through1848, the US Army occupied the Presidio of San Francisco. The Presidio Post began a long era directing operations to control and protect Native Americans as headquarters for scattered US Army organizations on the West Coast.

On March 27, 1847, the Presidio of San Francisco was formally occupied by American troops under the command of Major James A. Gardie. Some of the US Army's most illustrious names associated with the Presidio Post were General William T. Sherman, Lieutenant General Arthur MacArthur, Lieutenant General Phillip H. Sheridan, Lieutenant General Hunter Liggett, and Brigadier General Frederick Funston who commanded the Presidio Post during their careers. During 1914, General John J. Pershing, when in Command of the Eighth Brigade, was stationed at the Presidio Post before leaving on the Mexican Expedition. On August 27, 1915, it was here that his personal tragedy occurred by the death of his wife and daughters when a fire destroyed their home.

During 1853, work began at Fort Point that became a fine example of coastal defenses of its time. Fort Point, located at the foot of the Golden Gate at the Presidio of San Francisco, was the keystone of an elaborate network of fortifications to defend the San Francisco Bay. These fortifications now reflect 150 years of military concern for the defense of the West Coast.

During 1861 through 1865, the American Civil War involved the Presidio of San Francisco. Colonel Albert Sydney Johnston protected Union weapons from being taken by Southern sympathizers at the City of San Francisco. Later, Colonel Johnson resigned from the Union Army and became a General in the Confederate Army. He was killed at the Battle of Shiloh. The Presidio Post organized regiments of volunteers for the Civil War, and to control Indian uprisings in California and Oregon during the absence of Federal military personnel.

During 1869 through 1870, Major General George Henry Thomas, who was an American Civil War hero commanded the Division of the Pacific. General Thomas died during 1870 and was buried at Troy in New York.

During 1870 through 1880s, the US Army trained Union regiments during the Civil War at the Presidio of San Francisco, and maintained the defense for the Western frontiers during the Indian Campaigns. During the Spanish-American War, volunteers trained for service overseas on what is now known as Infantry Terrace.

During 1872 through 1873, the Modoc Indian Campaign involved some Presidio of San Francisco military personnel in this major battle; the last large scale US Army operation against Native Americans in the Far West.

During the 1880s, the US Army initiated a forestation program planting more than 80 thousand pine, cypress, and eucalyptus trees. Today, 89-percent of the Presidio of San Francisco's area is "green" with 25 species of plant life to include two varieties found nowhere else in the World. The Presidio Post had numerous areas that were available for the public to enjoy. The Presidio Post offered 70-miles of scenic roads, paths, and trails to include a six-mile historic trail and a two-mile ecology trail. There were many historic and scenic points of interest while driving or taking a hike. During January 1963, a dedication ceremony officially designated the Presidio Post as a registered National Historic Landmark. This honor identified the Presidio Post as a symbol of an important part of American history. The plaque marking the landmark stands near the Presidio Post flagpole, the site of General Pershing's former home. The Site was landscaped and adorned with two 18th Century Spanish cannons, two Civil War vintage cannons, and several cannon balls. During the first 100 years, the Presidio of San Francisco's 1400-acres were barren and bleak.

Since the 1890s, the Presidio of San Francisco was home to the Letterman Army Medical Center (LAMC), named during 1911 for Jonathan Letterman, the Medical Director of the Civil War era Army of the Potomac. LAMC provided thousands of war wounded with high quality medical care during every US foreign conflict of the 20th Century. Sections of the Letterman Army Hospital were preserved by the Thoreau Center for sustainability. The Marine Hospital operated a Cemetery for merchant seamen approximately 100 to 250-yards from the hospital property. Based on City of San Francisco municipal records, historians estimated that the cemetery was in use from 1885 through 1912. As part of the "Trails Forever" initiative, the Parks Conservancy, the US National Park Service, and the Presidio Trust partnered to build a walking trail along the south side of the Site featuring interpretive signs about its history._The Presidio Post had four creeks that are currently being restored by park stewards and volunteers to expand the former extents of their riparian habitats. The creeks are Lobos and Dragonfly creeks, El Polin Spring, and Coyote Gulch.

During 1890 through 1914, the Presidio of San Francisco military personnel became the Nation's first "park rangers" by patrolling the new Yosemite and Sequoia National Parks.

During 1898 through 1906, the Presidio of San Francisco became the Nation's center for assembling, training, and shipping out forces to the Spanish-American War in the Philippine Islands and the subsequent Philippine-American War (Philippine Insurrection). Letterman Army Hospital was modernized and expanded to care for the many wounded and seriously ill soldiers from these campaigns. The Philippine campaign was an early major US military intervention in the Asia/Pacific region.

During 1903, President Theodore Roosevelt visited the Presidio of San Francisco. His honor guard was from the African-American "Buffalo Soldier" 10th Cavalry Regiment, then at the Presidio Post. This regiment took a role in Roosevelt's famous charge of San Juan Hill in Cuba.

On April 18, 1906, while major San Francisco earthquakes followed by a devastating fire struck the City of San Francisco, the Presidio of San Francisco military personnel under the command of General Frederick Funston reported to the City's Chief of Police to assist refugees, maintain security, enforce Marshal Law, fight fires, and give aid, food, and shelter to refugees at the direction of the City Government. History has also noted that some military personnel also participated in the looting of stores and buildings devastated by the raging fires under the aegis of Marshal Law. Temporary refugee camps were also established on the Presidio Post grounds to provide food, tents, blankets, medical supplies, and attention for thousands of the City's homeless. General Funston had earned the Medal of Honor for his bravery in the Philippines.

During 1912, Fort Winfield Scott was established in the Western part of the Presidio of San Francisco as a Coast artillery Post, and the headquarters of the Artillery District of San Francisco.

During 1914, General John J. Pershing, was the Commanding General of the Eighth Brigade, at the Presidio of San Francisco before leaving on the Mexican Expedition. General Pershing commanded the Mexican Punitive Expedition to eliminate the threat of Pancho Villa, a Mexican rebel and bandit who conducted raids across the US border.

On August 27, 1915, General Pershing's family died in a tragic fire while he was away; it was here that his personal tragedy occurred by the death of his wife and daughters when a fire destroyed their home. As a result of the 1915 fire in General Pershing's quarters, the Presidio Fire Department was established as the first fire station staffed 24 hours per day on a military post. During World War I, the Presidio of San Francisco was an Officers' Training Camp for 11 Western States.

During 1915, part of the Panama-Pacific International Exposition was located on the Presidio of San Francisco waterfront that was expanded by landfill. Military personnel supported the Exposition with parades, honor guards, and artillery demonstrations. The Exposition was to celebrate the opening of the Panama Canal.

During 1917 through 1918, the Presidio of San Francisco rapidly expanded with new cantonments and training areas for World War I. Recruiting, training, and deploying military organizations again become the Presidio Post's primary mission. An Officers' Training Camp was organized here. The waterfront area was covered by quickly assembled buildings, and the railroad track into the Presidio Post was busy with wartime traffic. During the war, the 30th Infantry Regiment, "San Francisco's Own," whose motto, "OUR COUNTRY NOT OURSELVES," fought with distinction in World War I as a key fighting element of the 3rd Infantry Division who earned the title "Rock of the Marne." The 30th Infantry Regiment was frequently based at the Presidio Post.

During 1918 through 1920, the Presidio of San Francisco was the center to establish and trained the American Expeditionary Force Siberia. This was a little remembered force that moved into Siberia during the Russian Civil War. The mission of this Force changed often. It encountered hostility from another part of the Expeditionary Force in Japan, while fighting bandits, and protecting allied civilian personnel.

During 1920 through 1932, the Presidio of San Francisco became home to Crissy Field, the major pioneering military aviation field located on the West Coast.

Trail breaking transpacific and transcontinental flights occurred here. At Crissy Field, future General "Hap" Arnold developed techniques for the new military aviation. General Arnold later commanded the Army Air Corps during World War II. Crissy Field has undergone extensive restoration and now serves as very popular US Naval Recreational Area. It borders on the San Francisco Marina in the East and on the Golden Gate Bridge in the West. Crissy Field is now the Crissy Field Center (former Army Air Corps/Army Air Force Airfield) an Urban Environmental Education Center with programs for schools; public workshops; after-school programs; summer camps; and more. The Center is operated by the Golden Gate National Parks Conservancy and overlooks a restored tidal march. The facilities include interactive environmental exhibits; a media laboratory; resource library; arts workshop; science laboratory; gathering room; teaching kitchen; café; and a bookstore.

The landscape of Crissy Field was designed by Mr. George Hargreaves. The project restored a naturally functioning and sustaining tidal wetland as a habitat for flora and fauna, that were previously not in evidence on the Site. During 1919 through 1936, the project also restored a historic grass Airfield that functioned as a culturally significant military Airfield. The US National Recreational Park at Crissy Field expanded and widened the recreational opportunities of the existing 1 ½-miles of the San Francisco Bay shore for a broader number of Presidio of San Francisco residents and visitors. During 2008, as the Doyle Drive viaduct was deemed seismically unsafe and obsolete, construction was started on the demolition of Doyle Drive that is to be replaced with a flat, broad-lane highway with a tunnel through the bluffs above Crissy Field, called the Presidio Parkway. The project would cost $1 billion and was scheduled to be completed by 2013.

During 1941 through 1945, at the outbreak of World War II, the Presidio of San Francisco served as the Headquarter, Forth US Army and the Western Defense Command under Lieutenant General John L. DeWitt, Commanding General of the Western Defense Command. General DeWitt responded to public hysteria directed against all Japanese on the West Coast. General DeWitt recommended removing all Japanese, to include citizens, from the Western Seaboard. The Federal Bureau of Investigation and some Western politicians also expressed alarm, although no incidents of sabotage occurred. The Presidio of San Francisco was the center for defense of the Western US during World War II. The infamous order to intern Japanese-Americans, including citizens, during World War II was signed at the Presidio of San Francisco. President Roosevelt signed Executive Order 9066 on February 19, 1942, to direct removal of ethnic Japanese residents to internment camps. Until the Presidio Post's closure during 1995, the Presidio Post was the longest continuously operational military Base in the US.

During 1941 through 1946, World War II saw intense activity at the Presidio of San Francisco. It continued as a major Headquarters; Deployment Center; and Training Facility for most of its existence. The Western Defense Command was responsible for the defense of the West Coast. During WW II, this included supervising combat operations in the Aleutian Islands. The Presidio Post again was crowded with temporary barracks for military personnel. Letterman Army Hospital was filled with war-wounded military personnel arriving at the Presidio Post from the battle fields of Okinawa and Iwo Jima. A Japanese Language School was set up to train Japanese-Americans to be interpreters in the war against Japan. Ironically, some of the Japanese military personnel's families were interned in Camps for the rest of the war while they performed bravely in the Pacific Theater of War.

During 1946, the Sixth US Army had fought through 25 major assaults from New Guinea to the Philippines during World War II, and established the Headquarters, Sixth US Army at the Presidio of San Francisco. After World War II, the Presidio of San Francisco Command was re-designated as the Sixth US Army. It was responsible for US Army forces in the Western US for training, supplies, and deployment. The Headquarters, Sixth US Army was also garrisoned at the military Installation where military personnel would coordinate disaster relief efforts. During this year, President Harry Truman had offered the Presidio Post as the site for the future United Nations Headquarters. The United Nations Committee visited the Presidio Post for the purpose of examining its suitability for the Site, but the UN General Assembly ultimately voted in favor of its current New York City location instead.

During 1951 through 1953, the Korean War tasked the Presidio Garrison's operations, repair, and maintenance mission and functions. Letterman Army Hospital was mobilized to care for casualties from the war. The Presidio of San Francisco hosted ceremonies for signing the ANZUS Treaty that was a security pact between Australia, New Zealand, and the US. The Japan-US Security Treaty was signed at the Presidio Post, while the Japanese Peace Treaty was signed in downtown San Francisco.

During 1961 through 1973, the Presidio of San Francisco had a supporting role during the Vietnam War. Anti-war demonstrations took place at the Presidio Post's gates.

During 1968, Richard Bunch Shot, initiated the Presidio Post mutiny at the Presidio Stockade Prison.

During 1969 through 1974, the Letterman Army Hospital (LAMC) was modernized and the Letterman Army Institute of Research (LAIR) was built. During the 1980s, there were no military Posts or Bases closed largely because of procedural criteria established by the US Congress. On October 24, 1988, after several legislative efforts to break the deadlock failed, the US Congress introduced a military Post and Base closure procedure in Public Law 100-526 that was enacted. The original military Post and Base closure law was designed to minimize political interference. The new statute established a bipartisan Commission to make recommendations to the US Congress and the Secretary of Defense for Post and

Base closures and realignments. Lawmakers therefore had to accept or reject the Commission's report in its entirety. On December 28, 1988, the Commission issued its report recommending the closure of 86 military Posts and Bases, partial closure of five Posts and Bases, and the realignment of 54 Posts and Bases. On January 4, 1989, the Secretary of Defense approved all of these recommendations.

On April 26, 1988, the Department of the Army announced that it was formally studying the closure and realignment of 29 US military Posts and Bases to include the Presidio of San Francisco. This Study would become an annual process where the DA would attempt to establish a more efficient and effective organizational structure; reduction of non-essential overhead costs; and the use of military personnel, Civil Service employees, and equipment resources. These studies proposed actions on a Nationwide scale that would eliminate approximately 9000 positions (5100 military personnel and 3900 Civil Service employees), and would reduce annual operating costs by $129 million. Mr. Sorenson summarized from the theoretical perspective that the following expectations would emerge from a sequential look at closed military Installations:

- First, members of the US Congress with a Post or Base in their district would find ways to get around the BRAC "depolarization" process to preserve their military Installation;

- Second, Department of Defense military personnel would attempt to get "excess" Posts and Bases closed under conditions that they retain control over the final selection;

- Third, learning over time would also occur at the BRAC level. BRAC members (some with overlapping terms) would draw from previous failure to close Posts and Bases, and to craft more successful policies and procedures in subsequent years. Essentially, individual and organizational self-interest would drive all forms of behavior. For example, legislators would desire to avoid punishment for perceived income losses from military Post and Base closures; military organizations would want to reduce overhead expenses to avoid suffering unfair loses; Commission members would want to maintain the objectivity that was the primary reason for their very existence; and they all wanted to minimize losses by absorbing lessons from past experiences.[4]

During 1988, it took considerable political struggle to finally complete a military Post and Base closure round in the face of a decade of no Post and Base closures. Fortunately for President Bush, the BRAC 88 Post and Base closure list appeared a month after the defeated Democratic challenger Mr. Michael Sukiyakis. The bad news for the State of California was the BRAC closures, of more than the seven

---

4   David S. Sorenson, "Shutting Down The Cold War: The Politics of Military Base Closure." (St. Martin's Press, New York, July 1998), pp. 39-40.

military Posts and Bases highlighted in this Case Study, would economically affect the State of California hard. .

Since 1988, there has been four successive bipartisan DOD Base Closure and Realignment (BRAC) Commissions that recommended the closure of 125 major and 225 minor military Posts and Bases, and the realignment of missions, operations, and functions of 145. In actuality, the four BRAC rounds achieved 97 military Post and Base closings and 55 major realignments. This resulted in a net savings to taxpayers of over $16 billion through 2001, and over $6 billion in additional savings annually. The principal mechanism for implementing the policy in both statutes has been an independent, bipartisan Commission. In addition, two of the most pressing issues were to provide assistance to local communities economically impacted by military Post and Base closures, and to establish a cost effective program of environmental clean-up at military Posts and Bases prior to their disposition. Since the Commission approach adopted by the US Congress was successful, new Post and Base closure legislation was introduced that also relied on the services of an independent Commission. During 1990, the US Congress refined the process with another law (Public Law 101-510) that charged the DOD with drawing up an initial list of military Posts and Bases for consideration by the Commission. During 1991, 1993, and 2005, the Commission met in accordance with a statutory provision. The Defense Post and Base Closure and Realignment of 1990 (1990 Base Closure Act), Public Law 101-510 established the process where military Installations from henceforth would be realigned or closed

During 1990, it was apparent that politics still dominated the process, a situation that became more obvious when the US Congress rejected a preliminary military Post and Base closure list. Embarrassed by the initial failure of the process, the US Congress searched for political remedies. The US Congress wrestled with Post and Base closures seriously for the first time in 10-years when it reluctantly passed a limited Post and Base Closure Bill

The BRAC Act of 1990, as amended, specified the selection process for the nine Commissioners who were to be nominated by the President for Senate confirmation. In selecting individuals for nominations for appointments to the Commission, the President would consult with the Speaker of the House of Representatives and the majority leader of the Senate concerning the appointment of two members each, and would consult with the minority leaders of the House of Representatives and the Senate concerning the appointment of one member each.

During 1991, the Presidio of San Francisco sent its remaining military tenant organizations to war for the last time during Operation Desert Storm in the Gulf War. The role of the Headquarters, Sixth US Army ceased to coordinate deployment and manage training of National Guard and Reserve organizations in the Western US.

On October 1, 1994, the Presidio of San Francisco was transferred to the US National Park Service, ending 219 years of military use, and beginning its next phase of mixed commercial and public use. Both the Headquarters, Sixth US Army and the Presidio Garrison were deactivated.

During 1996, the Presidio National Recreation Park became privatized through Congressional action.

During 2001, the Letterman Army Hospital was demolished. Later on, the Letterman Digital Arts Center was constructed on the identical Site.

During 2004, the Presidio National Recreational Park has a large inventory of approximately 800 buildings, many of them historical. About 50-percent of the buildings on the Presidio National Recreational Park grounds have been restored and partially remodeled. The Trust has contracted commercial real estate management companies to help attract and retain residential and commercial tenants. The total capacity was estimated at 5000 residents when all the buildings had been rehabilitated. Among the Presidio of San Francisco's residents is The Bay School of San Francisco, a private Co-educational College Preparatory School located in the central Main Post area. Others include The Gordon and Betty Moore Foundation; Tides Foundation; Internet Archive; Arion Press; Sports Basement Presidio; and The Walt Disney Family Museum—a museum in the memory of Walt Disney. Many various commercial enterprises also lease buildings on the Presidio Post to include Starbucks Coffee. The San Francisco Art Institute maintained a small Student Housing Program at the MacArthur neighborhood during 2002 through 2007. The Presidio National Recreational Park area with an extensive Residential Leasing Program. During 2005, the Bay School of San Francisco opened in Building 35.

During 2007, Mr. Donald Fisher, founder of the GAP clothing stores and former Board Member of the Presidio Trust, announced a plan to build a 100,000-square-foot museum tentatively named the Contemporary Art Museum of the Presidio, to house his art collection. Mr. Fisher's plan encountered widespread skepticism and even outright hostility amongst San Francisco preservationists, local citizens, the National Park Service, the Presidio Trust, and City of San Francisco officials who saw the Presidio of San Francisco as "hallowed ground." Due to such criticism, Mr. Fisher withdrew his plans to build the museum at the Presidio Post and instead donated the art to the San Francisco Museum of Modern Art before his death during 2009.

During October 2008, artist Andy Goldsworthy constructed a new sculpture "Spire" at the Presidio of San Francisco. The sculpture is 100-feet tall and is located near the Arguello Gate. The sculpture represents the tree replanting effort that has been underway at the Presidio Post.

During 2009 through 2015, the demolition of the Doyle Drive viaduct was programmed to be replaced by an eight-lane boulevard to include two pairs of tunnels between Crissy Field and the Main Post and a pair of elevated viaducts, at a total project cost of approximately $1 billion. The original Doyle Drive was demolished from April 27-30, 2012. After a hard-fought battle, the Presidio of San Francisco averted being sold at auction and came under the management of the Presidio Trust, a US Government Corporation established by an Act of the US Congress during 1996.

During July 2013, the Presidio of San Francisco had reached a point of self-sufficiency; and the final set of buildings was under renovation. The Fort Scott Post would become home to the new National Center for Service and Innovative Leadership. The first youth program was piloted at the Center in partnership with the National Youth Leadership Council. The National Youth Leadership Training would serve a diverse mix of high school aged students from across the country to develop leadership skills and learn about educational inequity in America.

During its long history, the Presidio of San Francisco was involved in most of America's military engagements in the Pacific region. Importantly, it was the assembly point for US Army forces that invaded the Philippines during the Spanish-American War, America's first major military engagement in the Asian/Pacific region.

Presidio of San Francisco Closure

The purpose of the Base Closure and Realignment Act (BRAC) of 1990 was to provide a fair process that would result in the timely closure and realignment of military Installations within the US. Under the purview of the Act, the US Congress directed the DOD to reorganize its military Installation infrastructure to efficiently and effectively support its Force Structure; increase operational readiness; and facilitate new and more efficient ways of operating. Under the Act, an independent Commission known as the "Defense Base Closure and Realignment Commission" was established. Originally under BRAC, the DOD believed it would be able to divest itself of unnecessary military Installation infrastructure and use the resultant savings for improving its "war fighting" capabilities and quality of life for its military personnel. This would allow the DOD to rationalize Installation infrastructure with National Security imperatives into the 21st Century. At that time, the DOD anticipated that BRAC 05 would attempt to build upon processes used in previous BRAC efforts and gain similar benefits during the approaching BRAC rounds. All military Installations within the US and its territories were to be examined under BRAC. At that time, it was too early to determine how many military Installations would eventually be closed and there were no specific numbers or "targets" under BRAC. The Act required that the DOD would complete a comprehensive review before it determined what military Installations would be realigned or closed. Once the final selections were made by the DOD, an independent BRAC Commission would review the Secretary of Defense recommendations, hold public hearings, visit various military Sites, and ultimately forward closure and realignment recommendations to the President for approval.

The difficulty in implementing BRAC was that future National Security threats were difficult to forecast, and military Installations were impossible to recover once closed. Would closing additional military Installations risk the ability to respond to emergent, unforeseen military threats in the future? This development could force the reopening of closed military Installations. In an attempt to coordinate Post and Base closures and realignments with projected future threats, the BRAC process contained a comprehensive analysis of future threat considerations and developed strategies and Post and Base locations to counter these projections. The DOD did not necessarily agree with these BRAC assumptions. However, the DOD theory about eliminating too many infrastructures developed for some Posts and Bases closed under BRAC were based on two faulty assumptions:

- That prior Post and Base closures impacted the ability to mobilize;

- That prior Post and Base closures were cut too deeply. The DOD did not close military Installations or properties deemed excessive if these military Installations may be required in the future. The DOD accomplished an in-depth analysis and review of this subject and provided the results to the US Congress during 1999 (Report on the Effect of Base Closures on Future Mobilization Options, November 1999). This review examined the effects of prior military Installation closures and future mobilizations, and gave the DOD confidence in believing that reclaiming military Installation infrastructure would not be necessary.

Specifically, the above in-depth analysis and review found that the current military Installation infrastructure could accommodate a Force Structure equivalent to that of 1987 even after previous BRAC reductions. This review found that for the most part, only "re-constituted" assets of military Posts and Bases that were excessive had been closed to date under BRAC, demonstrating that it was more cost effective to rebuild or obtain these assets in the private sector than it was to retain them under the DOD. This review also found that "difficult to re-constitute" assets necessary to support reconstitution were either retained in the current inventory or transferred to military organizations such as the National Guard or Reserve that would ensure their continuous availability.

The BRAC process had its origins during the 1960s. Understanding that the DOD had to reduce its Force Structure that was created during World War II and the Korean War, President John F. Kennedy directed Secretary of Defense Robert S. McNamara to develop and implement an extensive military Post and Base Realignment and Closure Program to adjust to the realities of the 1960s. The

Office of the Secretary of Defense subsequently established the criteria to oversee the selection of military Posts and Bases without consulting the US Congress or the DOD. During the 1950s, under Mr. McNamara's guidance, the DOD closed 60 military Posts and Bases without the US Congress or other Federal Government agencies being involved. During 1965, in view of the political and economic ramifications of military Post and Base closures, the US Congress decided that it had to be involved in the process and passed legislation that required the DOD to report any ongoing military Post or Base closure programs. However, President Lyndon B. Johnson vetoed the Bill. Throughout the 1960s, the veto permitted the DOD to continue closing and realigning military Posts and Bases without Congressional oversight.

Socioeconomic and political pressures eventually forced the US Congress to intervene in the process of closing military Posts and Bases and the DOD's independence concerning this matter. On August 1, 1977, President Jimmy Carter approved Public Law 95-82. The law required that the DOD notify the US Congress when a Post or Base was a candidate for reduction or closure; to prepare studies on the strategic, local socioeconomic and environmental consequences of such action; and wait 60-days for a Congressional response. Codified as Section 2687, Title 10, US Code, the legislation along with requirements of the National Environmental Policy Act (NEPA) permitted the US Congress to prevent any DOD refusal to initiate military Post and Base Closure and Realignment studies and gave the US Congress an integral role in the process.

As socioeconomic pressures mounted, the drive to realign and close military Installations intensified. During 1983, the President's Private Sector Survey on Cost Control (Grace Commission) concluded in a report that economies could be made in military Post and Base structures and recommended the creation of a nonpartisan, independent Commission to study military Post and Base reorganizations, closures, and realignments. Although nothing developed on this recommendation, the Defense budget that had declined since 1985 and that was predicted to decrease in coming years prompted the Secretary of Defense to take decisive action. During 1988, the Secretary of Defense recognized the requirement to close excessive Posts and Bases to save money and therefore chartered a Commission to recommend military Posts and Bases for closure and realignment. During 1990, the US Congress approved the first BRAC that followed the Secretary of Defense's Charter.

A primary role of Installation Commanders during the BRAC process was to certify information used to conduct the analyses. To enhance fairness during the BRAC process by treating all military Installations on an equal basis, all information submitted to the Secretary of Defense and the BRAC Commission for use in making recommendations for military Post and Base closures and realignments would be certified by Installation Commanders as accurate and complete to the best of their knowledge and belief. Much of this information regarding military Installations and Federal agencies and facilities would be gathered in required data initiated by military Departments and sent to military Installations for processing.

In addition, Installation Commanders were authorized to attend meetings, in a liaison or representational capacity, with State and local officials, or other organizations that desired to develop plans or programs to improve the ability to discharge their National Security and Defense missions. However, the DOD officials were not authorized to manage or control such organizations or efforts. In their official capacity, the DOD officials were not to participate in activities of any organization that had as its purpose, either directly or indirectly, insulating military Installations from closure or realignment. The guidance was aimed at ensuring the fairness of the BRAC process. Local communities could request that military Installations in their area be considered for closure because they preferred to have Post and Bases in their area converted to non-military use. The BRAC Act of 1990, as amended, addressed this issue with the following guidance: "The Secretary of Defense would consider any notice received from a local Government in the vicinity of a military Installation that the Federal Government would approve of the closure or realignment of the military Installation."

The big thrust that came from Washington, DC was to increase the productivity of Civil Service employees. This would be a major gain for the American people and undoubtedly a way to put the brakes on the on-going spiraling inflation. The employee's desire and willingness to participate was considered a major factor in the improvement of productivity in the Federal Government. Due to this factor, the Administration faced the uphill task of reselling 2.8-million Civil Service employees on the idea that they were appreciated that they had the ability to produce, and that they were effective and efficient. The word "reselling" was emphasized because a large segment of the Civil Service personnel work force had resented the negative picture painted by many executives in the Executive Board and echoed by many members of the US Congress. The Federal Government could hardly expect a productive attitude and approach by Civil Service employees when they had been described as over-paid, under-worked, and too numerous:

- To define in detail those functions proposed for conversion to contractor operation;

- To present detailed schedules and a description of each task necessary to conclude contract specifications; procurement packages; proposal evaluations; and contract awards.

Prior experience; however, had shown contract sources to be far less effective in reacting to urgent, unscheduled work than an experienced Civil Service personnel work force. The managers and supervisors at the Presidio of San Francisco were concerned about plans to contract out public works positions along with everything else, and were very concerned about the possibility of a new contractor emerging every few years and the attendant new production during the break-in and learning periods. These astute observations applied to practically everything that was repair and maintenance in nature at the Presidio Post. Looking back over the past years, almost all of the repair and maintenance work was of the urgent and unscheduled type.

If the US Army believed that private contractors were going to respond as quickly as Civil Service employees had done in the past, they should have taken a good look at military Installations that were already under contract where it took weeks to get someone to fix even a critical problem. The US Army was spoiled by Civil Service employees who gave quick reaction, but did not get credit when credit was due. At least the Presidio of San Francisco military officials knew that was a fact and it proved that not everyone in the US Army agreed that contracting out was a panacea to correct production problems. Some two-years before BRAC was created, the DOD issued a Study that showed the socioeconomic impact of a quarter century of military Post and Base closures had been largely positive. The 1986 study also revealed real differences in job replacement after a military Post or Base closure. In some cases, there were dramatic gains in employment in a Post or Base closure. The Study found similar results at the Fort Ord Post, George AFB, Norton AFB, Beale AFB, Castle AFB, and Mather AFB closed by BRAC.

Several possible reasons for the unexpected results were the departure of military Spouses (opening up jobs for local citizens) and the shift by military retirees from the Base Exchange to stores in the local community. A study was accomplished concerning the impact of closing the Fort Ord Post in California. Placed on the BRAC 91 list, the Fort Ord Post was one of Monterey County's largest employers. Mr. Lewis J. Cole used an Economic Impact Forecasting System (EIFS) to estimate the impact of replacing the Fort Ord Post with Educational, Science, and Technology Centers. Mr. Cole determined that after a short term loss in the area's economy, such Centers would generate 13,000 new positions and 25,000 new students in local communities. Despite the loss of 16,000 military personnel and Civil Service employees, Mr. Cole projected that the local sale volume would increase by $235 million and in local income by $49 million. During 1992, after Mr. Cole's Study was published, the California State University at Monterey Bay was established on the Site of the Fort Ord Post.[5]

Every Civil Service employee at the Presidio of San Francisco knew that the battle being waged against the DA was not only limited to just initial operations, repair, and maintenance positions that were programmed for contracting out. It was pretty well understood in Washington, DC that the Administration was adamantly and completely in favor of contracting out most, if not all, of the Nation's Federal Civil Service employee positions. No Civil Service position was safe in the Federal Government as well as the Presidio Post. Although the Presidio of San Francisco escaped the first military Post closure and realignment

---

[5]   David S. Sorenson, "Shutting Down the Cold War: The Politics of Military Base Closure," (St. Martin's Press, New York, July 1998), pp. 73-75.

go-around, the Presidio Post's service and military tenant organizations were by no means safe from a proposed reorganization, consolidation, realignment, or contracting out. There was every indication that the Presidio Post's service and tenant organizations were already being scheduled for conversion to some private contractor operation, and it would be just a matter of time before they would be targeted for the Presidio Post closure or realignment.

In view of the findings of the Cost Study prepared by the Headquarters, Sixth US Army staff and the "Save the Presidio" Committee, it appeared that the US Army has prematurely reached a decision to realign the Headquarters, Sixth US Army staff to Treasure Island, discontinue the Presidio Garrison, and transfer the Presidio of San Francisco to the US National Park Service with contracting out repair and maintenance of Presidio of San Francisco facilities without first adequately determining that contracting out was an economically sound investment for the Federal Government. Therefore, the final decision to convert from an in-house capability to private contractor operation at the Presidio Post should have been deferred at some future date to allow planners and managers to adequately prepare a more detailed cost analysis of the proposed Headquarters, Sixth US Army realignment, discontinuance of the Presidio Garrison, and the transfer of the Presidio of San the US National Park Service.

Opposition to further military Post and Base closures concentrated on military personnel and Civil Service employee losses in local communities surrounding military Installations. But a RAND Corporation study found that some military Post and Base closures did actually generated jobs. During 1988. For example, the closure of the Fort Ord Post in California was expected to result in a 15-percent drop in the population of the surrounding communities, but the real drop was less than three-percent. Unemployment was expected to jump by seven-percent, but employment actually increased by 1-percent, and retail sales increased by two-percent instead of sliding by an expected 25-percent.

In the wake of the favorable response from the Headquarters, Sixth US Army staff, the "Save the Presidio" Committee lobbied in Washington, DC to request legislators and the Director of OMB to demand that all planning and preparation for the proposed Headquarters, Sixth US Army staff realignment to Treasure Island; the Presidio Garrison discontinuance; and the transfer of the Presidio of San Francisco to the US National Park Service be immediately canceled by public announcement. Many articles in local newspapers were published advising public citizens to write letters to appropriate Committees in the Senate and House to deny appropriated funds for the proposed Headquarters, Sixth US Army staff realignment; the Presidio Garrison discontinuance; and the transfer of the Presidio Post to the US National Park Service.

In defense of military Post and Base closures, one Committee representative briefed Senators and Representatives on the amount of time and money that had already gone into the Presidio of San Francisco's Closure and Realignment

Study, and pointed out that this money could never be recovered. The Committee representative also presented facts and figures to show that some military Installations were trying to operate with a loss of work force because of a freeze in hiring that caused some work to be contracted out. The Committee elaborated on previous reports from on-Site personnel to the effect that other military Installations were a disaster area because of the private contractor's lack of capability, inefficiency, and cost overruns to accomplish the workload. In sum, "The 1991 Post and Base closure list produced some clear winners and losers on the employment front. California lost approximately 27,000 positions from both military Post and Base closures and realignments. The closing of the Fort Ord Post on California's Northern Coast caused a decrease of over 16,000 military personnel and Civil Service employees alone."[6]

The initial Presidio of San Francisco Closure and Realignment Study indicated that 2349 military personnel and 2688 Civil Service employees at the Presidio of San Francisco could be transferred of eliminated. Military personnel and Civil Service employees from the Headquarters, Sixth US Army staff stationed at the Presidio of San Francisco were programmed to be realigned to Treasure Island in California; the Fort Ord Post at Monterey in California to was programmed to be realigned to Fort Lewis in Washington; the Letterman Army Medical Center was programmed to be realigned to the Oakland Naval Medical Facility at Oak Knoll; and the Letterman Army Institute of Research was programmed to be realigned to other US Army Research Centers elsewhere in the US. The initial announcement by the DOD that the Headquarters, Sixth US Army staff; Letterman Army Medical Center; Letterman Army Institute of Research; and several tenant organizations stationed on the Presidio Post were being considered for realignment that would cause the Presidio of San Francisco discontinuance brought forth a predictable, strong political outcry from the Mayor of San Francisco.

Aside from political efforts, there were no formal analytical efforts taken at that time to develop a case for the City of San Francisco as to why these actions should not take place. To be effective, both military and civilian politics and the facts had to work together for necessity as political contacts and lobbying were most important in getting legislative and Executive Board attention. A logical and effective presentation of the facts would become a necessity to provide the rationale for changing or overruling previous political decisions. During this period, military Posts and Bases were the focus of significant political priorities. They were classic cases of many of the dilemmas facing the divided American political structure to include local versus National interests and organizational interests versus elected leadership interests.

The originally planned and programmed Headquarters, Sixth US Army realignment; Presidio Garrison discontinuance; and the Presidio of San Francisco

---

6   David S. Sorenson, "Shutting Down the Cold War: The Politics of Military Base Closure." (St. Martin's Press, New York, July 1998), pp. 100.

transfer to the US National Park Service did not occur as originally intended. The more the Headquarters, Sixth Army staff argued against the Presidio Post closure, the more the Department of the Army added "nails" to the Presidio Post's demise. However, the remains of the 200-year old historic Presidio Post would still remain preserved and still accessible to the public. This was an important and viable result of the political process that took place after the Headquarters, Sixth US Army staff and the Presidio Garrison discontinuance; the reassignment of military personnel and Civil Service employees to other military Installations; and the Presidio of San Francisco transfer to the US National Park Service.

As a result, the City of San Francisco would obtain some of the newest housing stock after taking over the Naval Base at Treasure Island, and renting out hundreds of houses that added to City of San Francisco revenues. During July 1998, the San Francisco Police Department Field Operations Agency moved to Hunter's Point Naval Air Station. The component question in presenting the Headquarters, Sixth US Army staff's arguments for the possible prevention of the Presidio of San Francisco closure still remains at issue. Due to misleading publicity at the beginning of the Presidio Post closure process, the full impact of an aroused public did not begin to surface. The Electorates of the City of San Francisco did not comprehended that consideration was being given to the discontinuance of a 200-year old military Installation for the sake of what San Francisco's late Mayor Moscone had termed "false economy."

The historical and political reasoning that closed the Presidio of San Francisco has been presented in an attempt to adjudicate an understandable Presidio Post closure decision. The closures of the Fort Ord Post, George AFB, Norton AFB, Beale AFB, Castle AFB, and Mather AFB have been added to this Case Study to support the rational for the consolidation of the Headquarters, Sixth US Army staff and the Presidio Garrison that did not occur. The Presidio of San Francisco primarily contained a Headquarters organization and qualified to be realigned with another US Army Post or be discontinued. In the case of the Presidio of San Francisco, the Headquarters, Sixth USA Army staff and the Presidio Garrison was finally discontinued, and its administrative mission with military personnel and Civil Service employees realigned to the Fifth US Army at Fort Sam Houston in Texas. At this point, it is rather obvious that the Case Study investigation of the Presidio of San Francisco closure did come under the purview of the Base Closure and Realignment Act of 1988.

The Presidio Trust Act called for "preservation of the cultural and historic integrity of the Presidio of San Francisco for public use." The Act also required that the Presidio Trust would be financially self-sufficient by 2013. These imperatives have resulted in numerous conflicts between the need to maximize income by leasing historic buildings, and permitting public use despite most structures being rented privately. Further differences have arisen from the divergent needs of preserving the integrity of the National Historic Landmark District in the face of new construction; competing pressures for natural habitat restoration; and requirements for commercial purposes that impede public access. The Presidio Trust planned to create a promenade that would link the Lombard gate and the new Lucas Film campus to the Main Post and to the Golden Gate Bridge. The promenade would be part of a trail expansion plan that would add 24-miles of new pathways and eight scenic overlooks throughout the National Recreational Park. As of 2007, there was only a rudimentary Visitor's Center to orient visitors to the Presidio of San Francisco's unique history.

The Presidio Trust now manages most of the Park in partnership with the US National Park Service. The Presidio Trust has jurisdiction over the interior 80-percent of the Presidio Post to include nearly all of its historic structures. The US National Park Service manages coastal areas. Primary law enforcement throughout the Presidio Post is the jurisdiction of the US Park Police. One of main objectives of Presidio Trust's Program was to achieve financial self-sufficiency by fiscal year 2013. Thanks to high rents from residential and commercial tenants, this happened well ahead of schedule during 2006.

Immediately after its inception, the Presidio Trust began preparing rehabilitation plans for the Presidio National Recreational Park. Many areas had to be decontaminated before they could be prepared for public use. The Presidio Trust entered a major agreement with Lucas Film to build a new facility called the Letterman Digital Arts Center (LDAC), which is now the headquarters of Industrial Light and Magic and Lucas Arts. The Site replaced portions of what was the Letterman Hospital. During June 1999, Mr. George Lucas won the development rights for 15-acres of the Presidio Post after beating out a number of rival plans to include a leading proposal by the Shorenstein Company. A $300 million development with nearly 900 thousand square feet (84 thousand-square feet of office space and a 150-thousand-square-foot underground parking garage) with a capacity of 2500 employees. LDAC replaced the former ILM and Lucas Arts Headquarters in San Rafael. Lucas Learning Ltd., Lucas Online, and the George Lucas Educational Foundation would also reside at the Site. Mr. Lucas' proposal included plans for a high-tech Presidio Museum and a seven-acre "Great Lawn" that is now open to the public.

CHAPTER III

History of the Fort Ord Post

The Fort Ord Post was a Sub-Installation under the Presidio of San Francisco located on the historically rich Monterey Bay Peninsula in central California. During 1917, the Fort Ord Post's 27,827-acre Site was established by the US Army as a maneuver area and field artillery target range. The US Army also bought the present day East Garrison nearby lands on the East side of the Fort Ord Post to be used as maneuver and training grounds for Field Artillery and Cavalry troops stationed at the Presidio of Monterey. The military Post covered over 28,600-acres during its existence. The local topography made it ideal as an Infantry Training Center and it became its primary mission. During 1846, the Fort Ord Post was organized during the Mexican-American War. Mr. John D. Gloat claimed the Monterey area along with the rest of California for the US. During 1852 through 1898, the Fort Ord Post was in disuse. During 1879, while visiting the area, writer Robert Lewis Stevenson wrote: "The beaches are white with weathered whale bones." During 1991, the Fort Ord Post was selected for de-commissioning; however, the military Post did not formally close until 1994.

The Fort Ord Post's primary mission was to train combat troops. The military Post provided command, administrative and logistical support necessary to operate, repair, and maintain the Fort Ord Post's facilities and its Sub-Installations; namely, the Presidio of Monterey and Fort Hunter Liggett. The Fort Ord Post was near Monterey Bay at Monterey County in California, approximately 80-miles South of San Francisco. The military Post consisted of approximately 28,000-acres near the Cities of Seaside, Sand City, Monterey, Del Rey Oaks, and Marina. Laguna Ceca Recreation Area and Toto Regional Park bordered the Fort Ord Post to the South and Southeast. Land use East of the Fort Ord Post was primarily agricultural. During 1917, the Fort Ord Post was established as Camp Giggling and was a military training Post for Infantry troops.

The Fort Ord Post located on California's Central Coast was a biologically diverse and unique region. The range and combination of climactic, topographic, and soil conditions at the Fort Ord Post supported many biological communities. The 11 plant community identified at the Fort Ord Post included coast live oak woodland; central maritime chaparral; central coastal scrub; vegetative stabilized dune; Northern fore-dune grassland; landscaped valley needle-grass grassland; seasonally wet grassland; vernal pool; upland federal and wet federal central maritime chaparral were the most extensive natural community. The Fort Ord Post occupied approximately 12,500-acres in the South-Central portion of the military Post. Oak woodlands were widespread at the Fort Ord Post and occupied the next largest area about 5000-acres. Grasslands, primary located in the

34

Southeastern and Northern portions of the Fort Ord Post occupied approximately 4500-acres.

The other five community types generally occupied less than 500-acres each. The remaining 4000-acres of the Fort Ord Post was considered to be fully developed and did not support ecological communities. Special status biological resources included plant and wildlife tax and native biological communities that receive various levels of protection under the Federal Government; State of California; and community laws, regulations, and policies. Of the 11 plant communities identified at the Fort Ord Post, two were considered rare or declining and of the highest inventory priority by the California Department of Fish and Game. Special status tax that occurred or potentially occurred in the plant communities at the Fort Ord Post were identified for each Site to include 22 vascular plants, one invertebrate, four reptiles, one amphibian, nine birds, and two mammals.

The Fort Ord Post elevations ranged from approximately 900-feet above the means level (MSL) near Impossible Ridge, on the East side of the Post to sea level at the beach. The predominant topography of the area reflected morphology typical of the dune sand deposits that underlied the Western and Northern portions of the Fort Ord Post. In those areas, the ground surface sloped gently West and Northwest, draining toward Monterey Bay. Runoff was minimal due to the high rate of surface water infiltration into the permeable dune sand; consequently, well-developed natural drainage was absent throughout much of the area. Closed drainage depressions typical of dune topography were common.

The topography of the Southeastern third of the Fort Ord Post was notably different from the rest of the military Post. This area was relatively well-defined; Eastward flowing drainage channels with narrow, moderately to steep canyons. Runoff was into the Salinas Valley. The military Post was within the Coast Ranges Geomorphological Province. The region consisted of Northwest trending mountain ranges, broad basins, and elongated valleys generally parallel the major geologic structures. In the Coastal Ranges, older, consolidated rocks were characteristically exposed in the mountains but were buried beneath younger, unconsolidated alluvial fan and flu-vial sediments in the valleys and lowlands. In the coastal lowlands, these younger sediments commonly inter-fingered with marine deposits.

The Fort Ord Post was at the transition between the mountains of the Santa Lucia Range and the Sierra de la Salinas in the South and Southeast, and the lowlands of the Salinas River Valley to the North. The geology of the Fort Ord Post generally reflected the transitional condition; older, consolidated rock was exposed at the ground surface near the Southern Fort Ord Post boundary and became buried under a Northward thickening sequence of poorly consolidated deposits in the North. The Fort Ord Post and the adjacent areas were underlain, from depth to ground surface by one or more of the following older consolidated units:

- Mesozoic granite and metamorphic rocks;

- Miocene marine sedimentary rocks of the Monterey Formation Upper Miocene to lower Pliocene marine sandstone of the Santa Margarita Formation (and possible the Poncho Rico and/or Juristic Formation). Locally, these units were overlain sand obscured by geologically younger sediment to include: Clio-Pleistocene alluvial fan, lake and flu-vial deposits of the Paso Robles Formation;

- Pleistocene Elian and flu-vial sands of the Aromas Sand Pleistocene to Holocene Valley fill deposits consisting of consolidated sand, silt, and clay Pleistocene and Holocene dune, beach sand and alluvium.

Recent studies of the Fort Ord Post hydro-geology concluded that the military Post straddled two distinct ground water basins; that is, the Salinas and Seaside basins. The military Post included the Southwestern edge of the Salinas basin and the Eastern portion of the smaller Seaside basin. The Salinas basin under-lied the Northern and Southeastern portions of the military Post and the Seaside basin underlied the Southern and Southwestern areas.

The Selina ground water basin was relatively large and extended well beyond the boundaries of the Fort Ord Post. At the military Post, the Salinas basin was composed of relatively flat lying to gently dipping poorly consolidated sediments. Although relatively simple structurally, the sediments were strati graphically complex, reflecting a variety of deposition's environments. Aquifers within the Salinas basin at the military Post, from top to bottom, indicated that the unconfined aquifer, the confined upper 100 foot aquifer, the confined and unconfined lower 180-foot aquifer, confined 400-foot and 900-foot aquifers. The aquifer names reflected local historical water levels over many years and were not directly correlated to the water levels used by the US Army at the military Post Ground water extraction by the City of Marina, by the military Post, and by irrigation wells in the Salinas Valley had historically induced seawater intrusion into the lower 180-foot and 400-foot aquifers. Seawater intrusion continued to affect those aquifers. Intrusion into the upper 180-foot aquifer appeared to affect those aquifers. Intrusion into the upper 180-foot aquifer appeared to be limited to the vicinity of the beach at the military Post.

The extraction, by the City of Marina, of drinking water from the lower 180-foot and 400-foot aquifer was terminated. Drinking water for the City of Marina area was extracted from the 900-foot and 1500-foot aquifers. However, the Fort Ord Post's true origin of development dates back to 1917. During August of that year, the Federal Government purchased 15,000-acres next to the area known today as Giggling for $160 thousand. During this period, the property was known as the Giggling Military Reservation. The name Giggling originated from a German family that had held title to the property in that general area for several years. As a result, the Fort Ord Post's official title became Camp Giggling. The area was purchased at the Presidio of Monterey and known to the troops as the "devil's own acres." Since WW I, the property had been used as a military training and maneuver area. The area sometimes known as the Giggling Reservation consisted of 15,000-acres of Tanzanian scrub brush and sand.

During 1865 through 1902, the Fort Ord Post was inactive. It was not until after the Spanish-American War (Remember the Maine) that a Force Structure of significant size would garrison the military Post once again. During 1892, the 15th Infantry Regiment and the 9th "Buffalo Soldiers" Cavalry returned from duty in the Philippines were assigned to the military Post. Some small refinements were made to the military Post during this period. The Fort Ord Post began its evolution into what we would recognize today. The US Army troops occupied the military Post for a few months at the end of the Civil War when it was known as Ord Barracks.

The Fort Ord Post was founded as a Cavalry Post and became a major training facility during World War I. The military Post's 27,825-acre Site continued to be expanded by the US Army as a maneuver area and field artillery target range. During 1917, the US Army purchased from Mr. David Jacks title to what is known today as the East Garrison. As it developed, it was considered one of the Nation's permanent military Posts. It was bordered on the North by the City of Marina and on the South by Sand City minutes from Seaside, Monterey, Pacific Grove, and beautiful Carmel. The agricultural community of Salinas was 14-miles to the East. The City of San Francisco was 115-miles further to the North, and the City of Los Angeles was 340-miles to the South. Before the US Army's use of the property, the area was agricultural before administrative buildings, Barracks, Mess Halls, Tent Pads, and a Sewage Treatment Plant were finally constructed.

During 1938, additional agricultural property was purchased for the development of the Fort Ord Garrison. Concurrently, beach front property was also donated to the US Army. During the same year major changes marked the excelled growth of the Fort Ord Post. Colonel Homer M. Ironing, who was promoted to Major General at a later date, was in charge of the construction work and renovation. Utilizing the benefits of President Franklin D. Roosevelt's Works Projects Administration Program, Colonel Ironing supervised the expansion of the military Post into a large Camp about one-mile from the Giggling railroad spur and saw to it that the dense brush areas were cleared for future construction. Colonel Ironing worked with an original WPA appropriation of $800 thousand. That amount would grow to over $6 million for additional construction at the military Post.

During 1939, the military Installation was designated as Camp Ord. During 1940, the military Post was renamed Fort Ord. During the early 1940s, elements of the 3rd Infantry Division participated in exercises before building began in earnest. During the 1940s through 1960s, the Fort Ord Garrison was constructed starting at the Northwest corner of the military Post and then expanding Southward and Eastward.

On June 27, 1940, non-Divisional organizations added at the Fort Ord Post were the 19th Engineer Regiment (Combat) originally activated as the 39th Engineer Regiment (General Service) and was re-designated as the 19th four-days later. Other organizations that were assembled or activated at the military Post for inclusion in the Division were the 31st Field Artillery (activated on July 1, 1940), and the 32nd Infantry and 53rd Infantry (activated on August 1, 1940). The first joint US Army and US Navy maneuvers were held at the military Post. One of the military organizations was the 276th Field Artillery stationed at the Presidio of Monterey during the inter-war year, and became the first military organization of the new Division. The other organization that was stationed at the Presidio of Monterey was the 11th Cavalry, who soon moved to Southern California for duty on the Mexican Border. The 17th Infantry Regiment, a military organization traditionally associated with the 7th Infantry Division, was transferred from various military Posts throughout the Country and assembled at the Fort Ord Post.

On July 1, 1940, the 7th Infantry Division was activated at the Fort Ord Post by order of the War Department with the famous Brigadier General Joseph Stillwell as its first Commander since World War I.

On October 4, 1940, a total of 10,000 troops and 1000 vehicles, boats, and horses took part in the maneuvers. During 1940, Colonel Ironing gave instructions to build the first wooden Barracks and Mess Halls. This included the Tent City slabs in the East Garrison. The wooden barracks were supposed to be temporary, not to last much longer than five-years. The construction was so well accomplished; however, they are still standing today. It began moving into a Tent City at Camp Ord (later called East Garrison); while a more permanent military Post was hurriedly constructed in an area close to Highway 1, and was known as Camp Clayton.

World War II was becoming a real threat. As a result, the US Congress approved a peacetime draft. As Fall approached, Camp Ord was filling up with new recruits. The plans for a $1 million Soldiers' Service Recreation Complex was the result of this large population growth and was beginning to take shape. Its framework was the brainchild of the 7th Infantry's Division Commander, General Joseph W. Stillwell. His nickname was "Vinegar Joe" because of his strong personality. It was his belief that soldiers should have some place to go and relax after duty hours.

During October 1940, additional land was acquired that expanded the Fort Ord Post to approximately 30,000-acres. Facilities at the Hearst Ranch were acquired and later renamed Camp Hunter Liggett, and were constructed by elements of the 19th Engineers. By December 1940, the military Post had 1098 buildings finished or in progress, and just under $15 million in contracts had been negotiated for construction at the military Post. During February, 1941, a 1500 bed hospital on the new military Post opened. During the Summer of 1941, the Forth US Army conducted a large Command Post exercise. Another organization, the 250th Coast Artillery (National Guard) was assembled at Camp McQuaide near Watson Ville. The military Post later became a Coastal Artillery Placement Training Center, and then a large military confinement facility. These military Posts were located within the Presidio of Monterey Area.

During December 1940, the Headquarters, III Corp was located in the military Post buildings at the Presidio of Monterey. The Corps was comprised of the 7th Infantry Division and the 40th Infantry Division (National Guard) at Camp San Luis Obadiah. During January 1941, General Stillwell became the III Corps Commander. In spite of this transfer and subsequent duty in the China-Burma-India Theater, General Stillwell would be forever associated with the Division he activated and built. Brigadier General White, the Assistant Division Commander, was appointed as the new Commander of the Division. The growth of the military Post's boundaries continued to the size of 20,000-acres.

During the Fall of 1940, Camp Ord became known as Fort Ord. It was established as a permanent US Army military Installation. By the end of 1941, more than $12 million worth of improvements were contracted out. During 1940 through 1960, the continued growth of the military Post's Main Garrison took place over the next 20-years. The construction started in the Northwest corner of the military Post, expanded Southward, and then finally Eastward.

Between the end of World War I and pre-World War II, Camp Giggling was primarily used as a maneuver area for the 11th "Black Horse" Cavalry and artillery target range for the 76th Field Artillery. Both organizations were stationed at the Presidio of Monterey. During the Summer, the 30th Infantry Regiment came down from the Presidio of San Francisco to use the reservation for maneuvers as did other US Reserve and National Guard organizations. During 1933, the reservation's name was changed to Camp Ord. Its landscape was brush covered and almost impenetrable in many places, and simple dirt and gravel road connected the East Garrison and Giggling Railroad spur located on Highway #1. There was a water well; a caretaker's house in the center of the reservation; and a few bivouac sites. But other than these limited improvements, no additional changes were made at Camp Ord until 1938.

The Fort Ord Post was named after Major General Edward Cress Ord. General Ord's fame in the history book includes some information on being an Indian fighter. During 1847, General Ord was a Lieutenant with Major General J.C. Fremont's Army when the present Site of the nearby Presidio of Monterey was brought into existence. But actions as a Civil War Commander established his military career. General Ord distinguished himself during the Civil War in the Battle of Luke in Mississippi; military operations against Petersburg in Virginia; and the capture of Fort Harrison in Virginia. General Ord was interned at Arlington National Cemetery.

A construction project was started on the basis that it was high time to stop talking about suitable recreational facilities for Enlisted Men and doing something about it. General Stillwell picked the Site and the Engineers to construct the building. The first to be constructed in the complex was the Soldiers' Club. It was designed by 1st Lieutenant Savoy Stopwatch, 13th Engineers and 2nd Lieutenant Orville W. Pierce, 74th Field Artillery. During September 1943, with donations from Enlisted Men and from additional WPA grants, the building was finally finished. It would turn out that the $500 thousand Enlisted Men's Club was the only building to be completed in the proposed military Post recreation complex that called for a Gymnasium; Stadium; NCO Club; Tennis Courts; Athletic Fields; as well as a Chapel. When it first opened its doors, it was known as the Soldiers' Club. Later the club's name was properly changed to "Stillwell Hall." The military Post held a special place in General Stillwell's heart. He willed that his ashes be scattered along the scenic Monterey Peninsula beaches.

As military organizations moved into newly built barracks at Camp Clayton, tents at Camp Ord became available for National Guard units called to active duty during a National emergency. The 147th Field Artillery (South Dakota National Guard) arrived at Camp Clayton after a remarkable overland journey from South Dakota that began in a blizzard. The Artillery Regiments were later broken up that provided separate Field Artillery Battalions that were married with Regiments throughout the US Army to form Regimental Combat Teams used during and after World War II. During January 1941, the 76th Field Artillery. For example, was split into the 74th, 75th, and 76th Field Artillery Battalions. Throughout this period the Presidio of San Francisco and the Fort Ord Post were Regional Reception Centers for draftees called to active duty during general mobilization. As most of the draftees that arrived at the Fort Ord Post were from California and other Western States, the 7th Infantry Division (Light) had an unusually large percentage of Mexicans and Indians. Records indicated that there was a training establishment of some sort as there is mention of the 11th and 13th Training Battalions at Camp Clayton but it was unclear when and how these organizations were used. Many of the inductees were reassigned to combat units as they were activated without the benefit of basic training as we know it today.

Just prior to the Japanese attack on Pearl Harbor, the 53rd Infantry was transferred to the Presidio of San Francisco to replace the 30th Infantry that had been transferred after many years of active duty there. The 159th Infantry of the 40th Infantry Division from Camp San Luis Obadiah replaced them at the Fort Ord Post. Much of this information was culled from yellowing copies of the Presidio's Panorama Post newspaper. After the attack on Pearl Harbor and throughout the war years, the Panorama by necessity, omitted any mention of specific units or movements. The Fort Ord Post organizations guarded the coast and critical facilities in Central and Northern California for months after the attack.

When World War II commenced, the Fort Ord Post became a jumping off point for other training areas like Camp Roberts and Fort Hunter Liggett. The Fort Ord Post was also a staging area for many famous fighting Divisions and military organizations. The Fort Ord Post's honorable alumni include the 3rd Infantry Division, 6th Infantry Division, 7th Infantry Division, 27th Infantry Brigade, 32nd Infantry Division, 25th Infantry Division, and 43rd Infantry Division. During World War II, new innovative tactical training with weapons, artillery, air defense, and amphibious landings was in demand. The concept of combat readiness training was first introduced at the Fort Ord Post. During 1942, the WACs were formed to handle administrative and non-combat duties. After the D-Day invasion, many German soldiers were taken prisoner and were interned at the Fort Ord Post's East Garrison. The German Prisoners of War (POWs) made it easier around the Fort Ord Post by performing Kitchen Police (KP), barracks clean-up, uniform mending, street cleaning, garbage pickup, etc.

During January 1942, the Headquarters, 27th Infantry Division was activated at the Fort Ord Post before moving to Hawaii the following month. The precursor to XVIII Corps (Airborne), the II Armored Corps, was also born at the Presidio of Monterey during January of that year. During November 1942, the 3rd Infantry Division that went on to fame in the European Theater trained at the Fort Ord before heading off to the East Coast and the landings in North Africa. During the Fall of 1942, the 43rd Infantry Division was located at the Fort Ord Post before departing for New Zealand.

On February 8, 1943, Monterey had its own "colored" USO and (lest you think that awareness of black history was a new thing) the week was designated "Negro1 History Week." During March 1943, the first contingent of German POWs arrived at the Fort Ord Post. As the war went on, most of the larger organizations had already been activated and had deployed overseas or were deploying. Emphasis shifted from activating and preparing organizations for overseas movement to supplying individual replacements for existing military organizations. Problems with the readiness and training of individuals already sent overseas led to the formation of two Replacement Centers with specific intention of preparing replacements for ground combat forces for overseas movement. One was established on the East Coast at Fort Meade ion Maryland, the other was established at the Fort Ord Post in California.

On June 25, 1943, the 73rd Field Artillery Battalion was activated at the Fort Ord Post. This organization was assigned to General George S. Patton's Third US Army. There were other organizations not well known. But just as important to the war effort were the 2nd, 3rd, and 4th Engineer as well as the 533rd and 539rd Amphibian. These five Engineer and Amphibian Groups had trained at the Fort Ord Post before being shipped to the Pacific Theater of Operations. During the Summer of 1943, as the last major organizations departed the continental US for campaigns to such places as the Aleutians, room became available on the Fort Ord Post.

During August 1943, the US Army Ground Forces (like TRADOC) Replacement Depot II opened their doors. On October 10, 1943, the XVIII Corps was born at the Presidio of Monterey by the re-designation of the Headquarters, II Armored Corps. Another organization of interest, the 1st Filipino Infantry Regiment, was activated during April and eventually included a few veterans of fighting on Bataan that had been wounded, evacuated, and returned to active duty in the US. Black troops were also at the Fort Ord Post. Most were in smaller "colored" Quartermaster Companies.

On September 24, 1943, other notable events in the Monterey area during the rest of WW II included the opening of the Stillwell Hall Enlisted Club and the movement of the newly reactivated Headquarters, Forth US Army to the Presidio of Monterey from the City of San Jose in California. During 1943, the Forth US Army departed for Texas During August 1944, the Headquarters, III Corps departed and was replaced be a new type of headquarters that became a model for others headquarters around the Country. During the same month, the 1st Headquarters and Headquarters Detachment, Special Troops, Army Ground Forces, was established at the Fort Ord Post.

The Headquarters and Headquarters Detachment was responsible for servicing miscellaneous organizations in the US being deployed overseas; the Detachment was established to exercise command and control over these organizations. During the same month, there was an unsuccessful attempt by 500 German POWs to escape by tunnel; and Italian Service Companies consisting of former Italian POWs who had volunteered for military service with US Forces (Italy had surrendered) began arriving during September 1944. During 1943 through 1975, the Fort Ord Post was a Basic Training Center. After 1975, the 7th Infantry Division (Light) occupied the Fort Ord Post. Light infantry troops operated without heavy tanks, armor, or artillery.

WW II placed increased emphasis on amphibious warfare particularly in the Pacific Theater. The Fort Ord Post with access to the many beaches of the Monterey Bay became the home of an amphibious training organization designated the 18th Armored Group. Pictures in the Presidio Panorama newspaper of the various types of Amphibious equipment used in and around the Fort Ord Post as the war progressed revealed the evolution of amphibious warfare during WW II from simple over-the-side Higgins boats to sophisticated tracked vehicles and drop ramp landing craft. The Fort Ord Post "amphibious" participated in the D-Day landings in all of the US Army operations in the Pacific. On April 11, 1944, new equipment for amphibious warfare was tested and reviewed by the Landing Vehicle Board established by the US Army. During October 1945, the Amphibious Equipment Branch was suspended shortly after WW II.

During January 1945, the III Corps returned to the Presidio of Monterey from Fort McPherson After VE Day, preparations were underway for intensified operations in the Pacific culminating in the invasion of Japan. A combined Army-Navy Civil

Affairs Staging Area (CASA) was established to prepare military personnel. Another Headquarters, XXXVI Corps was formed at the Presidio of San Francisco. After the first Atomic bomb was dropped during August, 1945, this Corps was replaced by the famous VII Corps returning from Europe in preparation for service against Japan and had most recently been at Camp San Luis Obadiah. As WW II wound down, the Discharge Center that originally had been at the Presidio of Monterey was moved to Camp Beale (later Beale Air Force Base). The Fort Ord Post continued its training capacity after WW II. After the allies defeated the axis and WW II came to its conclusion, the Fort Ord Post took on a much slower pace. During 1946, the Fort Ord Post officially became a training facility for basic combat and advance Infantry training. This would be its primary mission for the next 30-years.

During 1947, the Fort Ord post became home to the 4th Replacement Training Center. On July 15, 1947, the 4th Infantry Division was reactivated and took up residence at the Fort Ord Post. During June 1950, the 4th Infantry was responsible for training military troops that were going to be reassigned to the Korean conflict. On September 22, 1950, the 4th Infantry Division moved to Fort Denning in Georgia. It was replaced by the 6th Infantry Division who took over the mission of training troops for assignment in Korea. During the 1950s, many Civil Service employees were hired with most of them ex-military personnel. The 6th Infantry Division continued this task until January 1956. On June 5, 1957, the 5th Division was reassigned from Germany and moved into barracks until it was deactivated.

During the 1950s, the Sixth US Army took up quarters at the Fort Ord Post. The Fort Ord Post became known as the main US Army Infantry Training Center. This would be its primary mission for the next 30-years. Its activity increased with the training of troops headed for Southeast Asia. During the Vietnam conflict, it became the major Training Center in the Nation. It was the highest overall training of combat ready military troops in the Fort Ord Post's history. It once again was home to basic combat, advanced Infantry and basic training for over half a million Enlisted Men. During 1964, a Drill Sergeant School was opened.

The military buildup at the Fort Ord Post created a housing demand that resulted in the creation of the Cities of Marina, Sand City, and Seaside. There was continued growth at the Fort Ord Post; the concrete barracks were constructed on "The Hill" and the airfield was built. During March 1946, this author vividly remembers the days at Fort Meade in Maryland when German POWs made my bed and shined my shoes while awaiting honorable discharge from the US Army after WW II. The German POWs were paid a monthly salary for their manual labor, walked around the military Base without guards, and were happy to be in the US. Some German POWs did not even want to return to Germany. As a result, military personnel could concentrate on their training for overseas duty. The largest congregation of military personnel at any one time was 50,000; the average population of military personnel was closer to 35,000.

During 1971, the Defense Department first considered an all-volunteer US Army with Project VOLAR. The WACs were abolished when women were given the same assignment rights and advantages as enlisted personnel. During 1973, the last American troops departed for Vietnam. Another training era had ended. On October 25, 1974, the 7th Infantry Division (Light) occupied the Fort Ord Post; Light Infantry stationed at the Presidio operated without heavy tanks, armor, or artillery. During 1975, the military Post became home to the 7th Infantry Division that conducted training exercises on the military Installation. During 1976, the military Post officially curtailed all training archives. During 1948 through 1975, the total number of military personnel trained at the military Post was estimated at 1.5 million. Daring 1976, the Fort Ord Post officially curtailed all training archives.

During 1978, the Headquarters, Fort Ord Garrison staff participated in the Installation Restoration Program; a program established by the DOD to identify, investigate, and control the migration of hazardous contaminants at military Installations and other DOD facilities. During March 1994, the US Army, the EPA, and the State of California signed an Interim Action Plug-in ROD to address Sites with limited soil contamination by soil excavation. The Plug-in ROD identified the criteria each potential Site must be evaluated against. If a Site met the criteria, the US Army could re-mediate the Site by soil excavation according to the Plug-in ROD. The interim actions were focused on addressing primarily surface soils contaminated with fuels and waste oils from motor pools. Soils would be excavated and then treated at a treatment area using bio-remediation. During 1994, a total of 16 Sites had been cleaned-up under the Interim Action Plug-In ROD. During April 1995, a No-Action Plug-in ROD was signed. The ROD was designed for Sites where soil-sampling results indicated levels were below concern. A 30-day public comment period was held for Sites that met the No-Action criteria. A total of 10 Sites had met the No-Action ROD criteria.

During 1984, an investigation into the nature and extent of contamination in the Nietzsche Army Airfield practice fire area began. During September 1995, the ROD was signed. Ground water clean-up standards were established in the ROD that must be met through the existing pump and treat system. The selected remedy was consistent with the initial action described above. This Site was addressed in multiple stage removal actions, interim actions, and long-term remedial phases focusing on clean-up of the entire site to include ground water plumes, the Fort Ord Post landfill, and unexploded ordnance. The US Army initiated an investigation into the nature and extent of ground water contamination. Findings showed an area of contamination known as the Nietzsche Army Airfield practice fire area. During 1988, the US Army installed a ground water and soil treatment system that has been operational. The contaminated ground water was treated through carbon adsorption. A mixture of treated ground water and necessary nutrients was sprayed on the contaminated soil adjacent to the ground water treatment plant to facilitate the completion of soil treatment. During 1988, the ground water treatment system was installed; the selected remedy was consistent with the initial action described above.

During 1985, the 7th Infantry Division (Light) became the US Army's premier Division. The "Base Realignment and Closure Act" had already been passed. The 7th Infantry Division (Light) joined coalition troops sent to the Middle East to defeat Iraq (Desert Storm). During its history, the military Post became home to a succession of Infantry Divisions and served as a Center for Basic and Advanced Combat Training.

During 1988, the Fort Ord Post was being considered as Property-in-Excess.

During 1989, the 7th Infantry Division (Light) was deployed to Panama to restore order and captured Dictator Manuel Norine. The Cold War ended with Russia. One of their last deployments was made to the 1992 Los Angeles riots. The military Post closed its gates and became part of US military history. A total of 121 military Posts and Bases had been closed since the passing of the BRAC 88 Act.[7] When the Cold War ended, the Fort Ord Post was being considered as "Property in Excess."

During 1990, the US Army began further investigations into the nature and extent of on-site and off-site soil and ground water contamination as well as ecological or health threats that could be present in the soil. The investigation identified three waste disposal Sites, firing ranges, and a vehicle maintenance that required extensive clean-up actions.

Since 1994, a total of 16 sites were cleaned-up under the Interim Action Plug-in ROD, and since 1995, 10 additional sites had met the No-Action ROD criteria. During April 1995, a No-Action Plug-in ROD was signed. The ROD was designed for Sites where soil-sampling results indicated levels were below concern. During September 1995, the ground water clean-up standards were established in the ROD that had to be met through the existing pump and treat system. The selected remedy was consistent with the initial action as described above. Sampling results indicated levels at the Fort Ord Post were below concern. A total of 10 had met the No-Action ROD criteria. A 30-day public comment period was held for Sites that met the No-Action criteria.

The EPA placed the Fort Ord Site on the National Priorities. Several areas of contamination existed at the Fort Ord Post. The military Post contained leaking petroleum underground storage tanks, containers of waste oil and various automotive chemicals, chemical storage areas, oil-waste separators, target ranges, and military Post landfills. One on-Site area was a 150-acre landfill that was primarily used to dispose of residential waste, as well as small amounts of commercial waste generated by the military Post. Other areas included a former fire drill area, motor pool maintenance areas, small dump Sites, and small arms target ranges. An 8000-acre firing range and other limited areas on-site posed threats from unexploded ordnance. Approximately 40,000 citizens

---

[7]   www.Fort Ord.com

obtained drinking water from wells located within three-miles of the Site. The Salinas River alluvial basin, El Toto Creek, and Monterey Bay bordered on the site. During 1990, the US Army signed a Federal Facility Agreement with the EPA and the State of California to address on-Site and off-Site contamination at the Fort Ord Post. The US Army clean-up program had three elements:

- The US Army excavated one portion of the military Post landfill (Cell A) on the North side of Imping Road, and consolidated materials from this Site into the larger landfill South of Imping Road;

- The US Army put a cover over the consolidated landfill to keep all surface water (such as rainfall) from reaching the materials in the landfill;

- The US Army built a treatment facility to treat the contaminated ground water. The treatment plant began operating during the Fall of 1995.

The US Secretary of Defense announced that the Department of the Army would begin a process to reduce the number of nationwide military Installations; the Fort Ord Post was one of the first Posts slated for closure. The Fort Ord Post was identified by the US Environmental Protection Agency (EPA) as a Federal Government "Super fund" Site on the basis of ground water contamination discovered on the military Post. The Headquarters, Fort Ord Garrison signed an Inter-agency Agreement with the Environmental Protection Agency (EPA) and the State of California to address on-Site and off-Site contamination

After military Post and Base closure rounds that shuttered scores of military Installations around the Nation, some observers predicted that the BRAC 05 Post and Base Closure and Realignment round would be the biggest and worst ever. Over the next year, BRAC would become a huge issue. The threatened shutdown of military Posts and Bases during an election year was sure to spark a political melee. In addition, Defense Secretary Donald Rumsfeld was already in the midst of transforming the military services while engaged in campaigns in Iraq, Afghanistan, and elsewhere. Mr. Tim Ford, Executive Director of the National Association of Installation Developers (NAID), a group that works with communities that lost a military Post or Base to BRAC dreads the prospect. Mr. Ford stated: "Trying to predict a BRAC is like betting on a horse race. No one really knows. It is a decision based on military values. There are no guarantees. I am sure they are doing some kind of analysis, but they did not reveal that analysis to the public."

During 1991, the Defense Base Realignment and Closure Commission recommended that the Fort Ord Post be downsized to a small military facility. The Commission recommended that the Fort Ord Post be closed and that the 7th Infantry Division (Light) military personnel be realigned at Fort Lewis in Washington. As part of that action, the US Army prepared several documents that identified future land re-use for the military Post following closure. The BRAC identified the principal sources of information and documents prepared by the US Army under the BRAC action; these documents were used in this Remedial Investigation and Feasibility Study to identify future land re-use scenarios at the military Post. The future land re-use scenarios were used to form the basis for appropriate exposure assumptions in conducting the risk assessments and for feasibility studies. The principal documents used in establishing these future land uses included the US Army's Environmental Impact Statement prepared to comply with the National Environmental Policy Act; the US Army's Installation-wide Multi Species Habitat Management Plan (HMP) prepared to comply with the Endangered Species Act; the local community's Re-Use Plan prepared by the Fort Ord Re-Use Authority; and the results of the real estate screening process.

Politics marked the BRAC 91 process despite the efforts to rationalize Post and Base closures. But there were other inequities. While California suffered during the closure of the aforementioned seven military Installations at the same time, Texas had only one Base closure. The military Post was selected for closure and placed on the Post and Base Realignment and Closure (BRAC) list. The US Air Force had the largest number with 14 Base closures. In contrast, the US Army had the fewest military Post closures with eight military Posts making the final list. Among those included was the Fort Ord Post in California. The military Post was the home of the 7th Infantry Division; a so-called "Light Infantry Division." These Infantry Divisions were created during the Cold War period, and some management officials in the US Army saw them as products of the "defense reformers" who rose to prominence during the Carter Administration. The military Post was located on scenic US Highway 1 about six-miles North of Monterey and was once home to 25,000 military personnel and Civil Service employees. During 1993, the military Post was home to the 7th Infantry Division that was inactivated. About 750-acres of the military Post included three housing areas; Post Exchange; and Commissary that were annexed to the Presidio of Monterey. They served the Defense Language Institute; the Naval Postgraduate School; and the Coast Guard Station. About 50-percent of the military Post's remaining property was turned over to the US Bureau of Land Management for re-use as open space. The Coastal Weapon Range became part of the California State Park system.

During September 1993, the 7th Infantry Division (Light) was inactivated and the m military personnel were reassigned to other military Installations. During September 1994, although the Fort Ord Post was closed, the US Army retained approximately five-percent of the property for a Presidio of Monterey (POM) Annex and US Army Reserve Center. The POM Annex was on a 785-acre parcel near Giggling and North-South Roads. The Annex, Ord Military Community was on a 785-acre parcel near Giggling Road and General Jim Moore Boulevard. The US Army retained a 12-acre parcel near Imping Gate at Reservation Road for continued use as a US Army Reserve Center. The military Post is often cited as an example of what can be accomplished during a Post or Base closure or realignment. On September 20, 1994, the Fort Ord Post was officially closed. The responsibility for remaining US Army activities were transferred to the Presidio of Monterey. The Directorate of Environmental and Natural Resources, Presidio of Monterey, managed the clean-up of the military Post under contract with the US Army Corps of Engineers. The US Army planned to permanently retain 812-acres of the military Post's 27,827-acres for other Federal Government use.

The City began protecting itself from BRAC intervention. Since then, there had been numerous attempts to close the DLI that were fought over and defeated. Mayor Dan Albert stated: "I do not even think about what might be done if the DLI and NPS were realigned by BRAC 05." Mayor Albert was a legendary former football and basketball coach at Monterey High School who stated: "Defeat was not an option worth considering. I do not even think about losing." And neither did Representative Sam Farr. The Carmel Democrat deliberately got himself on the Committee that approved military construction projects. He had managed to fortify the local economy with new dorms and classrooms at DLI, and even completed a $2.1 million "academic" style fence for the US National Park Service. The Fort Ord Post closure was such a local catastrophe that the City of Monterey began its own campaign to ensure it did not lose its other two military Posts and Bases; that is, the home of the Defense Language Institute (DLI) and the Naval Postgraduate School. Losing either of these military Sites would have been a City disaster. According to the most recent City analysis, the total military presence here that included smaller facilities; for example, Fleet Numerical Weather Station and the Accounting Center both located at the Fort Ord Post meant a total loss of 10 thousand employees and $1 billion in local spending. To assist the local military Post and Base defray costs, the City took on firefighting duties at both Sites and public works duties at the Presidio of Monterey in an arrangement that was neither a subsidy nor a profit machine according to officials at the City of Monterey.

For Mayor Albert, the presence of the DLI and NPS went beyond socioeconomics. Mayor Albert stated: "The economy is one thing; there is a huge payroll with the DLI and the Naval Postgraduate School. During 1770, when the City of Monterey was founded, the Presidio of Monterey was founded at the same time. The military presence has been part of the community ever since." During the Fort Ord Post closure, the City hired several Management Consultants, and it probably would again if needed according to City officials. Mayor Albert finally stated: "We are going to do everything we can to retain the DLI and Naval Postgraduate School. In the next year, I think it will become the big issue. It is my number one concern."

During early 1994, the DOD issued guidelines for the formation of Restoration Advisory Boards at military Installations undergoing remediation and restoration. The RABs would be the vehicle for "achieving dialogue between Federal Government decision makers and the community." The guidelines described in detail how community RAB members were to be selected; what role RABs would play in clean-up planning and implementation; and even "how to" lessons on communications skills that make for better meetings. As a result, the RABs have been organized at numerous military Installations and facilities. The military services have admitted taken responsibility for and committed it to correcting its toxic legacy was indeed a big step forward. In recognizing that Stakeholders must be given a significant role in the clean-up process is also to be praised.

During March 1994, the EPA and the US Army signed an Interim Action Plug-In Record of Decisions ROD) between the US Army and the State of California to address Sites with limited soil contamination by soil excavation. The Plug-in ROD identified the criteria each potential Site must be evaluated against. If a Site met all the criteria, the US Army could rectify the Site by soil excavation according to the Plug-in ROD. The interim actions were focused on addressing primarily surface soil contaminated with fuels and waste oils from motor pools. Soils were excavated and then treated at a treatment area using bio-remediation. During September 1994, the ROD was signed.
Ground water clean-up standards were established in the ROD that would be met through the existing pump and treatment system.

The US Army completed an investigation focusing on ground water and soil contamination originating from the Fort Ord landfill. Monitoring wells were installed; surface soil samples collected; and soil/gas samples taken. During the Fall of 1994, the US Army selected a remedy ROD) that included capping the landfill and installing a ground water pump and treatment system. Construction of the ground water treatment system was completed and was operational. The US Army had installed an active military Post landfill gas extraction and treatment system to capture and remediate methane and other volatile organic compound gases that were being generated by decaying materials in the landfill. The US Army continued to monitor landfill gases to ensure that they did not pose a health hazard. The US Army has initiated a Remedial Investigation and Feasibility Study of another area of ground water contamination, the so-called "carbon tetrachloride plume operable unit" near the City of Marina. Contaminants slightly above regulatory standards were found in off-Site ground water. This area of contamination was not being used for drinking water. Potential source areas were also being investigated. The military Post was officially closed. The US Army planned to retain 812-acres of the military Post's 27,827-acres.

The Fort Ord Post closed and was no longer officially an Infantry Training Post although training operations by the US Army would still take place at several military Installations. The 20,000-acres on the Central Coast of California now have a State University where portions would be developed into research facilities and resorts. A majority of the 20,000-acres that were used as training grounds would remain as natural reserves. The US Army would also retain parts of the military Post for several functions to include Annexes for the Defense Language Institute and the Presidio of Monterey. Several contaminated and unexploded ordnance areas within the Military Post were fenced off and would be continuously monitored.

When the Fort Ord Post closed, 2800 Civil Service employees lost their positions and 7500 military family members left town. After a decade, the Fort Ord Post's re-use is far from a success story. In fact, the debacle of the Fort Ord Post's and Monterey's efforts to preserve its remaining military Posts serves as somewhat contrasting national examples of the BRAC phenomenon. Both Monterey City Manager Mr. Fred Mercer and the Fort Ord Re-Use Authority Executive Officer Mr. Michael Housemaid sat on the NAID Board. Monterey would host the annual meeting of the NAID during August that was attended by some "significant" military personnel and DOD officials with BRAC 05 topping the agenda for that meeting. Monterey's efforts to become a community partner with DLI and NPS would serve as an example for communities eying their own possible BRAC. Mr. Ford stated: "Communities all over the Country were doing the same things you see in Monterey, especially places that have a major military service presence that plays a significant role in the local economy."

After the Fort Ord Post closed, public access to the Fort Ord lands increased dramatically. The US Army was conducting various actions to clean-up known and suspected Munitions Response (MR) sites to make it safe for the public to access the military Post. Munitions Response actions were proceeding in areas where there were explosive threats to the public. The MR Remedial Investigation and Feasibility Study (MR RI/FS) Program would investigate various clean-up alternatives and recommend remedial actions that would ensure eventual safe re-use of MEC Sites. The US Army was coordinating these Munitions Response Programs with the Fort Ord Post Realignment and Closure (BRAC) Clean-Up Team that consisted of the US Army, US Environmental Protection Agency (EPA), and California EPA-Department of Toxic Substances Control (DTSC).

On June 14, 1994, the 7th Infantry Division Light was deactivated.

During 1988 through 1995, after painful criticism from closing 97 major US Air Force Bases, US Army Posts, US Navy Stations, and smaller facilities, the US Congress during 2002 agreed to the next BRAC round but put it off until 2005. In the US Congress, military Post and Base closures were particularly unpalatable. Mr. Ford stated: "They would rather do anything else than say 'Yes' to a Base closure." So the US Congress replied: "Let us have a BRAC to end all criticism." The other factor fueling BRAC fear of military Post and Base closures was, according to Washington information, that the DOD believed that DOD was 25-percent in an excess capacity in the military network of military Installations. That meant nearly 90 military Posts and Bases could be closed. Mr. Ford stated: "Some 130,000 Civil Service employees were lost last time around." However, some 90,000 civilian employee positions were re-created through military Post and Base re-use. Presumptive Democratic nominee Senator John Kerry had hinted at postponing BRAC stated: "The whole thing could get upended following the Presidential election." The aftermath of a BRAC was evident in the white elephant known as the Fort Ord Post. On May 15, 2005, a list of military Installations eligible for closure was released by the DOD. The military Posts and Bases that were economically crucial to their neighboring communities, but extraneous and costly to the DOD were on that list.

During August 1996, the changes were documented in the Explanation of Significant Differences (ESD). The consolidation was completed and the main landfill was capped, with the exception of one cell that remained partially open in order to receive lead contaminated soils from the clean-up of small arms ranges throughout the Fort Ord Post. The US Army proposed to consolidate wastes from several areas around the main landfill that would provide more clean land for re-use.

During 1995, "some of the more dangerous contaminants on military Post land were the thousands of tons of unexploded ordnance that has accumulated for decades at many military Posts estimated at 620 sites. The magnitude of the problem was indicated by the fact that 55,000-acres of former Fort Ord Post property was so contaminated with unexploded munitions that it would have to remain the property of the Federal Government to perpetuity. Firing ranges at the military Post in California had accumulated so many spent lead bullets that much of the beach area (to become a State Park) had taken on a gray color. A far more serious problem existed at the military Post's 8000-acre impact range where the Bureau of Land Management proposed to limiting access to the 8000-acres in order to minimize risks to the public. The cost of cleaning-up ammunition at the Fort Ord Post could exceed $300 million and would take at least 10-years to accomplish."[8]

During 1997, the US Army completed the RI/FS and ROD allowing them to first clean-up the lead contamination; ensure ground water pump and treatment systems were operational; and address human health concerns by soil excavation and placement in the Fort Ord Post landfill that was simultaneously being rectified (capped). The action included remediating Sites 2 and 12 maintenance and disposal areas by soil excavation and ongoing ground water remediation, and Sites 16, 17, and 31 disposal areas by soil excavation.

During 2000, a comprehensive RI/FS was initiated-the first such RI/FS nationally. The RI/FS evaluated ordnance detection equipment and procedures, risk assessment approaches, and long-term monitoring methods to name a few. The RI/FS split into different tracks (0-3) to allow for sites at various phases of investigation to move through the decision making process faster. For example, Track 0 sites were those sites that UXO was not suspected and required no action, whereas Track 3 sites that UXO was suspected but no investigation occurred. Track 0-Plug-in ROD was expected to be signed during late 2001 or early 2002. The clean-up was completed with the dunes being re-contoured and re-vegetated.

---

8   David S. Sorenson, "Shutting Down the Cold War: The Politics of Military Base Closure," (St. Martin's Press, New York. July 1998), pp. 82-83.

The US Army finalized a military Post clean-up ecological risk assessment that suggested the initial clean-up was protective of ecological species as well.

During 2001, the US Army installed an active landfill gas extraction and treatment system to capture and rectify methane and other volatile organic compound gases that were being generated by decaying materials in the military Post landfill. The US Army addressed the clean-up of UXO through removal actions as discussed above.

On June 19, 2002, a Record of Decision (ROD) for Track 0 was signed. Track 1 Sites are Sites where munitions and explosives of concern were suspected but no further remedial action were deemed necessary to protect human health and the environment. On September 15, 2004, the Track 1 Proposed Plan was issued for public comment and the ROD was scheduled to be signed during 2005. Track 2 Sites were Sites where munitions and explosives of concern were found and a removal action was conducted for clean-up. The first of several Track 2 RI/FS reports were due to be issued for the area explosives of concern were known to be present but no clean-up had been conducted during 2005. By 2007, the final Track 3 ROD was expected to be completed with UXO clean-up work continuing for at least 10-years.

During September 2002, an interim action ROD was signed to allow the US Army to initiate clean-up actions at several ranges that contained extremely sensitive and dangerous UXO amidst thick vegetation that needed to be removed first so the UXO could be seen and cleared. Prescribed burns were selected as the safest method to clear vegetation while also protecting special status plants. To minimize smoke impacts to the community, the US Army developed a specific set of meteorological conditions where a burn would be conducted such that smoke would disperse and have offered temporary relocation to all residents of the County during each burn.

During December 2002, most of the excavated soils were placed at the Fort Ord Post landfill that was closed. The US Army was excavating treatment disposal options for additional Site 39 small arms ranges by soil excavation. Additional Site 39 soils were intended for the landfill if the capacity existed. Site 3 Beach Small Arms Firing Range was situated within 3.2-miles (780-acres) of dunes along the coastline of Monterey Bay at the Western boundary of the military Post. Results of the investigation indicated lead from small arms was the main contaminant at this Site.

The US Army addressed the clean-up of unexploded ordnance through removal actions and remedial actions. During 2000, a comprehensive RI/FS was initiated— the first such RI/FS nationally. The RI/FS evaluated ordnance detection equipment and procedures, risk assessment approaches, and monitoring methods to name a few. The RI/FS for munitions Sites at the Fort Ord Post utilized a tracking process to allow for sites at various phases of investigation to move through the decision making process faster. According to this tracking process, a munitions Site on the military Post was assigned to one of four Tracks: Track 0 through Track 3. Track 0 Sites were Sites that have no evidence of use of munitions and explosives of concern.

The US Army had transferred over 10,000-acres, with 7212-acres going to the Bureau of Land Management. The other major recipient of the military Post land was the California State University (CSU) system. The CSU Monterey Campus was located on the Site of the former military Post and was expected to expand in the future. Clean-up activities were not affected by military Post closure activities except to the extent that they were accelerated to facilitate more rapid land transfers. The Fort Ord Garrison was a permanent military Installation under the operational control of the Headquarters, Sixth US Army at the Presidio of San Francisco.

On October 24, 2003, the first prescribed burn took place. The burn escaped the initial boundaries and 1000-acres were burned. The US Army studied the October 2003 burn to understand both what went right and what went wrong. Ordnance has been cleared from the surface of the entire burned area and subsurface clearance was ongoing.

During 2004, a soil vapor sampling and Extraction System Pilot Study was conducted to address the Vaduz Zone above the carbon tetrachloride plume area. The pilot study was successful and appeared to have removed significant mass from the Vaduz Zone. The next prescribed burn took place during 2005. The US Army awarded a fixed price contract for the management and completion of the ground water clean-up remedy at Operable Unit 1.

During 2005, the US Army expected to complete the draft Remedial Investigation and Feasibility Study Report for the carbon tetrachloride plume operable unit. The ground water treatment systems at the fire practice area; the military Post landfill; and Sites 2 and 12 areas; the capping of the landfill and removal and treatment of landfill gas; a pilot soil vapor extraction system for volatile organic compounds in the Vaduz Zone above the carbon tetrachloride plume; and the removal of soil and debris reduced the potential of exposure to contaminants. UXO removal actions, fencing, warning signs, and patrols had further reduced exposure to UXO. Contaminated ground water was not being used for drinking water. The final Track 3-ROD was expected to be completed with UXO clean-up work that would continue for at least additional 10-years.

The US Army had transferred over 13,000-acres, with 7212-acres going to the Bureau of Land Management. The other major recipient of the military Post property was the California State University (CSU) system. The CSU Monterey campus was located on the Fort Ord Post and was expected to expand in the future. Clean-up activities were not affected by military Post closure activities, except to the extent that they were being accelerated to facilitate more rapid land transfers for private use.

The DOD transferred much of the sprawling 28,000 sandy acres of agriculture land and Monterey Bay beach front except for 800-acres the US Army retained as a Reserve Center and an Annex for the Presidio of Monterey. The State of California sanctioned the Fort Rod Re-Use Authority (FORA) to oversee the hands-off, and the military Post now housed the new and growing California State University Monterey Bay campus. The Campus takes up 1365-acres, leaving much of the former military Post property unused. Recent developments have begun to provide housing for military personnel stationed at nearby military Installations and improved facilities; landscaping; infrastructure; and access. However, many challenges remained. The area's unique geography houses a sensitive environment and protected species such as the threatened California Tiger Salamander. The clean-up of a wide variety of potentially unexploded ordinance, toxic spills, and abandoned and dilapidated buildings would take years and considerable funding. However, the area's geographic desirability and high housing prices argue well for the military Post's future. The military Post was officially closed. The US Army planned to permanently retain 812-acres of the military Post's 27,827-acres for other Federal Government use.

The Fort Ord Post included three housing areas. The Post Exchange and Commissary were annexed to the Presidio of Monterey. They served the Defense Language Institute; Naval Postgraduate School; and Coast Guard Station. About 50-percent of the military Post's remaining property was open space. The Coastal Weapons Ranges would become part of the California State Park System. The new California State University at Monterey Bay and the University of California at Santa Cruz new Research Center opened its doors on former military Post property, and the Monterey Institute of International Studies was programmed to take over the Officer's Club and several other buildings. The military Post's airfield was turned over to the City of Marina. The US Army continued to occupy 277 buildings to include 600 family housing units, Community Club; Commissar; Post Exchange; and a small Medical Clinic.

Unlike the Presidio of San Francisco closure that had an administrative mission, the 1991 Defense Base Realignment and Closure Commission still recommended that the Fort Ord Post be closed and that troops of the 7th Infantry Division (Light) be realigned to Fort Lewis in Washington. The military Post was one of several military Installations subordinate to the Headquarters, US Sixth Army. As part of that action, the US Army prepared several documents that identified future land uses for the military Post to follow Post closure. The BRAC identified the principal sources of information and documents prepared by the US Army under BRAC action; these documents were used in this Remedial Investigation and Feasibility Study that identified future land use scenarios at the military Post. The future land use scenarios were used to form the basis for appropriate exposure assumptions to conduct Risk Assessments and Feasibility Studies. The principal documents used to establish these future land uses included the US Army's Environmental Impact Statement prepared to comply with the National Environmental Policy Act; the US Army's Installation-wide Multi-species Habitat Management Plan (HMP) prepared to comply with the Endangered Species Act; the local community's draft Re-Use Plan prepared by the Fort Ord Re-Use Authority; and the results of the real estate screening process.

The Base Closure and Realignment Act of 1988 promulgated the US Army's interest to solicit industry and secure competitive offers to convert part of the support functions and activities from in-house to contractor operation. The magnitude of the functions for contracting out conversion could be equivalent to that performed by assigned Civil Service employees. Underlying BRAC, contracting out functions and entire activities performed by Civil Service employees was usually caused by personnel ceilings established within Federal Government agencies. In theory, contracting out resulted in tangible savings by reducing overhead costs per man-year. The paradox; however, was far from the truth. At any given time, any Federal Government agency, the Office of Personnel Management (OPM) or its predecessor the US Civil Service Commission (USCSC), and the Office of Manpower and Budget (OMB) could give the exact number of people directly employed by the Federal Government.

However, there was no one in the Federal Government, from the White House down, who had any specific data of man-days or man-years bought by Federal Government agencies from private contractors. For decades, the DOD has attempted to amass information concerning man-days purchased from private contractors. So far, these attempts have been a dismal failure. The problem was that each Federal Government agency had varying degrees of personnel ceilings. The US Congress has established manpower ceilings for the DOD based on elaborate hearings. However, there were other Federal Government agencies with little or no personnel ceiling restraints. In addition, the OMB accepted the Congressional ceilings and established their own ceiling that is commonly called the Bureaucratic versus Democratic Government. The US Congress decided the manpower needs for Federal Government agencies and in turn, a power group in the OMB, far removed from the Electorate, made its own questionable decisions for manpower manning requirements.

For many years, Personnel Specialists who followed the Civil Service personnel ceiling control process believed that OMB restraints were cleverly devised to throw more Federal Government work to private contractors. There was no doubt that the biggest reason private contractors were used in the Federal Government was due to Civil Service personnel ceilings. However, Civil Service personnel ceilings used by the Federal Government merely deceived the taxpayer. That is, the average taxpayer believed the Federal Government used less manpower when actually the Federal Government paid more for total labor requirements that included statistics on the number of both direct hire and contractor personnel. For example, productivity is measured every year in the Federal Government by comparing a constant workload to the authorized number of Civil Service employees. With contracting out decreasing the number of employees in this equation, Federal Government agencies could now portray false productivity figures to partially justify minimizing yearly cost-of-living pay raises for Civil Service employees.

The revised or reduced Civil Service employee ceiling usually required management in Federal Government agencies to contract out for labor, as man-years were the problem and not dollars. Thus we find the Federal Government in the paradoxical situation of giving up the role of the model employee. For example, the employer with appropriate training; compensation; work hours; upward mobility; retirement program; insurance; etc., for the lowest private contractor bid for furnishing labor. Of course many private contractors can and did equal the Federal Government's model employer role. But to obtain the contract of furnishing labor to the Federal Government at the lowest possible cost, the majority of profit-motive companies had to bid as low as possible, pay minimum wages, hold fringe benefits to a minimum, and leave training of employees up to the Federal Government. There were many Federal Government agencies where Civil Service employees, well trained and fully qualified, faced a reduction-in-force (RIF) to be replaced at the same work bench with lower-paid, less qualified employees furnished by these so called "flesh merchants." After contracting out for labor occurred at worldwide military Installations, there could be little wonder what the effect would be on Civil Service employee's morale, productivity, and discipline.

The Defense Language Institute was located on the Presidio of Monterey (POM). Permanent party military personnel assigned to the Institute lived in military housing on a portion of what previously the Fort Ord Post. Also located on the Annex were the Commissary; Post Exchange; Main Chapel; Youth Services Center; Army Community Service; AAFES Gas Station; Thrift Shop; Library; Child Development Center; Grammar School; and a Middle School. A local community Task Force was formed to address the impacts of this announcement and prepare a strategy report. This report helped set direction for many activities that were to follow. Following completion of the report, the Task Force disbanded and a new group was formed to develop a Presidio Post Re-Use Plan.

A new group called the Fort Ord Re-Use Group (FORG) was established. The Fort Ord Re-Use Plan was in initial preparation stages when special State legislation was passed changing FORG into a governing body known as the Fort Ord Re-Use Authority (FORA). FORA became responsible for planning, financing, implementing, and regulating a Post Re-Use Plan to receive former military Post property from the Department of the Army for development by local communities. Warm and dry summers and cool, rainy winters characterize the area's climate. The Pacific Ocean was the principal influence on the climate causing fog and onshore winds with moderate temperature extremes. Daily ambient air temperatures typically ranged from 40-degrees to 70-degrees Fahrenheit, but temperatures in the low 100s did occur. Fog was common during the morning throughout the year.

Winds were generally from the West. The average annual rainfall of 14-inches occurred almost entirely between November and April. Because the predominant soil was permeable sand, runoff was limited and stream flow only occurred intermittently and within the very steep Canyons in the Eastern portion of the military Post According to Mr. Farr's office, Mr. Farr had directed $82.4 million to local military construction projects. Mr. Farr stated: "I probably know more about BRAC than anybody in Congress. 'Pork' alone will not save military Posts or Bases." After the last BRAC round, Mr. Farr convened with Post, Base, and local Government officials to ponder whether the remaining military facilities were relevant to the military service, whether they had a unique role that could not be found elsewhere, and whether being in the Monterey area was critical. Mr. Farr liked to point out that General John Abigail, Commanding General of the US Central Command that oversees military operations in the Middle East and Central Asia stated: "He considered the DLI and NPS National treasures." Justifying a Monterey address can be subjective when other places may have more room and are cheaper.

In previous BRAC rounds, there was some thought in moving the DLI at Fort Huachuca in Arizona because it's the next place many DLI graduates go for military Intelligence Training. Mr. Farr stated: "That faculty protesting an exodus to the desert caused the idea to be reconsidered. For NPS, the requirement to stay in Monterey was harder to pin down. It's here and it's growing because of its cross relationships with DLI, the Monterey Institute of International Studies and CSUMB. We have put hundreds of millions of dollars into DLI and NPS." One thing that could argue against keeping the Post in Monterey is the high cost of housing; as the military provided a locally adjusted military Post housing allowance for service members who wanted to live off Post. Mr. Farr also dismissed the cost-of-living argument, as the US Navy for one, had Bases in expensive coastal areas like San Diego. Mr. Farr stated: "He did not believe that DLI or NPS would close. Rather he relied on a tactic used by Captain James T. Kirk of Star Trek that went: 'Change the rules so your side wins.'"

The ground water treatment systems at the former fire practice area; a landfill; Sites 2 and 12; capping of the landfill; and the removal of soil and debris reduced the potential of exposure to contaminants and unexploded ordnance (UXO) removal actions. Fencing and patrols further reduced the public exposure to UXO. The US Army investigated the carbon tetrachloride ground water plume. Potentially responsible parties (PRPs) refer to companies that were potentially responsible for generating, transporting, or disposing of the hazardous waste found at the Site. Information about the PRPs for the Site was not yet available. The US Army has held monthly community involvement workshops to keep the public up-to-date on progress at the Site. The US Army maintained a web-Site that contains valuable Site information to include upcoming community involvement workshops.

"A RAND Corporation study of the communities surrounding the Fort Ord Post revealed population growth and increases in the value of housing and retail sales after military Post and Base closures. The study found similar results at the George AFB and the Castle AFB."[9] For the military, other disruptions also stemmed from Post and Base closures. For example, military Golf Courses were closed to include some famous courses such as the Presidio of San Francisco and the Fort Ord Post both in California."[10] "Military efficiency was also hampered by political interference in military operations and funding due to efforts to mitigate negative military Post and Base impacts. For example, Section 8090 of the Defense Appropriations Act of Fiscal Year 1997 appropriated $7 million for the California State University Monterey Bay at the Fort Ord Post Site."[11]

On-Site ground water was contaminated with Volatile Organic Compounds. Contaminants were detected in ground water samples collected from the Fort Ord Post. On-site soils in several vehicle maintenance and motor pool areas, and a 150-acre landfill and other minor dump Sites were contaminated with chemicals that were spilled on the ground. In addition, soils at target ranges were contaminated with lead. These contaminated soils have been addressed significantly, reducing or eliminating the potential threat to public health. Unexploded ordnance on an 8000-acre firing range and at limited on-Site areas also posed severe safety hazards for the public visiting the site.

A Multi-Range Area (MRA) was located in the South-Central portion of the Fort Ord Post. Lands within the boundaries of the MRA were expected to have the highest density of ordnance and explosives (OE), with specific target areas having the highest densities. OE is defined as bombs; warheads; propellants and all similar and related items, and component explosives that constituted a threat to be re-activated and present an imminent safety hazard. These ordnance and explosives Sites were posted with warning signs that stated: "Off-limits to Unauthorized Personnel."

Both time-critical and non-time-critical removal actions to address unexploded ordnance both in-side and out-side the 8000-acre firing range were ongoing while the Ordnance and Explosives Remedial Investigations and Feasibility Study was underway. The US Army developed a Site Security Program to increase education, fencing, sign age, and overall security to prevent the public from coming into contact with unexploded ordnance until final actions were complete.

---

9   David S. Sorenson, "Shutting Down the Cold War: The Politics of Military Base Closure," (St. Martin's Press, New York, July 1998), p. 74.

10 David S. Sorenson, "Shutting Down the Cold War: The Politics of Military Base Closure," (St. Martin's Press, New York, July 1998), pp. 86-87.

11 David S. Sorenson, "Shutting Down the Cold War: The Politics of Military Base Closure," (St. Martin's Press, New York, July 1998), pp. 224.

During 1993, an archival investigation was conducted to locate areas where Munitions and Explosives of Concern (MEC) had been used. Since 1993, additional archive searches, follow-on interviews, and visual inspections conducted indicated that approximately 12,000-acres were known or suspected to contain MEC. There was 29 Munitions Response (MR) sites were identified in the Phase One Engineering Evaluation and Cost Analysis (EE/CA). The Phase II EE/CA established a process to evaluate the remaining sites. The areas range in size from less than one-acre to more than 1000-acres, although most of the areas were less than 200-acres. To date, approximately 3000-acres have been investigated or received response actions designed to minimize the explosive safety risk.

The Fort Ord Post had been established since 1917 until the inactivation of the 7th Infantry Division (Light) during 1994. The Fort Ord Post was primarily a combat training and staging facility for the Infantry with many areas of the military Post being used for Ordnance training. The Department of Defense Ammunition and Explosive Safety Standards stated that real property that is known to be contaminated with ammunition explosive chemical agents must be decontaminated with the most appropriate technology to ensure the protection of the public consistent with the proposed end use of the property. This standard was incorporated into US Army Regulations 385-64 (US Army Explosives Safety Program). During 2003, the US Army began implementing new terminology nationwide to describe its Ordnance Up Program at the military Post such as Administrative Record Documents, Fact Sheets, minutes of meetings, and pages within the web Site that were created prior to 2004 to include the old terminology. The new terminology was being incorporated into newly written materials as they became available.

The Fort Ord Post removal process was documented in the EE/CAs and prepared in accordance with the Comprehensive Environmental Response, Compensation and Liability Act (CERCLA). These documents received thorough regulatory and public review. An Impact Area was located in the South-Central portion of the military Post and was designated as a Munitions Response (MR) Site. Lands within the boundaries of the impact area were expected to have the highest density of MEC, with specific target areas having the highest densities. Types of MEC found at the military Post included artillery projectiles; rockets; hand grenades; land mines; pyrotechnics; bombs; demolition materials; and other items. Known MR Sites were posted with warning signs and were off-limits to unauthorized people.

Unexploded ordnance (UXO) can be very unstable and may be a serious safety hazard. DANGER and NO TRESPASSING signs were posted around areas where UXO could be present. The most dangerous areas were fenced and signs were posted. The safety of public citizens living, working, and recreationing on the Fort Ord Post was the top priority of the military Installation. It was the military Post's policy that no person would be injured by munitions and explosives of concern (MEC), regardless of the circumstances. Immediately following the military Post closure, the military Installation examined site security in areas suspected of containing MEC to ensure appropriate measure were in place to effectively reduce the explosive threat to the community until removal actions could be completed. The following measures were completed to reduce the explosive threat to the community by:

- Conducting removal actions; and installing a four strand barbed wire fence around the impact area;

- Posting "Danger" and "No Trespassing" signs on the fencing; security patrols; and establishing a public education program.

A "Trespassing Incident" form was developed to assist the US Army respond to trespassing incidents in restricted areas. Trespass in restricted areas on the Fort Ord Post was a serious threat to public safety. As a result of the US Army's use of military munitions on the Fort Ord Post, employees working on or re-using the military Post's property could encounter unexploded ordnance (UXO). Therefore, training was recommended for anyone excavating on the military Post, and required for all Civil Service employees and private contractor employees entering restricted munitions response sites. The US Army Corps of Engineers (USACE) offered training to all private contractors, property owners, and Civil Service employees involved in intrusive (digging) activities on the military Post. The training would orient attendees on UXO avoidance, the visual characteristics of UXO, and the precautions necessary if encountered. Attendees would be provided the procedures for contacting authorities if UXO were encountered:

- It was free;

- It would take about 20-minutes at the USACE facility;

- The USACE would make special arrangements for (come to your job Site) training groups of 15 or more personnel.

The US Army had continued Munitions Response (MR) actions under the time-critical and non-time critical processes, as described in the National Contingency Plan (TCRA). The US Army began conducting Time-Critical Removal Action (TCRA) shortly before the military Post closure. Subsequently, Phase One and Phase Two Engineering Evaluation and Cost Analysis (EE/CA) were prepared to transition into the Non-Time Critical Removal Action (NTCRA) process. The EE/CA identified removal objectives, and analyzed and compared removal alternatives. The effectiveness, feasibility, and cost of the solutions were weighed, and only the most qualified technologies were formally considered. From this analysis, the recommended removal alternatives were clearly described as the alternatives that best satisfied the evaluation criteria.

Additionally, selected alternatives complied with applicable or relevant and appropriate requirements to the extent possible. After all recommended solutions were published in an EE/CA; a one 30-day public comment period was required. However, the US Army had held four public comment periods and several public meetings for the two EE/CAs. The US Army responded to all regulatory agency and public concerns to achieve acceptable solutions. The Non-Time Critical Removal Action was documented in Action Memorandum Phase Two EE/CA. Prior to conducting a NTCRA at a Site, Site specific clean-up plans were presented to regulatory Government agencies and the public in a Notice of Intent (NOI) for a 30-day public review period.

The review period began with the announcement in local and major newspapers of the availability of the NOI. Once a clean-up was completed at a Site, an After-Action Report was prepared to document what was found and what corrective action would be taken. Those documents were available at the Fort Ord Administrative Record and in the local information repositories. Once an area had been identified as potentially containing MEC (through archives search or interviews), the area was inspected by an Ordnance Safety Specialist for any evidence of past MEC use. This inspection was documented in a report that may or may not recommend further action. If further action was recommended, the investigations continued to verify the presence and determine the extent of MEC. This was called Site characterization, and typically involved investigating all portions of the site and excavating every piece of detected metal to determine if it was an MEC item or trash. The information would be analyzed using statistical methods to determine the types and distribution of MEC at the site that would enable the Project Manager to determine the appropriate clean-up approach. Once the clean-up approach was published in an NOI, the entire removal area would be surveyed for any metallic item that could be detected, and all of the detected items would be excavated to determine if they were an MEC item or trash. All of the unexploded ordnance discovered during the investigation and removal operations would be destroyed by detonation.

In addition to continuing munitions response actions to address any immediate threat to the general public, the US Army conducted the MR RI/FS Program under the CERCLA remedial action process. The MR RI/FS would recommend actions to be taken to ensure safe re-use of the Fort Ord Post property. The US Army would re-evaluate past investigation and removal actions, and would determine if additional actions were necessary. For areas where MEC investigation or removal had not occurred, the MR RI/FS would evaluate risks, vegetation clearance methods and MEC detection technologies, and develop remedial alternatives. The evaluations would be conducted in separate studies, and each study would undergo regulatory and general public review. Then, remedial alternatives would be developed and compared using nine evaluation criteria specified in the NCP to include:

- Protection of human health and the environment;

- Compliance with regulations;

- Long-term effectiveness and permanence;

- Reduction of toxicity, mobility, or volume through treatment;

- Short-term effectiveness;

- Implementation;

- Cost;

- State acceptance;

- Community acceptance.

An alternative that best satisfied the nine evaluation criteria would be selected and presented to regulatory agencies and the public in a proposed plan during a 30-day public comment period. After all the comments were considered, a Record of Decision would document the remedial action to be implemented for each area. All MR RI/FS documents were made available at the Fort Ord Administrative Record and in the local information repositories.

The Fort Ord Post has continued munitions response removal actions under the time-critical and non-time critical processes as described in the National Contingency Plan (NCP). Removal actions complied with the substantive requirements of applicable, relevant, and appropriate regulations (ARs) to the extent practicable. The non-time critical removal process included the preparation of an EE/CA. The EE/CA identified removal objectives and analyzed and compared removal alternatives. The effectiveness, feasibility, and cost of the solutions were weighed, and only the most qualified technologies were addressed. From the analysis data, the recommended removal action alternative was clearly described as the alternative that best satisfied the evaluation criteria.

Although the public was involved throughout the entire project, peak involvement occurred during the EE/CA process. The US Army responded to all public concerns to achieve an acceptable solution. The selected EE/CA removal alternatives were either a surface removal or removals of MEC down to a depth of four-feet but each must remove the imminent explosive threat. The US Army recognized that there were limitations in the detection of MEC. The US Army was in the process of transitioning from CERCLA removal actions into CERCLA remedial actions. The US Army would be re-evaluating its removal action results to include the MEC detection capabilities in a Remedial Investigation and Feasibility Study (RI/FS). The RI/FS would evaluate MEC detection systems addressed in the EE/CAs to be used in future work at the Fort Ord Post.

During the Site characterization and removal, the US Army's Munitions Response (MR) contractor performed quality control (QC) by randomly re-checking areas that have already been investigated. If the contractor failed the QC check, then they would re-accomplish the grid. A US Army Ordnance Safety Specialist would then perform quality assurance (QA) by randomly checking a minimum of 10-percent of the grid that the contractor has completed. If the QA inspection did not pass, the contractor would have to re-accomplish the grid. Once the QC/QA checks were completed, all fieldwork and the results of investigation and removal action were documented in an After Action Report that would be made available for regulatory agency and public review. The work would also be re-evaluated during the Military Response Remedial Investigation and Feasibility Study.

The RI/FS would also likely recommend language to be included in property transfer documents to notify the recipient of the location of the Site, sampling efforts and results, and response action results. Removals were conducted to the depths that were appropriate for the given MEC characteristics. Once an area had been identified as potentially containing MEC (through archives searches or interviews), the area was inspected by an Ordnance Safety Specialist for evidence of MEC. The inspection was documented in a report that may or may not recommend further action. If further actions were recommended, the Site was characterized to verify the presence and determine the extent of MEC. Site characterization (also known as sampling) was accomplished by using one of two methods.

The first method of grid sampling divided the area into grid squares (approximately 100-feet x 100-feet) and selected a minimum of 10-percent of the grid squares that were investigated using magnetometers to a depth of four-feet. Every piece of metal detected by the magnetometers was excavated to determine if it was MEC. The second method of grid sampling was performed using a computer program called Site Stats/Grid Stats. This program used a statistical method to determine the presence or absence of MEC. All discovered unexploded ordnance was detonated on the Fort Ord Post. The US Army was transitioning from CERCLA removal actions to CERCLA remedial actions. The US Army was in the process of developing a Work Plan that would outline the strategies to address remediation of unexploded ordnance at the military Post.

Deputy Defense Secretary Rudy De Leon told a convention of developers: "The closing of a military Post does not have to be a never ending disaster for the surrounding community." During the early 1990s, Secretary De Leon pointed to the example of the US Army's Fort Ord Post in California that was deactivated as part of the BRAC process. Secretary DeLeon stated: "The surrounding area, that included Monterey, had made enormous progress since the closure." Two new institutions of higher learning-California State University at Monterey Bay and the University of California at Santa Cruz Research Center had opened their doors on the Fort Ord Post property. Secretary DeLeon stated: "In all, more than $3 billion had been invested in the Site, creating in excess of 10,000 new positions, far exceeding the 2000 Civil Service employee positions that were there when the military Post was closed."

The future of land use in Monterey County would be determined by the future of land use in the Salinas Valley. The Salinas Valley contained tens of thousands of acres of the most economically productive farmland in the World. It was also the most developed part of Monterey County. It is flat and it had water. It was just the kind of place that large-scale residential and commercial developers would like to put their hands on. Practically nowhere in California had that kind of farmland been saved when development pressures arrived. It was not saved in the Santa Clara Valley. It was not saved in Los Angeles County or Orange County. It's being lost right now in every County in California as developers seek new land to build on. The future of land use in the Salinas Valley would be determined in large part not by what Monterey does, but by what the Cities of the Salinas Valley accomplish. The Planning Commission in the City of Greenfield went to work on the City's housing element, set its meeting schedule for the year ahead, and considered the City's Redevelopment Plans. If interested in the larger and long-term issues, it would be a good time to get acquainted with some of the individuals who were going to have an impact on the future of land use in this part of the World. The future of land Monterey County would be determined by the future of land use in the Salinas Valley. What happened to that incredibly productive farmland really is key, and development threats in that farmland, and hence in the Monterey County agricultural industry that are the very real threats? However, farmland protection is not the only issue. Another key question was: "What will finally happen to the Fort Ord Post?"

The Monterey County Board of Supervisors met to consider an allocation of 52.5-acres of potable water from what it called its "Fort Ord allocation." If the Board approved the water allocation, Monterey Peninsula College would be able to develop a Public Safety Officer Training Facility. This was an interesting project in and of itself. Water makes development possible. One reason that the farmlands of Salinas are such an inviting target for developers is that they already have water on site. It took about the same amount of water per-acre to grow a crop of lettuce or a crop of homes. If the people of Monterey County would rather develop on the military Post, that would make good planning sense as they would have to address the water issue.

A land use policy has a big impact on our lives as it affects the environment and the economy. It affects the social relationships and how we live together. The economy, environment, and equity are the three "Es" of a land use policy. A land use policy is the product of community decision making. However, public citizens do not always appreciate this. Individual landowners do carry out individual projects, and those individual projects do affect the community greatly. However, it's simply not legally true that property owners can do whatever they want. Where land use is involved, individuals need to get permission from the community before they do any alterations to the land. That is why we have the so-called "permit process." Ultimately, the rules governing land use reflect community choices. In this particular system, involvement with the local Government was necessary. Most land use decisions are discriminatory at the local level. If you are interested in land use policy, and how that relates to the future of your community, you should get involved in local Government.

Citizen participation is the key to land use policy. Ultimately, land use decisions reflect community choices. To have an impact on the future of the community, where land use policy is involved, you will need to increase the rate of your participatory heartbeat. It takes some training to do that, just like those aerobic fitness programs take work to raise our physical heartbeat. However, better physical health and better community health are available to all of us if we will do the work. How the Fort Ord Post would be developed would have a profound impact on the future of Monterey County. Properly developed, the military Post could help bring positions and affordable housing together on the Monterey Peninsula. The decision that the County made about its East Garrison lands had to be recognized as a critical choice.

The Fort Ord Dunes State Park was established to perpetuate forever for the public use, inspiration, aesthetic enjoyment, and education. It is in an area along the Central California Coast of unique natural beauty and scientific significance to include sandy beaches and coastal dunes. All scenic, natural, cultural, and recreational resources would be managed as a whole, preserving and restoring the natural character of the State Park in accordance with ecological principles. Located on Monterey Bay, the State Park has four-miles of shoreline with 886-acres. The State Park was also an area of contrasts. Millions of people saw it as they drove by on State Highway #1, but it has been closed to the public for decades. The land was open and relatively undeveloped, yet the past development of the land for small arms training has significantly altered the landscape. The US Army deserves credit for preserving the open space character of the land, yet they used the land for the most utilitarian purposes to include sewage treatment and storm water disposal. The full force of the Pacific Ocean pounds the beaches and bluffs and yet they are composed of tiny grains of unconsolidated sand. The vegetation was dominated by African ice plant, yet the area was highly valued for its habitat value for endangered species. The area was revered for its beauty; however, the Site does include over 100 abandoned buildings.[12]

Much of the beauty of the Fort Ord Dunes State Park was in its potential. There was a commonly shared vision that the State Park could become an area of outstanding environmental quality that was available for the public to enjoy. You can just imagine the different opportunities this State Park represented. Four-miles of undeveloped coastline in view of the Monterey Peninsula, one of which was the most popular tourist destination in the World, adjacent to the nation's largest National Marine Sanctuary, and the largest component of California's

---

[12]   www.Fort Ord Closure.com

newest State seashore. Exotic plants, abandoned buildings, and contaminated soils are problems we do not have to dread or face; however, they are challenges that need to be addressed and overcome. The establishment of the State Park represented the US commitment to the environment to our quality of life, and to our faith in the future and the public. The 7th Infantry Division was, in the end, transferred to Fort Lewis in Washington when the Fort Ord Post closed. It's noteworthy to add that the US Army did not close any of the other large Infantry or Armor Posts during 1991.[13]

Did the US Army put military items like explosives, poisonous gases, or bio-medical supplies in the landfill? During its operation, the landfill was used for disposal of normal household garbage and municipal waste. As the landfill was being closed, the US Army used some soil taken from other clean-up Sites as part of the foundation soil to support the cap that now covers the landfill. This soil was taken from contaminated Sites known as Sites 2 and 12, and from clean-up of the beaches that were used during Fort Ord Post's operation as small arms (rifles and hand guns) training ranges. The US Army screened the soil from the beaches for spend bullets; however, very small particles of lead still remain in the soil. Because the contaminants are contained under the landfill cover, ground water will not reach them and they will not move out of the landfill into either the air or ground water. Explosives and live munitions were not allowed to be landfilled but it was a normal practice to dispose of inert scrap metal in a landfill.

Just what is a landfill? A landfill is where municipalities dispose of household garbage.

What is stored in the landfill? Landfills were used to dispose of household garbage. Unfortunately, before scientists knew they were dangerous, citizens used to discard items like paint cans, paint thinners, cleaning solvents, and other household products that we now describe as "hazardous materials," as part of their household garbage. As a result, many older landfills "leak" into the ground water beneath them, and this is contamination that had to be removed.

Why does a landfill produce gases? All landfills generate gases when organic waste decomposes. This results from the action of anaerobic bacteria on the organic matter present in the waste. Landfill gas as chiefly composed of methane and carbon dioxide with small amounts of other organic gases.

Are these gases unsafe? These gases would be unsafe only if you were exposed to very large amounts. The US Army had installed underground monitoring probes and also took air samples to be sure the gases were at safe levels.

---

[13] David S. Sorenson, "Shutting Down the Cold War: The Politics of Military Base Closure," (St. Martin's Press, New York, July 1998), pp. 128-129

What was the US Army doing to get rid of the gases? The US Army had installed a landfill gas extraction and treatment system adjacent to the landfill. The system sucks in methane and other gases from a series of extraction pipes around the perimeter of the landfill. These were then transported in pipes to a facility where potentially harmful compounds were removed.

What homes were closest to the landfill? The landfill was located near the Frederick Park student housing. The boundary of Cell F of the landfill was located 368-feet from the nearest house at the end of Gettysburg Court, and about 700-feet from the nearest homes on Fredrickson Court.

Was there a health risk from exposure to these gases? During 2002, a health risk assessment based on measurements made showed a slightly elevated health risk, but only if they had been exposed to the highest readings for a period of six-years, 24-hours a day. The amount of increased risk was small enough that it fell in a range where the US Environmental Protection Agency said that further study was appropriate, but no action was required until these studies were completed.

A technical review was conducted by Summit Irresolution's, Inc. on behalf of Ecological Consultants for the Public Interest (ECPI). Summit conducted the review as part of a technical assistance team for the Fort Ord Toxics Project. The review addressed the technical content of the Engineering Evaluation/Cost Analysis-Phase I, for the Fort Ord Post, and Monterey County in California. The purpose of the Summit review was to evaluate the Engineering Evaluation and Cost Analysis (EE/CA) from a public interest point of view. For the purposes of this evaluation, the public interest was interpreted to be the adequate protection of human health and the environment. The review was general in nature and focused on the methods used to achieve the goal and objectives as well as the organizational format and presentation of the technical material. The review was summarized by presenting both general and specific comments. The general comments precede the specific comments and were intended to address significant aspects of the document as a whole. Specific comments were tailored to sections within the EE/CA.

Generally speaking, the EE/CAs appeared to have accomplished the task of comprehensively documenting available information; conducting safety-specific risk evaluations; establishing criteria for evaluating alternatives for reducing risk associated with ordnance and explosives (OE); and making recommendations for specific land areas at the Fort Ord Post. However, clarification on a number of general and specific technical, procedural, and organizational issues were warranted in order to provide a basis for evaluating the adequacy and completeness of EE/CA actions and the recommended alternatives. Concurrently, these various statements would present an inconsistent focus for the reader. These documents would have benefited from concise Goal and Objectives Statements that would have clearly stated what the EE/CAs was trying to accomplish. Based on the review and analysis of these documents, an adequate Goal Statement should have read: "The goal of the EE/CA is to evaluate technically and administratively feasible alternatives for optimally reducing the risk associated with the public exposure to and interaction with OEs at the Fort Ord Post." The objectives for accomplishing the goal should have been defined:

- To document available information pertaining to the nature and extent of OE at the Fort Ord Post;

- To identify areas where future investigations may be warranted;

- To identify risk for Sites where adequate information was developed;

- To provide decision criteria for evaluating and recommending the most feasible alternatives.

Using a defined goal as a preventive focus, each task could be evaluated relative to its effectiveness and or relevance to accomplish the goal and objectives. The EE/CA was prepared based on background information and Site characterization data that relied on a statistical means of sampling. As stated in the document, the statistical sampling did not diminish the potential risk to the public at the Fort Ord Post, nor did it intend to demonstrate that the Site was safe. This was a critical issue. While it was true that the report was prepared using the standard of care that was customary in the environmental profession, the statistical sampling and analysis protocols that supported the basis for the report represented the most important component of the overall program. Without a valid, conservative, systematic, and statically verifiable program of Site investigation and data analysis, the EE/CA exercise that was based on the Ordnance Explosive Cost Effective Risk (OECert) evaluation model would become academic. The report would benefit from a discussion in the introduction that established a level of confidence regarding the Site characteristics program conducted by other independent contractors. This discussion should have included a reference to sampling and analysis methods; protocols; regulatory guidance; statistical analysis methods; quality assurance; and quality control. It was understood that this figure was intended to convey the overall process and should therefore explain the relationship between the Phase I and Phase II report. Completion of the Phase I report would imply that a significant stage in a series of events had been accomplished for the overall goal of the EE/CA. A significant amount of work would have been accomplished, documented, and presented in Phase I of the EE/CA. It was unclear; however, what the criteria were for distinguishing between Phase I and Phase II of the EE/CA.

It appeared on the surface that a significant amount of baseline characterization work still remained to be accomplished for large portions of the military facility; that is, archives review; field sampling; data analysis; and evaluation of alternatives. This document would benefit from an explanation of the decision criteria established for the phased approach and what distinguished Phase I from

Phase II of the EE/CA. It was stated several times throughout this document that the Ordnance Explosive Cost Effective Risk evaluation was developed by QuantiTech, Inc. under contract with the US Army Engineering and Support Center at Huntsville in Alabama (CEHNC). This document also noted that "the risk analysis model was identified for use by CEHNC," and "the use of the OECert tool for the purposes of the EE/CA had not been validated by Earth Tech." Because the model was developed specifically under a contract with CEHNC, it appeared that there was a conflict of interest using this model as an exclusive interpretation of risk. Furthermore, since the title included a reference to the model as a "cost effective" risk evaluation and a large portion of the data was directly related to cost, it appeared cost was integrated as a primary factor in the model. Based on this interpretation, it was unclear why the Ordnance Explosive Cost Effective Risk evaluation had not been evaluated independent of the cost.

This document provided: "a summary of detection technologies for Site investigation and characterization with emphasis on future work being accomplished at the Site." Previous detection methods had exclusively employed the use of the magnetometer. It was unclear why only the magnetometer was being used for previous investigations when the presentation of additional investigative techniques for consideration implied potential application of a vast variety of methods. An up-to-date literature search of available technologies and techniques for detecting UE at the Fort Ord Post had been conducted. At a minimum, the documents should have been reviewed, in addition, an evaluation of the limitations of the previous investigation work that provided the basis of Phase I of the EE/CA. If alternative detection technologies proved to be more appropriate (as implied in the document), strong consideration should have been given to identifying Phase I Sites where additional work should have been accomplished to reduce risk.

The alternatives that were evaluated for reducing risk involved those that consider physical exposures and the hazards associated with direct OE interaction; for example, safety issues. Although a cursory statement was made regarding the DOD removal response authority, a statement that addressed the issue surrounding potential impacts to human health through alternate exposure scenarios should have been made to clarify what risks the EE/CA addressed.

This document stated that: "new information and further discoveries would inherently affect the findings and recommendations of the EE/CA." This document provided an explanation of the administrative mechanism to address new information on the context of the EE/CA. The discovery of chemical identification sets at Site 13B earlier that year; for example, represented a significant issue. The document should have been made to clarify what role Phase II or other phases would play in addressing new information, and how the new information would affect the conclusions drawn as part of Phase I.

This document indicated that: "Phase II of the EE/CA would provide a presumptive remedy at areas of the Fort Ord Post where recommendations were not made for the Phase I EE/CA." Based on the lack of site characterization data for a number of Sites scheduled for investigation in the Phase II work, it was premature to conclude that any remedial approach was "presumptively appropriate" until more data was available. The document should have clarified that a "presumptive remedy," if appropriate, would only be chosen for Phase II Sites where thorough, accurate, and complete data sets had been developed that would indicate that one or more response actions outlined in Phase I of the EE/CA.

This document presented: "an introduction and recommendations for Sites." This document stated: "sufficient quantitative data did exist on these Sites to perform risk evaluations . . . to provide recommendations based on those evaluations made." This document did not provide a qualifying statement that provided a level of confidence or assurance that "sufficient quantitative data" referred to data obtained during a rigid and systematic process of investigation, characterization, and interim remedial action. Although the EE/CA report made reference to previous reports by private contractors, the EE/CA would benefit from a more comprehensive general statement regarding the adequacy of the characterization data being used as a basis for risk evaluation and remedial alternative evaluation.

This document stated that: "Earth Tech contracted with QuantiTech to evaluate the risk of public exposure to OE at selected areas of the Fort Ord Post." This document did not adequately define "exposure" and should have provided a comprehensive understanding of this term.

This document stated that: "QuantiTech determined that the OE density estimate ranged from 12.01 per-acre to 0 per-acre at Sites 1, 2, 4a, 6, 9, 13a, 14SE, 17, 20, and 22." It was unclear and inappropriate how Sites 1, 4a, 9, 13a, and 22 could be attributed to a 0 density value when these Sites required further sampling investigation. This document should have clarified the rationale used here or should have modified this document accordingly.

This document referred to: "pertinent regulatory guidance documents." This document should have been listed in the references as a basis for analysis. This document stated that "the use of the OECert tool for the purpose of this EE/CA had not been validated by Earth Tech." It was unclear whether this comment referred to validation of the model itself, or validation of its appropriateness for use in the EE/CA. This comment should have been clarified and justification provided for its use in either case.

This document stated that: "should Site conditions or future land uses change substantially, the conclusions drawn and recommendations made for the EE/CA study areas could change substantially from present conditions." This document did not provide an explanation of the criteria established for determining when substantial changes could or would occur. Nor was there an explanation of the administrative mechanism for addressing new information in the context of the EE/CA. These issues should have been thoroughly addressed.

This document stated that: "removal of all OE was not considered practicable, given technical limitations." Generally speaking, this statement would reflect a number of concerns related to the quality of the data used to develop the EE/CA. At a minimum, it should have provided the public with a summary of the technical limitations; for example, detection technology, removal technology, etc., independent of costs as a basis for evaluating the merits of recommendations.

This document stated that: "the milestone schedule included information pertinent to the successful completion of this project." It would have been more beneficial from a presentation of a more comprehensive conceptual schedule that communicated the overall schedule for subsequent phases of investigation, characterization, risk evaluation, and remedial measures for the entire military Installation.

This document referenced: "a 20-year time frame for effectiveness of institutional controls." It was unclear why this time frame would have been selected. It should have provided some clarification for the long-term effectiveness.

The community was vitally concerned that Re-Use Conversion Plans succeed; and policy makers often cited the Fort Ord Post as a "model" of military Post or Base closure and realignment. The Fort Ord Post was also known to have serious environmental problems. These problems may have interfered with planned conversion and re-use. All interested parties such as the DOD, Federal Government regulators, State of California, environmental activists, and the communities surrounding the military Post strongly supported environmental restoration at the former Fort Ord Post, either for its own sake or because it was a key to implementing a promising and attractive Re-Use Plan. More generally, the DOD had acknowledged that toxic contamination of military Installations was widespread. The DOD had committed itself to restoring the environment at these military Installations. The DOD also understood that its traditional way of relating to communities that were contiguous to its military Installations was no longer a workable public relations solution. It had embraced the idea that all Stakeholders must be given a voice in the clean-up process. To this end, the DOD had issued guidelines for the formation of Restoration Advisory Boards (RABs), and RABs for set-up at numerous military Installations undergoing closure or realignment.

Environmental restoration was a pre-condition for realizing various aspects of the Fort Ord Re-Use Plan; in turn, achieving meaningful Stakeholder participation seemed necessary if restoration was to be accomplished in an orderly and timely fashion. The adequacy of the DOD's new enhanced Stakeholder participation policy was then of central importance. Therefore, a critical examination of the development of basic RAB concepts produced early results for an in-depth investigation of the implementation of the Fort Ord Post concept.

Examining policy design resulted in DOD's RAB guidelines showed that the DOD continued to deeply distrust public participation in its affairs and that this distrust was operationalized in a host of public details that, in variety of ways, constrained and weakened the public's role in restoration decision making. The RAB concept rested on several flawed assumptions about the nature of contemporary American communities. If the goal and objectives of RABs were to forestall community resistance and out-of-control "panic organizing," those flawed assumptions could mean that RABs may prove irrelevant to the goal of preventing such outbursts of community mobilization, even if RABs are implemented fully and in good faith. Examining the Fort Ord Post's policy and implementation, the actual working of that RAB fell far short of good guidelines.

Although the findings were necessarily provisional, RAB policy was quite new and the Fort Ord Post RAB had existed for more than one-year; both policy design and policy implementation would improve as the DOD learned from its experience that there may be cause for concern. Experience suggested that communities can get spooked, lose trust in restoration decisions and decision makers, and organize to halt the restoration process. If RABs are poorly designed and implemented, the fact that they have been organized at a military Installation may do nothing to prevent such outbursts. Once under way, such events can take on a life of their own with tremendous momentum. Such events unconstrained can bring restoration to a halt, thereby delaying, if not outright blocking, the conversion of closed military Posts or Bases in several new economic uses.

During the past several years, the Federal Government began to close many military Installations and facilities. Five waves of military Post and Base closings had been announced. In California alone, 22 military Posts and Bases have closed or are in the process of closing. From the point of view of National interest, military Post and Base closings are rational and desirable. The military Post and Base closings can; however, mean severe socioeconomic hardship for the communities where military Posts and Bases are located. Such communities face the prospect of lost revenue, lost positions, closed stores, failing property values, and out-migration. It was estimated that the closure of the Fort Ord Post alone would cost the local economy $423 million annually. Understandably, communities felt threatened when a local military Post or Base was slated for closure. If, however, the Federal facility is not merely abandoned but is put to re-use, the closure does not have to be the harbinger of local decline. It can, instead, be the vehicle for a burst of vigorous local socioeconomic development.

At the Fort Ord Post, the local Re-Use Authority had developed a plan that promised to generate 60,000 employee vacancies and 20,000 housing units. Because military Post or Base closures could mean socioeconomic ruin for local economies, conversion had great political support. On July 2, 1993, the President announced a five part program to: "aggressively reinvest in communities and create employee vacancies where military Installations were being closed." The notion of military Post or Base conversion was attractive because it promised to reconcile conflict between Federal Government and local Government interests. Desirable though it may have been assumed, socioeconomic conversion is a complex, difficult, and uncertain process. During my research, it was especially interesting in how military Post or Base conversion was affected by the presence of toxic contaminants at the closing military Installation.

The military Installations and facilities it's now known have serious environmental problems. Contaminants range from wastes that resemble hazardous wastes found at private sector industrial sites (solvents, paint strippers and thinners, corrosives, and heavy metals) to more exotic military wastes; for example, pyrotechnics; radioactive materials; nerve agents; and unexploded ordnance. As early as 1975, the DOD began to identify and clean-up contamination at some military Posts and Bases. Restoration took on new urgency when military Posts and Bases began to close and communities expressed their desire that closing military Installations be made available for other uses. Each potential new use for some parcel of a closed military Post or Base required a certain minimum level of cleanliness, though that level could vary greatly depending on whether the parcel was intended to become an Industrial Park or a new Community College Campus. If the proposed Site for conversion was contaminated, restoration seemed to be a necessary pre-condition if re-use goals were to be realized. Mr. James M. Strock, California Secretary for Environmental Protection. The military Post closed its gates and became part of US military history. stated: "Without environmental clean-up, it was a 'pipe dream' to think these military Posts or Bases could be quickly converted to civilian re-use."

In addition to making military Posts or Bases suitable for re-use, restoration was said to have two other socioeconomic benefits. If clean-up funds went to local firms, restoration could be partly offset by the transitional shock of the military Post or Base closure. Environmental clean-up at military Installations could also contribute to national economic growth if these efforts spur the development of new remediation technologies and encourage the private sector to invest and create a large, sophisticated globally competitive remediation industry.

Though interest in cleaning up military Installations was high and growing, policy makers had to deal with a series of impediments or hurdles if they were to succeed. The cost and technical complexity were often mentioned as a serious problem. In this respect, focus was on a third concern; that is, securing Stakeholders trust and their consent to let the restoration process go forward. Local Stakeholder's perception of risk was a concern because as many studies have shown, the public had developed a deep distrust of technology and of the officials and experts, both in the Federal Government and in industry's trial. Chemicals no longer mean progress and material well-being; rather, they evoke images of 55 gallon drums leaking toxic wastes; of cancer, miscarriages and birth defects;

of contaminated communities; and ruined lives. Distrust of technology and fear of toxic contamination developed first in the context of communities dealing with civilian industrial Sites; however, with news coverage of contamination at several nuclear weapons plants, reports of contamination at many, if not most of military Installations and facilities, such attitudes generalized to military Installations and facilities of all kinds. The public's view of military Installations and facilities shifted from trust and studied indifference to disenchantment and the presumption of contamination guilt. Recent revelations that the military had, early during the Cold War, made some of the public into de facto nuclear guinea pigs, unbeknown to them and without their consent, did nothing to improve the public's view of the military establishment's regard for public health and safety.

The fabric of trust between military Posts and Bases and their surrounding communities was everywhere in doubt, if not actually torn. The public felt vulnerable. Consequently, even a minor event during the restoration process may occasion a flare up of concerned fear. Residents living near the contaminated military Post or Base seemed disinterested or indifferent may protest, organize, and refuse to let the restoration process go forward. Expressions of concern about such potential surges of community panic and mobilization were found throughout literature on remediation at military Installations and facilities. Implication guides for re-use planning were clear enough. If restoration was a pre-condition for re-use, and if there was a real danger that public distrust may bloom into community panic and mobilization that brings restoration to a halt, receptions of environmental risks may be one of the most important potential impediments to successful conversion.

Realizing re-use goals would require the development of mechanisms that could secure local Stakeholder's trust and consent; and officials charged with the clean-up of military Installations and facilities would have to realize the need to address the public's fear. They realized that the more traditional format for public participation. commonly referred to as "decide-announce-defend" did not work. Public citizens, typically, have not felt that they can really affect the course of things that opportunities provided them for comment, and "participation" is little more than window dressing belated attempts to secure their consent to decisions others have already made. New ways to bring Stakeholders into the process had to be found.

Considerable thought and effort had gone into developing the DOD's new Stakeholder participation policy. The RAB model was at that point, new and untested. It was not known if that model was well conceived or if it was being properly implemented. RABs must now be studied in detail to assess how they actually function. The work aimed to contribute to what will certainly be an ongoing effort to evaluate and improve the RAB concept. The RABs should be examined at two different levels to examine the adequacy of the DOD's RAB model. Could RABs "increase credibility and improve community acceptance and support," thereby smoothing the way for environmental restoration and subsequent economic re-use as the DOD had hoped? To put it more starkly, can the presence of a RAB forestall explosive outbursts of community panic and oppositional organizing? To date, the DOD has taken two approaches to this question. First, to identify key moments in the actual development of RAB policy; and to ask how the policy changed from the first proposal to the final guidelines. Second, the DOD explored conceptually the possibility that every version of the RAB concept implicitly rested on erroneous assumptions about the nature of contemporary political consciousness.

How were the DOD's guidelines being implemented "on the ground?" How were community members chosen? Did community members reflect or represent the diverse segments and interests present in the surrounding community? What actually happens during RAB meetings? How did the RAB alter or impact the restoration process? Did RAB community members report back to the community as they are supposed to? To answer all of these questions, you have to undertake a long-term, in-depth investigation of the RAB at the Fort Ord Post. Why the Fort Ord Post? Because the Fort Ord Post was a large 120,000-acre military Post on California's Central Coast near Monterey. During 1992, the Fort Ord Post was selected for closure. The military Post was an excellent Site for studying the DOD's enhanced Stakeholder participating policy for the following reasons:

- The Fort Ord Post was physically the largest military Post for closure in California, and was of prime socioeconomic importance in its region;

- The community had been vitally interested in the conversion of the Fort Ord Post in non-military uses; and conversion planning was Well advanced;

- Containment at the Fort Ord Post was serious. The military Post was a "Super fund" Site. The military Post also had a serious unexploded ordnance problem that affected at least 8000 of its 20,000-acres. Effective and timely restoration was necessary if ambitious conversion plans were to be realized;

- Clean-up at the Fort Ord Post began 10-years prior and is now well advanced;

- Environmental awareness in the surrounding community was quite high, and a RAB was organized shortly after DOD guidelines were promulgated;

- The surrounding community had a high proportion of African-Americans, Latinos, and Asians that provided the opportunity to examine environmental justice issues;

- The Fort Ord Post had been singled out as a "model;" first of conversion planning, and now of community and Stakeholder participation in restoration.

There was an examination of two critical moments in the development of RAB policies. The first was the consensus recommendations of the Federal Facilities

Environmental Restoration Dialogue Committee, presented in its Interim Report during February 1993, commonly referred to as the Keystone Report. The second was the SSAB guidelines that were jointly issued by the DOD and US Environmental Protection Agency during May 1994. Both documents rejected past models of Stakeholder's participation; that is, decide-announce-defend. Both called for a more open process, earlier and fuller Stakeholder participation. The differences; however, were quite important. The DOD and EPA guidelines acknowledged that they were based on the work of the Keystone group and that they should modify the Keystone's recommendations in several ways.

The Keystone's model for a community Stakeholder organization was called a Site-Specific Advisory Committee, or SSAB, that did not give that Committee power to actually make remediation or restoration decisions. But taken together, several of its recommendations gave that Advisory Committee an activist view:

- Its definition of the relevant Stakeholder sounds quite like Jesse Jackson's Rainbow Coalition-Individual residents that live in the communities;

- Representatives of citizen, environmental and public interest groups;

- Workers or representatives of workers; and representatives of Indian nations;

- Only community representatives can be members of SSAB. Defense officials and regulators were relegated to ex officio status. This underscored the intent to make SSAB independent of official;

- The SSAB was given wide discretion to establish its own agenda. The SSAB could address;

- The SSAB could address important issues related to clean-up such as land use, level of clean-up, acceptable risk, and should have the discretion to hear presentations on the social, economic, cultural, aesthetic, and worker health and safety effects, and may hear presentations on other environmental management decisions that SSAB members regard as relevant and appropriate. The SSAB was given technical assistance funding that would allow it to independently review and comment on technical reports and documents being developed by Federal Government facility managers and their contractors.

Keystone finally stated that Federal Government agencies and regulators must be accountable to the SSAB; respond to recommendations and advice; and provide information were recommendations or advice could be implemented; where recommendations needed to be modified in order to be implemented; or that recommendations cannot be implemented.

The DOD and EPA guidelines devoted a great deal of space to matters of what one might call a democratic form, carefully detailing the process for selecting community members, and providing something like a primer course in how to practice good communication skills during meetings. The substance of the guidelines; however, established an advisor body that had significantly less independence and less authority than the body envisioned by the Keystone report. The guidelines made it crystal clear in the very typesetting that the Restoration Advisory Board was not a decision making body. That differed from Keystone only in emphasis, but it did betray a fear of losing control that is evident in a host of guideline details:

- The definition of Stakeholder was broadened in ways that made it less activist or populist. The DOD and EPA definition included, in addition to the interests named by Keystone, "current Technical Review Committee members. For example, Federal Government officials; Post and Base officials; Federal Government and State regulators; local Government; business communities; and homeowners associations:"

- RAB membership included not only community Stakeholders but included regulators; the DOD and EPA; Post and Base officials; State officials, consultants, and private contractors;

- The RAB was provided with a strong Co-chairmen; one of whom would be a Post or Base official;

- What the RAB was allowed to address was restricted. RABs were explicitly forbidden to deal with land-use issues;

- RAB members did not get funding for independent technical evaluations;

- Post and Base officials were to be responsive to RAB members of the community and feel that issues should be "brought to the table," but again, what was emphasized was the form or process of "openness," the explicit call for accountability found in the Keystone Report that was absent.

Accordingly, comparison of the two documents suggested that even as the DOD acknowledged that it could no longer operate in the traditional military manner, insulated from civilian supervision and input, it was hardly ready to embrace the process of a democratic, public participation, but instead would regard these changes with considerable dread and ambivalence. That ambivalence was embodied in the DOD and EPA guidelines that mandated Stakeholder participation at the same time that it moved to ensure that the DOD would continue to be in firm control. One general concern was that the DOD's effort to maintain firm control even as it invited greater Stakeholder participation may have, in the long run, undermined the credibility and legitimacy of RABs, especially when they needed that credibility and legitimacy most when distrust was rising and the potential for polarization and conflict was growing. More specifically, there was concern over the implications of the shift from SSAB involvement in re-use land-use planning in the Keystone model to the firm separation of restoration and re-use issues in the DOD and EPA guidelines. Conceptually, this separation made little sense to this author.

The intended re-use determined the minimum clean-up goal of the Installation, so one might argue that Re-Use Plans were primary and restoration secondary and derivative. On the other hand, technical and financial constraints may have determined the level of clean-up that could be achieved, independent of any re-use rational that would build in maximum organizational communications between re-use and restoration planning bodies, rather than to seek to compartmentalize them. Furthermore, there was a concern that such efforts to compartmentalize and limit the scope of RAB deliberations was only to enhance feelings of powerlessness, both among RAB members and in the local community supposedly represented by the RAB, thereby increasing the possibility that the RAB would have little credibility and legitimacy.

It's fairly clear that enhanced Stakeholder participation policies arose because policy makers were concerned about uncontrolled surges of community mobilization, moments of mass panic and rage that, once developed, would be tremendously difficult to contain and that if they did develop, make restoration effects much more difficult. The hope was that such moments of unproductive gridlock, familiar enough in the comparable case of clean-up of civilian Sites could be prevented with the introduction of a more open, inclusive Stakeholder participation process. There was some concern that the whole RAB concept, even the more populist Keystone version, was based tacitly on an unrealistic, fictitious notion of how communities in contemporary American society actually function. The notion that 12 to 20 citizen representatives could engage in ongoing, two-way communications with "the community" would assume that a community actually existed, that there was a collective entity that paid attention, that had the infrastructure for discussion and opinion formation, a community that is in effect, vibrantly alive and actively engaged with its collective interests. It's much more plausible to offer a quite different image of the community. To simplify matters a great deal, imagine that communities exist, for the most part, in one of two "digitalized states." The "O-State," disorganized, inattentive, the vast bulk of individuals paying almost exclusive attention to private, immediate, daily life interests and concerns; and the "I-State," panic mobilization. Consider the Monterey Bay communities that surround the Fort Ord Post. This is a region where everyone agreed there was a high degree of environmental consciousness and concern. How does one reconcile that with facts such as: "there have been only small handfuls of comments submitted when the public had been asked to comment on the proposed Fort Ord Restorations Plans; there were only 19 applications for 12 community member's positions on the RAB?" Such co-existence of seemingly irreconcilable conditions in public attitude and behavior toward environmental problems was the norm, not the exception. Public interest and concern was ambiguous, seemingly self-contradictory, both present and absent at the same time. Mr. Szasz discussed that in some detail in his book; but such contradictions are typical of what we labeled above the "O-State." If so, the vibrant, engaged community that is the un-acknowledged pre-condition for the SSAB and RAB was not the normal state of American communities. If so, we would then argue that, even at their best, RABs would not function as envisioned:

- If a community is in "O-State, "the most communities would get is self-appointed activists who participated in the name of the community," but did not communicate with anyone because the community was not attentive or interested, and because there was no ongoing, functioning infrastructure in the community for activists to interact with;

- If panic subsequently ensued, and the community rapidly shifted to an "O-State, "you could equally and plausibly select anywhere up to 5000 communities that have been inflamed by grass-roots toxic organizing, it is not the unlikely that officials could successfully contain the mobilization by pointing out that they had earlier, and earnestly tried to get the community involved by forming a RAB, and so forth. Experience suggested that, at this point, such arguments would do nothing to change what would be by then, quite well formed and quite frozen perceptions;

- On the other hand, if the community stayed in "O-State," the RAB, present or not, properly or poorly implemented, would not materially affect things in one way or another.

This line of reasoning would suggest that, as presently conceived, RABs would have little effect on community acceptance or consent no matter what the course of events. It suggests that if the intent of RAB design was to prevent, or at least lessen the likelihood, of rapid shifts in communities to an "I-State," the whole question of Stakeholder participation had to be reconsidered from the ground up.

During 1994, the RAB at the Fort Ord Post was established. The military Post had a Technical Review Committee (TRC) made up of defense officials, their contractors, and Federal and State regulators. Community members were added to convert the TRC into the RAB. On May 11, 1994, the first meeting that community RAB members were present took place. It was of course, too early to tell how the RAB at the Fort Ord Post would affect the long-term prospects for successful restoration and military Post conversion. There had only a handful of meetings. The RAB bylaws were still in draft form; many important things, to include how Sub-committees would be defined and how they would operate were yet to be decided. Both the DOD and the community Co-chairs had experienced recent turnover. A report would be given with more confidence once the process has settled down and followed the process for several years. However, based on observing numerous meetings and on initial interviews, a number of observations could be realized:

- Although the DOD lavished considerable attention on proper membership election procedures, the results at the Fort Ord Post were at best mixed. Few people applied to serve as RAB community members. The selection process did seem to have succeeded in having a wide variety of viewpoints represented on the RAB;

- Some community members were "fast-trackers" who trusted and respected military personnel and wanted to see pieces of the military Post cleared for civilian use ASAP;

- Others worried more about environmental risks and were not convinced that the DOD and regulators were seriously interested in citizen input. In other ways, the selection process was less successful. The most visible problem was that minorities were under-represented at the military Post surrounded by communities that had significant Latino, African-American, and Asian populations;

- Meaningful participation. RAB's legitimacy rested on the claim that even if RABs were not empowered to make decisions they could have some significant, meaningful impact on the course of restoration at a military Installation. At the Fort Ord Post, claims of significant impact had been undermined in several ways;

- Site characterization and remediation had been occurring at the Fort Ord Post for a decade. The clean-up work was well under way at several of the most polluted Sites (OU1 and OU2). At least at the Fort Ord Post, the DOD's implementation of new Stakeholder mechanisms came after some of the most important decisions had been made;

- Community members could participate meaningfully only if they had some basic ability to understand technical issues to include geography and hydrology of the Fort Ord Post, the nature of the contamination present, and various restoration options;

- Workshops were held to get community RAB members "up to speed" and able to participate. Interviews suggested that these workshops were not uniformly helpful. Some interviewees said they learned a great deal, but a majority said they still did not feel confident that they understood the issues or that they could offer meaningful input;

- The meeting format had not been conducive in meaningful participation.

Typically, most RAB meetings consisted of the DOD officials and their contractors presenting detailed updates on either the investigation or the restoration at numerous individual locations at the Fort Ord Post. The DOD's guidelines emphasized the need to practice good communication skills at RAB meetings as the community would feel that the process was legitimate when its representatives were listened to and their input was respected. There were numerous instances; however, when RAB meetings were not run in an open manner. The military Post and Base officials were quick to squelch certain lines of inquiry, were dismissive of criticism, and seemed irritated when community members raised issues. Some of the community members interviewed did not believe that the administrative process was open or legitimate:

- According to both Keystone and the DOD, RABs would provide the vehicle for two-way communications between military Post and Base decision makers and community Stakeholders. This suggested that there was not much substantive communications from RAB community members with military Post and Base decision makers. Only a small minority of RAB community members systematically reported to anyone in the community about what was going on at RAB meetings;

- Most did so only haphazardly; and some not at all.

The Fort Ord Post RAB was at a very early stage in its development. New community members might have improved minority representation; community members might have gained confidence and take a more active role at meetings. They might have developed more sustained ways of reporting back to the community. Difficulties such as failure to live up to the ideals of policy design were to be expected at the beginning of implementation. What was seen raised concerns, especially if other researchers reported similar developments at other RABs.

Many of the findings were necessarily tentative. As with any new untested policy, it was expected that the DOD would modify and improve its guidelines as experience with RABs accumulated. Implementation at the Fort Ord Post would also look different once the RAB got through its start-up phase and settled into routine operation, and as members gained experience. There would be no surprise if things never settled into a routine if the current organizational tensions generate with chronic discontent and periodic crises. It would be unwise to extrapolate the course of things at the Fort Ord Post from what had been observed.

Nonetheless, the work was sufficient to raise concern. A community such as the one surrounding the Fort Ord Post may never "boil over" and travel down the road of panic mobilization and gridlock. If it did not, none of the problems of the recent efforts to enhance local Stakeholder participation would matter. The community would remain quiescent, largely inattentive, and would give tacit consent. Restoration decisions and implementation would remain largely in the hands of the DOD, its private contractor, and various regulators. Once the required level of restoration was achieved, the road would be open to implement Re-Use Plans.

But in the event that things did go wrong and there was panic, both the DOD's effort to limit the theoretical power of the RAB and the numerous implementation problems that are evident at a site such as the Fort Ord Post would become important. It was likely that at those moments the presence of a RAB would not be able to forestall the spiral of suspicion, fear, rage, and protest. Restoration and along with that, socioeconomic conversion, might well be brought to a halt. How should the DOD rework its Stakeholder participation policy if further research at the Fort Ord Post and experience at other Federal Government facilities confirm the tentative findings? Since the analysis was at this point, tentative and provisional, it would have been inappropriate to specify the alternative in detail and with great confidence. But briefly, if the above analysis held up, policy revisions along three points might be indicated:

- Re-think how RABs were supposed to represent "the community." This point addressed the argument that the RAB model rested on an unrealistic notion of the state of American communities and RABs, consequently, would prove largely irrelevant to whether or not communities would mobilize and, if they did, the trajectory that mobilization would take. Realistically, the DOD could do little about the paradoxical qualities of the American community, but its current RAB model, its insistence that RAB community members be selected as individuals, were not to represent an organized element of the community in any direct sense, and act and vote on the RAB as individuals only exacerbates its helplessness. It would have been far better to adopt the polar opposite model and build RAB membership in a way that explicitly brought in and represented all of the relevant segments of the community that were already in existence at the time the RAB was formed. This would not only increase the likelihood that RAB members took matters back to the community, as intended, but would also tend to give the RAB legitimacy when and if community panic occurred;

- Give RABs more autonomy, more scope, and more authority. In brief, push the guidelines back toward the Keystone model. The danger in weakening RABs was, as indicated above, that they are likely to be seen as lacking credibility and legitimacy, especially in moments when the public trust was low and cynicism high, just when one would like to be able to calm the community by pointing out to the existence of the RAB as proof that the DOD has been solicitous of public concerns;

- In fact, one can imagine that a structurally dis-empowered RAB would itself become a target at such point and would be a rhetorical target, pointed to as an example of officials' duplicity and lack of good faith. The DOD may worry about the loss of control, the extra time, effort, and trouble it would take to work with RABs that had real decision making authority and that were in fundamental ways really autonomous, but that may have been the only way to achieve a kind of legitimacy RABs must have in order to do what they were originally intended to do;

- Take implementation guidelines seriously to include such matters as following guidelines for membership selection and practicing good communications skills. It was clear that at the Fort Ord Post, the DOD officials needed better training in such skills as providing information, running meetings in an open and democratic fashion, and always of single importance, listening and communicating real respect toward civilian Stakeholder's views and concerns;

- By the end of 1992, the DOD had identified 1800 active military Installations or facilities containing 18,795 Sites requiring evaluation for possible clean-up. On the basis of its own analysis, the DOD had concluded that 40-percent of these 18,795 Sites did not require further clean-up work. The DOD also identified over 7300 formerly used or DOD owned Sites with the potential for inclusion. The DOD has screened out approximately 3000 of those Sites. The GAO based this on the DOD's Defense Environmental Restoration Program Annual Report to the US Congress;

- According to the DOD's 1993 Annual Report to Congress, the DOD identified nearly 20,000 potentially contaminated sites on 1722 military Installations and 8000 potential sites on 1632 formerly used military Installations in the US. Of the 20, 000 Sites, the DOD had determined that 9245 Sites on current military Installations and 6189 Sites on formerly used military Installations required no further action. Of the 10,449 active Sites on current military Installations, 5507 Sites were on 244 military Installations considered as high priority. The DOD had initiated or completed the study phases; that is, preliminary assessment, Site inspection and the remedial investigation feasibility study at 7445 of the 19,694 Sites; 3825 Sites had reached the remedial design/action phase. As of March, 1994, none of the 92 NPL Installations and 10 former used NPL Installations had all Sites cleaned-up;

- There were 2521 potential Sites on 149 military Installations scheduled to be closed. There were 17 losing military Installations that were listed on the NPL and another five were proposed for listing. There were 862 potential Sites on closing NPL Installations with 518 in the design/remedial action phase. As of September, 1993, 21 Sites had remedial actions completed and no further action was required at 85 Sites. The DOD had 254 high priority military Installations that contained 7446 Sites. The EPA had designated 102 of these military Installations as NPL or "Super fund" Sites that included 5029 individual contaminated Sites. Another 25 military Installations with 760 sites were proposed NPL Sites;

83

- Types of hazardous wastes found at most military Installations included solvents and corrosives, paint strippers thinners, and heavy metals such as lead, cadmium, and chromium found at most industrial operations. Other substances such as nerve agents and unexploded ordnance were found at some military Installations. Contamination usually resulted from improper disposal, leaks, or spills. The primary contaminant found in a majority of all the DOD and private sector waste Sites were petroleum products or petroleum related products such as solvents;

- Beyond such common contaminants, military Site hazardous wastes also present special problems not found at private sector Sites. The DOD facilities often had many wastes in common with private Sites, but faced a clean-up challenge due to the large quantity and variety of wastes. In addition, military unique compounds such as pyrotechnics, explosives, and propellants were atypical of private industry and required special remedial investigative procedures and responses. Unique military wastes included exotic fuels, explosive compounds (TNT, DNT, etc.);

- Military chemicals included mustard gas, white phosphorous, Agent Orange, etc., and mixed waste to include low-level radiation hazardous waste;

- Finally, the Fort Ord Posts had extensive problems with unexploded ordinance (UXO).

Mr. James M. Souby, Executive Director of the Western Governors' Association testified at a Congressional hearing that: "there are some two million-acres of land managed by the Bureau of Land Management; 15 National wildlife refuges; and some 900 formerly used Defense Sites that were contaminated by UXO." UXO include, as is did at the Fort Ord Post; rockets; rifle grenades; 60mm mortar shells; armor-piercing ammunition; cannon rounds; howitzer rounds (high explosive; white phosphorous and illumination); and land mines. The DO-IT Military Munitions Working Group mentioned the obvious when it stated: "The risk from unexploded ordnance, both surface and subsurface, in the range area is very high." Speaking about UXO contamination at the Fort Ord Post, Mr. David Wang of the EPA told a Congressional Committee: "Until new technology is developed that can effectively locate and remove all buried UXO at a reasonable cost, re-use was impossible."

The US military continue to field the best prepared and best equipped organization in the World. BRAC would enable the US military to match Facilities-to-Forces; meet the threat and challenges of a new Century; and make the wisest use of limited Defense dollars. BRAC would facilitate multi-service missions by creating joint organizational and basing solutions that would not only reduce waste by maximizing military effectiveness. Consolidating facilities would save billions, allowing the DOD to focus funds on maintaining and modernizing facilities needed to better support our Force Structure; recruit quality military personnel and Civil

Service employees; modernize equipment and infrastructure; and develop the capabilities needed to meet 21ˢᵗ Century threats.

The DOD's military personnel and Civil Service officials would not be allowed to participate in any organizational meetings for the purpose (express or not) of insulating a military Installation from closure or realignment to ensure the fairness and rigor of the BRAC deliberative process. In coordination with DUSD (I&E), who is the sole releasing authority for information on BRAC 05 to the news media, military Post and Base Commanders and their PAOs were encouraged to respond to questions within the scope of this guidance. To protect the integrity of the BRAC 05 process and to ensure that accurate information was provided, Office Secretary of Defense, military departments, and Defense agencies would designate key individuals to respond to community and Congressional inquiries. Unauthorized discussion, dissemination of information, or speculation regarding BRAC by DOD officials and contractors was strictly prohibited.

External Stakeholders such as communities had an extraordinary interest in the BRAC process and consistent with DOD's need for internal deliberation should have received timely access to data that could be made public as the BRAC analytical process unfolded. Timely and consistent information from all the DOD elements would minimize confusion and foster trust. PAOs would continue to release the same type and amount of information on their military Installation as they were currently doing, but could not release in whole or in part, data and information requested under BRAC. It's important to note that local Post and Base Commanders were not in a position to evaluate entire mission requirements and cross-service implications of their individual functions as they may affect DOD; and local military Commanders were not in a position to answer questions requiring them to speculate or discuss BRAC issues that were subject to internal DOD deliberations. While information normally provided to the public would continue to be provided, even if it was the subject of a BRAC data issue, its relationship to BRAC was not releasable.

The DOD officials could not participate in their official capacity in activities of any organization that had as its purpose either directly or indirectly, insulating military Posts and Bases from realignment or closure. The guidance was initiated to ensure the fairness and rigor of the BRAC deliberation process. Invitations to participate in such organizations should have been discussed with an Ethics Counselor. In a liaison or in a representative capacity, the DOD officials could attend meetings with State and local officials, or other organizations that may seek to develop plans or programs to improve the ability of military Installations to discharge their National Security and Defense mission. However, the DOD officials could not manage or control such organizations or efforts. Many former influential Federal Government officials and retired General or Flag Officers would become involved with organizations attempting to insulate military Posts and Bases from possible closure or realignment.

These officials were allowed to participate in this manner and due to their participation, organizations were not allowed any greater or lesser information or access; public information concerning the current BRAC process and past experience with prior BRAC rounds was available. Contents included the text of the current Defense Base Closure Act; reports of the Secretaries of Defense and Defense Base Closure and Realignment Commission during BRAC rounds; GAO reports on the status of military Posts and Bases closed and realigned during prior rounds; and information on assistance available to communities with military Posts and Bases that had been closed. The DOD officials were encouraged to refer the media, community representatives, and other interested parties to the public web-Site for further information about what happened during prior rounds and the process for BRAC 05. Additional information relating to BRAC 05 would become available and posted to the BRAC web-Site as the process proceeded. In a report to the US Congress, Secretary of Defense Donald H. Rumsfeld certified that the military service had approximately 24-percent of excess military Post and Base capacity to support the Force Structure.

The US Army had the most military Posts that met the Base closure criteria (29-percent); followed by the US Air Force (24-percent); and the US Navy/USMC at 21-percent). Greenfeld's report stated that if the BRAC 05 round of military Post and Base closures produced a 20-percent reduction, the DOD would see a net savings of approximately $5 billion by 2011 and re-occurring annual savings of approximately $8 billion. The four previous military Post and Base closure rounds had already saved military departments $6.6 billion every year. Nevertheless, there was a movement to derail the next round of military Post and Base closures by convincing the public it was cheaper to keep military Posts and Bases open and lease land to earn money; thus expanding what is known as Government Owned Contractor Operated (GOCO) facilities. This would "rob" local communities of business taxes and rarely produce net profits as cozy relationships resulted in contracts where the Federal Government paid for property maintenance.

Small military Posts and Bases were inefficient to operate since each military Post or Base had a Housing Office; Equal Opportunity Office; Public Affairs Office; Chapel; Library; Auto Shop; Medical Dispensary or Hospital; Dental Clinic; Commissary; Post and Base Exchanges; Post or Base headquarters; Military Police; Decal Office; Fitness Center; Reception Center; Swimming Pool; Child Care Center; Enlisted and NCO Club; Officers' Club; Teen Club; Family Support Center; Temporary Lodging; Education Center; Dining Hall; Maintenance Office; Golf Course; Post and Base Theater, Post Office; and various Recreational facilities. Therefore, shifting "tenant" units to larger military Posts or Bases with room for growth would save money and manpower in the long run, although moving units required money for realignment and some new construction. The Reserve, National Guard, and civilian activities at closed military Posts and Bases could continue as they did elsewhere without a military landlord. Base closures allowed the elimination of outdated organizations that had been preserved as positions were programmed by the US Congress.

During March 2005, the BRAC 05 base closure round began when the President and the US Congress appointed the nine member Base Closing Commission, and the Secretary of Defense submitted his list of military facilities to be closed on May 16th. It would take several members to add a military facility to that list, but just a simple majority to remove one. The President could approve the list and send it to the US Congress or reject it and send it back to the Commission. Neither the US Congress nor the President could make changes. If the President accepted the list, it would become law unless the US Congress voted against it within 45-days. This has never happened since Congressmen from spared districts would naturally believe the list was fair.

During BRAC 05, US Army Posts that were proposed for realignment or closure included: Carlisle Barracks, PA; Detroit Arsenal, MI; Fort Beauvoir, VA; Fort Buchanan, PA; Fort McPherson/Gilles, GA; Fort Monmouth, NJ; Fort Monroe, VA; Fort Polk, LA (realign); Fort Richardson, AK; Fort Sam Houston, TX; Fort Shafter, HI; Lima Army Tank Plant, OK; Natick Soldier Center, MA; Picatinny Arsenal, NJ; Redstone Arsenal, AL; Rock Island, IL; Sierra Army Depot, CA; and Yuma Proving Grounds, AZ.

During BRAC 05, US Air Force Bases that were proposed for realignment or closure included: Altus AFB, OK; Beale AFB, CA; Brooks AFB, TX; Cannon AFB, NM; Columbus AFB, MS; Ellsworth AFB, SD; Goodfellow AFB, TX; Grand Folks AFB, ND; Hanscom AFB, MA; Kirkland AFB, NM; Los Angeles AFB, CA; McConnell AFB, KS; Nellis AFB, NV; Seymour Johnson AFB, NC; Shaw AFB, SC; and Vance AFB, OK.

During BRAC 05, US Naval Bases that were proposed for realignment or closure included: Ingleside Naval Station, TX; Naval Postgraduate School; US Navy Air Station Meridian, MS; Naval Air Engineering Station Lakehurst, NJ; Naval Recreation Station Solomons Island, MD; Naval Surface Warfare Center Crane, NJ; Naval Surface Warfare Center Dahlgren Division, VA; Navy Supply Corps School, GA; New Orleans Naval Support Activity, LA; Pascagoula Naval Station, MS; Portsmouth Naval Shipyard, NH; and Saratoga Springs Naval Support Unit, NY.

During BRAC 05, US Naval Marine Bases that were proposed for realignment or closure included: Marine Corps Logistics Base Albany, GA; Marine Corps Logistics Base Barstow, CA (realign); Marine Corps Station Miramar, CA; Marine Corps Mountain Warfare School, CA; Marine Reserve Support Unit, Kansas City, MO; and Marine Corps Recruit Depot San Diego, CA (realign or closure). 0000000 The City of Marina developed a large part of land within its City limits building over 1000 new homes. A large strip mall along Highway #1 at the former North entrance to the Fort Ord Post opened and houses popular retail stores such as Target and Best Buy. A substantial amount of land on the East side of the Fort Ord Post was set aside for preservation as open space. This preserve included a network of hiking trails and other recreational amenities.

The Fort Ord Post's golf course became a public golf course. They have hosted PGA golf events and were recently renovated. A small portion of the military Post remained under US Army control and is called the Presidio of Monterey Annex. It included the Rod Military Community California National Guard; DOD Center; and gunnery ranges. The military still have a presence at the Fort Ord Post with California National Guard units; facilities administered by the Presidio of Monterey; Post Exchange; and Commissary to cater for military retirees who chose to settle in the area and were entitled to shop at such facilities. Management of the military housing was outsourced to private firms; however, the homes were still occupied by military personnel stationed at the Presidio of Monterey, Naval Postgraduate School, and retired military personnel.

Comparison with the Presidio Post Closure

During September 1994, the Fort Ord Post closed its gates and became part of US military history. The BRAC 91 Commission recommended closing the military Post and moving the units stationed at the Fort Ord Post to Fort Lewis in Washington. US Army elements from Fort Ord Post and Marines from Camp Pendleton participated in quelling the 1992 Los Angeles riots. Most of the land was returned to the State of California and became the home of the California State University, Monterey Bay. The remainder was given to the University of California, Santa Cruz to be developed into Monterey Bay Education, Science, and Technology Center (UC MBEST). The MBEST Center became a regional economic development effort focused on developing collaborative research-business opportunities in the Monterey Bay Area.

In sum, the historical and political reasoning that closed the Fort Ord Post has been presented in an attempt to adjudicate an understandable Post closure decision. The Fort Ord Post closure, of course, supports the rational for the entire historic Case Study. The Fort Ord Post did not have an administrative headquarters like the Presidio of San Francisco; however, its training mission did qualify the Post to be realigned with another US Army Post. In the case of the Fort Ord Post, it was finally discontinued and its training mission with military personnel and Civil Service employees realigned with a supportable mission to another US Army Post. At this point, it is rather obvious that the Case Study investigation of the Fort Ord Post closure did come under the purview of the Base Closure and Realignment Act of 1988.

CHAPTER IV

History of George Air Force Base

During April 1940, civic leaders from Victorville in California approached the US Army with a proposal to develop an airfield in the High Mojave Desert. They promoted the area's 360-day per year of sunny weather, abundance of wide open spaces, and the availability of support services from the nearby towns of both Victorville and Adelanto. During June 1941, as part of the buildup of the US Army Air Corps prior to the entry of the US during WW II, an agreement was made, and construction of a 22,200-acre airfield commenced with a ground breaking ceremony on July 12, 1941. In addition to the airfield, the building of a large support facility was carried out with barracks, various administrative buildings, maintenance shops, and hangars.

The Victorville Army Airfield was located within the City limits, eight-miles Northwest of central Victorville in California, and about 75-miles Northeast of Los Angeles in California. The airfield was established by the US Army Air Corps as an Advanced Flying School located in the Mojave Desert. The airfield was used during the postwar years primarily as a surplus aircraft storage facility by the Air Material Command. A large number of aircraft were flown to the airfield and parked out in the high desert. These included the Boeing B-29 Super fortress; Beechcraft AT-7 Navigator; and AT-11 trainers. During January 1948, the caretaker host organization was named the 2756th Air Base Squadron after the establishment of the US Air Force.

The Victorville Army Airfield consisted of a large number of buildings based of standardized plans and architectural drawings, with the buildings designed to be the "cheapest" temporary character with structural stability only sufficient enough to meet the needs of the service that the structure was intended to fulfill during the period of its contemplated war use. To conserve critical materials, most building facilities were constructed of wood, concrete, brick, gypsum board, and concrete asbestos. Metal was sparsely used. The Airfield was designed to be self-sufficient with not only hangars; but with barracks, warehouses hospital facilities dental clinic, dining halls, and maintenance shops. There was a library, social club for officers and enlisted personnel, and stores to buy living necessities. With over 250 buildings, together with water, sewer, electric and gas utilities, the airfield was home for over 4000 military personnel.

During February 1942, training began on Curtis AT-9s, T-6 Texan's, and AT-17s for Pilots, and AT-11s and BT-13s Valiant for Bombardiers. The US Army operated an advanced twin-engine Pilot Training School at the airfield, generally flying C-47 Sky Train Transports, B-25 Mitchells, and B-26 Marauder medium bombers.

The training School also trained replacement aircrew members in B25s and B-26s. On April 24, 1962, the first class of Flying Cadets graduated.

In addition to pilot training, a USAAF Bombardier Training School was established. Bombardier training was conducted by the 519th, 520th. 521st, and 522nd Bombardier Training Squadrons. The 516th, 517th, and 518th were the Twin-Engine Flying Training Squadrons. During April 1942, these training Squadrons were organized under the 36th Flying Training Wing that became the main flying operations command and control organization. The first Bombardier classes had to practice their target runs at nearby Muroc Army Airfield that was later renamed Edwards AFB. The pilots used Highway 395 as a landmark and guided North to the bombing range.

Waco CG-4 Glider pilots were also trained at the Victorville Airfield, with special emphasis on spot-landing and night flying. The gliders were an essential part of the June 6, 1944 D-Day invasion and hundreds of gliders carried combat troops and equipment landing sites at Normandy in France. To ease the over-crowded runways at Victorville Airfield, glider students practiced take-offs and landings at the El Mirage lake-bed and El Mirage Airfield. During January 1943, there were several oiled runways on the dirty dry lake and they worked efficiently until the lake-bed flooded.

During April, 1944, several changes were made at the Victorville Airfield with the 3035th Army Air Forces Base took over the administrative organization of the School during April. During March 1944, a School for P-39 Air cobra single-engine pursuit pilots was established. Also training for B-24 Liberator Bombardiers began, and during September, a Radar Training School for Bombardiers was established.

During 1945, with the surrender of Germany, the training mission at Victorville Airfield began to slow down, and on August 15, all training at the airfield ceased. After the Japanese capitulation, the Post Commander was notified around September 15th that the Victorville Airfield was to be placed on a standby status. On October 12, 1945, all flying missions at the Airfield ended and the Base was placed on standby status.

During November 1949, the George AFB was reassigned to the Continental Air Command. On October 10, 1950; George AFB was reassigned to the Air Defense Command. During November 1950, the George AFB was again activated as a combat training Base by the US Air Force with the outbreak of the Korean War. On January 1, 1951, the military Base was reassigned to the Tactical Air Command. The George AFB remained a combat training Base throughout the Cold War, and a number of bomber, glider, single engine, and jet fighter aircraft were flown by various organizations. The Tactical Air Command primarily trained pilots in front-line US Air Force fighter aircraft until being deactivated. The George AFB was closed by the Base Realignment and Closure Commission,

BRAC 92 at the end of the Cold War, and was eventually renamed the Southern California Logistics Airport.

On July 18, 1950, the 1st Fighter-Interceptor Wing was realigned from March AFB in California to George AFB in California. On November 30, 1951, with the exception of the Headquarters and Headquarters Squadron, and the three Fighter-Interceptor Squadrons, all, 1st Fighter-Interceptor Wing organizations and the Group Headquarters were reduced to a strength of one officer and one airman at which time the Wing moved from George AFB in California to Norton AFB in California. The 94th Fighter-Interceptor Squadron remained at George AFB until 1955 when it was realigned to Selfridge AFB in Michigan.

On June 2, 1950, the Victorville Army Airfield was named George AFB in honor of Brigadier General Harold Huston George. General George was a WW I fighter ace who directed air operations on Bataan at the beginning of WW II. On April 29, 1942, General George died in an aircraft accident near Darwin NT in Australia. A Curtiss P-40 of the 49th Fighter Group, piloted by Lieutenant Bob Hazard, was taking off as the second of two P-40s from Twenty Seven Mile Field, Southeast of Darwin in Australia, lost directional control in the prop wash of the lead fighter, striking a recently arrived Lockheed C-40 parked next to the airstrip killing General George. Time-Life war correspondent Melvin Jacoby and 2nd Lieutenant Robert D. Jasper, were standing next to the Lockheed. Other personnel received injuries; however, the P-40 pilot survived. During June 1950, the George AFB was named after the late General.

On June 25, 1950, the outbreak of the Korean War indicated that the US Air Force would soon see an increase in combat training requirements. By July 1st, the US Air Force had approved plans to increase to 95 Wings from the reduced force during the postwar years due to the demobilization after WW II. Experienced pilots in fighter jets were needed. The newly established Continental Air Command (ConAC) was assigned the dual missions of the Air Defense of the US as well as the employment of Tactical Air Forces to support contingency deployments around the world. ConAC activated the WW II training Base at Victorville in California, now renamed George AFB, and assigned it to the Air Defense Command.

When reactivated, the George AFB had been in mothballs for over five years, and many of the WW II buildings on it were deteriorating due to the temporary nature of the structures when they were built. A rapid refurbishment of the military Base was necessary to bring it up to postwar standards to include updating electrical telephones and electrical systems, barracks and support buildings, and extending the runway to accommodate jet aircraft. On October 1, 1971, the 35th Tactical Fighter Wing was reactivated at George AFB in California where it replaced the 478th Tactical Fighter Wing. The Wing's mission at George AFB was to take over the mission of retraining F-4 aircrews. During July 1973, with the arrival of F-105G aircraft from the 3878th Tactical Fighter Wing at

Karat RTAFB in Thailand, the Wing began training aircrews for radar detection and suppression of "Wild Weasel" missions in addition to other F-4 combat training. By 1975, with the arrival of new F-4G aircraft, the Wing was training aircrews exclusively in "Wild Weasel" operations for deployment to operational organizations at Okinawa and Germany. During 1980, the Wing received the new F-4G aircraft and its advanced "Wild Weasel" system. By July 1980, the last F-105G aircraft left George AFB leaving the 37th Tactical Fighter Wing with F-4G aircraft in its inventory for "Wild Weasel" training and operational missions. On March 30, 1981, tactical operations at George AFB were reorganized for mission requirements. The 35th Tactical Fighter Wing retained control of the 20th and 21st Tactical Fighter Training Squadrons and gained the 39th Tactical Fighter Squadron.

As the only "Wild Weasel" training Wing in the World, the Wing provided instructor pilots and qualified aircrews for the other two "Wild Weasel" Wings in the Philippines (3rd Tactical Fighter Wing) and West Germany (52nd Tactical Fighter Wing). As part of the training mission, the Wings participated in numerous tactical, maritime, tactics, suppression of enemy air defenses, force escort operations and dissimilar air combat training and with Air National Guard and Air Force Reserve Squadrons, and various allies. During 1985 through 1987, the Wing aircrews and ground personnel won the US Air Force Worldwide Fighter Gunnery Meet.

During 1985, with the inactivation of the 39th Tactical Fighter Squadron, the 35th Tactical Fighter Wing was redesigned the 35th Tactical Training Wing. However, the Wing retained the air defense augmentation responsibility. It provided operations and maintenance support for the close air support portion of US Army training exercises conducted at the US Army National Training Center at Fort Irwin in California from 1981 through 1990. The Wing also advised special Air National Guard organizations on F-4G operations from 1981 through 1991.

During 1988, the George AFB was scheduled in the first round (BRAC 88) for Base closure as approved by the US Congress under the Base Realignment and Closure Act. On October 5, 1989, operations at George AFB were again reorganized. The 37th Tactical Fighter Wing and the 35th Tactical Training Wing consolidated all operations under the newly redesigned 35th Tactical Fighter Wing. Under the reorganization, the 35th Tactical Fighter Wing regained control of the 581st Tactical Fighter Squadron and the 582nd Tactical Fighter Training Squadron. The George AFB was among a number of military Installations where environmental clean-up was placed on a "fast track;" Base property could therefore be quickly transferred to the community for re-use. Many of the old Base housing homes and buildings are currently being used by the US Army and US Marine Corps for urban warfare training.

During August 1990, the 35th Tactical Fighter Wing mobilized in support of Operation Desert Storm. On August 16, 1990, twenty-four F-4Gs of the 561st

Tactical Fighter Squadron left George AFB en-route to Shaikh Isa Air Base in Bahrain. Once in the Middle East, its deployed personnel established operational, maintenance, and living facilities for the 35th Tactical Fighter Wing (Provisional). These facilities eventually housed more than 60 active duty and Air National Guard F-4s and more than 2600 military personnel.

On January 17 1991, during Operation Desert Storm, the 561st Tactical Fighter Squadron flew 1,182 combat sorties for a total of 4,393.5 hours. The 35th Tactical Fighter Wing (Provisional) was credited with flying 3,072 combat missions for 10,318.r hours. The US Central Command relied heavily on the Wing's "Wild Weasels" to suppress enemy air defense systems. The F-4G aircrews were credited with firing 905 missiles at Iraqi targets, while the RF-4C aircrews shot more than 300,000 feet of vital reconnaissance film. During Operation Desert Shield and Desert Storm, the 35th Tactical Fighter Wing (Provisional) suffered no casualties. On March 23, 1991, the Wing's personnel began returning to George AFB with its pilots and aircraft following three days later.

During March 1991, the 35th Tactical Fighter Wing became the host for George AFB when the 831st Air Division inactivated. As a result, the Wing gained several support agencies to include the 35th Combat Support Group and associated Squadrons. On June 28, 1991, in support of the US Air Force reduction programs, the 21st Tactical Fighter Training Squadron was inactivated. That October, as part of the US Air Force reorganization plan, the 35th Tactical Fighter Wing was re-designated the 35th Fighter Wing. A month later, the Wing's Tactical Fighter Squadrons were designated Fighter Squadrons.

During December, 1992, the George AFB was officially decommissioned. During 1993, President Bill Clinton announced a "Five Part Plan" to speed up economic recovery in communities where military Posts and Bases were to be closed. One part of this plan called for improving public participation in the Post and Base environmental clean-up program. The George AFB was among a number of military Installations where environmental clean-up was placed on a "fast track" so that the Base property could be quickly transferred to the community for re-use. Many of the old Base housing homes and buildings are still currently used by the US Army and US Marine Corps for urban warfare training.

During 1992, the 35th Tactical Fighter Wing began downsizing in preparation for the George AFB closure. On June 5, 1993, thev20th Fighter Squadron moved to Holloman AFB in New Mexico, and by the end of June, the 561st and 562nd Fighter Squadrons were inactivated. On December 15, 1992, the 35th the 35th Fighter Wing inactivated and George AFB closed bringing an end to 21-years of continuance service and more than 34-years of total service for the 35th Tactical Fighter Wing. Since 2009, the California National Guard's 199th Reconnaissance Squadron has operated an MQ-1 Predator Remotely Piloted Aircraft (RPA) training facility at the Southern California Logistics Airport.

The George AFB has joined a small number of converted civilian facilities slated for fast track transfer five-years after the (BRAC 88) Base closure announcement for re-use. It is now the Southern California Logistics Airport (SCLA). During February, 1990, the airport was listed as a Superfund site calling itself a dedicated Air Cargo Facility with a 5000-acre multi modal business complex that integrated manufacturing, industrial, and office facilities. SCLA began efforts to extend the main runway to accept larger cargo jets and better serve more than 70,000 troops that annually passed through the Airport to and from the US Army's Fort Irwin Training Center. The Airfield now serves multi modal distribution functions, with interfaces to truck and rail shipping, through smaller hangers and global weakness in the air freight industry have countered some benefits of the successful runway expansion. A recent estimate found that approximately 20-percent of the George AFB's 7500 military personnel and Civil Service employees had already been replaced. Considering its relatively remote location in the Mojave Desert, many considered the George AFB's closure recovery fully successful

Comparison with the Presidio Post

Unlike the Presidio of San Francisco closure that had a primary admission mission. the 1991 Defense Base Realignment and Closure Commission still recommended that the George AFB be closed, and that military personnel and Civil Service employees be transferred to other military Installations and equipment resources be realigned. The George AFB primary mission was to provide facilities for aircraft storage and maintenance; air operations and coordination; and organizational training.

In sum, the historical and political reasoning that closed the George Air Force Base has been presented in an attempt to adjudicate an understandable Base closure decision. The George AFB closure, of course, supports the rational for the entire historic Case Study. The George AFB did not have an administrative headquarters like the Presidio of San Francisco; however, its training mission did qualify the Base to be realigned with another AFB. In the case of the George AFB, the 1991 Defense Base Realignment and Closure Commission still recommended that the George AFB be closed; and that its training mission with military personnel and Civil Service employees be realigned with a supportable mission to another AFB. At this point, it is rather obvious that the Case Study investigation of the George AFB closure did come under the purview of the Base Closure and Realignment Act of 1988.

CHAPTER V

History of Norton Air Force Bas

The Norton AFB was located within the City limits of San Bernardino in California. It began before WW II as the Municipal Airport San Bernardino under the Army Air Corp's jurisdiction. During the Summer of 1941, the Municipal Airport San Bernardino became a military training Base to meet the needs of the 30,000 Pilot Training Program. After December 7, 1941, within days after the attack on Pearl Harbor, combat-ready fighter planes arrived at the Municipal Airport San Bernardino to protect the Los Angeles area from enemy attack. During WW II, the primary mission became the repair and maintenance of military aircraft.

On March 1942, the Municipal Airport San Bernardino was renamed the San Bernardino Army Air Field; and the San Bernardino Air Depot was established there.

On June 2, 1942, the first military aircraft arrived at the San Bernardino Army Air Field.

During March 1943, all runways were completed. By December 1943, night flying was initiated.

During WW II, the San Bernardino Army Air Field provided administrative and logistical support for the US Army Desert Training Center (DTC). The DTC was a massive training facility was organized in the Mojave Desert, largely in Southern California and Western Arizona. The DTC's primary mission was to train US Army and Army Air Corps military personnel and military organizations to live and fight in the desert; to test and develop suitable equipment; and to develop tactical doctrines, techniques, and training methods. The Air Transport Command used the airfield during WW II.

During 1948, the San Bernardino Army Air Field was transferred to the newly established US Air Force. The Norton AFB became a Processing and Separation Center for the millions of servicemen being discharged at the end of WW II.

During 1940 through 1960, the major secondary mission at Norton AFB was to provide military logistical support for the Headquarters, Air Defense Command in Southern California.

During the late 1940s, the USAF moved into the jet age, Norton AFB began overhauling jet engines during 1951, and the Air Material area became one of three USAF jet overhaul centers by 1953. To accommodate the largest Strategic

Air Command bombers, the main runways were extended 10,000 feet by 1954. B-45 Tornado upgrades were also performed at Norton AFB during the late 1940s.

During 1950, the Air Defense Command activated the 27th Air Division (Defense) at Norton AFB that was assigned to the Western Air Defense Force. Its primary mission was the air defense of Southern California and later Southern Nevada. By 1953, the area of control included a small portion of Arizona. The 27th Air Division controlled both Aircraft Interceptor Squadrons, as well as general surveillance anti-aircraft Radar Squadrons.

During 1950, the San Bernardino Army Air Field was renamed Norton AFB after Captain Leland Francis Norton, a WW II bomber pilot, when on his16th combat mission, his A-20 Havoc was struck by anti-aircraft fire on May 27, 1944 near Amiens in France. After ordering his aircrew of his crippled aircraft to bail out, Captain Norton perished with his Havoc aircraft. Captain Norton's portrait hung in the Officer's Club until the Norton AFB closed.

During 1955, the 27th Air Division established a manual Air Defense Control Center (ADCC) (P-84) at Norton AFB to monitor and control aircraft in Southern California. The manual site was replaced during 1959 by a Semi-Automatic Ground Environment (SAGE) Data Center (DC-17).

During 1956, the Norton AFB in California became the home of the 63rd Military Airlift Wing that provided airlift and food services to World-wide air and ground combat units. During 1966, the Headquarters, Aerospace Audio-Visual Service (AAVS) was established at the Norton AFB to provide audio-visual services to the US Air Force and DOD agencies. The Norton AFB also quartered numerous tenant organizations to include the Headquarters, Air Force Inspection and Safety Center; Military Airlift Command; Non-Commissioned Officer Academy-West; and the Headquarters, Ballistic Missile Organization.

On November 29, 1957, General Thomas D. White disclosed the development of an anti-missile called the "Wizard;" the assignment of intercontinental and intermediate missile programs to the Strategic Air Command and the transfer of the 1st Missile Division to the Strategic Air Command. The San Bernardino Air Force Depot in California would also assume support services for long-range ballistic missile programs.

During 1960 through 1986, for the majority of its operational lifetime, the Norton AFB was a logistics depot and a heavy-lift transport facility for a variety of military aircraft, equipment, and supplies as part of Air Material/Air Force Logistics Command. The Norton AFB expanded its depot support mission by supporting Titan and Atlas Intercontinental Ballistic Missiles (ICBM) with depot level logistic support. SAMSO, the Space and Missile Systems Organization, also managed the Minuteman and Peacekeeper Programs, was located at Norton AFB from the 1960s. Upon Norton AFB closure, the mission was transferred to the Los Angeles Air Force Station and later to the Los Angles AFB.

During the late 1960s, discrete C-130 Hercules modification tests were conducted out of Area II at Norton AFB with the 1198th Operational Evaluation and Training Squadron operating four highly classified C-130E (I) special operations test beds modified at Lockheed Air Services, at nearby Ontario Airport under projects "Thin Slice" and "Heavy Chains." Their electronics sorties were developed for and identical to those of the MC-130 Combat Talon, with the addition of Forward Looking Infrared, and 1198th DEATS test missions were flown out of Takhli Royal Thai AFB in Thailand under project "Heavy Chain" with the aircraft painted all black.

During 1966, the Los Angeles Air Defense Sector (LAADS) was inactivated and the designation returned to the 27th Air Division, at Luke AFB in Arizona under the Forth Air Force as part of a consolidation with the inactivating Phoenix Air Sector DC-17 at Norton AFB that was inactivated a few months later on June 25, 1966. Its mission being consolidated with SAGE Data Center DC-21 at Luke AFB in Arizona under the 27th Air Division.

During 1966, a change in mission from the Air Force Logistics Command (AFLC) to the Military Airlift Command (MAC) meant that the Norton AFB became one of the six MAC strategic airlift Bases supporting the US Army and Marine Corps' airlift requirements among other military missions. A new MAC passenger terminal was built to replace the WW II facility to handle passenger traffic primarily to and from Southeast Area.

During February, 1969, the SAGE system was an automated complex network linking Air Force and later FAA General Surveillance Radar Stations into a centralized Center for air defense, intended to provide only warning and response from a Soviet nuclear attack. It was initially under the Los Angeles Air Defense Sector (LAADS) established on February 1, 1959 with the reorganization of the 27th Air Division.

During 1970, a railroad system interchanged with the Pacific Electric/Southern Pacific Branch line on the South side of the military Installation. When Base rail operations were discontinued during the late 1970s, the Base diesel locomotive, a General Electric center cab B/B 9090, USAF 8580, was donated to Orange Empire Railroad Museum at Perris in California.

During 1986 through 1994, the Norton AFB continued as part of Military Airlift/ Air Mobility Command. The Norton AFB hosted numerous Air Force Reserve transport organizations. The Norton AFB produced the "Air Force Now" films, shown at monthly Commander's Call at USAF Bases around the World. The Norton AFB hosted numerous US Air Force Reserve transport organizations. The

Office of the Inspector General and the Directorate of Aerospace Safety were also located at Norton AFB.

During 1988, the Norton AFB was selected for closure by the Base Realignment and Closure Commission, and finally closed on March 31, 1994. Detachment 10 of the Ballistic Missile Organization remained until September 1995.

During 1996, the SAGE Direction Center closed along with the other ADC facilities at Norton AFB. Being vacant, it became the home of the Aerospace Audio-Visual Service. The windowless, temperature controlled SAGE structure was perfect for film storage. It was also the home of the Air Combat Service. The Norton AFB was finally closed during April 1994 as a result of BRAC 88 intervention; the facility was essentially abandoned, and may remain so today. Many adjacent smaller structures have been demolished, and likely it remains standing is due to its heavily reinforced concrete and steel construction.

Finally, the Norton AFB aviation facilities were converted into the San Bernardino International Airport. The 63rd and 445th Military Airlift Wings realigned three of the four Squadrons (C-141 Star lifter, C-21, and C-12 Huron aircraft) to nearby March AFB in California, while the remaining Squadron (C-141 Aircraft) was realigned to McCord AFB in Washington. Operational control of the airport and surrounding facilities were turned over to a Consortium consisting of several nearby Cities to manage and oversee its operations. However, airport conditions did not lend themselves to any airlines desiring to start service to a new airport in the greater Los Angeles area. But improvements in recent years to the runway and terminal facilities as well as infrastructure support such as widening of area roads have been made and the airport is still looking for a Carrier willing to begin operations. Charter as well as private flights operate from the San Bernardino International Airport and it is also used as a base for firefighting airplanes. Civilian operations were expanded to provide maintenance, storage, and logistical support for various missile programs. In the long run, the Norton AFB closure was attributed to environmental waste, inadequate facilities, and air traffic congestion due to air traffic from Ontario International Airport 20-miles West, and the Los Angeles International Airport 60-miles West.

Recently, private development on the former Base has assisted in turning the basically unused land into jobs and revenue for the City of San Bernardino as several Companies have opened distribution centers on the property. Mattel opened a distribution center during 2004, consolidating three other smaller centers from around Southern California into a single location. Slater Brothers Markets also built a new headquarters as well as a centralized warehousing facility. The completion of the project during 2007 consolidated the headquarters and a warehouse near the City of Colton as well as several other warehouses that have been located around the Inland Empire into a single location. Industrial buildings used by Pep Boys Auto and Kohl's are also located on the premise.

Comparison with the Presidio Post Closure

Unlike the Presidio of San Francisco closure that had a primary administration mission, the 1991 Defense Base Realignment and Closure Commission still recommended that the Norton AFB be closed and that military personnel and Civil Service employees be transferred to other military Installations and equipment resources be realigned. The Norton AFB primary mission was to provide facilities for aircraft storage and maintenance; air operations and planning and coordination; and organizational training. The Norton AFB was placed on the DOD's Base Closure List the same year that the DOD signed the Federal Facilities Agreement with the EPAA.

In sum, the historical and political reasoning that closed Norton Air Force Base has been presented in an attempt to adjudicate an understandable Base closure decision. The Norton AFB closure, of course, supports the rational for the entire historic Case Study. The Norton AFB did not have an administrative headquarters like the Presidio of San Francisco; however, its training mission did qualify the Base to be realigned with another AFB. In the case of the Norton AFB, the 1991 Defense Base Realignment and Closure Commission still recommended that the Norton AFB be closed; and that its training mission with military personnel and Civil Service employees be realigned with a supportable mission to another AFB. At this point, it is rather obvious that the Case Study investigation of the Norton AFB closure did come under the purview of the Base Closure and Realignment Act of 1988.

CHAPTER VI

History of Beale Air Force Base

The Beale AFB was located outside of Linda, about 10-miles East of the towns of Marysville and Yuba City and about 40-miles North of the State Capital at Sacramento in California. The Beale AFB was large in terms of land, and had five gates to provide access on all sides of the military Base. Visitors entered the military Base through a main gate that local merchants, citizens, and the Beale Military Liaison Committee donated $100 thousand to construct. The Beale AFB was home for approximately 4000 military personnel. The Beale AFB was also a census-designated place (CDP) at Yuba County in Northern California. The Beale AFB was at an elevation of 197-feet. The 2010 US census reported the Beale AFB population at 1319.

The Beale AFB covered nearly 23,000-acres of rolling hills in Northern California. The military Base's natural resources were as rich as its significant cultural and historical heritage. Native Americans lived on this land; the mortar bowls they carved into the bedrock lie embedded in a shallow stream. German POW's were held captive on the military Base during WW II. A block of barred prison cells still stand at Beale AFB; however, the drawings of the POWs remain vivid on the walls of the prison cells. To preserve these and other historical areas, the Beale AFB proudly maintains 38 Native American Sites, 45 homestead Sites, and 41 WW II Sites.

Camp Beale also housed a German POW Camp, and served as the Main Camp for a series of satellite POW Camps around Southern California. Some Branch POW Camps were established at Arbuckle in Colusa County with 200 German POWs; Chico Butte County with 475 German POWs; Napa in Napa County with 250 German POWs; and Windsor in Sonoma County with 250 German POWs. All of the Camps provided agriculture manpower to local farms and ranchers. German POWs at Camp Beale also provided manpower for military Installation repair and maintenance.

The 9th Reconnaissance Wing was the host organization assigned to the Air Combat Command that was part of the Twelfth Air Force. The Wing was considered to be one of the show places of the US Air Force. The Wing was a Reconnaissance, Command and Control, and Intelligence military organization assigned to the US Air Force Reserve. The Wing was responsible for the stand up and total force integration of the Air Force Reserve Command's newest multi-mission Wing that included Command and Control, Reconnaissance, and Intelligence forces in support of Air Combat Command, Pacific Air Forces, and the Air Force Intelligence, Surveillance, and Reconnaissance Agency.

The 9th Reconnaissance Wing collected intelligence information essential for Presidential and Congressional decisions critical to the National Defense. To accomplish this mission, the Wing was equipped with the nation's fleet of U-2 Dragon Lady RQ-4 Global Hawk unmanned aircraft and the MC-12 Liberty Recognizance aircraft, and associated support equipment. The Wing also maintained a high state of readiness in its combat support and combat service support forces for potential deployment. The Wing also maintained a high state of readiness in its combat support and combat service forces for potential deployment in response to theater contingencies.

During 1940, the Camp Beale area consisted of grassland and rolling hills, and the 19th Century mining town of Spencerville. During this period, Marysville City officials encouraged the Department of War to establish a military Installation in the area. During 1942, as a result the Federal Government purchased 87,000-acres for a training Post for the 13th Armored Division, the only unit of its kind to be entirely trained in California. Camp Beale also held training facilities for the 81st and 96th Infantry Divisions, and a 1000 bed Hospital. Dredge materials from the area's abandoned gold mines were used to build streets at Camp Beale. As a complete training environment, Camp Beale had tank maneuvers; mortar and rifle ranges; Bombardier and Navigator training; and chemical warfare training. During WW II, Camp Beale at its peak quartered 60,000 military personnel.

During 1942, Camp Beale was formerly named after Edward Fitzgerald Beale, an American Navy Lieutenant and a Brigadier General in the California Militia who was an explorer and frontiersman in California.

During 1948, Camp Beale had a mission to train bombardiers and navigators in radar techniques.

On April 1, 1951, Camp Beale became Beale AFB; steeped in history; it was in the forefront of the USAF's future in high technology. The Beale AFB established six bombing ranges of 1200-acres, and the US Navy also used the Beale AFB for training. The Beale AFB trained Aviation Engineers and operated an Air Base Defense School. These additional activities led to rehabilitation of existing military Base facilities and construction of rifle, mortar, demolition, and machine gun ranges.

During 1952, the Beale AFB in California was placed in an inactive status for conversion to an operational military Base. The Headquarters, Aviation Engineer Force administered the Beale AFB for the next six-years while a runway was laid down, and appropriate support facilities such as hangers, maintenance shops, warehouses, barracks, and other infrastructure was laid out and constructed. The 2275th Air Base Squadron was the coordinating organization during construction. The Beale AFB stopped being used as a bombing range and the Federal Government declared portions of the Camp Beale/Beale AFB in excess, eventually transferring 60,805 acres. Eventually, excess land from the former Army Camp was sold off to the public. On December 21, 1950, 40,592-acres on the Eastern side of the Base were sold at auction. An additional 11,213-acres were transferred to the State of California from 1962 through 1963, and now comprise the Spencerville Wildlife and Recreation Area. During 1964 through 1965, other 9,000-acres were sold at auction. In deeds for the former Camp Beale property, the Federal Government recommended that the property have surface use only.

On January 30, 1959, the US Air Force announced plans to conduct surveys in the vicinity of the Beale AFB in California to determine the feasibility for a missile Base. During September, 1959, Colonel Paul K. Carlton Commander of the Beale AFB 4126th Strategic Wing, announced that the Beale AFB would be the fifth HGM-25A Titan I missile Installation. Three complexes with three weapons each would be located 25-miles Southwest, 27-miles West, and 71-miles Northwest of the Beale AFB near the respective communities of Lincoln, Live Oak, and Chico. On April 1, 1961, the US Air Force activated the 851st Strategic Missile Squadron (Titan). On February 28, 1962, the first missile was moved to the 4A complex at Lincoln where workers had difficulty placing the missile into the silo. On April 20, 1962, follow-on missile installations went smoothly and the last missile was lowered into the Chico complex 4C.

On February 8, 1959, the Strategic Air Command (SAC) established the Beale AFB in California as an operational AFB. The 4126th Strategic Wing was activated to disburse its B-52 Stratofortress heavy bombers over a larger number of military Bases, making it more difficult for the Soviet Union to destroy the entire fleet with a surprise first strike. During May 1959, Colonel (later General) Carlton assumed command of the recently activated 4126th Strategic Wing. The first two KC-120 Stratotanker aircraft arrived two months later on July 7, 1959 as part of the 903rd Air Refueling Squadron. On January 18, 1960, the 31st Bombardment Squadron with its B-52E Stratofortress aircraft arrived at the Beale AFB to become part of the Wing. The 14th Air Division moved to the Beale AFB from Travis AFB in California one week later. Half of the aircraft were maintained on as 15-minute alert, fully fueled and armed, and ready for combat. As an expedient, the US Air Force considered Strategic Wing (Provisional) organizations when they transitioned from B-52E aircraft to B-52G aircraft.

On December 21, 1959, 40,592-acres on the Eastern side were at auction.

On May 24, 1962, during a contractor checkout, a terrific blast rocked Launcher 1 at back in operational service. Today, the site has had all three launch silos capped, but some developments have taken place on the launch area with a retention pond, some trees, and some single story buildings being erected. It appears to be in use for some type of quarrying/grading material that is transported to construction sites at the Chino area.

During September 1962, the 851st Strategic Missile Squadron (Titan) became the host Titan I Squadron to achieve alert status. On March 9, 1963, after damages were repaired, the Chico complex became operational. Two months later after the Squadron became fully operational; SAC subjected the Squadron to an Operational Readiness Inspection (ORI). The 851st Strategic Missile Squadron (Titan) became the first Titan I organization to pass. On May 16, 1964, Defense Secretary McNamara directed the accelerated phase-out of the Atlas and Titan IICBMs. On January 4, 1965, the first Beale AFB Titan was taken off alert status. Within 3-months, the 851st Strategic Missile Squadron (Titan) was deactivated.

All three missile sites still remain in various stages of abandonment. Site "A" is now being encroached by newly built single family homes as the suburbs of Lincoln. The underground structures of approximately 30-acres of the facility are currently owned by the Placer County who use the site to store and maintain road maintenance equipment. Since the site was deactivated, groundwater has inundated the facility, flooding the underground spaces. Site "B", located in a rural area, is remarkably well preserved with all three launch sites still capped and what appears to be the concrete Control Center still standing.

During 1862 through 1964, additional 11,213-acres were transferred to the State of California and now comprise the Spencerville Wildlife and Recreation Area.

On October 15, 1964, the Department of Defense announced that the Beale AFB would be the home of the new supersonic reconnaissance aircraft—the SR-71 "Blackbird." On January 1, 1965, the 4200th Strategic Reconnaissance Wing (Provisional) was activated in preparation of the realignment. On July 8, 1965, the new Wing received its first aircraft—a T-36 Talon. The first SR-71 aircraft did not arrive until January 7, 1966. The SR-71 aircraft was developed from the Lockheed A-12 reconnaissance aircraft during the 1960s for the Central Intelligence Agency by the Lockheed Skunk Works as a black project. During reconnaissance missions, the SR-71 operated at high speeds and altitudes to allow it to outrace threats. If a surface-to-air missile launch was detected, standard evasive action was simply to accelerate.

During 1964 through 1965, another 9000 acres were sold at auction. In deeds for the former Camp Beale property, the Federal Government recommended that the property have surface use only.

On June 25, 1966, the 9th Strategic Reconnaissance Wing was moved from Mountain Home AFB in Idaho and reassigned to the Beale AFB. The 9th Strategic Reconnaissance Wing had been its host organization at the Beale AFB. With the activation of the 9th Strategic Reconnaissance Wing at the Beale AFB, the Wing absorbed the assets of the 4200th Strategic Reconnaissance Wing (Provisional). This allowed the Wing to stay with the 14th Strategic Aerospace Division. With the arrival of the SR-71 aircraft, the strategic bombardment mission at the Beale AFB was downsized, being replaced by the strategic reconnaissance mission.

During 1967, the Wing performed strategic reconnaissance in Southeast Asia frequently deploying the SR-71 aircraft to Kadena Air Base in Okinawa where it operated over areas of the Pacific and Asia. During 1970, the Wing provided photographic intelligence for the Son Tay prison camp raid named "Operation Ivory Coast" in North Vietnam. Following the Viet Nam War, the SR-71 aircraft established a level-flight-at-altitude record at 85,131-feet and a straight course speed record of 2,194 miles per hour.

Until June 30, 1976, the 17th Bombardment Wing continued global strategic bombardment alert when it was inactivated as part of the phase-out of the B-52 aircraft at the Beale AFB in California. The Wing's EC-135 tanker aircraft were subsequently reassigned to the 100th Air Refueling Wing that the Strategic Air Command (SAC) moved to the Beale AFB from Davis Monthan AFB in Arizona as part of SAC's phase-out from Davis Monthan AFB. The mission of the 100th Air Refueling Wing was primarily to refuel SR-71 aircraft of the 9th Strategic Refueling Wing. Concurrent with this action, the 100th Air Refueling Wing's U-2 aircraft at Davis Monthan AFB would merge with the 9th Strategic Reconnaissance Wing and its SR-71 operations at the Beale AFB. The first U-2 aircraft arrived from Davis Monthan AFB on July 12, 1976 until January 26, 1990 when budget restrictions forced the retirement of the SR-71 aircraft. The Beale AFB was the home of two of the world's most unusual aircraft. The 100th Air Reconnaissance Wing remained at the Beale AFB until March 15, 1993; its assets being absorbed by the senior 9th Air Reconnaissance Wing that became a composite Wing under the one-Base, one Wing concept.

On July, 1, 1976, the U-2 aircraft joined the SR-71 aircraft in the 9th Strategic Reconnaissance Wing giving the organization two of the most recent unique aircraft in the world. The "Dragon Lady" had gained national and international recognition with flights over the Soviet Union, China, Cuba, and Southeast Asia. The U-2 aircraft was the perfect complement to the SR-71. The "Blackbird" could penetrate highly defended areas, take a quick look, and depart at high speeds. The "Dragon Lady" could spend more time on station and furnish a longer look at the desired target. The U-2 aircraft was much less expensive to fly. During 1989, the US Air Force decided the SR-71 was too expensive to operate and retired the "Blackbird" on January 1, 1990. Although the "Blackbird" made a brief revival during the mid-1990s, the "Blackbird" aircraft is still retired. During 1990 through 1991, the Wing deployed the largest contingent of U-2 aircraft to Saudi Arabia to support Desert Shield/Desert Storm. The "Dragon Lady" tracked Iraqi troop and armor buildups, assessed bomb damage, and monitored a massive oil spill in the Persian Gulf. The U-2 pilots alerted ground stations of Scud missile launches, and guided fighter aircraft to destroy Scud launchers. Following the Gulf War, the U-2 aircraft stayed at Saudi Arabia to monitor Iraqi compliance with the peace agreement. During 1998, the "Dragon Lady" set a weight-to-altitude record, and during 1999 won the Collier Trophy—aviation's most coveted award.

On September 1, 1991, the 14th Air Division inactivated and the Second Air Force, with a lineage stretching back to WW II, activated at the Beale AFB in California. On July 1, 1992, following the disestablishment of SAC, the Second Air Force inactivated and re-activated at Keesler AFB in Minnesota as part of the Air Education and Training Command (AETC) the same day. The 9th Strategic Reconnaissance Wing was transferred to the newly established Air Combat Command (ACC) and was designated as the 9th Reconnaissance Wing operating the U-2 aircraft and the T-30 Talon aircraft, while the KC-130Q tanker assets and the 350th Air Refueling Squadron were transferred to the newly established Air Mobility Command (AMC).

During July 1994, the 350th Air Rescue Squadron transferred from the Beale AFB in California to McConnell AFB in Kansas taking the last of the KC-135Q tankers.

During 1997, tanker aircraft returned to the Beale AFB in California when the 940th Air Refueling Wing, an Air Force Reserve Command unit, operationally gained by Air Material Command, transferred to the Beale AFB in California with its KC-135R aircraft following the Base closure of its former home station at Mather AFB in California because of the Base Realignment and Closure BRAC 88 realignment action.

During 1998, tanker aircraft returned to the Beale AFB in California when the 940th Air Refueling Wing, an Air Force Reserve Command organization, operationally gained by the Air Material Command, transferred to the Beale AFB in California with its KC-135R aircraft following the Base closure of the former home station at Mather AFB in California because of the Base Realignment and Closure (BRAC 88) realignment action.

During 2001, the historic 12th Reconnaissance Squadron joined the Wing as the parent organization for the RQ-4 "Golden Hawk" aircraft. An unmanned, remotely piloted high altitude reconnaissance platform, the ": Golden Hawk" could linger over the target for 24-hours.

During 2008, the Beale AFB received the Block 20 model. By the end of 2008, under the subsequent BRAC 05, the 940th Air Rescue Wing's KC-135R aircraft were realigned and the last aircraft departed the Beale AFB in California as the 94th converted to an associate Reconnaissance Wing mission in partnership with the 9th Air Rescue Wing operating the RQ-4 "Global Hawk."

During 2010, the Beal AFB received the Bock 30 model. The MC-130W "Liberty" was moved to the Beale AFB and there was two Squadrons operating the aircraft. The 489th Reconnaissance Squadron conducted training while the 427th was primarily the operational Squadron.

Comparison with the Presidio Post Closure

Unlike the Presidio of San Francisco closure that had a primary administration mission, the 1991 Defense Base Realignment and Closure Commission still recommended that the Beale AFB be closed and that military personnel and Civil Service employees be transferred to other military Installations and equipment resources be realigned. The Beale AFB primary mission was to provide facilities for aircraft storage and maintenance; air operations planning and coordination; and organizational training. DOD signed the Federal Facilities Agreement with the EPAA.

In sum, the historical and political reasoning that closed the Beale Air Force Base has been presented in an attempt to adjudicate an understandable Base closure decision. The Beale AFB closure, of course, supports the rational for the entire historic Case Study. The Beale AFB did not have an administrative headquarters like the Presidio of San Francisco; however, its training mission did qualify the Base to be realigned with another AFB. In the case of the Beale AFB, the 1991 Defense Base Realignment and Closure Commission still recommended that the Beale AFB be closed; and that its training mission with military personnel and Civil Service employees be realigned with a supportable mission to another AFB. At this point, it is rather obvious that the Case Study investigation of the Beale AFB closure did come under the purview of the Base Closure and Realignment Act of 1988

CHAPTER VII

History of Castle Air Force Base

The Castle AFB was a former US Air Force Strategic Air Command Base located Northeast of Atwater, Northwest of Merced, and about 123-miles Southeast of the City of San Francisco. It was first known as the Air Corps Basic Flying School Merced. During September 1941, it became one of the Airfields that were established to meet the needs of the 30,000 Pilot Training Program. As the original name indicated, it provided air training for beginning Pilots and aircrews. During April 1942, it was renamed Merced Army Air Field. During 1995, the military Base was located in unincorporated Merced County, and was closed after the end of the Cold War. It is now known as the Castle Airport Aviation and Development Center. The history of the Castle AFB was very eventful.

The Castle AFB contained an airfield, aviation support buildings, warehouses, 1707 dormitory beds, and a 52 bed hospital. Two housing areas separated from the military Base included 933 family housing units. Most of the Castle AFB was within the unincorporated part of Merced County. Part of it, however, lied within the City of Atwater. The 11,800-foot runway was 300-feet wide, and was the 4th longest civilian runway in the State of California. During January 1996, the nearest airport was in Merced with a 5900-foot runway. Castle Airport opened as an uncontrolled day-use airport. The Castle Airport was designated as general Aviation Airport with fueling and Pilot services provided by Trajan Flight Support. Primary use of the Airport was general aviation; however, large commercial aircraft companies showed significant interest in its use. The Castle Airport was being positioned for use as a Heavy Cargo/Maintenance/Training/Manufacturing Facility. General aviation activity had been amply provided for with the premier terminal in the area and community hangar and tie-down facilities.

The Castle AFB was named after Brigadier General Frederick Castle (1908-1944). General Castle was Air Commander and leader of more than 2000 heavy bombers in a strike against German Airfields. On Christmas Eve 1944 near Liege in Belgium, seven Messerschmitt's set General Castle's B-17 afire. General Castle remained at the controls while his aircrew bailed out. General Castle bravely refused to release his bombs over territory occupied by friendly forces, and died with the Co-pilot when their B-17 exploded. General Castle rode his flaming B-17 to his death while leading the biggest bombing mission of World War II during the Battle of the Bulge.

When the Castle AFB closure was announced, a group of dedicated enthusiasts in the Atwater-Merced area formed a non-profit organization called the Castle Air Museum Foundation, Inc. Their purpose was to assume custody of the Aircraft.

It was their dream to build an Air Museum where faithfully restored historic Aircraft could be exhibited for public enjoyment. "Other things of historical value were in military Air Museums. The Castle AFB in California had 44 rare aircraft on display to include a B-24, a B-36 and a SR-71 all restored and maintained by devoted volunteers. The B-36, the largest bomber ever built, was not in flying condition and was not easily movable."[14] These aircraft are a tribute to the men and women who maintained and flew them. You can read the history of each Aircraft, view the statistics, and see a photo of the Aircraft as they are displayed on the Air Museum grounds. The Castle Air Museum prepared a comprehensive booklet for teachers and educators containing a variety of informative sections from the Castle Air Museum background, to classroom activities and worksheets for 4th to 6th Grammar School students.

The Castle AFB Air Museum stands as a tribute to the men and women of the past who put their lives on the line for our freedom. In order to maintain this tribute for present and future generations, the Air Museum has many needs. During 1995, the Air Museum has been self-supporting operated by the Castle Air Museum Foundation since the Castle AFB closed. Although most of the Aircraft belong to the US Air Force Museum, funds were not provided for repair and maintenance. You can walk among the 45 restored Aircraft on the grounds and indoor Air Museum. The sights include entrance to the Air Museum featuring vintage uniforms, interesting artifacts, and displays. Money to operate the Air Museum, maintain the aircraft and grounds, and add to the collection comes from admissions, memberships, fund-raising events, and donations. The Air Museum was designed to inform interested people about the environmental clean-up and restoration that was being performed at the former Site known as CERCLA, and the regulation known as NCP. The information contained herein is largely of a general nature suited to giving an overview of the Castle AFB program.

The Castle Air Museum Foundation has been in existence since the US Air Force established the Base Museum during 1981. It had been supported by nearly 600 citizens, many of whom are military retirees. During 1995, when the Castle AFB closed, the Foundation assumed all responsibility for managing and displaying the Museum's collection of 44 planes that were on loan from the US Air Force, among them a B-24, a B-36, and a SR-71. Just before Base closure, the US Air Force conveyed two buildings and about 20-acres to the Foundation under a public benefit conveyance sponsored by the US Department of Education. Visitation to the Museum, currently at 80,000, was expected to increase as the newly opened Challenger Learning Center attracts more visitors. In addition, the US Space Camp Foundation in Huntsville, Alabama had opened an Aviation Challenge Program at the Castle AFB in California.

---

[14] David S. Sorenson, "Shutting Down the Cold War: The Politics of Military Base Closure," (St. Martin's Press, New York, July 1998), p. 90

In addition, the US Space Camp Foundation at Huntsville in Alabama had opened an Aviation Challenge Program. CEDAR (California Economic Diversification and Revitalization) is an Internet information project of the California State Library and its California Research Bureau, the Trade and Commerce Agency, with funding from the Economic Development Administration of the US Department of Commerce. Businesses located near closed military Bases may be eligible for tax credits under the Local Agency Military Base Recovery Act (LAMBRA). Through Regional Workshops and State Summit meetings, you can learn how the Defense industry in the State of California makes a significant contribution to National Defense, California's economy, and World stability through the Partnership for Preparedness Companies developing dual-use technologies by providing a wide range of services and resources.[15]

On September 20, 1941, the Airfield was open as the Army Air Corps Basic Flying School; one of the Airfields utilized to meet the needs of the Pilot Training Program. As the original name indicates, it provided basic air training for beginning Pilots and aircrews. Many Pilots and aircrews were trained during WW II to include a number of Women's Air Service Pilots (WASP). On January 13, 1958, the 2777-acre Castle AFB Site was established. During 1994, the Castle AFB's primary mission was transitional training for new B-52 Pilots and aircrews.

With the end of WW II, the 444th Bombardment Group (Heavy) returned to Merced Army Air Field from West Field in Tinian with four Squadrons (344th, 676th, 677th, and 678th) of wartime B29s. The 444th operated from Merced Army Air Field for about six-months with the 678th Bombardment Squadron being re-designated as the 10th Reconnaissance Squadron and its Aircraft being converted to the RB-29 configuration.

On May 6, 1946, the three other B-29 Squadrons inactivated with the 10th Reconnaissance Squadron being relocated to Davis-Monthan Army Air Field in Arizona where it turned in its RB-29 aircraft. On November 16, 1947, the 444th Bombardment Group (Heavy) was finally inactivated. After World War II, when most other airfields were winding down, the Merced Army Air Field was expanding to accommodate large Air Tanker Squadrons that were coming to service, and remained a Training Center for Pilots and aircrews

On June 21, 1946, the 93rd Bombardment Group (Heavy) was activated at the Merced Army Airfield starting a 50-year relationship with the airfield. The 93rd Bombardment Group (Heavy) was a former 8th Air Force B-24 Liberator Group that was assigned to Merced for Boeing B-29 Superfortress training. The 3rd Bombardment Group (Heavy) was one of SAC's first 10 Bombardment Groups. There were three initial operational Squadrons (328th, 329th, and 330th) that absorbed the equipment and Aircraft of the inactivated 333th Bombardment Group.

---

[15] www.Castle AFB Closure.com

On October 1, 1946, the Merced Army Air Field was put on "minimal" operations on a "caretaker status" with control from the military facility at Colorado Springs Army Air Field. The 93rd Bombardment Group (Heavy); however, remained active The Group along with the 509th Composite Group at Roswell Army Air Field in New Mexico was all there was of the Strategic Air Command at that time. The Castle AFB remained in this status until May 1947 when it was reactivated. On May 1, 1947, the Castle Army Airfield was reactivated by the Strategic Air Command. On July 28, 1947, the 93rd Bombardment Wing (Heavy) was established and took over responsibility from the 93rd Bombardment Group. During 1947 through 1948, the Wing flew the Boeing B-29 Superfortress, but soon received the upgraded version of the B-29, the Boeing B-50A. During 1948, the entire Wing deployed to Kadena in Okinawa to become the first Strategic Air Command Bombardment Wing to deploy in full strength to the Far East.

On January 13, 1948, the Merced Army Air Field was officially renamed Castle AFB as part of the US Air Force when it became a separate military service. General Castle was posthumously awarded the US Congressional Medal of Honor for his heroic action. The former Merced Army Airfield was named in his honor, and the history of Castle AFB is now noteworthy to document.

During 1948, the Convair B-36 Peacemaker entered the Strategic Air Command's inventory. The huge airplane dwarfed the earlier bombers. The 93rd Bombardment Wing (Heavy), along with all other B-29 and B-50 Bombardment Groups was designated "Medium." Only the B-36 Bombardment Groups were configured as "Heavy."

On June 27, 1949, the Air Force Reserve 447th Bombardment Group was activated at Castle AFB, and equipped with the B-29s formerly assigned to the 93rd Bombardment Wing (Heavy). The 447th Bombardment Group remained active until 1951 when the Group was activated and the aircraft and military personnel sent to the Far East Air Force as replacements for combat losses during the Korean War. With the Group's departure from the Far East, the 447th Bombardment Group was inactivated.

During October 1950, the Wing began aerial refueling operations that provided aerial refueling and navigational assistance for the July 1952 movement of the 31st Fighter-Escort Wing from the US to Japan, the first jet fighter crossing of the Pacific Ocean during the Korean War.

During 1943 through 1955, the Wing flew Boeing KC-97 Stratotankers, and jet-propelled Boeing KC135 tanker that came on line during 1957.

On January 25, 1955, the first flight of the B-52-B models was made, and initial delivery to the 93rd Bombardment Wing (Heavy) at the Castle AFB occurred during the summer of 1955. Even though the 93rd Bombardment Wing was considered an operational unit, its primary mission was transition training for new B-52 aircrews. The "B" models were used by the 95th, 99th, and 22[n] Bombardment Wings. In addition, the 93rd Bombardment Wing would eventually use the "B" model. Eventually, the "B "models (RB-52-B's included) were used by the 90th, 95th, 99th, and 22nd Bombardment Wings.

On February 16, 1956, trouble began when a B-52 exploded in midair near Tracy in California, while on a flight from nearby the Castle AFB. The crash made National headlines in part because of the B-52s then unprecedented cost of $8 million. Several months later an in-flight explosion claimed a second Castle B-52 and the lives of five aircrew members. On January 16, 1957, five B-52s thundered down the Castle AFB runway. Their mission was simply to show the World that the B-52 had the capability of becoming the first jet aircraft to circle the World non-stop. Supported by nearly 100 KC-97 tankers flying from Canada, Morocco, Saudi Arabia, Philippines, and Guam, the three-B-52s led by Lucky Lady III, finished the mission at March AFB in California on the morning of January 18th. Their flight time of 45-hours, 19-minutes was less than half that required by B-50 Lucky Lady II just eight-years prior.

During 1981, the US Air Force dominated the military Base closure list with no fewer than 11 major Bases being proposed. What was more surprising was that only two of the five (Loring AFB in Maine and Wurtsmith AFB in Michigan) were 'Northern-tier' Bases, while the others (Carswell AFB in Texas, Castle AFB in California, and Eaker AFB in Arkansas) were Sunbelt Bases.[16]

On June 1, 1992, the 93rd was relieved from assignment to SAC and was reassigned to the newly formed Air Combat Command (ACC). It was then re-designated as the 93rd Bomb Wing and its B-52G aircraft given the ACC tail code of "CA" and carried blue tail stripes. On May 3, 1994, the 328th Bomb Squadron was in activated and the Wing was placed on non-operational status. However, the 93rd Bomb Wing continued to supervise the Castle AFB closure.

On September 30, 1995, the 93rd Bomb Wing was inactivated with the Castle AFB closure. On January 28, 1996, just four months later; it was re-designated as the 93rd Air Control Wing and was reactivated at Robbins AFB in Georgia.

On June 11, 1996, the 93rd Bomb Wing was equipped with the E-8C Joint Surveillance Target Attack Radar System (Joint STARS), and accepted the first production aircraft.

---

[16] David S. Sorenson, "Shutting Down the Cold War: The Politics of Military Base Closure," (St. Martin's Press, New York, July 1998), p. 99. . The military Post closed its gates and became part of US military history.

During 1996, the Federal Bureau of Prisons leased 660-acres at the Castle AFB.[17] Given the cost of building new prisons at both local and Federal Government levels, this replacement idea was sure to spread.

During the middle of 1998, the Federal Bureau of Prisons began construction of a new $70 to $80 million, 1000 bed high-security Federal Penitentiary at the Castle AFB. Also included in the Plan was a150 inmate Minimum-Security Satellite Camp. The initial Bureau Plan at the Castle AFB included a 1600 inmate Medium-Security Federal Correctional Institution. The Federal Bureau of Prisons was a potential claimant where it operated several prisons located on or near closed military Posts or Bases. However, the Federal Government needs to change and there is currently a more urgent need for a High-Security capacity.

Since September 11, 2001, as we entered the 21st Century, the State of California's response to the ever changing needs of the OD was critical to the health of the economy and the Nation. OMBRR provided ongoing assistance and support to maintain active military Installations and mitigate the effects of Post and Base closures and realignments. How bad was the Post and Base pollution problem? At the Castle AFB, 26 toxic waste Sites were found on the Installation's 2777-acres. They involved both surface and subsurface contamination to include solvents, waste oil, pesticides, cyanide, PCB, TCE, and other volatile organic compounds that made the military Base's drinking water unsafe to drink.[18]

During 2008, Federal Government plans to convert the dormant military Installation to civilian commercial use has become an active political issue. The military Installation has been identified as the preferred location for the Central Maintenance Facility for the proposed California High-Speed Rail System.

The end of the Cold War brought many changes to the US Air Force. For example, Castle AFB was selected for closure under the Defense Base Closure and Realignment Act of 1990 during Round II of the Base Closure Commission deliberations BRAC 91.

On January 22, 1995, the US Air Force completed the transfer of the Castle AFB in California from military control to private ownership on one of the military Base's former housing areas being accepted as a retirement village. During September 1995, the Atwater Retirement Village II, LLC, accepted the final parcel of property completing a process that began when the Castle AFB closed. On December 19, 2006, portions of the 2777-acre Castle AFB were transferred by deed to private ownership over the years with the largest portion, nearly 1900-acres, going to the Mercer County Board of Supervisors.

---

[17] David S. Sorenson, "Shutting Down the Cold War: The Politics of Military Base Closure," (St. Martin's Press, New York, July 1998), pp. 60-61.

[18] David S. Sorenson, "Shutting Down the Cold War: The Politics of Military Base Closure," (St. Martin's Press, New York, July 1998), p. 78.

Mr. Dexter Cochnauer, Senior Representative at AFRPA's Western Regional Execution Center in Sacramento, California stated: "The transfer was not only important for the US Air Force, but also for the local community as well. The community can now take advantage of US Air Force assets to spark economic growth." The Castle AFB is now home to a variety of businesses; a Federal Bureau of Prisons Facility; a University of California Campus; and an Air Museum. The County of Merced and the local redevelopment authority for Castle AFB, had plans for further redevelopment at the military Base to include re-use of the Airfield as an Airport; construction of new educational facilities; residential development; and bringing in new businesses.

Mr. Cochnauer stated: "The County had very ambitious plans for redevelopment. It will be interesting to come back in a few years and see how much the Castle AFB has changed." AFRPA has also made significant progress with the environmental clean-up of Castle AFB. Working alongside the Environmental Protection Agency and the California Department of Toxic Substances Control, the US Air Force signed the final Record of Decision, outlining the clean-up of soil and ground water Sites on the Base during July 2006. The local Restoration Advisory Board that provided community input on the clean-up formally adjourned satisfied by the progress made at the Castle AFB.

During the Base Realignment and Closure round (BRAC 91), Castle AFB was a Strategic Air Command Installation that was once home to B-52 Stratofortress bombers, and was selected for military Base closure. Since the Castle AFB closure, the US Air Force Real Property Agency was charged with the environmental clean-up of the military Base and making the property available for re-use. Federal Government agency officials worked closely with City regulatory agencies and private citizens of Atwater and Merced to reach military Base closure goal and objectives.

Mr. Phil Mook, AFRPA's Lead Environmental Engineer for Castle AFB's Clean-Up Program stated: "Everyone was extremely pleased with the clean-up progress at the Castle AFB. All major decisions were made; the ground water treatment was operating properly and successfully; and we are on the home stretch toward Site closeout." While all property at the Castle AFB has been transferred, the US Air Force remained responsible for the last residue of clean-up with no threat to human health.[19]

During 1981, the US Air Force dominated the military Base closure list with no fewer than 11 major Bases being proposed. What was more surprising was that only two of the five (Loring AFB in Maine and Wurtsmith AFB in Michigan) were

---

[19] www.Castle AFB History.com

'Northern tier' military Bases, while the others (Carswell AFB in Texas, Castle AFB in California, and Eaker AFB in Arkansas) were Sunbelt Bases.[20]

The Castle AFB had entered the 21st Century in response to the downsizing of existing military Posts and Bases became more critical to regional economic health. The mission of the Office of Military Base Retention and Re-Use (OMBRR) was to provide ongoing assistance and support to those communities with active military Installations, and to ensure their continue viability and retention. The State of California had the largest number of military Installations in the Nation with 36 major and 25 minor facilities and military Installations, DOD laboratories and testing facilities

Comparison with the Presidio Closure

Unlike the Presidio of San Francisco closure that had a primary administration mission, the 1991 Defense Base Realignment and Closure Commission still recommended that the Castle AFB be closed and that military personnel and Civil Service employees be transferred to other military Installations and equipment resources be realigned. The Castle AFB primary mission was to provide facilities for aircraft storage and maintenance; air operations and planning; and organizational training.

In sum, the historical and political reasoning that closed the Castle Air Force Base has been presented in an attempt to adjudicate an understandable Base closure decision. The Castle AFB closure, of course, supports the rational for the entire historic Case Study. The Castle AFB did not have an administrative headquarters like the Presidio of San Francisco; however, its training mission did qualify the Base to be realigned with another AFB. In the case of the Castle AFB, it was finally discontinued and its training mission with military personnel and Civil Service employees transferred to a supportable mission at another US Air Force Base. At this point, it is rather obvious that the Case Study investigation of the Castle AFB closure did come under the purview of the Base Closure and Realignment Act of 1988.

---

[20] David S. Sorenson, "Shutting Down the Cold War: The Politics of Military Base Closure," (St. Martin's Press, New York, July 1998), p. 99.

CHAPTER VIII

History of Mather Air Force Base

During 1918, the Mather Field was established as an Airfield and Pilot Traing School. The Airfield was named for Carl Mather, a World War I Test Pilot. The Airfield was located 12-miles East of Sacramento in California. It was built during World War I as a Pilot Training Base and was used by the Army Air Corps for various purposes during the years between wars. Following World War I, the Mather Field was used intermittently to support small military uniorganizations

During 1941, the Airfield was expanded and became a training Base for single-engine Pilots and Navigators. The Mather Field had three auxiliary Airfields that were located at Lincoln, Elk Grove, and Franklin. During World War II, the Mather Field was used for Pilot and Navigator training as well as Observer and Bombardier training. During 1943, the training of B-25 bomber crews began; and from 1944 through 1945, Mather Field became an aerial port of embarkation to the Pacific in preparation for the expected transfer of large numbers of men and aircraft from Europe to the Pacific. The Mather Field's primary mssion was to provide a Center for Pilot, Navigator, and Bombardier training. The 5716-acre Mather Field was located in the unincorporated portion of Sacramento County in California.

The operational history of the Mather Field was also very historical and is worth mentioning. During April 1945, military orders came through transferring the 509th Ground Support Squadron to Tinian Island in the Marianas Group of Islands in the South Pacific. During late April and May, 1945, there was a gradual staging of these support organ izations. They quickly packed up their tools and assorted equipment and boarded troop trains for the West Coast where ships were waiting to transport them to Tinian. Some ground crews, to include that of "The Great Artiste," stayed behind and would fly with the Airplane to Tinian. During early June, 1945, the aircrews received military orders to proceed to Tinian. The flight plan of "The Great Artiste" took it to Mather Field in California where the aircrews would spend a few days processing paperwork for overseas duty. Next, they proceeded to John Rogers Field in Honolulu where the B-29 would be checked over and refueled. Next, on to Kwajalein Island in the Pacific for another refueling, and then to North Field on Tinian Island.

The addition of the ground crew as passengers on the flight to Titian presented real problems. As the biggest Airplane in the World, the B-29 was a sophisticated bomber, and not just a transport plane. It was designed to carry about 10 aircrew members; not 20. Even without additional passengers, the B-29 was crowded. In the nose, the Bombardier was squeezed into a very small space, surrounded with delicate equipment to include the Norden Bomb Sight, a small table, and various controls. On the flight deck, the Pilot and Co-pilot seats were surrounded with sophisticated instruments and gauges. Behind the Co-pilot, facing the rear of the plane, the Flight Engineer had a small seat in front of his controls where he could monitor fuel supply and adjust the four-engines for maximum performance. Behind the Pilot, the Navigator had a small chair and table for his charts, maps, and radar scope. Next to the Flight Engineer, the Radio Operator had a small chair and table. The removal of the forward gun turret opened up a little room, but not much. However, there was some open space in the rear cabin area created by the removal of the gun turrets and machine guns. On June 4 1945, with Major Sweeney in command, "The Great Artiste" buzzed Wendover Field for the last time and headed for Mather Field in California. "The Great Artiste" was joined by three other B-29s also headed to Titian. The following account by Lieutenant Fred Olivi, the Co-pilot of "The Great Artiste," sheds light on the intense security surrounding the mission of the 509th Composite Group.

It was at the Mather Field that Lieutenant Olivi first learned what it meant to be the only Second Lieutenant among higher ranking officers. He was put in charge of security for "The Great Artiste" whenever it was on the ground. Since they were scheduled to remain the night at the Mather Field, this meant that he was responsible for protecting the B-29 aircraft. The ground crews were normally assigned to guard duty. Lieutenant Olivi was new at this role as "Officer of the Day" and very awkward when he had to inspect their weapons. However, the Sergeants helped him work out a reasonable schedule. Checking on the ground crew throughout the night also meant Lieutenant Olivi did not get much sleep. This kind of armed security for our ultra-secret, modified B-29, at one of our own military Bases, in our own Country, may seem strange. But before they left Wendover Field, Colonel Tibbets had issued strict orders that no unauthorized person was to get "near" one of the B-29s. And only members of the 509th Ground Support Squadron were authorized. "Authorized persons only" also meant everyone, to include General Officers. Later in the evening, the Commanding General of the Mather Field had heard about the strange looking B-29s without gun turrets and decided to drive out to the Airplane and take a look.

The guard on duty immediately realized that the General was not an "authorized" person because he was not with the 509th Ground Support Squadron. After some heated words, the General told the Airman that he was going to board the B-29, and that the Airman had better get out of the way if he knew what was good for him. Generals of course, like their Roman General counterparts, like to play God with their subordinates and forget that even a General Officer has some limitations in using their rank as authority in issuing an order. The Airman pulled back the bolt on his Carbine and aimed at the General's chest. He pleaded with the General saying that he would shoot if he had to. The General finally stated: "I'm going to nail your ass to the wall." The General finally got back in his jeep and roared off. Although the General later complained both to Colonel Tibbets and General Groves, the General was told that: "they were sorry but

B-29s of the 509th Ground Support Squadron were strictly off limits to everyone as it was a matter of National Security."

During 1958, a Strategic Air Command (SAC) B-52 Squadron was assigned to the Mather AFB. During the 1950s through the 1980s, the Mather AFB continued to be a Training Center for military personnel. By 1990, the primary mission of the Mather AFB was to provide formal long-range and over-water Air Force Navigator training. The Mather Field historically operated its own Housing; Schools; Hospital; Commercial and Recreational facilities; as well as an operational Airfield. The majority of on-Base development occurred during the 1940s through the 1960s. Expansion and improvements continued throughout the 1980s, but ceased during 1988 after the Mather AFB closure was announced. Following the Mather AFB closure announcement, the Sacramento County Board of Supervisors initiated Re-Use Planning activities with the appointment of the Sacramento Area Commission on the Mather AFB conversion. The major element of the recommended Re-Use Plan initiatives included retention of aviation use. During 1963 through 1989, the 320th Bombardment Wing (H) flew B-52s out of the Mather AFB.

Om September 30, 1993, the Mather AFB was closed. The Mather AFB was located in the un-incorporated portion of Sacramento County, 12-miles Southeast of downtown Sacramento in California. The Mather AFB was composed of 5716-acres and 970,000-square feet of buildings and auxiliary facilities. The Mather AFB included an 11,300-foot runway and a parallel 6100-foot runway; four aircraft hangars; office and industrial structures; 18 dormitory buildings; and 1271 units of single family housing. As the home of the 323rd Flying Wing, the Mather AFB was a Center for Pilot, Navigation, and Bombardier training. In addition to the 11,300-foot runway, this 5716-acre complex in the heart of the Highway 5 corridor, possessed diverse aviation and industrial facilities, open space, and housing.

The Mather AFB closure would result in the displacement of 7600 military personnel and Civil Service employees, and the diversion of over $150 million of income from the Sacramento County socioeconomic economy. The California Army National Guard [CAARNG] aviation organizations were based at the Mather Army Aviation Support Facility (AASF) located at the former Mather AFB at Sacramento; the AASF in Stockton, the California Aviation Classification Repair Depot (AVCRAD) in Fresno; and the Armed Forces Reserve Center (AFRC) at Los Alamitos. All military Sites included hangar facilities, aircraft parking aprons, and armories. The Mather Army Aviation Support Facility (AASF) was located Southeast of US Highway 50 on the Mather AFB, about 12-miles East of the State Capitol proper in Sacramento. Interstate 5 provided North and South access, and Interstate 80 provided East and West access. The Mather AASF was located in Sacramento County and Congressional District #5. The AASF containment was part of the flight line operations area. The AASF facilities (armory and hangars) were located on a 30-acre parcel located within the Mather Regional

Park (business and light industrial development area). The Mather Airport has become a joint-use facility, with military operations located on the North side of the runways. The local demographics provided a good recruiting population. The military personnel and Civil Service employees made positive contribution to the local economy in terms of salaried jobs and personal purchases.

Although the Mather AFB was identified for closure by BRAC 88, sale negotiations between the US Air Force and the Sacramento County did not begin until 1992. At this time, the County and two large area home builders, Lewis Homes Enterprises and Elliott Homes, proposed to renovate the 1271 Wherry and Capehart housing units for use as affordable and senior citizen housing. Five-years later, a revised plan was necessary due to property deterioration, increased costs, and concerns of the public community. Only Lewis Homes Enterprises remained involved with the project. On October 31, 1996, the US Air Force conveyed 757-acres at the Mather AFB to the Sacramento County.

The local Regional Development Agency charged with the design and implementation of the Mather Re-Use Plan was the Redevelopment Agency of the County of Sacramento (RACS). RACS had the same responsibility for McClellan AFB and the Sacramento Army Depot both in California. On March 14, 2000, RACS approved the first five-year updated Implementation Plan for the Mather AFB Redevelopment Plan during January 2000 through 2004. On November 22, 2000, the initial five-year Implementation Plan for the McClellan AFB/ Watt Avenue Redevelopment Plan was adopted along with the Redevelopment Plan. On December 9, 2003, the final draft of the Mather Airport Master Plan version of December 2004 was presented to the Sacramento County Board of Supervisors and was subsequently approved. The time line established by the Board of Supervisors for the implementation of the Master Plan for conversion was during January 2005 through 2009.

The Mather Airport offered Air Cargo Companies superior facilities and one of the longest runways in the Country. Mather Field development, a multifaceted property, presented opportunities for many different users and boasted a list of distinguished tenants such as McGraw Hill; Sutter Connect; Advance PCS; State of California Office of Emergency Services; Sacramento County Office of Education; Federal Aviation Administration; TRACON; Sacramento County Public Works Division; Veterans Administration Medical Center; United Parcel Service; and several other related companies.

These facilities were not the Mather Airport's only significant attribute. The former Mather AFB included extensive parklands that created the appearance of a modern Industrial Campus favored by many Companies seeking new offices. During 1996, a total of 1434-acres on the East side of the property were set aside for establishing the Mather Regional Park, an increasingly popular destination that boasted among other things, a top-flight public Golf Course. Improvements of the property continued through the expenditure of a $10.8 million Federal

Government grant. The money was used to transform the Mather Airport main entrance from a military style gate to one more suitable for a commercial Business Park. Also funded were landscaping of the major arterial streets in the area and construction of a new General Aviation Terminal at the Sacramento Mather Airport and the adjacent main Base area, now called Mather Commerce Center. Together they comprised some 600-acres of developed and developable property conveniently located along the Highway 50 corridor, Sacramento's second largest Employment Center after downtown. These attributes have already attracted 53 employers with over 2800 employees in the Mather Redevelopment Area, and many more employers were considering making a move to the property that is bounded on the North and West by urban development and on the East and South by undeveloped land.

The County has also engaged the development firm of McCuen Properties LLC as its exclusive agent in the redevelopment efforts at the Mather Airport. McCuen Properties LLC was currently working with SACTO (Sacramento Area Commerce & Trade Organization), with local real estate brokerage firms, and with National and International Site location consultants to provide potential user Companies with information on the benefits of locating a business facility at the Mather Airport. To facilitate tenant service, McCuen Properties LLC had established an on-Site marketing Center and Property Management Office.

The Mather Airport suitability for use as an Air Cargo Facility cannot be overstated. The lack of available funds was one major reason the Cargo Airport was not expanding at an optimum rate. The Mather Airport was on a pay-as-you-go plan. Each project had to pay for itself through growth of anticipated jobs and tax revenues. The Air Cargo operations at the Mather Airport were ready to expand when infrastructure modifications were made. The goal of the Mather Re-Use Plan through 2009 included total estimated redevelopment investment projects that totaled $25.45 million. The CMB believed the significant public investment would make the Mather Airport area a prime target for private enterprise investment capital.

The Mather Army Aviation Support Facility (AASF) is now located Southeast of US Highway 50 on the former Mather AFB, about 12-miles East of the State capitol proper at Sacramento in California. Interstate 5 provided North and South access and Interstate 80 provided East and West access. The Mather AASF is located in Sacramento County and Congressional District Five. The AASF was part of the former Mather AFB flight line operations area. The AASF facilities (armory and hangars) were located on a 30-acre parcel located within the Mather Regional Park (business airport and light industrial development area). The Mather Airport was a joint-use facility with military operations located on the North side of the runways. The local demographics provided a good recruiting population for the Mather AASF. The new civilian Installation also made a positive contribution to the local economy in terms of salaried jobs and personal purchases.

The Mather AASF consisted of a hangar, armory, operations building, and an associated administrative facility. The existing buildings and pavement (rotary and fixed wing and vehicle parking) were inadequate in size and condition to support the assigned units. The armory and administrative building were situated along Macready Drive and Superfortress Avenue, just North of the AASF hangar and Aircraft parking. Additional Aircraft parking was located to the East of the Armory. The taxiways and runways lied to the South of the facility.

Since 1982, the Mather AFB was located in the suburbs of Sacramento in California and has had a clean-up program. During 1987, the Mather AFB was placed on the NPL, and was placed on the Base closure list during 1988. As a result, the Mather AFB's clean-up started well before CERFA or President Bill Clinton's "Five Point Plan" incorporated a re-use emphasis.

During 1988, the Mather AFB announced closure was a significant loss to the Sacramento Region. The negative effects of this action were exacerbated by the closures of the two nearby military Posts and Bases; that is, Sacramento Army Depot and McClellan AFB. In the case of Mather AFB, closure of the 5716-acre military Base meant the loss of 76 00 jobs, 1271 housing units, and $150 million in annual income to the Sacramento area. From the date of the announcement, it was recognized that the special tools and authorities provided by redevelopment law would be instrumental in converting the Federal Government facility to civilian use. During the past years, significant steps in that conversion effort have been completed and the Mather AFB is now emerging as a major Business Park; Air Freight Hub; and Recreational Center that is restoring many of the Civil Service positions that were eliminated.

During 1988, immediately following the military Base closure announcement for the Mather AFB, Sacramento County officials formed a Commission to plan for the re-use of the Mather AFB not unlike the "Save the Presidio" Committee. The Sacramento Area Commission on Mather Conversion (SACOM-C) and its Sub-committees grew to over 150 members. Simultaneously with the SACOM-C preparation of a Re-Use Plan, the Rancho Cordova Chamber of Commerce began preparation of a Re-Use Plan.

During 1990, the primary mission of the Mather AFB was to provide all formal long-range and over-water US Air Force Navigator training. The Mather AFB historically operated its own housing schools; hospital; commercial recreational facilities; as well as an operational Airfield. The majority of on-Base development occurred during the 1940s through the 1960s. Expansion and improvements continued through the 1980s, but ceased during 1988 after the Mather AFB closure was announced.[21]

---

[21] www.Mather ADB Closure.com

On April 3, 1991, the Sacramento County Board of Supervisors authorized the execution of an agreement with Leigh Fisher Associates (LFA) for the development of the Airport System Policy Plan and the Mather Airport Master Plan. The purpose of the Airport System Policy Plan was to review and refine policies relating to the general operation and development of the four Airports that comprised the County Airport System. The Agreement with LFA established the Mather Airport Master Plan that would be built upon potential roles established for Mather Airport in the System Policy Plan.

During April 1991, under the revised procedures, the DOD recommended the closure of 42 Posts and Bases and the realignment of 28 Posts and Bases. The Commission made several adjustments to the DOD list and proposed 14 Post and Base closures and 48 Post and Base realignments. The President and US Congress accepted the Commission's recommendations for the current round of Post and Base closures and realignments. The US Congress retained essentially the same requirements and procedures as during December 1991. The US Congress amended the Defense Base Closure and Realignment Act to require that the Secretary of Defense submit his recommendations for closures and realignments to the Commission by March 15, 1993. The Secretary's recommendations were to be based on the DOD's selection criteria and a six-year Force Structure Plan. A key amendment to the Defense Base Closure and Realignment Act was a requirement that the DOD certify the data presented to ensure its accuracy.[22]

During the Fall of 1991, the Board of Supervisors endorsed a comprehensive Re-Use Plan and forwarded the plan to the US Air Force. During March 1993, the US Air Force issued a Record of Decision for the disposal of the Mather AFB. On May 5, 1995, the Mather Airport was officially reopened as a commercial Airport. The Airport area included runways and aprons consisting of approximately 2875-acres. During September 1995, the Mather Regional Park was established. The Park encompassed approximately 1432-acres on the East side of the property; included an 18-hole championship Golf Course; and a potential for a variety of recreational opportunities. During October 1996, the Economic Development Conveyance was finalized transferring 775-acres. This property was ideal for commercial development. As we entered the 21st Century, the Mather AFB was well on its way to becoming a vibrant Business Park; thriving Air Cargo Hub; and Recreational destination.[23]

During the Fall of 1991, the ultimate plan approved by the Sacramento County Board of Supervisors represented a consolidation of the SACOM-C and Rancho Cordova Chamber of Commerce Re-Use Plans. In addition to the Air Cargo and General Aviation Airport, Sacramento County operated a 1600-acre Regional Park

---

[22] Charles A. Bowsher, Comptroller General of the US, "Military Bases, Analysis of DOD's Recommendations and Selection Process for Closures and Realignments," (GAO, Washington, DC, April 15, 1993), p. 11.

[23] www.Mather AFB History.com

containing among other things an 18 hole championship golf course; recreational lake; hiking trails; and an abundance of property for future development of recreational facilities that would benefit the entire community. A 770-acre Economic Development Conveyance (EDC) of the developed Mather AFB area and two large undeveloped areas on the East side of Mather AFB were completed. Following the Mather AFB closure announcement, the Sacramento County Board of Supervisors initiated Re-Use-Planning activities with the appointment of the Sacramento Area Commission on Mather Conversion. A major element of the various recommended Re-Use Plans included retention of aviation use. The initial step in conversion was made when the Board of Supervisors endorsed a comprehensive Re-Use Plan and forwarded the plan to the US Air Force.

During March 1993, the US Air Force issued a Record of Decision for the disposal of the Mather AFB." About 18-months later, the US Air Force issued a Record of Decision for the disposal of the military Base. For example, the Mather Aviation facilities were subsequently transferred to the County.

The 1993 Secretary of Defense recommendation changed the realignment location for the 940th from the McClellan AFB to the Beale AFB both in California. The proposal to redirect the 940th Air Refueling Group to the Beale AFB in California would save $21.2 million. Even with the temporary facilities construction costs ($1.1 million) and termination costs ($3.0 million) at McClellan AFB in California, the savings were substantial to support the Secretary's recommendation. The Commission's recommendations found the Secretary of Defense did not deviate substantially from the Force Structure Plan and final criteria. Therefore, the Commission recommended the 940th Air Refueling Group with its KC-135 aircraft be re-directed to the Beale AFB in California vice the McClellan AFB in California. Because of the rapidly approaching closure of the Mather AFB in California, the 940th would temporarily relocate to McClellan AFB in California while awaiting permanent "bed down" at the Beale AFB in California.

During late 1993, the Mather AFB still had a training mission located 12-miles Southeast of Sacramento in California. The Mather AFB closure caused an estimated 3000 military personnel and Civil Service employee losses to the area. The consolidated Re-Use Plan was subsequently approved with over 150 members submitting input. The Sacramento County Board of Supervisors took control of the project and various departments were responsible for implementation of the Re-Use Plan. During early 1995, the Mather Airport lease was signed. The County Board had funded a $17 million line of credit for the Mather Airport to look for new tenants and improvements. The County was marketing the Airport as an additional cargo Airport in central California.

On September 30, 1993, the Mather AFB was finally closed. The Mather AFB was located in the unincorporated portion of Sacramento County, 12-miles Southeast of downtown Sacramento. The Base was composed of 5716-acres and 970,000-square feet of buildings and auxiliary facilities. The military Base included an 11,300-foot runway and a parallel 6100-foot runway; four aircraft hangars; office and industrial structures; 18 dormitory buildings; and 127 units of single family housing. The Mather AFB was home to the 323rd Flying Wing and a Center for Pilot, Navigator, and Bombardier training. In addition to the 11,300-foot runway, the 5716-acre complex was in the heart of the Highway 50 corridor and possessed diverse aviation and industrial facilities; open space; and housing.

During March 1995, the Mather AASF lease for 2875-acres was signed. The County Board of Supervisors voted to accept the long-term Airport lease with the US Air Force subject to a modification of the lease to assure the County and future tenants of Mather Airport uninterrupted telecommunication, electrical, and natural gas service and continued maintenance of Base water, storm drain, and sanitary sewer systems. The US Air Force agreed to operate the electric, gas, and telephone systems for a period of 18-months, with the County paying its fair share for use and maintenance of these systems until a private entity would take over.

During February 1997, Trajen Flight Support began to modify a 420,000 gallon steel fuel storage tank located at the former Mather AFB tank farm. By Summer, Aircraft fuel storage was available from the 40-year old tank that is fed directly from an underground Santa Fe Pacific gas pipeline. Since the Commercial Airport opened several years ago, the number of large transport category Aircraft reusing the airfield was constrained by the limited fuel storage capacity of fuel trucks. Trucks can only hold and transport 8000 to 10,000 gallons of fuel while a large cargo airplane can require 10,000 to 15,000 gallons.

On May 5, 1995, the Mather Airport was officially opened as a commercial Airport and is currently operated by the County Department of Airports as an Air Cargo and Aviation Center. The Airport area, to include runways and aprons, encompassed approximately 2875-acres. The Mather Airport currently offers a full service FBO, 24-hour Air Traffic Control, and one of the longest runways in California at 11,300-feet. Various buildings at Mather Airport were currently available for lease to include 31,217-square feet of office space; 26,600-square feet of hangar/shop/office space; 81,000-square feet of warehouse space; and a 17,600-square foot ramp side air cargo sort facility. In addition to the available space, over 200-acres of land were available for new construction at the Mather Airport. Airborne Express, Integrated Airline Services, Kitty Hawk, and Emery Air Freight already had operations at the Mather Airport.

Since May 5, 1995, the Mather Airport (officially called Sacramento Mather Airport) had been open as a public use Air Cargo and General Aviation Airport. Managed by the Sacramento County Department of Airports, the Airport facilities included two parallel runways, one 11,300-foot long and the other 6100-foot long with 40-acres of exclusive air cargo ramp space.

On May 5, 1995, the Mather AASF's were subsequently transitioned over to the County. The Mather Airport was officially reopened as a Commercial Airport. The Airport area included runways and aprons consisting of approximately 2875-acres.

During September 1995, the Mather Regional Park was established. The Regional Park encompassed approximately 1432-acres on the East side of the property to include an 18-hole championship Golf Course and potential for a variety of Park and Recreational opportunities. The California Army National Guard (CAARNG) aviation organizations were based at the Mather AASF located at the former Mather AFB in Sacramento; the AASF in Stockton; the California Aviation Classification Repair Depot (AVCRAD) in Fresno; and the Armed Forces Reserve Center (AFRC) in Los Alamitos. All Sites included hangar facilities, aircraft parking aprons, and armories.

During April 1996, Airborne Express and Emery Worldwide moved their operations from Sacramento International Airport to the Mather Airport.

During October 1996, the Economic Development Conveyance was finalized transferring 775-acres. This property was ideal for commercial development. As we entered the 21ˢᵗ Century, the Mather Airport was well on its way to becoming a vibrant Business Park; thriving Air Cargo Hub; and Recreational destination. "Former US Air Force and US Naval Air Bases were especially useful because runways provided the capability for Air Cargo flights to deliver parts and fly out finished goods. The Mather Airport at the former Mather AFB has both Airborne Express and Emery Air Freight operating on its 11,300-foot runway."[24]

During November 1996, the Federal Aviation Administration (FAA) announced that it would build an Air Traffic Control Facility on 32—acres at the Mather Airport.

During September of 1997, construction began and the facility opened during late 2000. It consolidated operations that are now in older, smaller facilities at Oakland; Monterey; Stockton; McClellan AFB; and Sacramento that control flight scheduling at all major Airports in Northern California. Approximately 300 people were employed. The US Air Force approved the request by the Veterans' Administration for the hospital and 28-acres. The Office of Management and Budget (OMB) reviewed the request after analyzing a Price-Waterhouse Study on VA needs in Northern California. The Study supported the use of the Mather hospital as a VA facility. The VA had moved most of the caseload from its downtown Sacramento Outpatient Clinic to the Mather Airport.

---

[24] David S. Sorenson, "Shutting Down the Cold War: The Politics of Military Base Closure, St. Martin's Press, N ew York, July 1998), p.65.

During the Fall of 1997, the Mather AASF was rapidly developing its operations as a Cargo Depot. By the second year of operations as a Cargo Depot, the airport was operating at a level of activity initially expected by its 7th year.

During March 1998, a new Airport Terminal opened. More than 40-percent of the unfinished terminal space was leased to Trajen Flight Support, the Airport's fixed base operator. The Mather Airport was also attracting some commercial Cargo Carriers operating under military contract. These Carriers were using the Mather Airport as a substitute for Travis AFB whose Airfield was already operating at full capacity.

During March 1998, the United Parcel joined Airborne, Emery, and BAX Global United in operating the Mather Airport.

During April 1998, two years later the United Parcel Service relocated its operations and 125 employees from Sacramento International Airport to the Mather Airport effectively doubling the Air Cargo weight coming through Mather Airborne Express. During May 1998, air freight shipments at the Mather Airport topped 11 million pounds that was an increase of 4-percent in one year. Emery Worldwide originally used half of a large warehouse building for its sorting operation but was building a 28,000-square foot facility to be completed during the Spring of 1999. During the Summer of 2003, the BAX Global joined other Cargo Carriers.

On July 1, 2000, two operational upgrades initiated facilitated the expansion of the Mather Airport and the Air Cargo facility of the Sacramento County Airport System. The first was an Air Traffic Control Tower staffed on a 24-hour basis under the Federal Aviation Administration's Contract Tower Program. The Air Traffic Controllers at contract towers were certified by the FAA and complied with the same standards the agency has for its own controllers. The FAA and the County Airport System were funding the daily operational cost of the tower under a cost-sharing agreement with the FAA paying for 16-hours of daily service and the System paying for the remaining eight-hours. The second upgrade was opening an Airport Fire Station at the Mather Airport staffed with the Airport System's personnel and equipment on a 24-hour basis. The resulting benefit was that fire and rescue response time had been reduced from seven-minutes to between two and three-minutes.

During early 2000, the selections stemmed from the AIR-21 Legislation signed into law that increased the total number of airports eligible for Federal Airport Improvement Program (AIP) funding from one to 15. The Mather Airport, formerly the Site of the US Air Force's Navigator Training Program, has two runways (11,300-feet and 6000-feet) that made it appealing to freight operators. Like the Presidio closure, the Secretary of Defense changed the recommendations of the 1991 Commission regarding the Mather AFB. The 94th Air Refueling Group (AFRES) with its KC-135 aircraft were redirected to Beale AFB in California vice McClellan AFB in California. Because of the rapidly approaching closure of the Mather AFB, the 94th Air Refueling Group (AFRES) would be temporarily realigned to McClellan AFB in California while awaiting permanent "bed-down" at Beale AFB in California.

During 2001, the FAA selected three military Airports for conversion to Commercial Airports only for joint-use status as part of a program designed to increase system capacity and reduce air traffic control delays. The Airports were Gray Army Airfield at Killeen in Texas; March Inland Port at Riverside in California; and Mather Airport near Sacramento in California under the FAA's Military Airport Program (MAP).

During June 2007, with nearly 80 Sacramento employees initially using half of an unoccupied hangar at Mather Airport until its new 32-square foot permanent Air Cargo Facility was completed. Initially, airborne operations consisted of a DC-8 that landed in the morning and departed in the evening. Packages were unloaded on the airport apron, sorted in the hangar, and then transferred to small aircraft and vans for delivery.

The Mather AFB was a large military Installation divided into 19 re-use parcels and only three OUs. One OU contained 59 of the 69 contaminated Sites at Mather AFB. The clean-up process was based on OUs and involved a nearly base-wide effort, with sequential stepping through CERCLA's lengthy investigating protocols. As a result of the complexity and costs associated with thoroughly investigating an entire military Base, approximately $50 million was spent on characterizing the Site; however, virtually no remedial action was taken. On this basis, there was no evidence that the CERCLA process corresponded to either a re-use-driven or a risk-driven approach. Instead, the Mather AFB clean-up approach appeared to have been protocol driven.

Forecasted estimates implied that more than $150 million would be expended before clean-up would be completed at the Mather AFB. The analysis suggested that by focusing efforts on the most important re-use parcel that crossed boundaries, along with other Sites where contamination could spread, a combined re-use and risk-based strategy should be pursued. Although you cannot argue that the total costs to clean-up the entire Mather AFB would be reduced, an interim goal could be set and achieved at costs well below that required for total Mather AFB clean-up. This required moving away from the current designation of Mather AFB as a single clean-up project. In effect, to replace the goal and objective of cleaning up the entire Mather AFB that was both too expensive to provide a realistic policy objective.

Since Base closure, the County of Sacramento has operated the Aviation facilities at the Mather AFB. The Mather AFB is now Sacramento Mather Airport operated by the County of Sacramento that was another Installation eyed for its trade and distribution potential. Despite substantial later successes, the Mather AFB in some respects began as one example of what can go wrong in closing a Post or Base. Relatively new to the business of selling real estate, the US Air Force thought it could make money on the sale of Mather AFB's 1000 housing units. Rejecting Sacramento County's $3 million bid, the US Air Force held firm to its $25 million asking price, and negotiations stalemated. By the time the buildings were finally sold years later for $2.5 million, most were so damaged by deterioration and vandalism that they had to be destroyed.

The Secretary of Defense had justified moving the 91st Air Refueling Group to Beale AFB in California as more cost effective. The original 1991 realignment cost was $33.7 million. The estimated cost for this re-direct was $25.5 million for a projected savings

Findings of the 1988 DOD Realignment and Closure Commission had recommended the closure of the 323rd Flying Training Wing hospital and the retention of the 940th Air Refueling Group at Mather AFB in California. The 1991 Defense Base Closure and Realignment Commission recommended the realignment of the 940th Air Refueling Group from Mather AFB in California to McClellan AFB in California, and recommended the 323rd Flying Training Wing hospital remain open as an annex to McClellan AFB in California. The Secretary of Defense justified moving the 91st Air Refueling Group to Beale AFB in California as more cost effective. The original 1991 realignment cost was $33.7 million. The estimated cost for this re-direct was $25.5 million for a projected savings of $21.2 million. There were no formal expressions of concern from the community. The following are organizations that were stationed at the military Installation:
Company A, 1-140th Aviation Battalion (32 people); 126th Medical Company (-) (Air Ambulance) (130 people); Company D, 1-140th Aviation Battalion (32 people); Detachment 1, Headquarters and Headquarters Company 1-140th Aviation Battalion (123 people); Detachment 32, Operational Support Airlift Command (eight people); and the 126th MED CO had fifteen UH-60s. Company A, 1-140th AVN BN was transitioning from eight UH-1s to eight UH-60s. Detachment 32, OSAA had one C-12 Aircraft maintained by two private contractors.

Comparison with the Presidio Closure

Unlike the Presidio of San Francisco closure that had a primary administration mission, the 1991 Defense Base Realignment and Closure Commission still recommended that the Mather AFB be closed and that military personnel and Civil Service employees be transferred to other military Installations and equipment resources be realigned The Mather AFB primary mission was to provide facilities for aircraft storage and maintenance, air operations planning and coordination, and organizational training. DOD signed the Federal Facilities Agreement with the EPAA.

In sum, the historical and political reasoning that closed Mather Air Force Base has been presented in an attempt to adjudicate an understandable Base closure decision. The Mather AFB closure, of course, supports the rational for the entire historic Case Study. The Mather AFB did not have an administrative headquarters like the Presidio of San Francisco; however, its training mission did qualify the Base to be realigned with another US Air Force Base. In the case of Mather AFB, it was finally discontinued and its training mission with military personnel and Civil Service employees realigned with a supportable mission of another US Air Force Base. At this point, it is rather obvious that the Case Study investigation of the Mather Air Force Base closure did come under the purview of the Base Closure and Realignment Act of 1988.

CHAPTER IX

Presidio of San Francisco Closure and Realignment Study

The Presidio of San Francisco Closure and Realignment Study included a general description of the Headquarters, Sixth US Army staff and the Presidio Garrison with sufficient details to allow reliable policy decisions to be incorporated in the final investigation. In addition, this Case Study is sufficiently detailed to document the implementation of the Presidio of San Francisco Closure and Realignment Study with future development of later actions to be accomplished as the proposed consolidation of the Headquarters, Sixth US Army staff and the Presidio Garrison progressed.

In compliance with governing procedures, a cost analysis was completed in advance of, and in addition to, the cost analysis performed by US Army Forces Command in connection with the evaluation of private contractor proposals in response to the Request for Proposal (RFP). Contractor source selection was accomplished through Boards and Committees, with members drawn primarily from the Headquarters, Sixth US Army staff and the Presidio Garrison that performed specific analytical, evaluation review, and advisory functions. A final decision concerning the consolidation of the Headquarters, Sixth US Army staff and the Presidio Garrison into a single command would be required before the scheduled realignment date. Due to the increasing complexity of the planning associated with greater depth of detail, it became impractical to continue planning for three possible courses of action, i.e., consolidation, realignment, or discontinuance. As a result, major reorganization actions would be required in either case as a result of implementing the Presidio Closure and Realignment Study.

During the later period, the National Council of Technical Services Industries (NCTSI) had been organized and chaired by Mr. Roy Ash. A major purpose of this association was to lobby for more contracting out by the Federal Government. On November 27, 1972, in a letter to President Richard Nixon, the NCTSI urged Federal Government agencies to rely on contracting out as a means to reduce the number of Civil Service employees. The NCTSI claimed that there were more than 300 thousand Civil Service positions in the DOD alone that could be contracted out. Since Mr. Ash accepted a position as Director of OMB, he was in a position to translate theNCTSI's wishes into Federal Government policy. On November 29, 1972 a Mr. T.E. Russell Jr., the Acting Executive Director of NCTSI, wrote to President Nixon stating: "We believe that elimination of all Federal Government in-house activities that are obtainable from private industry offer a great potential for reducing the size of Civil Service employees and achieving economy and efficiency. For example, in DOD alone there were more than 300 thousand Civil Service employees on the payroll performing commercial or industrial type activities that could be obtained from the private sector."

One of the major components of the initial Presidio of San Francisco Closure and Realignment Study was the possible conversion of military personnel and Civil Service employees to contractor operation, thereby reducing the budget costs and reducing expenditures for the Federal Government. Before the Base Closure and Realignment Act of 1988 was enacted, Representative Jerome Waldie, (a Democrat from Antioch, California), revealed the Office of Manpower and Budget (OMB) plan. The action, according to Representative Jerome Waldie, was one of the many targets on the horizon to affect the then popular Congressional objective to attain economies of scale in response to infamous reports of overspending in the military services. Other similar plans had come from Representative Chet Holifield's (California) Bills that were in Committee. One such bill called for a Federal Office of Procurement that would allow such an agency to contract out to private firms, military personnel and Civil Service employee positions as they saw fit, as long as the US Congress did not object. On December 28, 1973, it was announced if the OMB plan disclosed by Representative Waldie had been implemented; it could have eliminated 185,000 Civil Service positions from the US Air Force alone.

Just what the effects would have been on the US Army and the US Navy was unknown; as was the Presidio of San Francisco, as this particular plan was never implemented. According to Mr. Roy Ash, then Director of the OMB and former management official of Litton Industries, the OMB planned to save the Federal Government $626 million. Representative Waldie stated: "It would wreak havoc with the Civil Service system," and in Representative Waldie's opinion "would have more serious consequences at the Presidio of San Francisco than the Presidio Closure and Realignment Study to realign the Headquarters, Sixth US Army staff to Treasure Island;" a location that was later rescinded when the US Congress balked.

The Headquarters, Sixth US Army staff and the "Save the Presidio" Committee were disturbed by the OMB proposal that had already drawn fire from some US Air Force and US Army spokesmen and praise from others. During September 1973, the plan was submitted to Mr. James Schlesinger, the Secretary of Defense. The plan included an estimate that 96,000 military personnel and 89,000 US Air Force Civil Service employees could be eliminated and converted to contactor operation. According to the briefing papers submitted to the OMB by the US Air Force, the OMB believed that the establishment of a favorable climate in the US Congress was essential to their proposed implementation because of the strong resistance to change that was expected by military Installations, State and City Governments, employee Unions, and concerned citizens.

The Companies representing NCTSI were no longer content just to perform contract work for the Federal Government. They were literally trying to take over the Federal Government. The Presidio of San Francisco conversion was just the "camel's nose in the tent;" the inch that could become a mile. If private industry could convert 300,000 Civil Service positions, they would want 300,000 more and so on. The appetite of the rich and powerful Corporations knows no bounds. However, the technical duties involved in repairing and maintaining the Presidio of San Francisco, according to Federal Government law, had to be performed by Civil Service employees unless there was a specific exception. And in this instance, there was no such exception. In effect, the Presidio of San Francisco Closure and Realignment Study endorsed by the Headquarters, Sixth US Army staff and the "Save the Presidio" Committee entailed a reorganization of organizations at the Presidio Post, and not just a realignment of the Headquarters, Sixth US Army, and transfer of operation, repair, and maintenance of the Presidio Post to the National Park Service. However, no such reorganization could be carried out without the consent and approval of the US Congress. Legal experts believed a decision to file a lawsuit did not rest with the "Save the Presidio" Committee but with Civil Service employees. Assuming Civil Service employees were to file a lawsuit, it would be accomplished on behalf of Civil Service employees at all military Installations.

One labor Union spokesman had already been heard from. For example, Mr. Kenneth Lyons, President of the National Association of Government Employees (NAGE). Mr. Lyons stated: "The plan would put Federal Government operations and Civil Service positions up for sale to the Nation's corporate giants, and would lead to the traumatic displacement of thousands of career Civil Service employees." Mr. Lyons stated: "The plan would be a windfall for private Corporations such as Litton Industries as they line up at the US Treasury to rake off the profits they would derive from assuming the positions performed historically and faithfully by Civil Service employees." The OMB believed that the multi-function approach was not effective and would generate a negative attitude to the Armed Services toward the concept of contracting out for military Post and Base repair and maintenance. Their belief was that while the OMB proposal was large enough to attract bids from major Corporations, the effect of a switch to a single manager operational approach was designed to eliminate competition from smaller business firms in favor of corporate giants. By June 1975, the initial OMB plan was proposed to be implemented at five AFBs and ultimately at 70 AFBs.

The proposal would have eliminated 75-percent of US Air Force Civil Service positions unless rehired by private contractors. Representative Waldie stated: "The US Air Force's tentative response was to oppose all but 1000 of the proposed reductions in Civil Service positions." Waldie stated: "Similar OMB proposals were submitted to US Army and US Navy officials for study and recommendations by the end of the year." The OMB proposal and Representative Holifield's Bills would have eliminated a great many more Civil Service positions if approved by the US Congress. Seniority and retirement benefits accrued by Civil Service employees would have been lost if and when their positions were terminated and not regained even if they were rehired by private contractors. Therefore, this was

131

the prime reason for the Headquarters, Sixth US Army staff and the "Save the Presidio" Committee to be so adamant about their determination to oppose the Presidio of San Francisco Closure and Realignment Study. Instead, a combined Headquarters, Sixth US Army staff with the Presidio Garrison at the Presidio of San Francisco was the preferred organizational method; as compared with the realignment of the Headquarters, Sixth US Army staff; discontinuance of the Presidio Garrison; and the transfer of the Presidio of San Francisco to the US National Park Service. The clash between organizational methods of approach between the OMB with local political and military officials led observers to believe that organizational guns at the Presidio of San Francisco would not be politically silenced. They were trained next on the OMB sweeping conversion plan for 70 US Air Force Bases or whatever Director Roy Ash had in mind.

The Headquarters, Sixth US Army staff had been directed by the DOD to initiate its own comprehensive study to measure the effects of the proposed realignment of the Headquarters, Sixth US Army staff; discontinuance of the Presidio Garrison; transfer of the Presidio Post mission and functions to the US National Park Service; realignment of the Letterman Army Medical Center to the Oakland Naval Medical Center at Oak Knoll; and the realignment of the Letterman Army Institute of Research to medical research facilities in the US. The DA's study of the proposed Headquarters, Sixth US Army staff realignment was finalized by the US Army Forces Command at Atlanta in Georgia with heavy input from the Headquarters, Sixth US Army staff.

The Presidio of San Francisco Closure and Realignment Study included a detailed review of existing operations to measure the efficiency and effectiveness of all available resources. For example, space, personnel, and support services. However, there were important economic factors left out of the Presidio of San Francisco Closure and Realignment Study that may have thoroughly justified a reorganization of military activities at the Presidio of San Francisco. The major savings projected as a result of realigning the Headquarters, Sixth US Army staff, discontinuing the Presidio Garrison, and transferring the Presidio of San Francisco to the US National Park Service came from the elimination of approximately 550 to 650 military personnel and Civil Service employees. However, there were serious questions about whether all of the reductions could be implemented since the US Army planned to retain a vast majority of the land and buildings at the Presidio Post after the Headquarters, Sixth US Army staff realignment.

The Headquarters, Sixth US Army realignment; however, was highly questionable for several reasons. Primarily, serious seismic hazards existed at Treasure Island as the island had been sinking into the San Francisco Bay and a major earthquake could result in liquefaction. In order to meet existing seismic and code requirements, new construction costs would be extremely high. Re-construction of the sea wall around Treasure Island was somehow not included in the original Headquarters, Sixth US Army staff construction estimate. The buildings identified for use by the Headquarters, Sixth US Army staff would be costly to operate. For example, an old hangar building with extremely high heating costs. The US Army Forces Command had counted on savings of $11.7 million in future construction expenditures outlined in the Presidio Master Plan with the majority of construction involved in new buildings and facilities. Although the Master Plan was approved, it was superseded by the 1978 Omnibus Parks Bill that specifically prohibited new construction at the Presidio of San Francisco. Therefore, construction costs should not have been portrayed as a saving to the DA. The cost to operate excess portions of the Presidio Post as part of the Golden Gate National Recreation Area was also not included in the US Army Forces Command Closure and Realignment Study. One time construction costs were estimated at $9.2 million and annual operating costs were initially estimated at $2.5 million by the Golden Gate National Recreation Area.

General Forrester had intended to write to General Robert M. Shoemaker, Commanding General, US Army Forces Command as to the status of the "Save the Presidio" Committee at the onset of Mr. Fleishell's appointment as Co-chairman.[25] General Forrester wanted to address the activities and intentions of this Committee and how he planned to relate to it. His initial impression was that the Mayor's Committee would be a constructive influence in the overall study process and perhaps provide a model for military and community cooperation. General Forrester had formed a task force to study the possible use of Presidio of San Francisco facilities by the DOD, the DA, and other Federal Government agencies located in the City of San Francisco and Bay Area. He was convinced management action could be taken to make the Presidio Post a more economically efficient and effective military Installation.

General Shoemaker forwarded a proposed press release to the Chief of Public Affairs, DA on September 6, 1978. There was a need to release conditional approved information concerning the current status of the Presidio of San Francisco Closure and Realignment Study. One of the news releases was proposed for issuance in the City of San Francisco and Bay Area. The intent was to provide a status report that was propitious to the DA to be prepared at US Army Forces Command level. The DA release approval was requested due to US Army sensitivities regarding military Post and Base closures and realignments. The proposed public affairs action would provide external and internal publics with official information to fill the void that would have otherwise existed between the time the military Post or Base closure and realignment was announced and the decision made. The

---

[25] Letter from Lieutenant General Eugene P. Forrester, Commander, Sixth US Army, to (Commander, Headquarters, US Army Forces Command, Atlanta, Georgia), December 19, 1979.

proposed news release addressed the following misconceptions that had surfaced in the affected area:[26]

- Fear that the US Army was trying to hide military Post or Base closure and realignment results;

- Fear of instant military Post or Base closures;

- That citizens had no input to the decision making process. The proposed news release of September 6, 1978 advertised to the public that the US Army's study regarding the Headquarters, Sixth US Army staff realignment; Presidio Garrison discontinuance; transfer of the Presidio of San Francisco mission and functions to the US National Park Service; or making the Presidio Post a Sub-Post under the Fort Ord Post had remained in the data collection phase.

During April 1978, the Presidio of San Francisco Closure and Realignment Study announced by the US Army was part of a detailed review of existing operations at some 29 military Installations. The review was an annual process whereby the US Army attempted to attain a more efficient and effective structure by studying the reduction of any non-essential overhead costs; the use of military personnel and Civil Service employees; equipment resources; and the number of single mission military Posts and Bases. To develop and process an investigation of this magnitude would become a lengthy and complex endeavor that would be conducted at several US Army organizational levels. Before data was to be submitted to the DOD for review and approval, information would be continuously scrutinized and verified by the Headquarters, Sixth US Army staff and the US Army Forces Command. In addition to fiscal management considerations, the US Army studied factors related to the Equal Employment Opportunity Act; the National Environmental Policy Act; various Appropriations and Authorization Acts; and other National Policy Acts involving resource utilization, Federal Government assistance, and employee placement rights.

The US Army Forces Command conducted environmental studies of all proposed US Army military Post closures and relocations to include the Oakland Military Traffic Management Command terminal; Presidio of San Francisco; Letterman Army Medical Center; and cumulative impacts of Department of the Navy relocations in the area. The US Army considered alternative actions to reduce the Presidio of San Francisco activities to the minimum necessary to maintain family housing and US Army Reserve Centers, and to transfer the Presidio Post's mission and functions to the US National Park Service. Comments were solicited during the investigation from interested members of the US Congress, Federal

---

[26] Letter from Colonel Patrick D. Chisolm, Jr., Chief of Public Affairs, US Army Forces Command, Atlantic, Georgia, to (Chief, of Public Affairs, Department of the Army, Washington, DC, September 6, 1978.

Government agencies, State and City Government officials, and special interest groups. The public participation represented implementation of the President's announced Government-wide policy to include local viewpoints into the earliest periods of decision making. Any decision regarding the Presidio of San Francisco other than the status quo would be implemented in a phased basis to mitigate military personnel and Civil Service employee, environmental, and socioeconomic impacts.[27]

The realignment of the Headquarters, Sixth US Army staff and the discontinuance of the Presidio Garrison would have resulted in the involuntary separation of more than 50 permanent Civil Service employees that was more than10-percent of the permanent Civil Service work force. The separation rule for RIF was now applicable. As a result, a request for Voluntary Early Retirement Authority (VERA) was submitted to DA for approval on October 9, 1991. The responsibility for achieving both external and internal change fell to General Forrester. General Forrester played a critical, pivotal role in the change process as he had to "orchestrate" the change. Not only did General Forrester take the lead in the implementation of the strategies that emerged from the policy development process, implementation required internal changes to ensure that military personnel, Civil Service employees, and financial resources were in place to implement the anticipated changes.

Changes ran the gamut from planning and defining problems to proposing solutions to those problems. In addition, changes implied altering policies as well as practices and procedures. Changes could be understood either as a phenomenon that were the result of individual changes, or the result of systemic or organization level changes. Societal or systemic level changes often had more to do with what might be considered politics or broad policy concerns. To fully understand the DA directed changes, three issues were discussed. General Forrester was the originator of change; individual systematic changes in the context of US Army relations; and problems associated with successfully achieving planned changes

The Headquarters, Sixth US Army staff had been directed by the DOD to initiate its own comprehensive study to measure the effects of the proposed realignment of the Headquarters, Sixth US Army staff to Treasure Island; discontinuance of the Presidio Garrison; the transfer of the Presidio of San Francisco mission and functions to the US National Park Service; the relocation of the Letterman Army Medical Center to the Oakland Naval Medical Center at Oak Knoll; and the relocation of the Letterman Army Institute of Research to US Army medical research facilities elsewhere in the US. The DA study of the proposed Headquarters, Sixth US Army staff realignment was finalized by the US Army Forces Command at Atlanta in Georgia with heavy input from the Headquarters, Sixth US Army staff.

---

[27] Editorial, "Proposed News Release," US Army Forces Command, Atlanta, Georgia, September 6, 1978.

However, there were important socioeconomic factors left out of the Presidio of San Francisco Closure and Realignment Study that would have thoroughly justified realigning other Federal Government agencies located in the City of San Francisco and Bay Area to the Presidio of San Francisco. The Headquarters, Sixth US Army staff realignment; however, was highly questionable for several reasons. Primarily, serious seismic hazards existed at Treasure Island as the island had been sinking into the San Francisco Bay and a major earthquake could result in liquefaction. In order to meet existing seismic and code requirements, new construction costs would be extreme.

The principal objective of the Presidio of San Francisco Closure and Realignment Study was to identify areas that would provide a potential for tangible savings through transfer of Federal Government agencies to the Presidio of San Francisco. The initial analysis of the Headquarters, Sixth US Army staff and Presidio Garrison at the Presidio of San Francisco indicated that there were incompatibilities in the command and operating support relationships, and that economies could result with a less complex organizational structure. Consolidation of similar or related areas of work responded to this objective. The organizational alternative to remain at the Presidio Post was also highly considered in terms of its potential monetary savings from a realignment of Federal Government agencies in the City of San Francisco and Bay Area to the Presidio Post.

The Presidio of San Francisco Closure and Realignment Study also examined numerous possible alternative organizational structures, and studied in detail several alternatives that appeared markedly superior to the status quo of the Headquarters, Sixth US Army staff realignment to Treasure Island. Included in these examinations were financial management; anticipated work mix and workload; program management; engineering support; customer interfaces; data systems integration; and identification of functional distribution. In the final stages of the Presidio of San Francisco Closure and Realignment Study, the recommended management actions were incorporated into the Alternative Proposal. The advantages of the Alternative Proposal over the status quo of the Headquarters, Sixth US Army staff realignment to Treasure Island were considered to be:

- Clarification of command and support relationships;

- An increase in economy;

- A more realistic capability to respond to the assigned mission;

- An increase in responsiveness to users;

- An improvment in internal management;

- An improvement in the realignment of organizations and missions for assigned programs at the Presidio of San Francisco.

The Alternative Proposal to the Headquarters, Sixth US Army staff realignment to Treasure Island appeared superior. The Presidio of San Francisco Closure and Realignment Study would:

- Save no less than 127 Civil Service employee positions effective September 30, 1992 due to the internal reorganization of the Headquarters, Sixth US Army staff and realignment to Treasure Island;

- Consolidate staff and administrative functions while lowering overhead costs in general;

- Merge program management for a singular point of work input;

- Derive the benefits of single command management to facilitate more efficient resource utilization.

Because of its geographic isolation from the Presidio of San Francisco, Treasure Island building facilities were not feasible. However, a realignment of the Headquarters, Sixth US Army staff would cause the discontinuance of the Presidio Garrison and the transfer of the Presidio Post to the US National Park Service by implementing the Presidio of San Francisco Closure and Realignment Study. Realignment actions would have to be accomplished as a part of whatever reorganization was to be implemented. The potential for economical savings was evidenced by the implicit interdependence of the Headquarters, Sixth US Army staff and the Presidio Garrison mission and functions. No change in mission would be required for any of these organizational entities. Functional issues that may have proved troublesome under the organizational structure were the same as those identified for the realignment to Treasure Island, except they may have been intensified due to the independence of command. The Alternative Plan; however, did provide for potential savings through the merger of mission and support efforts. An in-depth study revealed a potential for some tangible savings from the elimination of duplication of effort. Contracting out of functions responsive to the Presidio of San Francisco Closure and Realignment Study's goal and objectives could have been accomplished in such a consolidated Headquarters, Sixth US Army staff and Presidio Garrison reorganization. "No one saved from a Post or Base closure during 1991 could breathe a sigh of relief. BRAC 93 was already being planned as the BRAC 91 list was being published."[28]

---

[28] David S. Sorenson, "Shutting Down the Cold War: The Politics of Military Base Closure." (St. Martin's Press, New York, July 1998), p. 129.

Alternative Closure and Realignment Plan

The Alternative Plan of remaining at the Presidio of San Francisco provided one means for improving the existing command and operating support relationships vis-a-vis the Commanding General, Sixth US Army and the Commander, Presidio Garrison. The Alternative Plan deviated from and would require modification of governing directives. The alternative, while entailing significant disruption of the existing organization, afforded the best opportunity to consolidate like functions and thus affect some meaningful savings. As a result, no change in missions and functions of existing organizations would be required. The alternative provided for the consolidation of functions desirable for coherence of command and operating support, and for the improvement in effectiveness and economy. Additionally, the capacity for contracting out in response to the goal and objectives established by the Presidio of San Francisco Closure and Realignment Study without loss to US Army control over contracted out functions had flexibility because of the serrated nature of the dual command structure. Through such a Closure and Realignment Study, the realignment could minimize loss of US Army control over contracted out functions, and maintain working level relationships between Command and operating support entities. For these reasons, Alternative Plans were investigated in-depth.

The Presidio of San Francisco Closure and Realignment Study contained the Headquarters, Sixth US Army staff proposed realignment; discontinuance of the Presidio Garrison discontinuance; and the transfer of the Presidio of San Francisco to the US National Park Service was finally submitted to the US Army Forces Command for approval. The plan contained the analysis of detailed implementation for the execution of the Study. The Study considered implementation for a consolidated command composed of the Headquarters, Sixth US Army staff and the Presidio Garrison, plus the relocation of Federal Government agencies in the City of San Francisco and Bay Area to the Presidio of San Francisco. Several alternate opportunities were also identified for reducing expenditures that would not have required the Headquarters, Sixth US Army staff proposed realignment; Presidio Garrison discontinuance; and the transfer of the Presidio of San Francisco to the US National Park Service. The Fort Baker Installation could be closed or realigned to the Presidio Post or transferred to the Golden Gate National Recreational Area. The Oakland Army Terminal could have been closed or realigned to the Presidio Post. The US Army Corps of Engineers District and Regional Offices could be moved out of commercial office space in the City of San Francisco and realigned to the Presidio Post. Selected agencies such as the National Park Service Regional Office could be moved out of commercial office space and relocated to the Presidio Post. And repair and maintenance improvements to include contracting, consolidation, and elimination of functions currently performed by Presidio Garrison military personnel and Civil Service employees could be implemented.

Having committed themselves, the Headquarters, Sixth US Army staff and the "Save the Presidio" Committee thought they had complied with the spirit and intent of the Study. However, managers and supervisors at both the Headquarters, Sixth US Army staff and the Presidio Garrison had hoped the US Army Forces Command would not "hold their feet to the fire" for the exact monetary savings expected. During the Summer of 1988, the Secretary of the Army, Clifford L. Alexander, announced in a draft press release the proposed realignment of all US Army activities at the Presidio of San Francisco. Enclosed in the draft press release was a Questions and Answers handout for the press (See Appendixes, Appendix B). The Headquarters, Sixth US Army staff at the Presidio Post was programmed to be realigned to the Naval Station at Treasure Island. Major troop units would be relocated to the Fort Ord Post in Monterey and Fort Lewis in Washington. The Letterman Army Medical Center and the Letterman Army Institute of Research would continue in operation. The Presidio Post family housing and the two US Army Reserve Centers would be retained at the Presidio Post. The operating support activities at the Presidio Garrison would be reduced to the level necessary to support the remaining organization. That portion of operating support facilities no longer required would be closed and declared excess by the US Army. Fort Baker being a Sub-Installation of the Presidio of San Francisco would also be closed and declared excess by the DA.

Under the provisions of Public Law 92-589, if the US Army decided to implement realignment proposals, the Presidio of San Francisco would become the joint responsibility of the US Army and the US National Park Service. Under the law establishing the Golden Gate National Recreational Area, all excess land on the Presidio Post would be transferred to the Department of the Interior for inclusion in the National Park system. The realignment was part of a concentrated effort by the US Army to improve efficiency and cost effectiveness of military operations. One of the main determining factors was that the Presidio Post had single-mission operations and was an administrative Post. That is, it contained a major Command headquarters organization. The collocation of US Army and US Navy elements at Treasure Island with certain common administrative and logistical support functions would achieve this objective without sacrificing the military mission in the City of San Francisco and Bay Area.

Being a single mission organization, the Headquarters, Sixth US Army along with the Presidio Garrison was seriously considered for consolidation, realignment, or discontinuance. The primary mission of the Headquarters, Sixth US Army was to command the Presidio Garrison; support assigned troop tenant units; reinforce training units; support mobilization designated detachments to include supervision of recruitment, organization, stationing, and training; arranging for administrative and logistical support for military tenant organizations; and to exercise command of US Army Reserve Training Divisions and US Army Reserve Forces Schools. However, changes in mission were already being reprogrammed beyond the control of the Presidio of San Francisco Closure and Realignment Study.

The Headquarters, Sixth US Army was reprogrammed to be realigned to Fort Carson in Colorado instead of Treasure Island due to the unsatisfactory conditions at Treasure Island. The revised mission would also delete Reserve component forces responsibilities and concentrate on command over active duty components of the US Army in the Sixth US Army geographic area of responsibility. On October 1, 1992, the Headquarters, Sixth US Army staff would be downsized as a result of a declining Continental US mission and, with the downsizing of responsibilities, there would be many changes in personnel authorizations. The reorganized Headquarters, Sixth US Army mission would focus on training, operations, mobilization, and deployment of Reserve component forces. The Headquarters, Sixth US Army would continue to provide military assistance to civil authorities; land defense of the Continental US; continuity of Operation Plans; military support of Civil Defense; Counter-Narcotics Support; Earthquake Disaster Support; and Boise Inter-agency Fire Fighting Support. Most Reserve related missions and responsibilities, military personnel, and Civil Service employees would be transferred to the newly formed US Army Reserve Command located at Atlanta in Georgia.

General Forrester had intended to write to the Commanding General, US Army Forces Command as to the status of the "Save the Presidio" Committee and Mr. Fleishell's appointment as Co-chairman.[29] General Forrester wanted to address the activities and intentions of this Committee and how he planned to relate to it. His initial impression was that the Mayor's Committee would be a constructive influence in the overall study process and perhaps provide a model for the US Army and community cooperation. General Forrester had formed a task force to study the possible use of the Presidio of San Francisco facilities by the DOD, the DA, and other Federal Government agencies in the City of San Francisco and Bay Area. General Forrester was convinced management action could be taken to make the Presidio Post a more economic and efficient military Installation.

The Headquarters, Sixth US Army staff in the meantime had requested approval to conduct a RIF in the Civil Service employee workforce. The Headquarters, Sixth US Army staff was programmed to lose an estimated 377 to 204 authorized positions as a result of downsizing the Headquarters, Sixth US Army staff due to the transfer of mission and functions to the newly established US Army Reserve Command. Effective September 30, 1992, the RIF was primarily due to substantial Fiscal Year 1992 budget reductions that would reduce the Civil Service employee workforce by 127 Civil Service positions. By September 30, 1992, of the 127 Civil Service positions to be eliminated, it was estimated that approximately 59 Civil Service employees would be involuntarily separated. The remaining Civil Service employees would be placed in lateral positions at the Presidio of San Francisco,

---

[29] Letter from Lieutenant General Eugene P. Forrester, Commander, Sixth US Army, Presidio of San Francisco, to (Commander, Headquarters, US Army Forces Command, Atlantic, Georgia), December 19, 1979.

other Federal Government agencies, or would be expected to leave voluntarily through the retirement or other attrition.

These estimates were based on projected Force Structure changes, cuts in programs, projected funded workload, and the President's Fiscal Year 1992 budget. The estimated number of positions eliminated could have increased if budget proposals were changed, or if personnel departures did not occur as projected. On September 6, 1978, General Shoemaker forwarded a proposed press release to the Chief of Public Affairs sat the DA. There was a need to release conditional approved information concerning the current status of the Presidio of San Francisco Closure and Realignment Study. One of the news releases was proposed for issuance in the City of San Francisco and Bay Area. The intent was to provide a status report that was propitious to the DA to be prepared at the US Army Forces Command level. The DA release approval was requested due to US Army sensitivities regarding Post and Base closures and realignments. The proposed public affairs action would provide external and internal publics with official information to fill the void that would have otherwise existed between the time the Presidio Post closure and realignment was announced, and the decision was made. The proposed news release addressed the following misconceptions that had surfaced in the affected areas:

- That the Department of Defense was trying to hide military Post and Base closure and realignment results;

- Fear of instant military Post and Base closures;

- That citizens had no input in the decision making process.

On September 6, 1978, the news release advertised to the public that the US Army's Study regarding the Headquarters, Sixth US Army staff proposed realignment; the Presidio Garrison discontinuance; the transfer of the Presidio of San Francisco to the US National Park Service; or to be realigned as a Sub-Post under the Fort Ord Post remained in the data collection phase. During April 1978, the US Army announced that the Presidio of San Francisco Closure and Realignment Study was part of a detailed review of existing operations at some 29 military Installations. The review was an annual process whereby the US Army would attempt to attain a more efficient and effective structure by studying the reduction of any non-essential overhead costs; the socioeconomic utilization of military personnel; Civil Service employees, equipment resources; and the number of single mission military Posts and Bases.

To develop and process a Study of this magnitude would become a lengthy and complex endeavor that would be conducted at several US Army headquarters levels. Before data could be submitted to the DOD for review and approval, information was continuously scrutinized and verified by the Headquarters, Sixth US Army staff and US Army Forces Command. The Presidio of San Francisco

Closure and Realignment Study would take from 23 to 46-weeks to complete. Variations in study duration were a result of procedures required in connection with the environmental analysis portion of the Study. The environmental analysis would require another four to nine-months to complete. Since the Presidio Post proposed realignment constituted a major Federal Government action significantly affecting the quality of the human environment, and the proposed Study was environmentally controversial, the Headquarters, Sixth US Army staff would be required to prepare an Environmental Impact Statement. One of the elemental parts of the statement was a formal public comment and review period. The US Army Forces Command conducted several environmental studies of proposed US Army Post closures and realignments to include the Presidio Post; Oakland Military Traffic Management Command terminal; Letterman Army Medical Center; and Department of the Navy realignments in the area. The US Army considered the alternative action to reduce the Presidio Post activities to the minimum necessary to maintain family housing and US Army Reserve Centers, and to transfer the Presidio of San Francisco to the US National Park Service. Comments were solicited during the Study from interested members of the US Congress, Federal Government agencies, State and City Government officials, and special interest groups.

The public participation represented implementation of the President's announced Federal Government-wide policy to include local viewpoints into the earliest periods of decision making. Any decision regarding the Presidio of San Francisco, other than the status quo, would be implemented in a phased basis to mitigate military personnel, Civil Service employee, environmental and socioeconomic impacts. The continued Headquarters, Sixth US Army staff location at the Presidio Post was subsequently expected to result in the involuntary separation of more than 50 Civil Service employee positions, or more than 10-percent of the Civil Service work-force at the Headquarters, Sixth US Army. The separation rule for RIF was applicable. On October 9, 1991, as a result, a request for Voluntary Early Retirement Authority (VERA) was submitted to the DA for review and approval.

Additional Office Space at the Presidio

Because of the facts that strongly supported maintaining the Presidio of San Francisco status quo, the Headquarters, Sixth US Army staff took another hard look internally to see what they could do to make operation more efficient and cost effective. They discovered office space in excess of 200 thousand square feet that could be used by the DOD, the DA, and other Federal Government agencies in the City of San Francisco and Bay Area. A total of 75 thousand square feet were initially found and another 125 thousand square feet through more effective utilization of office space. The Headquarters, Sixth US Army staff could not criticize itself for this under-utilization as they were under different pressures and had different resources. However, under investigation, the Presidio Post was found to be under-utilized as a military Installation. The data generated by the Headquarters, Sixth US Army staff would be relied on heavily to refute portions of the Presidio of San Francisco Closure and Realignment Study.

"Save the Presidio" Committee Involvement

As a result of the DA announcement that the Headquarters, Sixth US Army staff would be realigned; the Presidio Garrison discontinued; and the Presidio of San Francisco transferred to the US National Park Service, Mayor George R. Moscone appointed a "Save the Presidio" Committee to represent his office and citizens of the City of San Francisco. On July 12, 1978, the Mayor took exception to the DA policy and wrote to several leading citizens of San Francisco wanting to know the extent of resources they were willing to commit to this important rebuttal. At that time, the Presidio Post accounted for $150 million spent in the City of San Francisco, and generated a payroll of over $169 million with 6000. to 7000 military personnel and Civil Service employees. The Presidio of San Francisco was a very unique military Post that had played a significant role in San Francisco's history dating back to the founding of San Francisco over 200-years ago. However, the DA was convinced that the Presidio Post should be closed because of economic considerations. Although Mayor Moscone supported economy in Federal Government agencies, he considered the role of the Presidio Post in the socioeconomic, cultural, and historical vein of San Francisco.

The Mayor met with several Federal Government officials to determine the steps the City of San Francisco could take to present its case against the Headquarters, Sixth US Army staff realignment. The Mayor's objective was to preserve one of San Francisco's most beautiful and enduring military Posts and not allow it to become a victim of short sighted planning and decision making by the US Army.[30] Ms. Dianne Feinstein who was serving on the San Francisco City Council when Mayor Moscone was assassinated on November 27, 1978 was subsequently appointed Mayor by vote of the City Council. Mayor Feinstein continued Mayor Moscone's initiative in her new administration to save the Presidio Post, and initiated a stepped-up campaign to preserve San Francisco's historic Presidio Post as a military Installation with appointment of well-known business and civic leader Mr. Melvin ("Mel") Swig as Co-chairman of the San Francisco "Save the Presidio" Committee. Mr. Swig would share direction of the Committee with Mr. J. Edward Fleishell, a prominent local attorney, longtime resident and Director of the City's Anti-litter Program who had been appointed as Chairman of the Committee.

The Committee had approximately 800 subscribers and had raised $6,000 in voluntary contributions to carry out its mission. Mr. Fleishell had announced the

---

[30] Letter from the late Mayor George R. Moscone, City of San Francisco, to (Mr. Howard Freeman, San Francisco, and California), July 12, 1978.

143

intention of the City to conduct an independent study to ensure the most efficient and cost effective use of military facilities in the City of San Francisco and Bay Area. Mr. Fleishell wanted the DA and the City of San Francisco to benefit from this study and would conduct his assessment accordingly. Citing the ties that had bound the City of San Francisco with military forces at the Presidio of San Francisco over many years, Mayor Feinstein made it clear that she was taking positive steps to retain its military personnel, Civil Service employees, and the Presidio Post as a valuable part of the community.

Mayor Feinstein's appointment of Mr. Swig followed her announcement before a combined Federal Government campaign luncheon that she was strengthening the Citizens' Committee organized by the past Mayor Moscone for the purpose of countering reported sentiment within the Department of Defense to realign, substantially reduce operations, or discontinue the Headquarters, Sixth US Army at the Presidio of San Francisco. The Committee, that included more than 400 foremost citizens on its roster, had also contracted with the consulting firm Touche Ross & Company to conduct what Mayor Feinstein described as a "thorough and professional study to determine the best use of the Presidio Post and to protect the rights and interests of the citizens of the City of San Francisco and Bay Area that would be affected by the DOD study." Mayor Feinstein wrote to Secretary of Defense Harold Brown referring to the DA announcement of April 26, 1978 of her intentions to study a series of proposed military Posts and Base closures and realignments to include alternatives affecting activities at the Presidio Post.

Mayor Feinstein stated that the City of San Francisco remained adamantly opposed to the proposed Headquarters, Sixth US Army staff realignment, and supported the retention of the Presidio of San Francisco under its current configuration and operation by the DA Mayor Feinstein was confident that the Presidio of San Francisco Closure and Realignment Study would conclude that there would be no significant changes in the best interest of the US Army and the City of San Francisco and Bay Area. However, Mayor Feinstein was concerned with the prospect that any peripheral areas declared excess under law would be transferred to the Department of the Interior as part of the Golden Gate National Recreation Area. Given the limited resources available to the Department of the Interior, the US National Park Service shared her concern that any property proposal for transfer might ultimately deteriorate under a caretaker status. Mayor Feinstein requested the President's Economic Adjustment Council immediately undertake an analysis of the situation to ensure that any proposed consideration by the US Army would guarantee a continued high level of operation, repair, and maintenance of this valuable resource.[31]

The Deputy Secretary of Defense replied to Mayor Feinstein's letter regarding the proposed Headquarters, Sixth US Army staff realignment and the discontinuance

---

[31]   Letter from Mayor Dianne Feinstein, City of San Francisco, to (the Honorable Harold Brown, Chairman, President's Economic Adjustment Committee, Washington, DC), December 5, 1978.

of the Presidio Garrison. While the Deputy Secretary clearly understood the City's opposition to significant changes in the current status of the Presidio of San Francisco, there were opinions of more players to be considered. The DA expected to have the preliminary study completed during early 1979 at the time the Deputy Secretary would have the opportunity to review their work. The Deputy Secretary assured Mayor Feinstein that he would take no final action to the proposed realignment of the Headquarters, Sixth US Army staff to Treasure Island, the discontinuance of the Presidio Garrison, and the transfer of the Presidio Post's mission and functions to the US National Park Service until Mayor Feinstein and other interested local officials had full opportunity to react to any proposal. Because the Department of the Interior's position in this involvement, as well as other non-Defense Federal Government interests, the Deputy Secretary thought the Mayor's suggestion to have the President's Economic Adjustment Committee become involved was a good idea. The Deputy Secretary had asked the Director of the Economics Adjustment Committee to arrange meetings with the Mayor of San Francisco, US Army personnel, US National Park Service officials, and other interested Federal Government agencies in the City of San Francisco and Bay Area to explore what could be accomplished to keep the Presidio Post a viable part of San Francisco regardless of the DOD's outcome with no prejudice to the City of San Francisco's current opposition.[32]

An independent study was undertaken by Touche Ross & Company at the Mayor's "Save the Presidio" Committee's authorization that addressed such aspects of the Presidio of San Francisco closure to determine how the Presidio Post could be utilized more efficiently in terms of facilities for other Federal Government agencies now renting or leasing commercial space or property in the City of San Francisco and Bay Area. A careful assessment of the plans and capabilities of the US National Park Service should be asked to take over the Presidio Post from the DOD. Environmental, historical, and social considerations of a major RIF or Post closure should have been examined, such as the effect of such an action or obligation of the Federal Government to assist the City of San Francisco and Bay Area in time of emergency.

Mayor Feinstein pointed out that: "the serious emotional and socioeconomic impact of the Presidio Post closure and realignment were such that they dictated that the Committee dedicate an equally serious effort toward saving the Presidio of San Francisco and continued military use." The Mayor's "Save the Presidio" Committee was undertaking an appeal among its members and others for funds to finance the study. The "Save the Presidio" Committee also contracted for an independent study by Economics Research Associates that was an internally known consulting firm. The firm's charter took into consideration the socioeconomic impact analyses and economic adjustment study for the Presidio Post and private facilities; the interface with the City of San Francisco and Bay Area; and the

---

[32] Letter from the Deputy Secretary of Defense, Washington, DC, to (the Honorable Dianne Feinstein, Mayor, City of San Francisco, California), December 30, 1978.

important role that the Headquarters, Sixth US Army staff, Presidio Garrison, and the Letterman Army Medical Center had in the economy of the City of San Francisco and Bay Area.

Sixth US Army Intervention

General Forrester forwarded a letter to General Shoemaker to inform him of the Presidio Closure and Realignment Study progress. On March 2, 1979, General Forrester enclosed a copy of a contract for an independent study between the City's "Save the Presidio" Committee and the Management Consultant firm of Touche Ross & Company. General Forrester found nothing in the contract inimical to the interests of the Headquarters, Sixth US Army. Indeed, he interpreted the willingness of several hundred citizens, under the leadership of Mayor Dianne Feinstein, to undertake a campaign to ensure the US Army's continued presence in the City of San Francisco as a reflection of the City's positive attitude toward the Presidio of San Francisco and their role in this historic community. General Forrester intended to fully cooperate with the City of San Francisco and Touche Ross & Company, confirming his good faith and objectivity in all respects to the DOD study.

City of San Francisco Intervention

After the first six-months of the public announcement concerning the proposed realignment of the Headquarters, Sixth US Army staff; discontinuance of the Presidio Garrison; and the transfer of the Presidio Post mission and functions to the US National Park Service, the City of San Francisco continued monitoring the progress of the Presidio of San Francisco Closure and Realignment Study through the Mayor's "Save the Presidio" Committee. The Committee of distinguished San Francisco citizens, Co-chaired by Messrs. J. Edward Fleishell and Melvin Swig had from its inception avoided the emotional, parochial arguments that normally accompany a military Post and Base closure or realignment. Instead, the Committee concentrated on bringing a meaningful business-management perspective to the situation. Their goal and objectives were to demonstrate to the DA that Federal Government spending could be reduced without a costly realignment of military organizations stationed at the Presidio Post. To that end, the Committee engaged the international consulting and public accounting firm of Touche Ross & Company to assist the City of San Francisco in its efforts.[33]

The Committee commended the Headquarters, Sixth US Army staff in its efforts to reduce expenditures and improve the efficiency at the Presidio Post. The Presidio of San Francisco Closure and Realignment Study concerning the proposed

---

[33] Letter from, Mayor Dianne Feinstein, City of San Francisco, to (the Honorable Clifford L. Alexander, Jr., Secretary of the Army, Washington, DC), March 16, 1979.

realignment of the Headquarters, Sixth US Army staff; the discontinuance of the Presidio Garrison; the transfer of the Presidio Post mission and functions to the National Park Service; and the closure of Letterman Army Medical Center and the Letterman Army Institute of Research; was an important part of this Nationwide review restraint knowing how difficult it was to reduce Federal Government spending without internal US Army intervention and cooperation. The Committee shared their commitment to fiscal impairing operations. The Committee was fully aware of the difficulty of obtaining the informed, insightful suggestions necessary for DA to make its final decision on the Presidio Post closure or realignment.

Although the independent study by Touche Ross & Company had not been finalized, their initial estimates were that the US Army's approach was likely to produce savings comparable to those projected for the proposed realignment of the Headquarters, Sixth US Army staff to Treasure Island at a lower initial cost. Their study also indicated that savings could be achieved through operations improvements to include contracting out of certain operating Presidio Post support functions currently performed by US Army military personnel and Civil Service employees; consolidating support activities; increasing the number of tenant units at the Presidio Post; and eliminating functions on a selective basis. They provided a sound fiscal perspective regarding the best use of human resources at the Presidio Post. They outlined alternatives such as relocating the Corps of Engineers and the California National Guard to the Presidio Post; improving the management of Presidio Post operations, repair, and maintenance activities; and indicating that some of the anticipated savings could not be realized.

The City of San Francisco was deeply concerned about the expanded use of Treasure Island by the US Army or any other Federal Government agency. A massive investment by the Federal Government, in light of available seismic information, simply could not be justified. "Sometimes the military service operating a military Post can make a transfer easier by lowering the price of both buildings and property, sometimes to zero. The Fort Ord Post on California's Monterey Peninsula became the Site of a similar scheme. Part of the military Installation closed by BRAC 91, became home to California State University at Monterey Bay, largely because the Federal Government transferred the land to the State of California without charge, and sold family housing on the military Post for $1 per-unit. That allowed California State Monterey Bay to own probably the cheapest dormitories in college history."[34]

In the succeeding management improvement actions, the Headquarters, Sixth US Army staff highlighted 10 nearby Federal Government agencies that were paying $2.5 million annually in lease costs alone through the GSA. If they were to relocate to the Presidio Post, 81-percent of these costs or $1,987 million could be saved. The

---

[34] David S. Sorenson, "Shutting Down the Cold War: The Politics of Military Base Closure," (St. Martin's Press, New York, July 1998), pp. 62-63.

priorities for moving would depend on mission and rental costs that were five times greater in the City of San Francisco and Bay Area than at the Presidio Post. As priorities were determined, the Presidio Post would support Federal Government agencies within the space available. The savings to the Federal Government and to US taxpayers would be much more than the cost of rent. Depending upon cross-service agreements between Federal Government agencies, the Presidio Post could make available finance; transportation; printing; data processing; military personnel and Civil Service employee support that most of these agencies provided for themselves on an individual basis due to their isolation.[35]

The Civil Service employees working directly for the DOD comprised another important component of the State of California's employment base. According to DIOR data for September 30, 2003, many thousands were associated with the US Navy or Marine Corps, for example 10,213 were with the US Air Force, 7139 was with the US Army, and 7534 with other DOD agencies. During 2003, California housed 130,473 military personnel and 57,631 Civil Service employees. During Fiscal Year 2003, the DOD spent $13.3 billion on payrolls in the State of California to include $6.0 billion for active duty military personnel pay and benefits, $3.4 billion for Civil Service employee pay, $427 million for Reserve and National Guard pay, and $2.5 billion for retired military pay. Even with the reductions in military personnel and Civil Service employees, the DOD remained one of the largest employers in the State of California.

During 2004, the DOD affected the State of California in important ways beyond military personnel, Civil Service employees, military Posts and Bases. In addition, every year the DOD distributed hundreds of billions of dollars for contracts with private companies, Universities, and other organizations that were to do everything from dispose of waste on military Installations to the manufacture of Aircraft Carriers, Missiles, Airplanes, and satellite technologies. According to DIOR that calculated contracts slightly different than the Census Bureau. For example, the DOD awarded $203 billion in prime contract awards. Of those awards, California Companies and other recipients won $27.9 billion or 13.7-percent of all contracts. Other States with large total awards included Virginia with $23.5 billion (11-percent) and Texas with $21.0 billion (10-percent). On a per capita basis; however, California ranked 16th out of the 50 States with $786 in spending per person; District of Columbia $6,212 per person; Virginia $3,181 per person; and Connecticut $2,583 per person, are the District of Columbia and two States having the highest per capita prime contract awards.

Prime contract awards were not necessarily related to the presence of military Posts and Bases in a given area. However, the relative concentration of contract awards in the State of California was at least in some part linked to the large

---

[35] Message from Headquarters, Sixth US Army, Presidio of San Francisco, Subject: "Base Realignment Study." to (Commander, US Army Forces Command, Atlanta, Georgia), March 16, 1979.

military presence in the State. It is not a coincidence that California, Virginia, and Texas ranked first, second, and third in terms of both prime contract awards and military personnel. Furthermore, the State of California's disproportionate decline in Defense spending over the past 20-years was at least partly due to past military Post and Base closures. If California were to lose a significant number of military Posts or Bases in the upcoming closure round, the State would expect to lose some portion of DOD contract spending. For industries of any type impact the State of California's economy more than the military combined as DOD payroll and prime contract awards in the State of California accounted for $42 billion on Federal Government spending for Fiscal Year 2003. Duriung 2003, the agriculture industry, sometimes viewed as the State of California's largest industry, had an aggregate socioeconomic impact of $27.8 billion.

DOD-BRAC Intervention

The US Air Force had lost 2260 military personnel, 2839 Civil Service employee positions, and 1050 reserve drill authorizations in accordance with the 2004 Force Structure announcement. Many military Posts and Bases, active duty and reserve components, were affected by this realignment. Some units gained aircraft and missions while others pared down. Besides manpower reductions, the realignment formally announced the retirement of the C-9-A and KC-135-E "Stratotanker" aircraft. According to US Air Force officials, the 20 C-9s were retired because of reduced patient movement; range limitations; increased maintenance; and upgrade costs. The aero-medical evacuation mission became a requirement-based system using all passenger-capable aircraft. Of the Air National Guard and US Air Force Reserve Command's 43-year old KC-135-Es, 44 were retired being replaced with 24 KC-135-Rs from the active duty fleet. By the end of 2006, the US Air Force retired 68 of the KC-135-Es.

The National Defense Authorization Act for Fiscal Year 2002 authorized the DOD to pursue another BRAC round during 2005. On November 14, 2002, Secretary of Defense Memorandum initiated the complex analysis and decision process that involved virtually all levels of DOD management, from military Installations through Major Commands and component/agency headquarters to the Office Secretary of Defense. All military Posts and Bases would be considered and treated equally. All military Posts and Bases were expected to respond to a comprehensive series of data calls. Ultimately, the Secretary of Defense's closure and realignment recommendations would be reviewed publicly by an independent Commission, the President, and the US Congress. Because of the potential impact upon DOD components and local communities, BRAC was a subject of intense interest to all Stakeholders. As a one-time authority, closure and realignment decisions would support transformation of the DOD. To provide the Secretary of Defense, the Commission and the President with the optimal set of recommendations, the analytical work and subsequent deliberations must occur free from opinions, internal or external, based on non-certified data and speculation. Accordingly, the DOD officials would not participate in their official capacities, in activities of any organization that has as its purpose, either directly or indirectly, insulating military Posts and Bases from closure or realignment. Invitations to participate in such organizations would be discussed with appropriate Ethics Counselors.

In the US Congress, Post and Base Closures and Realignments are contentious and controversial. Commanders and their Public Affairs Officers had to be prepared to respond to questions and objectively communicate the details of the BRAC process to the general public. During 2005, the DOD had received Congressional authorization for a Post and Base Realignment and Closure round. BRAC was a means to achieve several goals; for example, eliminate excessive infrastructure; reshape military; pursue "jointness;" optimize military readiness; and realize significant savings in support of transforming the DOD. At a minimum, BRAC 05 would eliminate excessive physical capacity, the operation, sustainment and recapitalization that divert scarce resources from the DOD capability. However, BRAC 05 would make an even more profound contribution to transforming the Department of Defense by rationalizing the infrastructure with Defense strategy. BRAC 05 would be the means where the DOD could reconfigure the current infrastructure into one where operational capacity maximizes both "war fighting" capability and efficiency. By creating joint organizational and basing solutions, the DOD could facilitate multi-service missions; reduce waste; save money; free up resources to recruit quality people; modernize equipment and infrastructure; and develop the capabilities needed to meet 21st Century threats. The Secretary of Defense directed that the BRAC 05 process to formalize military Installations begin immediately. By May 16, 2005, after gathering information and completing a comprehensive analysis, the Secretary would submit recommendations for closing or realigning Posts and Bases as required by public law.

The following Questions and Answers were provided for response to queries only. Questions that could not be answered within the scope of this guidance would be taken without comment and forwarded with proposed answers to Office Assistant Secretary of Defense OASD (PA):

Q1: Should communities perceive military construction (MILCON) as an indicator of whether their military Installations would be realigned or closed?

A1: The presence or absence of funding for military construction is not an indication of military service intentions or future recommendations to the Secretary of Defense under BRAC. The DOD funds its military construction program based on its current highest priority requirements recognizing that it may make investments in military Installations that are ultimately selected for closure or realignment.

Q2: Would encroachment issues at Posts or Bases factor into the decision making process?

150

A2: In accordance with the requirements of the BRAC statute, the DOD would base all of its recommendations upon approved selection criteria that reflect military value as the primary consideration. The public law further required that the selection criteria address the ability of both existing and potential receiving communities' infrastructure to support forces, missions, and personnel. To the extent that encroachment limits a military Installation in fulfilling mission requirements, it would be factored into military value. The proposed selection criteria would be made available for general public review no later than December 31, 2003 and finalized by February 16, 2004.

Q3: There have been concerns and questions about environmental costs. Would environmental costs be factored to recommend a Post or Base for realignment or closure?

A3: In accordance with the requirements of the BRAC statute, the DOD would finalize all recommendations based on approved selection criteria that reflected military value as the primary consideration. The law further required that the selection criteria address the impact of costs related to environmental restoration as well as waste management and environmental compliance. The proposed selection criteria would be made available for public review no later than December 31, 2003 and finalized by February 16, 2004.

Q4: What was the closure results of the last four rounds of BRAC (88, 91, 93, and 95) from the total available to the number selected for BRAC action?

A4: The four prior rounds of BRAC resulted in recommendations to close 97 out of 495 major military Installations. BRAC 88 closed 16 major military Installations; BRAC 91 closed 26 major military military Installations; BRAC 95 closed 28 major military Installations; and BRAC 05 closed 27 major military Installations.

Q5: How much has the DOD saved through the previous rounds of closures and realignments?

A5: Through 2001, the four previous rounds produced a net savings (cost avoidance) of approximately $16.7 billion and approximately $6.5 billion annually thereafter. Independent studies have repeatedly verified that savings from BRAC far exceeded costs.

Q6: How much excess capacity did the DOD have?

A6: The DOD would not know its excess capacity until the completion of the BRAC process. During April 1998, the Department of Defense completed a report for the US Congress that estimated it retained approximately 20 to 25-percent in excess capacity across DOD.

151

Q. When will the DOD complete the BRAC analysis and make its recommendations available to the public?

A7: The National Defense Authorization Act for Fiscal Year 2002 established the following milestones for the BRAC 05 round: publish proposed selection criteria for a 30-day comment period by December 31, 2003; publish final selection criteria by February 16, 2004; and submit a report to the US Congress with the Fiscal Year 2005 budget justification along with a comprehensive military Installation inventory and Force Structure Plan. By May 16, 2005, the Secretary of Defense would forward recommendations for closure and realignment to the BRAC Commission at which time the information would be available to the public. By September 8, 2005, the BRAC Commission would forward its report to the President. The President would have until September 23, 2005 to accept or reject recommendations on an all or nothing basis and forward the recommendations to the US Congress. Once the President forwarded the recommendations to the US Congress, the US Congress would have 45-legislative days to enact a joint resolution rejecting all the recommendations or they become binding on the DOD.

Q8: Where would funds come from to perform BRAC analysis and evaluations?

A8: BRAC analysis and evaluations were performed within available resources. They are currently funded by Operations and Maintenance (O&M) funds.

Q9: Would near-term future new Force Structure bed-downs be incorporated into the 2005 BRAC process?

A9: Where the BRAC time line can accommodate operational imperatives, new Force Structure bed-downs would be incorporated in the BRAC process. Using the BRAC process offered the opportunity to make the most efficient and effective use of the capacity and capabilities of the DOD.

Q10: If a Post or Base was approved for closure or realignment, how long would it take?

A10: Under BRAC law, actions to close or realign a Post or Base would be initiated within two-years of the date the President transmitted the BRAC Commission's recommendations report to the US Congress, and must be completed within six-years of that same date.

Q11: Can Posts, Bases, and communities get an assessment of how they "scored" during BRAC 95"?

A11: How a military Installation "scored" in a previous BRAC round was no indication of how it might "score" during the next BRAC 05 round. In accordance with the BRAC statute, when considering military Installations for closure or realignment, the DOD considered all military Installations equally, without regard to whether the military Installation has been previously considered or proposed for closure or realignment by the DOD. However, for those interested in historical information, the Office of the Secretary of Defense maintained the documentation used by the previous BRAC Commissions. 1745 Jefferson Davis Highway, Crystal Square 4, Suite 105, Arlington, Virginia. The information was open to the general public; however, they asked that individuals call the office, 703-602-3207, before arriving to ensure a Federal Government representative was present. There was a copier available.

Q12: How will "jointures" be assessed during the next BRAC round?

A12: The BRAC law required that closure and realignment recommendations be based on published selection criteria that made military value the primary consideration. The law further provided that military value must include impacts on joint "war fighting," readiness, and training. On November 15, 2002, the Secretary of Defense established goals and priorities for the BRAC 05 round memorandum. A primary objective of BRAC 05, in addition to realigning Post or Base structure to meet post-cold war Force Structure, was to examine and implement opportunities for greater "jointness." To reinforce the idea that looking across traditional lines to examine the potential for "jointness," the Secretary of Defense established an internal BRAC 05 decision making body that was joint at every level. The Infrastructure Executive Council (IEC), chaired by the Deputy Secretary, and composed of the Secretaries of military Departments and their Chiefs of Services, Chairman of the Joint Chiefs of Staff, and Under Secretary of Defense (Acquisition, required or cost effective as a military Installation. Technology and Logistics) (USD (AT&L)), would be the policy making and oversight body for the entire BRACS 05. The subordinate Infrastructure Steering Group (ISG), chaired by the USD (AT&L) and composed of the Vice Chairman of the Joint Chiefs of Staff, the military department Assistant Secretaries for Installations and Environment, Vice Chiefs, and the Deputy Under Secretary of Defense (Installations an Environment) (DUSD (I&E)), would oversee joint cross-service analyses of common business oriented functions to ensure the integration of the BRAC process with the military Department and Defense agencies for specific analyses of all other functions.

Q13: How could communities be involved in BRAC to enhance their support to the Post or Base population and mission and their prospects during the BRAC 05 round?

A13: During May 2005, the Defense Base Closure and Realignment Commission would solicit community input once it has received the Secretary of Defense's Base closure and realignment recommendations.

Q14: If the final decision was to close or realign the Post or Base, with whom will community leaders work in the transition of the Post or Base from its current military mission to civilian use?

A14: Although an enormously complex undertaking that involved the DOD, other Federal Government agencies, and State and local Governments, each military Department would have a central point of contact at the closing activity to assist in coordinating the involvement of the various organizations. Additionally, the DOD's Office of Economic Adjustment was chartered to assist local communities with planning for the re-use of closing and realigning military Installations and in that capacity would provide individual community assistance.

Q15: How would property be disposed of or sold?

A15: The BRAC Statute provided the DOD with a variety of mechanisms for disposal of property at closed or realigned military Installations. While speculation cannot be given on which mechanism would be used at any given military Installation, in previous rounds of BRAC, Federal Government real property was made available by public benefit conveyances for airport, education, and homeless assistance; Federal Government transfers to Native American tribes; economic development conveyances to local redevelopment authorities; and public sales just to name a few.

Q16: How would the DOD decide re-use of the Post or Base?

A16: The DOD does not decide the re-use of military Installations. Once the property was declared surplus to the needs of the Federal Government, it was the job of the local community, through its designated local Redevelopment Authority, to plan for the re-use of the surplus property.

Q17: Some of the Posts and Bases had environmental contamination. Will the DOD clean it up?

A17: The DOD has a continuing obligation to perform environmental clean-up all of its military Installations regardless of whether a Post or Base was identified for closure or realignment.

Q18: During the time clean-up would take place after several years in many cases, would the military Post or Base property be vacant and unused until all the clean-up is completed?

A18: In previous rounds, from the time of the military Post or Base's selection for closure, several options would be available for property to be used until it was disposed so that the community could begin using military Post or Base facilities promptly and economic redevelopment could occur. Consistent

154

with public health and safety, once a contractual arrangement was in place, property could be leased or, in certain circumstances, deeded while the property was being environmentally prepared for transfer.

Q19: What comments were made by communities impacted by Post or Base closures?

A19: The communities affected by Post and Base closure and realignment decisions during the last four rounds of BRAC have successfully transitioned to productive economic development. The DOD was committed to working with BRAC 05 communities to assist in that success.

Q20: There are web sites on the Internet that indicate that a list of potential Post or Base closures already existed. Did the DOD maintain a list of military Posts or Bases it wanted to close?

A20: The DOD did not maintain a list of military Posts or Bases it may have considered closing. The BRAC analytical process would not result in departmental closure and realignment recommendations until May 2005.

Q21: How would the realignment of military forces at overseas Posts and Bases impact BRAC 05 efforts?

A21: On March 20, 2003, the Secretary of Defense directed the development of a comprehensive and integrated presence and basing strategy looking out 10-years. Results of that effort, to include rationalizing areas of potential excesses and identifying the utility of overseas Installations, were available to inform the BRAC 05 process.

Q22: What is BRAC?

A22: "BRAC" is an acronym that stands for Base Realignment and Closure. It is a process the DOD had previously used to reorganize military Post or Base structures to more efficiently and effectively support our forces, increase operational readiness and facilitation, and find new ways of doing business. The DOD anticipated that BRAC 05 would build upon processes used in previous rounds.

Q23: How does BRAC work?

A23: The closure and realignment process is governed by law; specifically by the Defense Base Closure and Realignment Act of 1990. The process begins with a threat assessment of the future national security environment, followed by the development of a Force Structure Plan, based on requirements to meet these threats. The DOD then applies published selection criteria to determine what military Installations to recommend for realignment and

155

closure. The Secretary of Defense publishes a report containing the closure and realignment recommendations, forwarding supporting documentation to an independent Commission appointed by the President, in consultation with Congressional leadership. The Commission has the authority to change the DOD's recommendations if it determined that a recommendation deviated from the Force Structure Plan and/or selection criteria. The Commission would then hold Regional meetings to solicit public input prior to making its recommendations. History has shown that the use of an independent Commission and public meetings make the process as open and fair as possible. The Commission would then forward its recommendations to the President for review and approval, who would forward recommendations to the US Congress. The US Congress has 45-legislative days to act on the Commission's report on an all-or-none basis. After that time, the Commission's closure and realignment recommendations would become law. Implementation would start within two-years, and actions wield be complete within six-years.

Q24: What is transformation?

A24: Transformation is shaping the changing nature of military competition and cooperation through new combinations of concepts, capabilities, people, and organizations that exploit our nation's advantages, protect our asymmetric vulnerabilities, and sustain our strategic position, that helps maintain peace and stability throughout the World.

Q25: Why is the DOD transforming?

A25: Over time, the Defense strategy called for the transformation of the US Defense establishment. Transformation is at the heart of this strategy. To transform the DOD, the DOD needed to change its culture in many important areas. The DOD budgeting, acquisition, personnel, and management systems must be able to operate in a World that is changing rapidly. Without change, the current Defense program would only become more expensive in the future, and the DOD would forfeit many of the opportunities available today.

Q26: How is BRAC transformational?

A26: BRAC provided a singular opportunity to reshape our infrastructure to optimize military readiness. The BRAC 05 process helped find innovative ways to consolidate, realign, or find alternative uses for current facilities to ensure that the US continues to field the best prepared and best-equipped military in the World. BRAC would also enable the US military to better match Facilities and Forces, meet the threats and challenges of a new Century, and make the wisest use of limited Defense dollars.

Q27: How many military Posts, Bases, and other military Installations would be closed?

A27: It is too early to say, but there are no specific numbers or "targets." Using specific selection criteria that emphasize military value, the DOD must complete a comprehensive review before it can determine what military Installations should be realigned or closed. During 2005, an independent Commission would review the Secretary of Defense's recommendations, hold public hearings, visit various sites, and ultimately send its recommendations to the President.

Q28: How much has been saved through previous BRAC rounds?

A28: During 1988 through 2001, the four previous BRAC rounds have eliminated approximately 20-percent of the DOD's capacity that existed and produced a net savings of approximately $16.7 billion that included the cost of environmental clean-up. Recurring savings beyond 2001 were approximately $6.6 billion annually. In independent studies conducted over previous years, both the GAO and the Congressional Budget Office have consistently supported the DOD's view that realigning and closing un-needed military Installations produced savings that far exceeded costs.

Q29: What is the time line for the next BRAC round?

A29: The National Defense Authorization Act for Fiscal Year 2002 established milestones for the BRAC 05 round; published proposed selection criteria for a 30-day comment period by December 31, 2003; published final selection criteria by February 6, 2004; and submitted a report to the US Congress with the 2005 budget justification on the following points: a Force Structure Plan based on an assessment of probable threats to National security over the next 20-years; the probable end strength levels and military force units needed to meet those threats; the anticipated levels of available funding; a comprehensive inventory of military Installations worldwide; a description of infrastructure necessary to support the Force Structure; discussion of excess capacity categories; economic analysis of the effect of realignments and closures to reduce excess infrastructure; Secretary of Defense certification of the need for BRAC; and the annual net savings that would result by 2011. By May 16, 2005, the Secretary of Defense would forward recommendations for closures and realignments to the BRAC Commission and the Commission would forward its report on the recommendations to the President by September 8, 2005. The President would have until September 23, 2005 to accept or reject the recommendations in their entirety. If accepted, the US Congress would have 45 legislative days to act on the recommendations.

Q30: Which Posts or Bases will be looked at in this round?

A30: All military Installations within the continental US and its territories (under the control of the Federal government) would be examined as part of this process. This included laboratories; medical; training; National Guard; Reserve; air station; and leased facilities.

Q31: Was BRAC just another example of budget priorities driving National Security planning?

A31: The legislation was quite clear that military value would be the primary consideration. The Secretary of Defense's guidance to military Departments emphasized that BRAC 05 would make a profound contribution to transforming the DOD by bringing the infrastructure in line with Defense strategy.

Q32: How would the Commission be selected, and who would serve?

A32: The BRAC legislation specified the selection process for Commissioners. The President was required to consult with Congressional leadership on nominations to serve on the Commission.

Q33: How have local communities affected by military Post and Base closures fared overall?

A33: The military Post and Base closures and realignments caused near term social and socioeconomic disruption. However, there were many success stories from previous military Post and Base closures. For example, at Charleston Naval Base in South Carolina, the local community, assisted by the DOD, was able to create approximately 4500 new jobs. Approximately 90 Federal Government, State, and private entities are re-using the Naval Base at Charleston. Since the closure of the Mather AFB in California more than 54 leases have been generated at the new Mather Field complex. Its prime location and one of the Country's longest runways had made it an active Air Cargo Hub for California's Central Valley and the Sacramento Region. Additionally, the Base now employs nearly 3700 personnel with its high technical businesses, manufacturing operations, educational centers, Federal Government agencies, and recreational facilities. At Fort Devens in Massachusetts, more than 3000 new jobs have been generated and 2.7-million square feet of new construction has occurred. With 68 different employers on-site, redevelopment ranges from small business incubators to the Gillette Corporation that occupies a large warehouse and distribution center and manufacturing plant. A military Post or Base closure can actually be an economic opportunity, especially when all elements of a community work together.

Q34: Will local Commanders and others in their official capacities be available to help assist in task forces or other efforts to influence BRAC decisions with regard to the military Post or Base?

A34: The DOD officials may attend meetings in a liaison or representative capacity with State and local officials, or other organizations that may seek to develop plans or programs to improve the ability of military Installations to discharge their National Security and Defense missions. The DOD officials may not manage or control such organizations or efforts. In their official capacity, the DOD officials may not participate in the activities of any organization that has as its purpose, either directly or indirectly, insulating DOD military Posts and Bases from closure or realignment. This guidance would ensure the fairness and rigor of the BRAC process.

Q35: Is the list of military Post and Base closures and realignments on the mil. com web site the official position of the Department of Defense?

A35: It's a privately operated web site with no ties to or support from the DOD.

Both the US Congress and the DOD recognized military value to be the primary consideration to reduce or restructure military Posts or Bases. The BRAC 05 process would find innovative ways to consolidate, realign, or find alternative uses for current facilities. All military Installations would be reviewed, and recommendations would be based on approved, published selection criteria and a future Force Structure Plan. Through the BRAC process, the DOD would ensure that the US continued to field the best prepared and best equipped military service in the World. BRAC would enable military organizations overseas to match Facilities to Forces; meet the threats and challenges of a new Century; and make the wisest use of limited Defense dollars. BRAC would facilitate multi-service missions by creating joint organizational and basing solutions that would reduce waste but maximize military effectiveness. Consolidating facilities would save billions allowing the DOD to focus on maintaining and modernizing facilities needed to support our military forces, recruit quality personnel, modernize infrastructure and equipment, and develop the capabilities needed to meet 21st Century threats. The DOD military and civilian officials would not participate in any meetings of organizations with the purpose (express or not) of insulating a military Installation from realignment or closure to ensure the fairness and rigor of the BRAC deliberative process. In coordination with DUSD (I&E), who is the sole releasing authority for information on BRAC 05 to the news media, local Commanders and their PAOs were encouraged to respond to questions within the scope of the PAO. To protect the integrity of the BRAC 05 process and to ensure that consistent and accurate information was provided, the Office Secretary of Defense, military departments, and participating Defense agencies would designate key individuals to respond to Congressional and community inquiries. Unauthorized discussions; dissemination of information; or speculation regarding BRAC matters by DOD officials and contractors were prohibited.

External Stakeholders such as communities have an extraordinary interest in the BRAC process, and consistent with the DOD's need for internal deliberation, should have received timely access to data that could be made public as the BRAC analytical process unfolded. Timely and consistent information from all DOD elements would minimize confusion and foster trust. The PAOs would continue to release the same type and amount of information on their military Installations as they currently did, but may not release, in whole or in part, data calls and information requested under BRAC. It's important to note that local Commanders were not in a position to evaluate the entire mission requirements and cross-service implications of their individual functions as they may affect the DOD, and local Commanders were not in a position to answer questions requiring them to speculate or discuss BRAC issues that were subject to internal DOD deliberation.

While information normally provided to the public would continue to be provided, even if it was the subject of a BRAC data call, its relationship to BRAC was not releasable. The DOD officials could not participate, in their official capacity, in activities of any organization that had as its purpose, either directly or indirectly, insulating Posts and Bases from realignment or closure. The guidance was aimed at ensuring the fairness and rigor of the BRAC deliberative process. Invitations to participate in such organizations would be discussed with appropriate Ethics Counselors. In a liaison or representational role, the DOD officials could attend meetings with State and local officials, or other organizations that wanted to develop plans or programs to improve the ability of military Installations to discharge their National Security and Defense missions. The DOD officials could not manage or control such organizations or efforts.

Many influential former officials and retired General and Flag Officers would be involved with many organizations attempting to insulate military Posts or Bases from closure or realignment. They were allowed to participate in this manner and due to their participation, the organizations were not allowed any greater or lesser information or access. Public information about the current BRAC process and past experience with prior BRAC rounds was available. Contents included the text of the current Defense Base Closure Act, reports of the Secretaries of Defense and the Defense Base Closure and Realignment Commissions in prior BRAC rounds, GAO reports on the status of military Posts and Bases realigned and closed in prior rounds, and information on assistance available to communities with military Posts or Bases that had been realigned or closed. The DOD officials were encouraged to refer the media, community representatives, and other interested parties to the public web site for further information about what happened in prior rounds and the process for BRAC 05. Additional information related to BRAC 05 would become available and posted to the DOD BRAC web site as the process proceeded.

In a report to the US Congress, Secretary of Defense Donald H. Rumsfeld certified that the Department of Defense had about 24-percent of excess military Posts or Base capacity to support the Armed Forces. The US Army has the most that needed to be closed (about 29-percent), followed by the US Air Force (about 24-percent, and the US Navy/USMC (about 21-percent). Secretary Rumsfeld's report stated that if the BRAC 05 round of military Post and Base closures produced a 20-percent reduction, the DOD would see a net savings of about $5 billion by 2011 and reoccurring annual savings of about $8 billion. The four previous military Post and Base closure rounds have now saved our military $6.6 billion each year. Nevertheless, there was a movement to derail the next round of military Post and Base closures by convincing the general public that it was cheaper to keep all military Posts and Bases open and lease land to earn money; thus expanding what is known as Government Owned Contractor Operated (GOCO) facilities.

This action would literally "rob" local communities of business property taxes and rarely produced net profits as cozy relationships resulted in contracts where the Federal Government paid for property maintenance. Small military Posts or Bases were inefficient to operate since each military Post or Base usually had a Housing Office; Equal Opportunity Office; Public Affairs; Chapel; Library; Auto Shop; Medical Dispensary or Hospital; Dental Clinic; Commissary; Post Exchange; Post or Base headquarters; Military Police; Decal Office; Fitness Center; Reception Center; Swimming Pool; Child Care Center; Enlisted and NCO Club; Officers' Club; Teen Club; Family Support Center; Temporary Lodging; Education Center; Dining Hall; Maintenance Office; Golf Course; Theater; Post Office; and various Recreational facilities. Therefore, shifting "tenant" organizations to larger military Posts or Bases with room for growth would save a great deal of money and manpower in the long run, although transferring organizations required money for relocation and some new construction. Reserve, National Guard, and Federal Government civilian activities at closed military Posts or Bases could continue as they do elsewhere without a military landlord. The military Post and Base closures also allowed the elimination of outdated organizations that has been preserved with jobs that were programmed by members of the US Congress.

During March 2005, the BRAC 05 Post and Base closure round began when the President, in conjunction with Congressional leaders, appointed the nine member Base closing Commission. Two months later on May 16th, the Secretary of Defense submitted his list of facilities to be closed. It would take seven members to add a facility to that list, but just a simple majority to remove a military facility. The President may approve that list and send it to the US Congress, or reject it and send it back to the Commission. Neither the US Congress nor the President could make changes to the list. If the President accepted the list, it became law unless the US Congress voted against it within 45-days. This has never happened since Congressmen from spared closure districts would naturally believe the list was valid.

US Army Posts proposed for closure or realignment during 2005 included: Carlisle Barracks, PA; Detroit Arsenal, MI; Fort Belvoir, VA; Fort Buchanan, PR; Fort McPherson, GA; Fort Monmouth ,NJ; Fort Monroe, VA; Fort Polk, LA; Fort

Richardson, AK; Fort Sam Houston, TX; Fort Shafter, HI; Lima Army Tank Plant, OK; Natick Soldier Center, MA; Picatinny Arsenal, NJ; Redstone Arsenal, AL; Rock Island Arsenal, IL; Sierra Army Depot, CA; and Yuma Proving Ground, AZ. US Air Force Bases proposed for closure or realignment during 2005 included: Altus AFB, OK; Beale AFB, CA; Brooks AFB , TX; Cannon AFB , NM; Columbus AFB , MS; Ellsworth AFB, SD; Goodfellow AFB, TX; Grand Forks AFB , ND; Hansom AFB, MA; Kirtland AFB , NM; Los Angeles AFB, CA; McConnell AFB, KS; Nellis AFB, NV; Seymour Johnson AFB, NC (realign); Shaw AFB, SC; and Vance AFB, OK.

US Naval Stations proposed for realignment or closure during 2005 included: Ingleside Naval Station, TX; Naval Postgraduate School, CA; Naval Air Station Meridian, MS; Naval Air Engineering Station Lakehurst, NJ; Naval Recreation Station, Solomons Island; Naval Surface Warfare Center, IN; Naval Surface Warfare Center Dahlgren Division ,VA; Navy Supply Corps School , GA; New Orleans Naval Support Activity, LA; Pascagoula Naval Station, MS; Portsmouth Naval Shipyard, NH; and Saratoga Springs Naval Support Unit, NY. US Naval bases currently proposed for closure or realignment during 2005 included: Marine Corps Logistics Base Albany, GA; Marine Corps Logistics Base, Barstow, CA; Marine Corps Air Station Miramar, CA; Marine Corps Mountain Warfare School, CA; Marine Reserve Support Unit, Kansas City MO; and Marine Corps Recruit Depot San Diego, CA.[36]

Letterman Army Medical Center Downsizing

In addition to the Headquarters, Sixth US Army staff downsizing and realignment issues, a continuous RIF had existed at the Letterman Army Medical Center at the Presidio Post. Since March 1998, the Medical Center had been under RIF procedures because of the Base Closure and Realignment Act of 1988 (Public Law 100-526, Act 102, Stat 2623). By 1995, it was announced that 652 (554 full-time permanent and 98 temporary) positions would be abolished and that the hospital would close. At the onset, 248 authorized positions were abolished. During July 1991, RIF's letters were sent to 219 employees causing 82 separations, seven reassignments, and 46 changes to lower grade. Since the July announcement, the number of involuntarily separated employees declined to 19 through the effort of the DOD Priority Placement Program (PPP), VERA, job fairs, voluntary retirements, and Civil Service employees seeking other employment. Notices were programmed to be delivered with an effective date no later than September 30, 1992, and to temporary employees on August 31, 1992, with an effective date no later than September 30, 1992.

Simultaneous with the Presidio of San Francisco Closure and Realignment Study, the Health Service Command at Houston in Texas conducted a study of the

---

[36]   www.Mather AFB Closure.com

possible realignment of the Letterman Army Medical Center to the Oakland Naval Medical Center at Oak Knoll, and the Letterman Army Institute of Research to US Army medical research facilities elsewhere in the Eastern US. Information regarding study assumptions was not made public, but many of the issues involved in the US Army study were reviewed in hearings by the Legislation and National Security Sub-committee of the House Committee on Government Operations. The testimony in those hearings focused on the specific proposal to close the Letterman Army Medical Center at the Presidio Post, to expand the Oakland Naval Medical Center at Oak Knoll to accommodate US Army patients; and to close the Institute of Research at the Presidio Post and realign to other US Army Medical Research facilities in the Eastern US.

The Sub-committee found certain facts concerning the realignment of the Letterman Army Medical Center that had a higher average daily patient workload, and a higher rate of utilization than Oak Knoll. The annual operating costs at the Letterman Army Medical Center were approximately $1.6 million lower than at Oak Knoll. The cost to make the Letterman Army Medical Center seismically safe would be from $2 to $8 million lower than at Oak Knoll. The closing of the Letterman Army Medical Center would significantly increase annual treatment costs for retired military personnel in the City of San Francisco and Bay Area since most patients would be required to seek private hospital care under the CHAMPUS Program. The closing of the Letterman Army Medical Center would also seriously impair the US Army's ability to recruit and retain Doctors, Nurses, and other medical professional employees.

In addition to these factors, the Letterman Army Medical Center played a key role nationally in the US Army's efforts to keep abreast of developments in the medical field. Because of its location in the City of San Francisco, the Letterman Army Medical Center had developed a close working relationship with San Francisco's many prestigious teaching hospitals. Through the Letterman Army Medical Center, medical personnel in the military services had direct access to nationally prominent consulting Physicians and medical researchers. The Letterman Army Medical Center closure would sever one of the US Army's key links to the civilian medical profession, and reduce its ability to attract and retain highly qualified medical personnel. In severing this link to the rest of the medical profession, the Letterman Army Medical Center closure would affect the entire system of US Army hospitals and post-graduate medical education. The Letterman Army Medical Center closure at the Presidio Post would also have a significant adverse impact on San Francisco's ability to provide emergency medical care following a major earthquake. If this action was taken in conjunction with the realignment of the Headquarters, Sixth US Army staff to Treasure Island, the City of San Francisco citizens would be in a rather precarious position following a serious earthquake. The Headquarters, Sixth US Army staff represented the Federal Government's organization for disaster relief would be stranded on Treasure Island, and the nearest military emergency medical facility would be across the San Francisco Bay with no land access.

The Sub-committee also found certain facts concerning the realignment of the Letterman Army Institute of Research. The closure of the Letterman Army Institute of Research would have an adverse impact as it was the most modern (1976) and versatile research laboratory in the US Army. The Letterman Army Institute of Research provided valuable support services to the Letterman Army Medical Center and should have been retained as long as the Medical Center remained open. The Letterman Army Institute of Research had been underutilized, but had the potential for supporting advanced research projects of the highest medical quality.

The closing of a fairly new medical facility would provide few benefits for the US Army, and would eliminate an important source of employment and medical expertise for the City of San Francisco and Bay Area. Existing US Army policies and procedures for the DOD analysis of the impact of military Post and Base closures could do little more than measure what these impacts would be, and suggest some mitigating measures that would spread out the impact over time. Unless the DOD offered strong, factual arguments for reconsidering these actions, the City of San Francisco and Bay Area was likely to suffer from irreversible impacts. At best, these socioeconomic and physical dislocations would be felt at different time periods, but the primary and secondary impacts would, nevertheless, be felt throughout the various neighborhoods of the City of San Francisco and Bay Area.

The GSA was also under increasing pressure in the City of San Francisco and Bay Area to maintain the leases already in existence due to increased rental costs. They indicated that they would welcome any efforts to increase the number of Federal Government agencies as tenants at the Presidio of San Francisco. There was sound operational and socioeconomic justification for the US Army to remain at the Presidio Post. The justification was even stronger by using efficiently all available resources such as space, military personnel, Civil Service employees, repair and maintenance services. During 1994, the Headquarters, Sixth US Army staff; however, was ordered to realign at Fort Carson in Colorado as Treasure Island was found to be a physically undesirable site.

Health Services Command Involvement

Stemming from the Committee's concern about information on the US Navy Medical Center at Oak Knoll and the Letterman Army Medical Center, the Committee decided to make a telephone call directly to the DOD to bring their concerns to an appropriate level of DOD management. The Committee did not ask the Headquarters, Sixth US Army staff for the information they wanted, nor did the Committee inform the Headquarters, Sixth US Army staff of their difficulties in obtaining the information they wanted because they felt that the Headquarters, Sixth US Army staff was not as close to the Letterman Army Medical Center Study as they were to the Presidio of San Francisco Closure and Realignment Study. On April 5, 1979, one of the members on the steering

Committee called the DOD to obtain the requested information and not satisfied called a contact on the White House that subsequently notified the DOD of the inquiry and directed the DOD to coordinate with the Mayor's "Save the Presidio" Committee in San Francisco and provide what information the DOD was authorized to release. On April 12, 1979, representatives from the US Army staff from the Health Services Command were in the City of San Francisco to brief the Mayor's "Save the Presidio" Committee.

The Closure and Realignment Study for the Letterman Army Medical Center and the Letterman Army Institute of Research was conducted by the Health Services Command located at San Antonio in Texas. The Health Services Command considered alternative plans ranging all the way from increasing the current use of hospital facilities to closing them. Some of the possibilities considered included realigning the Oakland Naval Medical Center at Oak Knoll, and transferring research functions to other US Army Centers in Maryland and Washington, DC. The Headquarters, Sixth US Army staff did not understand why the eminently successful procedures wherein the Mayor's "Save the Presidio" Committee cooperation with the Headquarters, Sixth US Army staff was disregarded. The new approach would only provide the typical "scrubbed down" publicly releasable generalizations that anyone could have provided the Committee. Certainly this approach irritated those in the DOD whom, in the best interests of the City of San Francisco, should not have been irritated. Someone in the expanded steering Committee may have been playing "politics" with this subject by trying to become the sole key player and communicator on the City of San Francisco's behalf. If the latest initiative was an example of how the Mayor's "Save the Presidio" Committee would proceed in the future, they would soon realize considerably less success than they had in the past with the assistance of the Headquarters, Sixth US Army staff. Successful cooperation as in the past might have been preferable to the questionable procedures of this latest initiative.[37]

Committee Involvement and Strategy

On April 26, 1978, and up to the time of the DA announcement that it was formally considering the proposal to close the Presidio of San Francisco, the Headquarters, Sixth US Army staff had been a good neighbor to the citizens of the City of San Francisco and Bay Area since 1847. During 1994, this proposal would realign the Headquarters, Sixth US Army staff to Treasure Island; discontinue the Presidio Garrison; and transfer the Presidio Garrison's repair and maintenance support mission and functions to the US National Park Service. Mayor Moscone decided that he would like the City of San Francisco to continue the relationship and would work with the DOD to develop more effective ways to reduce US Army

[37] Memorandum from Colonel H. Gordon Waite, Chief, Public Affairs, Headquarters, Sixth US Army, Presidio of San Francisco, Subject: "Mayor's Committee to 'Save the Presidio'" April 10, 1979.

expenditures in the City of San Francisco and Bay Area. If the Presidio Post would close, the land would revert to the US National Park Service after it was deemed excess to the US Army and other Federal Government agencies. Because of limited funds and manpower available to the US National Park Service, the removal of military personnel and Civil Service employees would undoubtedly have an adverse impact on the residential communities forming the South and East boundaries of the Presidio Post. Landscaping, trees, and shrubbery could not possibly be maintained, and the available of Military Police patrols would be drastically reduced.

Early in the planning stage, General Forrester being the senior US Army Commander in the Western US, had a meeting with the newly appointed Mayor Dianne Feinstein of San Francisco to provide her with a considerable amount of useful background information pertaining to the proposed realignment of the Headquarters, Sixth US Army staff to Treasure Island, discontinuance of the Presidio Garrison, and the transfer of the Presidio Garrison's repair and maintenance support mission and functions to the US National Park Service. However, the Presidio of San Francisco Closure and Realignment Study was being reviewed and amended by the US Army Forces Command located at Atlanta in Georgia. The US Army Forces Command was studying alternative plans ranging from a status quo to a RIF that would leave only military quarters and some US Army Reserve facilities at the Presidio Post in the hands of the US Army. In other words, the Presidio Post would revert to a status similar to that currently found at the Fort Mason Post in California. If the Headquarters, Sixth US Army staff would come under realignment, and the Presidio Post would come under BRAC closure, many of the tenant military organizations located at the Presidio Post would have to move to Fort Lewis in Washington, Fort Ord in California, and Fort Carson in Colorado.

The Headquarters, Sixth US Army staff was originally scheduled to be realigned to Treasure Island where the US Navy had over several years reduced its need for the use of buildings and facilities. When the US Army Forces Command and the Health Service Command completed their study, recommendations with study data were forwarded to the DA. The DA reviewed the study and forwarded recommendations to the DOD. When the DOD approved the recommendations, the DA would announce a "Preferred Alternative" and provide complete environmental and decision information to the US Congress, State of California, and the City of San Francisco officials. This announcement was projected for April 1979. A period of time was provided for local study and recommendations. During this time, dialogue with Federal Government agencies at Washington, DC would be appropriate and constructive. In the meantime, information or briefings on releasable information and technical advice would be provided to the City of San Francisco officials and other interested parties.[38]

General Forrester assisted in this endeavor by providing appropriate information and technical advice to allow the "Save the Presidio" Committee and the City of San Francisco officials to participate in the decision making process. As demonstration of the concern of San Francisco citizens over the proposed Presidio Closure and Relocation Study, Mayor Moscone visited Washington, DC shortly after the final DOD decision was announced. Mayor Moscone secured assurances from the Secretary of Defense and local members of the US Congress that the City's interests would be considered and that the City of San Francisco would be able to participate in the decision making process. The prior President of the Board of Supervisors, Ms. Dianne Feinstein, sponsored a resolution opposing the Presidio Post closure and realignment that was passed by the Board and forwarded to the Secretary of Defense. During December 1979, Mayor Moscone wrote to the Secretary of Defense reaffirming the City's adamant opposition to the realignment and requested that the City of San Francisco's President's Economic Adjustment Committee undertake a separate analysis where the City of San Francisco could participate in the final outcome.

The Economic Adjustment Committee responded that it would assist the City of San Francisco in a number of ways. Many interested organizations and groups expressed their concern and their commitment to assist the City of San Francisco. Some organizations, such as the Fort Point and Army Museum Associations had passed resolutions opposing the proposed realignment and Presidio Post closure, and forwarded their resolutions to officials in Washington, DC. Others organizations, such as the San Francisco Planning and Urban Research Association (SPUR), wrote letters dealing with specific subjects such as the Environmental Impact Study to specific agencies that would deal with these subjects. Several groups raised money to support opposition efforts. This demonstration of interest was encouraging but would be less effective if continued on an ad hoc basis rather than a coordinated and organized effort.

The City of San Francisco wrote letters to many San Francisco organizations and citizens that may have been interested in the Presidio of San Francisco realignment or closure, and asked if they would be willing to join the City's "Save the Presidio" Committee and pool collective resources and talents. Informal coordination by members of the Committee with some key organizations such as the 1100 members Association of the US Army and Presidio Post Society indicated a very positive response and a pledge of full cooperation. The City of San Francisco intended to organize the Committee fully and provide it with sufficient resources to assess and articulate the interests of the community. Based

---

[38] Letter from Lieutenant General Eugene P. Forrester, Commander, Sixth US Army, Presidio of San Francisco, to (the Honorable Dianne Feinstein, Mayor, City of San Francisco), December 21, 1978.

on the initial two mailings, the "Save the Presidio" Committee membership listed five hundred names and had amassed $6 thousand in contributions to support its activities. During January 1979, the Committee contracted with the leading international accounting and management firm of Touche Ross & Company to conduct a separate study for the City of San Francisco.

The initial study results that Touche Ross & Company had agreed to undertake for only $15 thousand was only half completed; however, the results were impressive. Based on their initial findings, the Mayor of San Francisco wrote a letter to the Secretaries of the US Army, Defense, and Interior informing them of the manner in which the City of San Francisco was organized and proceeding, as-well-as outlining what she considered to be the right of participation by the City of San Francisco. The Committee worked with the President's Inter Agency Economic Adjustment Committee on separate studies. The City of San Francisco officials obtained accurate, up-to-date seismic analyses of the Sites being considered by the initial study, and determined the significant environmental aspects to be studied in detail. The City of San Francisco directed considerable effort to an analysis of better, more-efficient use of the Presidio of San Francisco while retaining its environmental and historical integrity. The Committee and the Headquarters, Sixth US Army staff advocated communications on the Presidio Post closure to keep the City of San Francisco officials and the public informed; and the City of San Francisco officials tried hard to keep the public informed. The City of San Francisco officials had marshaled and used all of the political influence that represented the interests and desires of the citizens who would be affected by the Headquarters, Sixth US Army staff proposed realignment to Treasure Island; the Presidio Garrison discontinuance; and the transfer of the Presidio Garrison's repair and maintenance support mission to the US National Park Service. The City of San Francisco officials were convinced that this was a serious study on the part of the DOD that should not be taken lightly or considered one that would be easily overcome. The City of San Francisco officials intended that the Committee would be an effective representative of the City of San Francisco's interest.

In order to complete the City of San Francisco's study and provide money for a Management Consultant to assist in the future, as-well-as covering mailing and administrative costs, the City of San Francisco officials asked for additional contributions from concerned citizens to bring the "Save the Presidio" Committee fund to $20 thousand. The City of San Francisco officials asked its citizens to contribute money to assist in their continued effort to "Save the Presidio" and keep the public informed of the progress made. In the meantime, the City of San Francisco officials urged its citizens to write to their Senators and Representatives to let them know how many of their constituents were interested in saving this beautiful and historical part of the City of San Francisco.

Touche Ross & Company Involvement

On January 23, 1979, the Touche Ross & Company corresponded with the "Save the Presidio" Committee to discuss their concerns regarding the Headquarters, Sixth US Army staff proposed realignment; the Presidio Garrison discontinuance; and the transfer of the Presidio Garrison repair and maintenance support mission to the US National Park Service. They outlined their understanding of the situation and described the Management Consultant assistance they would provide to the "Save the Presidio" Committee. The Committee had requested an independent, objective study of the continued use of the Presidio of San Francisco and the Letterman Army Medical Center as a military Installation. The investigation was needed to assist the City of San Francisco and Bay Area representatives to respond to the DOD proposals for the Presidio Post closure, and the realignment of military tenant organizations at the Presidio Post.[39]

What the "Save the Presidio" Committee wanted was a Management Consultant from Touche Ross & Company to analyze and define the problems; articulated in such a manner that the casual and underlying mechanisms of the Presidio of San Francisco closure and realignment problems were understood; and then recommend remedial action. The Management Consultant would employ an extensive repertory of instrumentation to use as flexible as possible; use situations as they developed spontaneously to work through the tensions and resistance that are normally associated with them; and use him as a role model. The role of the Management Consultant made it sound more ambiguous and vague than the consulting process. This probably reflected reality for in the Management Consultant's approach, the processes of change and the change agent's interventions were less systematic and less programmed than in either the consulting or in the applied-research program. The behavior of different Management Consultants do vary, but they would typically serve as observers of the "process" and interpreters of the dynamics of the Committee's interactions to the degree that the Committee would express a readiness for such intervention. The Management Consultant encouraged the Committee to take careful risks, a step at a time, and to experiment with new behavior at the Committee level of support. Thus, the Management Consultant attempted to stimulate new behavior and also protect the membership of the Committee.

The Management Consultant played a much broader role in periodic data gathering And diagnosis, and in joint long-range planning. The key issues required an analysis of whether the closing of the Presidio of San Francisco was a sound business decision. Comments from the "Save the Presidio" Committee and the citizens of San Francisco and Bay Area were extremely important and were taken into account. In the latter case, the Management Consultant examined the desirability of the proposed realignment of the Headquarters, Sixth US

---

[39] Letter from Touche Ross & Company, San Francisco, California, to (Mr. William D. Evers, President, Committee to "Save the Presidio," January 23, 1979.

Army staff to Treasure Island with the point of view of the City of San Francisco. In addition, the Touche Ross & Company would document the process to be followed if Treasure Island was declared surplus. The Touche Ross & Company presented their analysis in a series of Fact Sheets summarizing the arguments and supporting data for each of the items indicated above. They reviewed the analysis with the Committee at the end of the phase of the engagement and determined if further research of the facts were required. During the last three to four-weeks of the investigation, the Management Consultant concentrated on developing a strategy for the City of San Francisco officials to respond to the DOD proposals. Specifically, the Management Consultant would work with the Committee to identify key arguments to be used by the City of San Francisco. The Touché Ross & Company agreed to provide up to three-days of effort at any time to assist the "Save the Presidio" Committee to respond to specific DOD studies and recommendations. They undertook the engagement with the understanding that if the DOD proposals substantially changed during the course of the project, it would be necessary to enlarge the scope of their review and renegotiate a new agreement.[40]

San Francisco Planning and Urban Research Association (SPUR) Intervention

On December 15, 1978, coinciding with the City of San Francisco's "Save the Presidio" Committee actions, Mr. John H. Jacobs, Executive Director of SPUR, corresponded with Dr. Jan F. Sassaman, Ph.D. of the Technical Staff of Environmental Assessment and Planning at McLean in Virginia. SPUR was concerned that the Environmental Impact Statement that was to be completed by the Headquarters, Sixth US Army staff would certainly consider the total public cost of any DOD action attendant to the proposed Headquarters, Sixth US Army staff realignment; the Presidio Garrison discontinuance; the transfer of the Presidio of San Francisco to the US National Park Service; and the required increase of US National Park Service budget necessary to operate and maintain the Presidio Post as a safe recreational area to include the preservation of historically significant buildings. SPUR had maintained a continuing and intensive interest in the Presidio Post for the past 20-years. SPUR vigorously objected over the past several years to numerous proposed uses of the Presidio Post such as cheap housing Sites for other Federal Government agencies for socioeconomic reasons. SPUR contested the DOD plans to use the Presidio Post far more intensively as a housing Site than that currently existed under GSA contracts.

In short, the relationship with the US Army officials over many years was not always a cordial one. This past relationship gave more emphasis to the belief that

---

[40] Letter from Lieutenant General Eugene P. Forrester, Commander, Sixth US Army, Presidio of San Francisco, to (General Robert M. Shoemaker, Commander, US Army Forces Command, Atlanta, Georgia), March 2, 1979.

the military presence at the Presidio of San Francisco was highly desirable and should continue as beneficial both to the City of San Francisco and the US Army in the indefinite future. In their view, any decision to remove all or a part of military activities from the Presidio Post could only be regarded as highly controversial. Undoubtedly others spoke of the adverse socioeconomic impact removal of this large base of employment in the City of San Francisco and Bay Area would have; therefore, SPUR did not elaborate on this, but simply stated that they believed "it would be inimical to the interests of the City of San Francisco and Bay Area for the US Army to remain at the Presidio Post."

The SPUR organization thought the most economical move in terms of expenditure of public entity dollars would appear to be either the release of US Navy property at Treasure Inland presently vacant and available, or the transfer of Treasure Island and its facilities to the City of San Francisco. Because of the limited access that made it a precarious military Installation, it would lend itself to the development of a senior citizen facility with easily and cheaply maintained security. The City of San Francisco and Bay Area was a desired place of residence for retired and well-aged personnel; however, facilities to accommodate the demand were quite inadequate. Such a consolidation of the Presidio of San Francisco and the elimination of needless expense of maintaining a separate military Post would serve the civilian population exceedingly well by providing facilities for an accommodated segment of the population.[41]

US National Park Service accepts Responsibility for the Presidio

Upon implementation of the Presidio of San Francisco Closure and Realignment Study proposal, the Presidio Post would become the joint responsibility of the US Army and the US National Park Service. Under the law establishing the Golden Gate National Recreational Area, any land at the Presidio of San Francisco declared excess to the US Army or other Federal Government agencies needs would be transferred to the US National Park Service. The Superintendent of the Golden Gate National Recreational Area estimated that restoration and repair of the Presidio Post facilities that would be released after theHeadquarters, Sixth US Army staff realignment would cost approximately $9.2 million, and that the continued repair and maintenance costs would cost approximately $2.5 million annually. These costs were not included in the US Army's study, but were later considered before the final closure decision was reached on the realignment of the Headquarters, Sixth US Army staff.

It would appear on the surface that the Headquarters, Sixth US Army was dumping a "white elephant" on the Department of the Interior. A full Environmental

---

[41] Letter from Mr. John H. Jacobs, Executive Director, SPUR, San Francisco, California, to (Dr. Jan F. Sassaman, Ph. D., McLean, Virginia), December 15, 1978.

Assessment Study would be needed to be accomplished by the US Corps of Engineers that would determine if hundreds of millions of dollars would be required to clean-up the mess made by 200-years of military occupation. For example, repaving the miles of roads on the Presidio of San Francisco would run into the tens of millions of dollars to repair and repave. Of course the Department of the Interior would try to recoup this cost from the US Army; however, it would eventually cost the US taxpayer in the end. On the other hand, the Golden Gate National Park Service would inherit one of the richest pieces of property in the Country where lots overlooking the Golden Gate Bridge could sell for $1 million each. These assets were lost, however, where previous law placed new minor restrictions on new construction on the Presidio Post and where amendments placed severe restrictions on new construction of all lands within the Presidio Post. As an example, "Members of the US Congress also prevented military Post and Base closings by refusing to authorize or appropriate US Air Force money to even study the Mather AFB closure in California."[42]

The Presidio of San Francisco Closure and Realignment Study became a significant issue for the Headquarters, Sixth US Army staff and the City of San Francisco. The study would be a serious, probably the most serious analysis that the Headquarters, Sixth US Army staff had ever undergone. It was not taken lightly for the best interests of all parties to be served. The "Save the Presidio" Committee was provided complete assistance, advice, and appropriate information to enable the Committee to fulfill their responsibilities and was assured that City of San Francisco officials would have the opportunity to participate in the decision making process. In furtherance of these objectives, members of the Headquarters, Sixth US Army staff worked with Mr. J. Edward Fleishell and Mr. Mark Buellin of the "Save the Presidio" Committee to draft a Memorandum of Understanding (MOU) that spelled out the manner of cooperation. Certain actions such as public petitioning of members of the US Congress were premature and not recommended in that the Study had not yet been finalized and forwarded by the US Army Forces Command to the DA.

Therefore, no one in Washington, DC knew what Major Command recommendations were nor did they know the details of the study's findings. Furthermore, the environmental impact assessment that was being performed by a contract civilian firm had not been completed and forwarded to the DA. Section 317(C), H.R. 12536 as amended, was signed into law on October 12, 1989. After reviewing the legislation, the DA informed OMB that new construction at the Presidio of San Francisco that was under the jurisdiction and control of the DA would be prohibited by Section 317(B) of the Enrolled Enactment. The DA was not previously given the opportunity to comment on this section. Although this provision may have restricted future performance of DOD missions at the Presidio Post, the DA did not request a change in the Enrolled Enactment since the US

---

[42] David S. Sorenson, "Shutting Down the Cold War: The Politics of Military Base Closure." (St. Martin's Press, New York, July 1998),

Congress in approving any new construction at the Presidio Post that might have been required could determine whether the prohibition should be overridden. In short, the DA did not decide to ask for a change in the law, but rather to continue planning and, if and when appropriate, request that the prohibition be wavered for construction where deemed necessary.

The previous law placed minor restrictions on new construction at the Presidio of San Francisco. The new amendment placed severe restrictions on new construction on all lands within the Presidio of San Francisco. The citizens of the City of San Francisco would gain little to transfer portions of the Presidio Post to the Golden Gate National Recreation Area. Almost 90-percent of the presiding 1440-acres was in open space and 75-miles of scenic trails and roadways were used daily by the general public. Over 300,000 public visitors tour the historic buildings on the military Installation, and over 70,000 retired military families were using Presidio Post support facilities. In short, the Presidio Post was already an important recreational facility for the City of San Francisco. The proposed Headquarters, Sixth US Army staff would not enhance public use after realignment and finally to its disestablishment.[43]

Concluding Comments

Monitoring and critiquing the primary elements of the Presidio of San Francisco Closure and Realignment Study while in motion and operation afforded a good evaluation of the DOD management theory and assumptions of a military Post or Base closure or relocation. In Chapter II, this author was motivated to write from an additional perspective what learned professors call the underlying characteristics, distinguishing features, foundations, or theoretical and practical underpinning in Organizational Development (OD). The plan could be characterized in several ways; as a process, as a form of applied Behavioral Science, as a normative change, and as incorporating a systems approach to a military organization. The results of the Presidio of San Francisco Closure and Realignment Study rested on a number of assumptions about Federal Government employees as individuals, as in groups, as in the total system, about the transitional nature of organization improvement, and about values. These assumptions tended to be humanistic, developmental, and optimistic. Assumptions and values held by the DOD; however, needed to be more explicit, for both enhancing working relationships with the City of San Francisco officials and for continuous review and evaluation.

The reason for a smoother process at the top tier was the improved service base evaluation process. The US Army first categorized its Posts and Bases by "mission category" that allowed a ranking of them by military importance. Those

---

[43]   Letter from Mayor Dianne Feinstein, City of San Francisco, to (the Honorable Clifford L. Alexander, Jr., Secretary of the Army, Washington, DC), March 16, 1979.

categories included: (1) fighting Installations; (2) training Posts and Bases; (3) industrial Posts and Bases; and (4) training Installations. However, the US Army still recommended the Fort Ord Post for closure; although it ranked 10ᵗʰ out of 13 military Posts.[44] As with any change effort, the chance to step back and assess what had occurred was critical. This assessment had two purposes. First, to ensure that the level and type of intervention was appropriate and correct. Second, to lay the ground work for institutionalizing OD practices into the routine of the organization. The discussion may well conclude that OD efforts in the public sector were a waste of time.

The list of constraints and inhibitions seemed insurmountable. Yet, those very difficulties were the justification for a search for better pairing of OD techniques and public sector management practices that suffered from poor management; low morale; loss of public support; and little public credibility is a military organization that had fallen into destructive habits and patterns, and furthermore, could see no way out from such behaviors. The readiness of the military Installation to accept changes implied by an OD process was necessarily proceeded by a change in these destructive habits and behaviors. In particular, the leadership needed to see an OD intervention through to institutionalization was likely absent from a military Installation that was in such serious need of revitalization. An OD intervention was part of the second phase of a revitalization process; and to introduce them earlier would be to risk failure.

The goal and objectives were to improve the overall capacity of the Installation to be effective that was both a managerial and political judgment. The OD process was oriented toward meeting both definitions as used by the Installation.[45] If there was anything that experience had taught, was that the problems, the possibilities, and public opinion that the Executive Board dealt with were in a state of constant flux and that, consequently, the policies that constitute a Federal Government planning program should have undergone continuing study and alteration. This was one meaning of the often repeated statement that Federal Government planning must be in a "continuous process." The experience of the 1980s and 1990s left no doubt that a Presidio of San Francisco Closure and Realignment Study that was not kept up-to-date would become worse than useless. Change could actually have been impeded. Some managers and supervisors concluded that Federal Government planning was more likely to succeed without a plan, or at least, without a comprehensive plan that was made publicly available. The danger of obsolescence, some supervisors and managers concluded, outweighed the study's advantages.

---

[44] David S. Sorenson, "Shutting Down the Cold War: The Politics of Military Base Closure." (St. Martin's Press, New York, July 1998), pp. 98.

[45] Raymond W. Cox III, Susan J. Buck, and Betty M. Morgan, "Public Administration in Theory and Practice," (Prentice-Hall, Inc., 1994), pp. 206-207.

However, it was apparent that there were techniques for keeping the Presidio of San Francisco Closure and Realignment Study current, and for providing a continuous re-examination of policy. The annual review and amendment procedure, along with periodic fundamental reconsideration of the study took its importance from the fact that recognized the need for constant study and frequent change, and provided a device for systematic alteration of the plan. The Executive Board was commended for its conformance with the plan, and the Executive Board's role in the preparation of the budget served the same general purpose.

Perhaps of even greater importance was the fact that the documentation of a deliberately formulated and explicitly stated policy in a study, that had been adopted by the Executive Board as an official Presidio of San Francisco policy document, that would expose inconsistencies; highlight the need for bringing former policy decisions into line with current thinking; and require Executive Board physical development issues. A study of this magnitude, given a systematic application of the above techniques should have become an instrument of alert reassessment of policy, and a means for maintaining Presidio Post plans abreast of changing times. The Presidio of San Francisco Closure and Realignment Study was not a perfect or ideal organizational intervention, but a result of what was initiated in DOD organizational development efforts. Although Post and Base Closure and Realignment programs would vary in their comprehensiveness, most of the military Posts and Bases would have many common features. The genius in creating the "Save the Presidio" Committee was that the perceptions, feelings, and cognitive inputs of Committee members were tapped to build an optimal and evolving organizational design for the unique circumstances faced by military personnel and Civil Service employees stationed at the Presidio of San Francisco.

The thrust of Committee activities was responsive to the data not to impose an organic system. In the process, the organization was likely to become more organic. The administration and the underlying assumptions of a wide variety of organizational sub-systems, and the formal aspects of the human social sub-system in particular, needed to be congruent with the realignment effort if sustained organizational improvements were to occur as a result of Committee action. This Chapter has looked closely at many of the techniques; at underlying management theory and assumptions; and at some of the pitfalls and challenges in an attempt to improve organizational realignment through behavioral science methods. When the interventions were finally based on appropriate diagnosis and historical workload, and utilized in a systematic, strategic fashion, they did assist the Headquarters, Sixth US Army staff in identifying and recommending organizational improvements.

The setting of this Case Study was a real military organization located within the City of San Francisco. Although the military setting was located on the Presidio of San Francisco, the setting could have been any of a wide range of military Installations or Federal Government agencies s all of which could have offered an appropriate setting for Organizational Effectiveness Programs. The locus of course is where there is a Post or Base that primarily has a repair and maintenance support mission; supports administrative organizations; that do not seek or embrace internal improvement; there are more opportunities for the bureaucracy to implement military Post or Base closures or realignments. Because the Presidio Post happened to primarily support a Headquarters organization and a few tenant organizations, the Presidio Post became a prime target for the Headquarters, Sixth US Army staff realignment to Treasure Island; the Presidio Garrison discontinuance; and the transfer of the Presidio Post repair and maintenance support mission to the US National Park Service.

In sum, the Presidio of San Francisco was first identified for closure by BRAC 88 intervention. However, the Presidio Post was only one of several military Posts and Bases that enjoyed a temporary respite after BRAC 93. The BRAC 93 continued to look at the Presidio Post closure decision again and again, and made fundamental changes to it. As a consequence, the Presidio Post got a new lease on life and a new set of problems. It would again be considered during BRAC 95 when it became apparent that even the BRAC 93 solution was inadequate. Few other military Posts or Bases held as much history as did the Presidio Post. As it turned out; however, the thought that the savings of realigning the Headquarters, Sixth US Army staff to Treasure Island became quite small. So a compromise was reached proposing to retain and consolidate the Headquarters. Sixth Army staff with the Presidio Garrison, while concurrently transferring the Presidio of San Francisco to the US National Park Service. The Presidio Post would be transferred from the US Army to the US National Park Service in the hope of preserving and developing the historical military Post.

During 1991, while operating under the guise of the US National Park Service, it would solicit some rather interesting proposals for non-commercial activities at the Presidio of San Francisco. The US National Park Service; however, found itself with inadequate resources to adequately repair and maintain the Presidio Post. To the rescue came Representative Nancy Pelosi (D-CA), who represented California's Eight District. Representative Pelosi attempted to get legislation through the US Congress that would create an independent agency to repair and maintain the Presidio Post as early as 1994. In its final form, the Bill created a seven member board appointed by the President to oversee the leasing of historic buildings to generate funds.[46]

The US Congress had established the BRAC 05 Commission to ensure the integrity of the military Post and Base closure and realignment process. On May 13, 2005, as directed by statute, the Commission was charged to provide an objective, non-partisan, and independent review and analysis of the list of military Installations recommend by the DOD. The recommendations provided by the DOD were extremely complex and interrelated, and would require an in-depth

---

[46] David S. Sorenson, "Shutting Down the Cold War: The Politics of Military Base Closure." (St. Martin's Press, New York, July 1998), pp. 144-151.

analysis and careful attention to detail. The Commission would follow a fair, open, and equitable process as set forth by statute. The Commission's mission was to assess whether the DOD recommendations substantially did not deviate from the Congressional criteria used to evaluate each military Post or Base proposed for closure or realignment. While giving priority to the DOD criteria of military value, the Commission did take into account the human impact of military Post and Base closures or realignments, and considered the possible environmental and other socioeconomic effects on the surrounding communities.

CHAPTER X

Methodology

The ultimate success of the Headquarters, Sixth US Army staff mission and functions depended on the ability of the Program Manager and Functional Manager to secure the willingness and desires of military personnel and Civil Service employees to give their best efforts in furthering the goal, objectives, and ideas that the Headquarters, Sixth US Army staff had been established. The responsibility of building strong group morale rested with each person in a managerial or supervisory capacity.

The Program Manager would be assisted in accomplishing the mission and functionss by the Human Resource Office staff comprised of Personnel Specialists in various functions of Human Resources. The most important factor in obtaining maximum sustained output was the employee's emotional reaction. That is, feelings toward the workload, associates, managers, supervisors, and the military organization. The Program Manager was accountable to the Executive Board for the planning and execution of programs imposed by the US Army, and for all aspects relating to performance of the assigned workload and was accordingly authorized to negotiate task assignments, review performance, and re-orient existing assignments as appropriate to workload requirements and socioeconomic resource constraints. The Program Manager was authorized to specify the scope and nature of task assignments to supporting functions, and to select among alternative ways of accomplishing program objectives. The Program Manager was responsible for maintaining close liaison with the Resource Management Office and Comptroller activities on these related matters.

The Functional Manager was accountable for the development and maintenance of the functional capability commensurate with both the qualitative and quantitative requirements of assigned and forecasted shortcomings, and for initiating appropriate remedies. The Functional Manager was required to determine manpower requirements, qualifications; disciplines; equipment resources; facility needs in terms of current and future capabilities; and to negotiate support of task assignments on the basis of improved socioeconomic resource constraints. The Functional Manager was accountable to the Program Manager for accomplishing assigned tasks to included output, quality, and matters of scope and timeliness. The Functional Manager was accountable to the Program Manager for accomplishing task assignments on time and within budget constraints, and generally for optimizing the use of assigned manpower and material resources. The Functional Manager was, accordingly, authorized to select military personnel and Civil Service employees to be assigned specific workload assignments, establish priority and scheduling mechanisms, and reject or negotiate modification of proposed assignments that exceeded the capability or capacity to perform. The Functional Manager was further authorized to determine the in-house contractor mix in their area, within the overall policy constraints established by managers and the Executive Board.

The emotional reaction of Civil Service employees during the Presidio of San Francisco Closure and Realignment Study had more effect on production than any other combination of physical working conditions that were tried, even more than the amount of salary received. This factor is known as "morale." Morale can be obtained only by good supervision using established management policies, and practices. Morale created in the employees is a feeling of personal satisfaction in their work, and a pleasant personal relationship among all those who would be associated in the reorganization. The results in terms of the employees were enthusiasm about the things the employees and their groups were accomplishing, and a desire to cooperate with those with whom the employees associated with.

It was the responsibility of the Executive Board to assist each and every supervisor and manager in building this spirit into a working team. The foremost task was the Personnel Management of employees, for high-caliber and strongly motivated employees constitute the most valuable asset of any large scale military organization. The enthusiasm, good will, and cooperation derived from sound conceptions about this vital resource were the basis for human satisfaction, improved operations, and for long range effectiveness. With payrolls comprising the largest single item in the operating budget of the Headquarters, Sixth US Army staff, Personnel Management had to be in the forefront of the Command goal and objectives. As the Headquarters, Sixth US Army staff reorganization became more complex under the proposed consolidation of the Headquarters, Sixth US Army staff with the Presidio Garrison, or a realignment of the Headquarters, Sixth US Army staff to Treasure Island with the concurrent discontinuance of the Presidio Garrison, the policies and relationships that made up the Human Resource Office required more attention and support from Command.

The management control process of the Executive Board, supervisors, and managers at the Presidio of San Francisco after the first RIF took maximum advantage of the two dimensional visibility afforded by the Matrix or Program Manager concept of organization. In this context, the Program Manager was in effect a management control tool that was continuously assessing performance relative to cost. The workload planning, assignments, and execution processes, together with the resources utilization process, were tailored to provide both the Program Manager and the Functional Manager with feedback information to allow adjustments in direction. For workloads that involved only operating support services, maintenance, repair, conceptualization was performed by the sponsor (user), and functional tasking was therefore inherent in the support request, that is, in the form of a Program Requirement Document (PRD).

The Program Manager's role was to ensure that support requirements were consistent with the functional capabilities and that shortcomings were properly addressed in terms of reduced requirements or increased capability development. For engineering cognizance workload, the Program Manager was responsible for conceptualizing US Army-wide engineering cognizance projects. In this process, the Program Manager considered unique capabilities, costs, responsiveness, and other relevant factors as engineering cognizance management agents. Through the use of participating field activities and private contractors, the in-house capability at the Presidio of San Francisco was greatly augmented. The Program Manager and the Functional Manager were responsible jointly for the quality of workload planning and execution.

The Personnel Study

Since December 1988, over three-years had passed when the Presidio of San Francisco Closure and Realignment Study were announced. On April 1, 1991, the Headquarters, Sixth US Army reached the 18-month deadline prior to the planned RIF of Civil Service employees at the Headquarters, Sixth US Army staff. Permanent promotions and appointments were not authorized. Hiring was limited to details, temporary promotions, and temporary appointments. On October 1, 1991, the Headquarters, Sixth US Army staff reached the 12-month plateau prior to the planned request for RIF and VERA. The Human Resource Office needed to identify employees eligible for retirement prior to conducting a mock RIF and to request DA approval and authority for RIF and relocation actions.

Effective September 30, 1992, the Headquarters, Sixth US Army staff underwent a major RIF as it downsized its strength to accommodate the loss of the Reserve forces mission. On October 1, 1997, by direction of the US Congress, the DA established the US Army Reserve Command. Since October 12, 1990, mission and functions for the Reserve force would be assumed by the newly established US Army Reserve Command. During October 1, 1990 through September 30, 1992, mission and functions of the Headquarters, Sixth US Army staff was significantly downsized. The Headquarters, Sixth US Army would no longer be resourced to maintain the headquarters staffing level beyond September 30, 1992. On September 5, 1991, a request for VERA for the Headquarters, Sixth US Army was submitted to the US Army Forces Command.[47] The request was based on the assumption, supported by the data collected from Civil Service employees, that VERA would lessen the adverse impact on the Civil Service employees during the transition to the US Army Reserve Command and the downsizing of the Headquarters, Sixth US Army staff. Effective September 30, 1992, a total of

---

[47] Letter from Colonel T. M. Crocetti, DCS/Personnel, Headquarters, Sixth US Army, Presidio of San Francisco, Subject: "Request for Voluntary Retirement Authority," to (US Total Army Personnel Command, Washington, DC), September 5, 1991.

127 of the 199 authorized Civil Service employee positions would be abolished, resulting in a RIF of approximately 96 permanent Civil Service employees.

On October 9, 1991, the reduction of permanent Civil Service positions warranted a request to OPM for RIF authority.[48] Colonel T. M. Crocetti, Deputy Chief of Staff for Personnel enclosed a questionnaire entitled Position and Personnel Impact (See Appendixes, Appendix C), a questionnaire entitled Reduction-in-Force (See Appendixes, Appendix D), and a copy of the Rights and Benefits of Civilian Employees (See Appendixes, Appendix F). Since the collective impact was expected to result in the involuntary separation of more than 50 or more permanent Civil Service employees, or 10-percent of the permanent work force at the Headquarters, Sixth US Army staff, the separation rule would be applicable. A request to the DOD Zone IV Coordinator for early registration in the DOD PPP was subsequently approved by the Coordinator who was responsible for the Western part of the US geographic area of responsibility.

Although the Headquarters, Sixth US Army did not received OPM approval to conduct a RIF in the Civil Service employee workforce because it was an election year, the US Army Forces Command approval was obtained to proceed with the RIF simply because the Headquarters, Sixth US Army Civil Service employee on-board strength dropped below the 50 Civil Service employee threshold. The Headquarters, Sixth US Army staff lost an estimated 127 Civil Service employees out of 199 authorized as a result of downsizing the Headquarters, Sixth US Army staff because of the transfer of mission and functions to the newly established US Army Reserve Command. These estimates were based on projected Force Structure changes; reductions in programs; projected funded workload; and the President's Fiscal Year 1992 budget. If further budget reductions were made, additional Civil Service employee reductions would be expected. Effective September 30, 1992, the planned RIF was primarily due to substantial Fiscal Year 1992 budget reductions that reduced Civil Service workforce authorizations.

Military organizations everywhere have become so big and so essential, and yet so difficult to control, that the Federal Government with all its degree of development and sophistication was still looking for answers to the perplexing questions of Personnel Management. Studies and recommendations for administrative reform were forthcoming in all but the most complacent of military organizations. Considering the obstacles of administration and resistance to change in the way of reform, remarkable progress was made in the improvement of Personnel Management. For efficient Personnel Management, the Headquarters, Sixth US Army staff was organized under the traditional military line and staff type of organization. At least as important as distinguishing various modern management relationships was the range of variation in formality. In contrast, the informal

---

[48] Letter from Colonel T. M. Crocetti, DCS/Personnel, Headquarters, Sixth US Army, Presidio of San Francisco, Subject: "Request for Reduction-in-Force Authority," to (Commander, US Army Forces Command, Atlanta, Georgia), October 9, 1991.

organization is characterized by the absence of rigid definitions of departmental functions, responsibility, and authority. It was generally evidenced by an absence of formal titles and delineations. In contrast, the Headquarters, Sixth US Army staff implied the rigid definitions of military officers and departmental functions; the strict delineation of authority and responsibility; and the specific delegation of duties. In the former, the Managers and Supervisors may have partial responsibility for managerial functions and final authority in none of them. In the latter, the Managers and Supervisors would be solely responsible, and their decisions would carry authority on the matters specified as within their military organization.

Personnel Management is that aspect of overall management that has as its goal and objective the effective utilization of the labor resources of the organization. It was previously thought that the primary mission of a Human Resource Office had accomplished their primary mission when it managed to keep all authorized vacancies filled. The primary mission of the Human Resource Office was believed to fill personnel vacancies. The inducement of wages and the fear of discharge were thought to be all that was necessary to bring out the maximum effort of the Civil Service employee. Today it's recognized that the functions of Personnel Management are not quite that simple. Wages and layoffs are not the only factors that influence an employee's efficiency and effectiveness at work. The Civil Service employee is a complex being, and his behavior and response are conditioned by acquisitiveness; worry; laws; hate; prejudice; joy; amusement; and the desire for peer recognition.

The definition for Personnel Management has broadened with use over the last quarter of a Century and today encompasses the entire human aspect of management. As defined, Personnel Management is a method of organizing and treating employees at work so that management would get the greatest possible realization of their intrinsic abilities, thus attaining maximum efficiency for themselves and their group, and thereby giving to the organization of which they are a part, its determining competitive advantage and its optimum results. The definition suggests that Personnel Management makes use of definite principles for organizing and treating employees at work and that by following these principles, the employees would develop to their full potential. It follows that the development would result in position satisfaction to them as employees and as members of a group, and they in return would give their best effort in those endeavors that adhere to these principles. If the Personnel Management Program was to accomplish the desired results at the Presidio of San Francisco, Civil Service employees would have to believe they were members of the team, and not just simply earning a living, and would also have satisfied the non-socioeconomic needs by giving life meaning, pride, and personal dignity.

This type of Personnel Management philosophy should have existed in the minds of Command and have been imparted by them to all members of the Human Resource Office management staff at the Presidio of San Francisco. The Presidio

Garrison Human Resource Officer could not do an effective job, regardless of his personal capabilities if the proper Personnel Management philosophy was lacking in Command leadership. The Human Resource Office activities also included the administration of the organization's public relations philosophy with respect to customers and the general public. Unless each of these groups thought well of the Human Resource Office and believed in its purpose and practices, the organization would not be able to realize its maximum potential.

The primary objective of Personnel Management may be expressed in terms of what they seek to prevent and what they seek to accomplish. The former objective was largely concerned with preventing labor unrest and dissatisfaction. The later was concerned with seeking out and utilizing the maximum capabilities of the Civil Service employees for the mutual benefit of the organization and the employees. To a considerable extent, the Human Resource Office activities reflected the importance given to the different functions of Personnel Management. The Human Resource Office existed to serve other departments on personnel matters such as classification, hiring, firing, training, employee development and relations.

During the proposed reorganization period, the relations between the Human Resource Office and other staff departments remained cordial. For maximum effectiveness, the Human Resource Office staff was not subservient to any other department head, but operated independent in matters affecting OPM rules and regulations. The Human Resource Officer had to be able to make decisions on his own. Along the same lines, nearly every manager and supervisor at the Presidio of San Francisco felt he was an expert on Personnel Management relations and were more than willing to offer advice in quantity. This posed a problem for the Human Resource Officer. Managers and supervisors usually saw employee problems along the lines of their effect on performance alone. The Human Resource Officer saw these problems along the lines of organization welfare and effectiveness and more likely considered long-run results.

The role of everyday Personnel Management in personnel affairs is less in the areas of personnel systems, pay and benefits, and employee consultation, but in the organization of work and in the assignment and utilization of the Civil Service employees. These principles suggested a style of Personnel Management that extended responsibility as far as the law allowed; that gave subordinates authority; yet gave them the opportunity to make mistakes. It meant delegation of authority based on faith and confidence in the natural motivation of their employees to do his or her best. However, as responsibility was shared down the line, personnel decisions would have to be shared laterally. And finally, the inhibitions of vertical authority by holding too much authority at the Command level would have to be reduced to satisfy public law and public demand.

When it came to the selection for promotion; providing opportunity for formal training; predictions of potential performance; and personnel decisions of some magnitude; managers and supervisors should not have been in the position of "playing God" that affected the lives and fortunes of Civil Service employees on the basis of their own limited perceptiveness, prejudice, or biasness. To avoid the worst alternative or reliance on an automatic seniority system as enjoyed by military officers, personnel decisions should have been shared decisions. The classical judgment of the manager or supervisor should have become one of a committee or panel who were familiar with the work situation and the personalities involved in the decision making process.

The term "scientific approach" connotes the research method, and not the prescription of some single right answers to a management problem. If Personnel Management was to continue to progress, it should have been based more completely on objective research rather than it was in the past. Too much management policy was still determined by trial and error; by intuition; by the compulsion to weather a crisis; and by military Command insistence. Local matters of leadership; motivation; pay and benefits; evaluation; incentives; training; employee complaints; and many others should have been dealt with intelligently where there were regular and systematic procedures for research as the standard basis for reconciliation. Trial and error; informed guessing; and exchange of professional opinions; while useful at times were not reliable or complete enough to serve as a continuing basis for solid progress in Personnel Management.

Deserving and developing public respect for Federal Government services is insistent now that most people have come to recognize that Federal Government organizations are here to stay. Personnel management in general and public personnel operations in particular, can never raise much above what the public expects of them. When they are viewed contemptuously, it makes the attraction of high caliber persons more difficult to the public service. Formerly, the source of the problem was the Command's objective of economy of operations and the tendency of the more thoughtless among them by ways of self-justification, to strike out at alternative modes of performance. The stock market, manufacturing, and commercial selling are not the attraction to young people. There is a yearning for reformation, impatience with injustice; poverty; war; and ecological mass suicide. There is a desire to be identified with aims and causes beyond self-interest. It is not clear how genuine these ideas are on the part of all that voice them. Nor is the role of the Federal Government in the renaissance of humanistic protestations been well articulated. Some who profess their interests in correcting societies wrong seem anarchistic in their attitudes, rejecting Federal Government regulations along with the rest of what is contemptuously called the "Establishment."

Finally, one of the management activities that gave promise of keeping the Federal Government an effective and potent force in modern society was the administration of public Personnel Management policy and procedures in a manner that would maintain and improve the quality and motivation of Civil

Service employees. The Human Resource Office recruited continually for new talent and fresh approaches as the public business was the foremost enterprise of the nation. No more fruitful or inspiring cause could be generated then in developing policies and conditions to enlist in the public service than enthusiastic participation of men and women with capabilities and concerns commensurate with its vast responsibilities.

The Behavioral Questionnaire

To illustrate the nature of the behavioral problems associated with the Headquarters, Sixth US Army staff, and a questionnaire was designed by this author to conduct a survey measuring the attitudes and perceptions of the managers and supervisors, technicians, and administrative employees stationed at the Presidio of San Francisco (See Appendixes, Appendix G). The questionnaire was designed to examine the answers at two different levels. First, it represented an attempt to gain some overall insight into the behavioral views held by managers, supervisors, technicians, and administrative employees, and to compare these view with "traditional" and "modern" organizational theories as discussed in earlier chapters. Second, since this Case Study includes questions about management policies used by the Headquarters, Sixth US Army staff and Presidio Garrison under investigation, it provided some interesting observations about the behavioral consequences that management had based its decisions on. Along these lines, management policies referred to only those policies and instructions published by the Headquarters, Sixth US Army staff in comparison with the regulatory material contained in the Federal Personnel Manual (FPM) published by OPM. In view of the small size of the questionnaire sample, no validity could be generalized beyond the particular activity studied. On the other hand, there was no reason to suppose that the Headquarters, Sixth US Army staff was much different from any other organization at military Installations or Federal Government agencies.

The questionnaire sample was drawn exclusively from the Headquarters, Sixth US Army staff at the Presidio of San Francisco. The questionnaire was developed to provide the framework for an analyses and a critique of organization and management goals and objectives, and for managers, supervisors, technicians, and administrative employees. In all, a total of 69 questionnaires were completed; six from managers, 30 from supervisors, and 33 from technicians and administrative employees. The questionnaire inquired into the attitudes and perceptions of managers and supervisors, technicians, and administrative employees regarding the objectives of organizational and management goals and objectives, and the use of management policies. It was considered desirable to include the management group for several reasons.

First, an interest in comparing the behavioral philosophies of the activity to place management policies in some perspective in regard to the attitudes and perceptions held by Civil Service employees in general. Second, sample the reactions of supervisors, technicians, and administrative employees in the implementation of management policies. Finally, it was hoped that answers to the managerial questionnaire would provide a basis for comparing the views of managers and supervisors against the employee's views that concerned the perceived role of management actions and attitudes at the Presidio of San Francisco. Chapters X through XIII address comments that summarize the findings of this Case Study. In addition, relevant portions of the questionnaire, together with a tabulation of responses, are portrayed in Appendix G.

Earthquake Survivability between the Presidio of San Francisco and Treasure Island Study

It has been the opinion of informed persons that surface access to Treasure Island was far too precarious to support a military Installation. With only one bridge to provide vehicular access, Treasure Island was vulnerable to bridge damage. For example, by aircraft; by vehicular fire; by corrosive materials; by explosive accidents; certainly by earthquakes; and finally, by blockage by militant and hostile demonstrators. On the other hand, the Presidio of San Francisco undoubtedly would provide disaster relief resources of considerable magnitude. For example, a major Hospital and Research Center; helicopter landing access in an emergency; the quick restoration of Crissy Field for fixed wing aircraft; easy and safe access from multiple points; a separate water supply; and open areas for military and civilian bivouacking. Contrast that with Treasure Island that is a manmade landfill island; subject to liquefaction during earthquakes; accessible by vehicles only; and over an extremely vulnerable bridge.

Because of the importance in the proposed Headquarters, Sixth US Army staff realignment to Treasure Island, the relocation was highly criticized by Mayor Dianne Feinstein. Treasure Island was constructed during the 1930s as a Site for the 1939 World's Fair. According to the engineer who supervised the construction of the island, the Site was designed as a temporary landmass to last approximately 40 to 45-years. Since its initial construction, the island had sunk seven-feet into the San Francisco Bay and continues to sink. The breakwater and levee encircling Treasure Island had seriously deteriorated over the years. The soil on the island was artificial fill and although it was never studied in detail, several prominent San Francisco Bay Area geologists believe that a major earthquake would result in the liquefaction of the island. Scientists generally agreed that the approaches to both the San Francisco-Oakland Bay Bridges were likely to collapse in a major earthquake that would block vehicular accesses to and from Treasure Island.

Other points of seismic vulnerability included the San Francisco Bay Bridge; the Road connecting the bridge and Yerba Buena Island; and the causeway between Yerba Buena and Treasure Island. Several geologists believed that at a minimum, the San Francisco Bridge would be closed to ascertain its stability after a major earthquake. Concurrently, additional construction on the island would violate the principles embodied in the Earthquake Hazards Reduction Act of 1977 that mandated Federal Government agencies to lead in a national effort to reduce the risks of life and property from future earthquakes.

The proposed realignment of the Headquarters, Sixth US Army staff had several other significant adverse impacts. The presence of the Headquarters, Sixth US Army staff itself in dealing with leaders in the business, media, and civic life in the City of San Francisco would be severely reduced. The ceremonial and historical value of the Presidio of San Francisco being the longest continually occupied military Installation in the US would be degraded. The traffic using the City of San Francisco streets at peak commute hours would be increased as personnel housed at the Presidio Post would drive to their jobs on Treasure Island. Congestion on the San Francisco Bay Bridge would be so severe that it would impede the growth of business in the City of San Francisco. Gasoline and energy consumption would be increased to accommodate the additional travel; and air quality in the region would be further degraded. The services provided to the Presidio of San Francisco by private contractors and Federal Government agencies such as the Postal Service would be hampered by the inaccessibility of this location. The Treasure Island Site would also impair military operations such as the mobilization of Reserve personnel in the event of an emergency at the City of San Francisco and Bay Area.[49]

Treasure Island and its approaches were excessively vulnerable to natural disaster and civil disturbances. The ability of the Headquarters, Sixth US Army staff to collaborate with the City of San Francisco and Bay Area disaster relief operations would be impaired during such outbreaks. The citizens of the City of San Francisco and Bay Area depended on the Presidio of San Francisco facilities as a major command headquarters for civilian and military activities during the first 24-hours and in the weeks following a major earthquake or civilian disturbance. This military relief support could not be relied on from Treasure Island.

On December 19, 1978, General Forrester forwarded a letter to the Commanding General, US Army Forces Command for information on the operational mission implications of realigning the Headquarters, Sixth US Army to Treasure Island.[50] General Forrester enclosed the proposed Emergency Operations Center Special Mission Considerations-Presidio of San Francisco Closure and Realignment Study (See Appendixes, Appendix A) that addressed requirements under Public Law 95-124, Earthquake Hazards Reduction Act of 1977, October 7, 1977. The most

---

49   Letter from Mayor Dianne Feinstein, City of San Francisco, to (the Honorable Clifford L. Alexander, Jr., Secretary of the Army, Washington, DC), March 16, 1979.

50   Letter from Lieutenant General Eugene P. Forrester, Commander, Sixth US Army, Presidio of San Francisco, to (Commander, US Army Forces Command, Atlanta, Georgia), December 19, 1978.

serious impact of the proposed move would be the ability of the Headquarters, Sixth US Army staff to respond to emergencies, particularly in the event of a major earthquake in the City of San Francisco and Bay Area.

When most urgently needed, the Headquarters, Sixth US Army staff at best, would be cut-off from the population needing assistance. Should an earthquake occur during other than duty hours, military personnel residing at the Presidio Post would be unable to reach their duty station? Even if the headquarters building at Treasure Island withstood the quake, electrical, water, and other utility systems would most likely be lost. In effect, the Headquarters, Sixth US Army staff would be unable to organize when it would be most needed by the City of San Francisco and Bay Area community. At worst, Treasure Island would not survive and the headquarters would sink into the San Francisco Bay. Treasure Island is an artificial island made of sand and silt dredged from the Bay. Since its construction date during 1938, it has dropped in elevation from 13-feet to four-feet above sea level. Experts estimated an earthquake of only 6.5 on the Richter scale would cause it to crumple and disappear in the water (The 1906 earthquake was rated 8.2).

On December 27, 1978, Colonel H. Gordon Waite, Chief, Public Affairs, Headquarters, Sixth US Army forwarded a letter to Colonel Patrick D. Chisolm, Jr., Chief, Public Affairs, US Army Forces Command in regard to a discussion with the Sixth US Army Engineer.[51] Colonel Waite was concerned that a potential public affairs problem would emerge with respect to the Presidio of San Francisco Closure and Realignment Study. The problem would involve embarrassment to the Sixth US Army, US Army Forces Command, the DA, the DOD, and possibly the Executive Board if a final decision was made to relocate Presidio of San Francisco activities to Treasure Island. The analysis was based on Public Law 95-124 (Earthquake Hazards Reduction Act of 1977) that directed specific consideration for structures "especially needed in time of disaster." The public law also directed the Executive Board to develop and implement an Earthquake Hazards Reduction Program, and to coordinate all of the public and private agencies concerned with earthquake hazards. The Executive Office of the President had published and disseminated the National Earthquake Hazards Reduction Program. Included were specific guidance and admonishment to all Federal agencies to include the DOD to mitigate earthquake hazards.

An internal Disposition Form (DF) written by Dr. Don Butler, a leading Seismologist who was a DA engineer stated flatly that extreme hazards would be incurred by the Headquarters, Sixth US Army realignment to Treasure Island. Eventually, the above derogatory information would become public knowledge as it was already widely known in engineering and scientific circles. In view of the specific

---

[51] Letter from Colonel Gordon H. Waite, Chief, Public Affairs, Headquarters, Sixth US Army, Presidio of San Francisco, to (Colonel Patrick D. Chisolm, Jr., Chief, Public Affairs, Headquarters, Army Force Command, Atlanta, Georgia,), December 27, 1978.

admonishment to the Federal Government and specifically the DOD not to incur additional earthquake hazards, and the fact that the information was available to the DA at the time of their recent In-Progress Review (IPR), embarrassment would result if the DA were found to be proceeding directly against the best interests of public law, the US Army, and the general public. The environmental assessment accomplished by the MITRE Corporation was based upon a document that omitted these critical documents and was considered a poor result on the US Army's investment. The Sixth US Army Engineer took the initiative and provided copies to the MITRE Corporation and in addition, alerted the Judge Advocate General at the US Army Forces Command to the untenable situation. There was reasonable cause for moderate and prudent individuals to have stopped the Study months before based on the known geological unsuitability of Treasure Island. Before more money, time, effort, and credibility were poured down a "rat-hole," it was time for a thorough Seismic Study of Treasure Island in compliance with public law and the Executive Program. The US Navy had requested funds from the US Army Forces Command to assist in this endeavor.

Mr. David P. Hill, Chief, Seismology Branch, Geological Survey, Department of the Interior forwarded a letter on December 29, 1978, to Colonel John Kern, Engineering Division, Headquarters, Sixth US Army in accordance with a request received through the Federal Disaster Assistance Administration.[52] Mr. Hill had emphasized that the Headquarters, Sixth US Army should have been aware that the high-shaking intensity predicted for Treasure Island in Map MF-709 was based on the fact that the "island" was built up of fill; no instrumental determinations of ground motion amplification had yet been made on the island. Coincidentally on the same day, a US Army Forces Command message was sent to the US Navy at San Bruno in California and the US District Engineer, at Mobile in Alabama answering a US Navy message that identified specific US Navy support anticipated in developing the scope and use of current geo-technical records in support of Seismic risk concerning Treasure Island land mass in Accordance with the Earthquake Hazards Reduction Act of 1977.[53]7777

The US Army appreciated the US Navy offer, however, the US Army had contracted with the MITRE Corporation to conduct Environmental studies to include the review of current geo-technical records in support of Seismic risk concerning Treasure Island land mass. Therefore, a second undertaking would have appeared inappropriate. The US Army Forces Command requested that current environmental projects were completed prior to considering decision to conduct further research in the Seismic conditions of Treasure Island.

---

[52]   Letter from Mr. David P. Hill, Chief, Seismology Branch, Department of the Interior, to (Colonel John Kern, Chief, Engineering Division, Headquarters, Sixth US Army, Presidio of San Francisco), December 29, 1978.

[53]   Message from Commander, US Army Forces Command, Atlanta, Georgia, to (WESTNAVFACENGCOM, San Bruno, California and US Army Corps of Engineers, Washington, DC), December 29, 1978.

In view of the December 20, 1978 announcement to form a DOD steering group to detect and prevent fraud, waste, and abuse, an examination of what appeared to be a case of prima facie evidence of unsuitability of site was most evident. A few people were going to take some lumps for this decision, but not as many or as hard as they would if an outside source stepped in and called a halt. It would have been easy to dismiss perceptions as partisan, but the primary purpose was to draw attention in a professional manner to a situation that, if not handled well, could have resulted in unfavorable public reaction.

On January 9, 1979, General Shoemaker forwarded a letter to General Forrester referring to the Presidio of San Francisco Closure and Realignment Study.[54] General Shoemaker shared General Forrester's concern over operational and other implications that could have resulted from implementation of the Alternative Study Plan opposing the realignment of the Headquarters, Sixth US Army staff to Treasure Island. The US Army Forces Command Staff Study Group was assigned the task of completing the required relocation documents and made every effort to identify mission and quality of life requirements as well as to identify some resource savings.

In those instances where the nature of the DA study directive conflicted with this philosophy, such problems were fully discussed and predominantly displayed in the study document. The data provided was considered for inclusion in the study. Action would have be taken to reflect the retention of the Commissary; Post Exchange; and other Morale; Welfare; and Recreational facilities at the Presidio of San Francisco to support active and retired military personnel and their dependents who remained in the City of San Francisco and Bay Area after relocation.

The Headquarters, Sixth US Army staff comments concerning operational and environmental implications would be provided to MITRE Corporation, at McLean in Virginia as input to the environmental report they were contracted to produce for the US Army Forces Command. General Forrester was commended for taking a great deal of personal and professional interest in the Presidio of San Francisco Closure and Realignment Study. General Forrester's continued support, and that of the Headquarters, Sixth US Army staff, helped to assure that a quality US Army Forces Command management proposal was presented to the DA.

On January 10, 1979, General Forrester forwarded a letter to General Shoemaker mentioning the serious reservations he had about Treasure Island as a location for the Headquarters, Sixth US Army staff in view of the disaster assistance mission

---

[54] Letter from General R. M. Shoemaker, Commander, US Army Forces Command, Atlanta, Georgia, to (Commander, Sixth US Army, Presidio of San Francisco), January 9, 1979.

in the event of a major earthquake in the City of San Francisco and Bay Area.[55] General Forrester had been made aware of documents that appeared to require a thorough Geological and Seismic analysis by the DOD if any site, especially in the Western part of the US, for which the establishment or expansion of a DOD activity was planned. These documents indicated that the analysis should be given prime consideration in Site selection.

Public Law 95-124 (Earthquake Hazards Reduction Act of 1977) and the implementing National Earthquake Hazards Reduction Program published by the Executive Office of the President had provided specific guidance to the DOD to consider Seismic hazards in decisions about the siting and construction of military Installations and facilities. These documents were not included in the MITRE Corporation in-Progress Review (IPR) on December 4, 1978. These documents were apparently overlooked at higher-levels as well as a leading DA Engineer/Seismologist rated Treasure Island as one of the least desirable and potentially most hazardous locations in the City of San Francisco and Bay Area. Moreover, mis-perception existed as to the extent of MITRE's contract as it called for a "review of existing records" that pertained to environmental assessment.

This review did not include Seismic data on Treasure Island because as the Headquarters, Sixth US Army staff had been informed by the Department of the Interior that "no instrumental determinations of ground motion amplification have yet been made on the island." The US Navy offered to assist the US Army at relatively low cost in preparing a technical Seismic risk study. Om December 29, 1978, the US Army Forces Command turned down the US Navy offer because of the MITRE study. The MITRE study; however, would have to rely on assumptions based on filled land without detailed technical data on the island.

General Forrester was concerned about maintaining credibility of the US Army as a whole, and the Headquarters, Sixth US Army staff in particular, in the conduct of this study. A loss of credibility would undermine the efforts to reverse trends and solve problems in Reserve strength maintenance, as well as damage US Army programs overall. Local leaders in the City of San Francisco and Bay Area perceived the Treasure Island alternative as impractical, and that the US Army study would eventually comprehend the final results. It appeared essential, regardless of the outcome of the decision, that the thoroughness and competence of the Headquarters, Sixth US Army study was evident to all concerned. Selected members of the Headquarters, Sixth US Army staff were invited to cooperate with the City of San Francisco and Bay Area by participating as technical advisers on the study group appointed by Mayor Moscone and continued by Mayor Feinstein. Although Mayor Feinstein opposed the realignment of the Headquarters, Sixth

---

[55] Letter from Lieutenant General Eugene P. Forrester, Commander, Sixth US Army, Presidio of San Francisco, to (Commander, US Army Forces Command, Atlanta, Georgia), January 10, 1979.

US Army staff; Mayor Feinstein apparently leaned toward an independent study to develop suitable alternatives.

On January 5, 1979, General Forrester met with Mayor Feinstein to discuss the exact nature of the coordination between the Headquarters, Sixth US Army staff and the "Save the Presidio" Committee. The Headquarters, Sixth US Army staff was committed to ensure that the provision of Army Regulation (AR) Number 5-10 regarding cooperation with local civic leaders were fulfilled with precision and at no compromise of the US Army. Cooperation and openness, within the proper guidelines and in proper channels, would have done much to ensure the productive intent of the US Army and preserve relationships with Western civic leaders essential to the success of the Headquarters, Sixth US Army mission in the City of San Francisco and Bay Area. The "Save the Presidio" Committee appeared destined to become the coordinating agent and spokesman for all of the interested groups in the City of San Francisco and Bay Area concerned about the future of the Presidio of San Francisco. Along these lines, the relationship between the Headquarters, Sixth US Army staff and the "Save the Presidio" Committee could have become a model of US Army and community cooperation that addressed a significant mutual problem.

On January 23, 1979, General Shoemaker forwarded another letter to General Forrester answering General Forrester's January 10, 1979 letter.[56] The impact stated in General Forrester's letter concerning Seismic Risk and vulnerability was recognized by the US Army Forces Command staff. During meetings at the DA on January 10 and 11, 1979, engineer representatives from the US Army Forces Command staff and DA seismic experts met to discuss these problems. This review produced the opinion that a comprehensive technical engineering analysis of the Seismic Risk offered by Treasure Island could cost as much as $1 million. It was questionable that the US Army could afford to obligate this amount to determine the Seismic Risk at Treasure Island when available information might suffice.

The study offer extended to US Army Forces Command by the US Navy would only parallel work that was already contracted out to be performed by the MITRE Corporation. The information obtained clearly established the potential risk to the current and proposed occupants of Treasure Island. General Forrester was convinced that the US Army should not move the Headquarters, Sixth US Army staff to Treasure Island. In the event the Headquarters, Sixth US Army staff was directed to move to Treasure Island, a comprehensive technical Seismic analysis would have to be required. In order to develop a complete environmental review at that time, the MITRE Corporation had been requested to document the scope of the technical Seismic analysis.

---

[56] Letter from General R. M. Shoemaker, Commander, US Army Forces Command, Atlanta, Georgia, to Commander, Sixth US Army, Presidio of San Francisco), January 23, 1979.

Earthquakes do not occur frequently, but the rules of the game established by the Executive Department mandated that Seismic considerations be made when determining new construction, and that the DOD determine the example. The proximity of the San Andreas and Hayward Faults, coupled with the fact that Treasure Island was man-made and extremely vulnerable to Seismic disturbances, appeared to rule out convincingly moving the Headquarters, Sixth US Army staff to Treasure Island.[57] The expanded use of Treasure Island by the DA or any other Federal Government agency would be a waste. A massive investment by the Federal Government in light of available Seismic information was not justified.

The validity of the cost data provided by the US Navy was questioned by the Headquarters, Sixth US Army staff. The Headquarters, Sixth US Army staff had to be absolutely sure that the estimated cost of construction and recurring operating costs were accurate and reflected the full support of activities that would relocate to Treasure Island. Otherwise, the Headquarters, US Sixth Army staff would find itself with inadequate support or increased costs that if accurately estimated would have changed the outcome of the study.

As the official representative of the Secretary of the Army in the 15 Western States that comprised the Sixth US Army area of responsibility, General Forrester was often requested to host domestic and foreign dignitaries both military and civilian on the West Coast. The Presidio of San Francisco offered an ideal setting for this task because of its historical significance and attractiveness. Visitors would leave with a most favorable impression of the Presidio of San Francisco and the Headquarters, Sixth US Army. They would not do so if the Commanding General, Sixth US Army was to satisfy this responsibility from less than impressive facilities at Treasure Island that was a prior a US Navy Installation.

Concluding Comments

The Headquarters, Sixth US Army Executive Board was very careful not to let managers show spurious profits and earnings. The problem was by the time the symptoms of trouble were obvious, the human organization would have deteriorated to a point where steps to correct it were difficult and costly. There was only one solution to this problem, and it did not lie in more precise accounting data. The solution was to obtain adequate periodic performance measurements of the character and the quality of the human organization. Judgment alone was notoriously inaccurate, and tended to be most inaccurate in those situations that were unsatisfactory or deteriorating. Performance measurements and compensation formulas were needed that would penalize managers financially when they permitted the quality of the human organization under their supervision

---

[57] Message from Headquarters, Sixth US Army, Presidio of San Francisco, Subject: "Base Realignment Study." to (Commander, US Army Forces Command, Atlanta, Georgia), March 16, 1979.

to deteriorate mission accomplishment, and reward them when they improved the quality of performance measurement standards.

It was not sufficient merely to measure morale and the attitude of employees toward the organization, their supervisors, and work accomplishment. Favorable attitudes and excellent morale did not necessarily assure high motivation, high performance, and an effective human organization. For example, favorable attitudes could be found where there was complacency and general contentment, and where production goals was low and there was little motivation to achieve high performance. Similarly, measurements of behavior that reflected the past condition of the human organization, while useful, were also inadequate for current performance appraisals. Such measurements such as employee absence and turnover tended not only to be insensitive performance measurements but also reflected changes in the human organization after they had become substantial. More sensitive and current performance measurements than those in effect were required by the organization.

The measurement of these variables was a complex process and required a high level of scientific competence. The Headquarters, Sixth US Army staff needed more adequate measures of organizational performance than they realized. The manager's primary responsibility required that they build an organization whose organizational structure, goals, levels of loyalty, personnel motivation, inter-action skills, and competence were such that the organization achieved its objectives effectively. The supervisors and managers needed a constant flow of measurement reporting on the state of the organization and the performance being achieved. These measurements would provide data that the supervisors and managers needed to fulfill the current serious gap in the information coming to supervisors and managers, and their organization.

In a landmark decision, US District Court Judge Joseph B. Waddy took a strong exception to the Federal Government's long standing practice of filling Civil Service positions with employees supplied by private contracting firms. His ruling was important to Federal Government employees everywhere, indicated his belief that such contracting out that involved billions of dollars annually and a million employees was illegal and should be subject to sterner review. However, it applied for the moment only to an injunction against NASA that undoubtedly would affect the decision.

During late 1967, the decision came in a lawsuit brought by the AFL-CIO American Federation of Government Employees, who challenged the legality of conversion to private contractor operations by which the National Aeronautics and Space Administration's (NASA) Marshall Space Center at Huntsville, Alabama that supplied 5000 private contract employees on its staff. The Court ordered the USCSC to review contracts under the tough standards of the so called "Pellerzi Rule" laid down in early 1967 by Mr. Leo M. Pellerzi, then Civil Service Commission General Council. If the ruling was strictly applied, these standards would rule out much of the "contracting out" of Federal Civil Service employees that had been practiced. The Waddy decision was one in a long series coming from NASA's 1967 order terminating the 764 Federal Civil Service employees while retaining 5000 private contract employees doing similar work.

The Waddy decision pointed out that the law creating NASA obliged it to appoint its members under Civil Service rules with the specific exception of 425 scientific, engineering, and administrative-type employees. The decision cited a 1968 report prepared by the Commerce Department Personnel Director Mr. John Wills, at the Civil Service Commission's request that quoted NASA officials as saying: "they relied on contract personnel primarily to ensure work force flexibility." Mr. Wills' contrary finding was that similar flexibility could be obtained by using Civil Service employees under temporary, when actually employed, or consulting appointments. The decision also cited a 1967 Comptroller General's review of three Marshall and six Goddard Space Center personnel services contracts, alleging that $5.3 million annually could be saved if the work was accomplished by Federal Civil Service employees.

More important, however, Waddy found that Marshall's private contract personnel worked side-by-side with Civil Service employees, performed similar duties, used the same Federal Government equipment, received their orders, directly or indirectly, from Civil Service supervisors, and handled a work-load that could have been accomplished by Civil Service appointees. On that basis, Waddy found the Marshall contracts in direct conflict with the Pellerzi Rule standards. And accordingly, granted the American Federation of Government Employees a partial declaratory judgment declaring the 1967 Marshall contracts null and void to the extent that they violated the rule. Now for the Pellerzi Rule itself, the rule that the Waddy order directed the Civil Service Commission to follow to evaluate contracts. As a result, direction was received to stop contract procurement actions related to the Presidio of San Francisco Closure and Realignment Plan that was underway and to preserve accurate records of program documentation, reports, and correspondence to utilize the work that was performed to improve the management and execution of those functions that were to be privately contracted out.[58]

The Alternative Plan was to consolidate the Headquarters, Sixth US Army staff and the Presidio Garrison into one organization. The reorganized Headquarters, Sixth US Army would be designed to provide a reasonable span of control and improved use of manpower resources while preserving the separation between command and support functions. Support functions were further divided into technical, engineering, repair and maintenance support at the Presidio of San Francisco. The adoption of this organization required the disestablishment of the Presidio Garrison. The discontinued functions within the Presidio Garrison

---

[58] Editorial, <u>Washington Star</u>, (Washington, DC), "<u>Judge Strikes a Blow Against Contracting-Out Jobs,</u>" December 5, 1973.

would be reorganized to form the several additional staff offices required on the Headquarters, Sixth US Army staff.

Guidelines would also be established to define the proposed contractible functions in accordance with the instructions contained in the Presidio Closure and Realignment Study. Continued competence and effectiveness of the organization to accomplish direct support to Reserve forces and other DOD users were the foundation of these guidelines. All functions that were performed by the Headquarters, Sixth US Army staff and the Presidio Garrison were inventoried, and manpower authorizations involved in performing these functions were identified. Support functions were also reviewed and analyzed in relation to guidelines to identify contracting out. There needed to be a good "fit" between technology, tasks, organizational climate, and human resources after the proposed Headquarters, Sixth US Army staff reorganization. Accordingly, different Presidio of San Francisco closures interventions may have different degrees of relevance under different substances. And those circumstances could vary by hierarchical levels; interdependency; skill and group process skills; time pressure; rapidity of external change; danger of external threats, technology, and values. A sustained, successful OD effort would have extensive ramifications throughout the system. Attention would have to be paid to the design and quality of a wide range of feedback Sub-systems.

The conversion of a significant portion of the workload performed by military personnel and Civil Service employees to contract operations required consideration of many factors. Major areas included maintaining continuing and viable management control; developing effective functional interfaces between private contractors and Federal Government organizations; determining the extent where services under contract would be included in the new contract package; minimizing the disruption of ongoing functions during the contract procurement period; and achieving the objectives of directed actions for the Presidio of San Francisco Closure and Realignment Study. All of these actions involved functions being performed by approximately 5000 personnel of whom approximately 2349 were military personnel to be relocated to several other military Posts, and 2688 Civil Service employees to be transferred or terminated.

Detailed private contract definitions required minor alterations of the mix between military personnel and Civil Service employees to correspond precisely to the staffing requirements of the functions involved. Several of the existing service contracts were included in contract actions for the Presidio of San Francisco Closure and Realignment Study. Consideration of the factors involved led to the conclusion that one major new contract should be awarded to cover the majority of functions to be converted to contract operations. It should be noted that the contract would be in addition to and separate from the existing contract for operation, repair, and maintenance at the Presidio Post. Where minimal or no functional interfaces existed, smaller military Post support functions would be

Sub-contracted to small business concerns or withheld from the major contract for separate awards.

Areas that historically provided an upward mobility source for minorities and women would be included in the major contract. With the planned inclusion of efforts performed under existing service contracts, the major new contract represented a level of effort provided by military personnel, Civil Service employees, and private contractors. Personnel Management policies throughout the implementation period of the Presidio of San Francisco Closure and Realignment Study would be directed toward minimizing the adverse impact on the permanent Civil Service work-force and maintaining a viable work-force capability.

The Presidio of San Francisco Closure and Realignment Study was not an irreversible decision. The Headquarters, Sixth US Army staff stated that perhaps considerable less than those Civil Service positions programmed for realignment would occur or that conversion efforts would be contracted out. The conversion cost had fluctuated up and down, and a senior responsible official in the US Army Forces Command stated the dollar figure could continue to fluctuate heavily up or down. The transfer date had slid, and it looked like it would slide again. The reported savings would no doubt be realized through a reduced private contractor payroll. The Committee stated that the transfer of military organizations and a contractor takeover of the Presidio Post would have a drastic effect on the local economy; and businessmen had already reported significant reductions in sales volume.

There were two other outstanding ways that appeared to be appropriate. The Presidio of San Francisco Closure and Realignment Study could have served to strengthen the leadership role. First, the very existence of the plan represented a permanent challenge to responsible US Army managers to accomplish what they had agreed needed to be accomplished in the plan. They would have participated in shaping the long-range program for the improvement of the US Army, and would have committed themselves to this program by adopting it as an official US Army program. The plan constituted an unrelenting test of the sincerity of their intentions; the degree of their effectiveness; and the measure of their accomplishment. The principles and policies of the plan had represented their "better selves" and, when faced with pressures toward expediency that arose in specific cases, the necessity to justify to themselves and to others any deviation from the plan would make them somewhat more able to render difficult decisions in favor of Federal Government-wide and long-run considerations.

Second, the Presidio of San Francisco Closure and Realignment Study could give a degree of unity to US Army leadership that would otherwise be lacking. This is especially important where the existence of the Executive Board left the Headquarters, Sixth US Army without a strong Executive and placed much of the responsibility for policy leadership on the members of the Executive Board. The preparation and amendment of the plan clarified important physical development issues, and provided the opportunity for the Executive Board to work out a set of broad policies and a general design for the future of the Presidio Post where the majority of its members could agree. The inevitable and healthy disputes that arose from week-to-week that would inevitable surround any subject as important and complex as physical planning, took on some degree of perspective where there existed a set of "compromises" in the plan that the Executive Board did agree on.

CHAPTER XI

Findings

A major issue behind the Presidio of San Francisco closure controversy was a component of the BRAC. It was the assumption that using private contractors to accomplish tasks at the Presidio of San Francisco instead of military personnel or Civil Service employees would reduce budgetary costs. California Congressmen and Presidio Post officials protested the realignment of the Headquarters, Sixth US Army staff to Treasure Island along with the discontinuance of the Presidio Garrison; and the transfer of the Presidio Post to the US National Park Service not only because it would have eliminated thousands of military personnel and Civil Service employees, but because they felt the legislation was motivated in favor of private industry. For example, the Director of OMB who would have implemented the Act was a former management official at Litton Industries and a potential private contractor. These matters were all addressed during the presentation of the Presidio Post realignment proposal when Presidio Post military advisers, City of San Francisco officials, and Federal employee unions joined the protests. The key to the OMB proposal was the conversion from a multi-function contract approach to a single-manager approach, with contractors and contractor employees reporting directly to the Presidio Garrison. However, the US Air Force in a prior study had objected to this outcome as they believed the outcome of the OMB proposed multi-function approach would attract private contractors with little or no corporate structure and no inherent managerial capability. That type of results would eventually add to the operating managerial burden of the Presidio Garrison Commander and his staff.

On January 29, 1979, Brigadier General Michael N. Bacharach, Chief of Staff, Headquarters, Sixth US Army presented Management Improvement Actions and the Presidio of San Francisco Closure and Realignment Study to General Forrester. This Study was directed by US Army Forces Command message, January 16, 1979, to actively participate in the supervision of Management Improvement Actions of the Presidio of San Francisco Closure and Realignment Study.[59] On March 21, 1979, General Shoemaker forwarded the Presidio Management Improvement Actions for the Presidio of San Francisco to the Chief of Staff at the DA. General Shoemaker stated: "Management improvement initiatives pertaining to the Presidio Post were developed to provide full and complete information as an aid in arriving at a decision concerning the Presidio of San Francisco Closure and Realignment Study." Operations at the Presidio Post and the economics involved

---

[59]   Letter from General R. M. Shoemaker, Commander, US Army Forces Command, Atlanta, Georgia, to (Chief of Staff, Department of the Army, Washington, DC), March 21, 1979.

in the utilization of leased commercial facilities by DOD agencies in the City of San Francisco and Bay Area was meticulously evaluated.[60]

The Presidio of San Francisco has been a prestigious US Army military Post looked upon with pride by soldiers and citizens of the City of San Francisco and Bay Area. Since the Headquarters, Sixth US Army was dedicated to Reserve components in 15 Western States; its location on the Presidio Post was symbolic of the importance the US Army placed on the Reserves and National Guard. Movement of the Headquarters, Sixth US Army staff to a US Navy Installation would probably have been perceived by the community and Reserve components as a degradation of emphasis on the Reserve Program. The realignment of the Headquarters, Sixth US Army to Treasure Island, discontinuance of the Presidio Post, loss of active component units, and closure of Fort Baker would degrade training support and reduced desirable training facilities for Reserve component units. Efficient and meaningful training was necessary for military personnel retention. Members of organizations remaining in the two US Army Reserve Training Centers at the Presidio Post looked forward to using the Post Exchange; Clothing Sales Store; and other military Post facilities on drill days. Loss of these facilities would lessen the attractiveness of the Reserve Program. The Headquarters, Sixth US Army was also very sensitive to any action that would deter active duty recruiting and retention efforts. The alignment of the Headquarters, Sixth US Army staff; the discontinuance of the Presidio Garrison; the transfer of the Reserve mission and staff functional responsibilities to the US Army Reserve Command; and the transfer of the Presidio Post repair and maintenance mission to the US National Park Service would have several adverse effects on recruiting, particularly in the highly populated City of San Francisco and Bay Area.

Concurrently, services such as Finance; Automatic Data Processing; Procurement; and Human Resources for tenant military organizations stationed at the Presidio of San Francisco would be degraded because of the transfer of support services to the Fort Ord Post. The degradation would be further exacerbated because of the understated manning levels and costs for support services. For example, the proposed Fort Ord Post Table of Allowances did not provide for military personnel or Civil Service employees to be retained at the Presidio Post to operate the Water Plant and the Sewage and Water Pumping Stations. There were other related omissions. Of particular concern was the level of support that could be provided Reserve Component units in Northern California by the Fort Ord Post. The Fort Ord Post's responsibility for support would more than double (increase of 94 units, 27 Reserve Centers, and four Area Maintenance Support activities). In addition, the Fort Ord Post Finance Center Office would have to provide Reserve pay support for the entire Sixth US Army geographic area of responsibility. The

[60] Letter from Brigadier General Michael N. Bakarich, Chief of Staff, Sixth US Army, Presidio of San Francisco, to (Commander, Sixth US Army, Presidio of San Francisco), January 29, 1979.

resource requirements identified for the Fort Ord Post needed to be carefully studied and fully coordinated with the Headquarters. Sixth US Army staff and the Presidio Garrison prior to finalization of the Presidio of San Francisco Closure and Realignment Study.

At the same time, the GSA in the City of San Francisco revealed that they were under considerable pressures to meet existing lease costs and constantly rising prices. The GSA welcomed the Headquarters, Sixth US Army staff's effort to increase office space utilization at the Presidio of San Francisco, and would accept any office space that would become available as a result of these initiatives. In addition, the Study also addressed the closure of East Fort Baker and the movement of additional tenant military activities to the Presidio Post. Subject to possible environmental impacts, the Presidio Post was in the unique position of being able to offer some realistic and practical alternatives to the rapidly escalating costs of the DOD agencies doing business in a major metropolitan market. San Francisco's Mayor Dianne Feinstein commended the Secretary of the Army on the Headquarters, Sixth US Army's effort to reduce expenditures and improve the efficiency of domestic Posts and Bases. Mayor Feinstein stated: "Studies of the Headquarters, Sixth US Army staff realignment; discontinuance of the Presidio Garrison; transfer of the Presidio Post repair and maintenance mission to the US Nation Park Service; and the closing of the Letterman Army Medical Center were an important part of the Nationwide review of internal US Army operations. As the Mayor of San Francisco, I share your commitment to fiscal restraint. I personally know how difficult it is to reduce Federal Government spending without impairing operations. And, I am fully aware of the difficulty of obtaining the informed, insightful suggestions necessary for your office to make its decision."[61]

The most effective way for the DA to reduce expenditures in the City of San Francisco and Bay Area was to implement management improvement initiatives at the Presidio of San Francisco rather than realigning the Headquarters, Sixth US Army staff to Treasure Island, discontinuing the Presidio Garrison, and transferring the repair and maintenance mission of the Presidio Post to the US National Park Service. First among these should have been the relocation of DOD agencies in the City of San Francisco and Bay Area to available office space on the Presidio Post. Because the aforementioned factors strongly supported maintaining the Presidio Post, the Headquarters, Sixth US Army staff took a strong look internally to see what they could do to make operations more efficient and effective. They discovered office space in excess of 200,000-square feet that could be used by other DOD or Federal Government agencies. The Presidio Post could immediately provide at minimal cost approximately 75,000-square feet of interior building space. An additional 125,000-square foot could be made available through the relocation of certain activities within the Presidio Post.

---

[61] Letter from Mayor Dianne Feinstein, City of San Francisco, to (the Honorable Clifford L. Alexander, Jr., Secretary of the Army, Washington, DC), March 16, 1979.

The National Guard was actively seeking a new site for its military facilities to make room for a waste water treatment plant at Fort Funston.[62] The best estimate was that this approach was likely to produce savings comparable to those projected for relocation to the Presidio of San Francisco at a lower initial cost. Additional savings could be achieved through operations improvements to include contracting out of certain Presidio Post operating support functions currently performed by the Presidio Garrison's military personnel and Civil Service employees; consolidation of activities performed by more than one tenant at the Presidio Post; and the elimination of support functions on a selective basis. Work was proceeding in these areas to provide a sound fiscal perspective regarding the best use of human resources and equipment at the Presidio Post. The alternatives to realign the Headquarters, Sixth US Army staff to Treasure Island; discontinue the Presidio Garrison:, and transfer the Presidio Post mission and functions to the US National Park Service were to relocate the Corps of Engineers and National Guard to the Presidio Post, and to improve the management of Presidio Post operations as some of the anticipated savings could not be realized.

The Presidio of San Francisco's work-force of 2500 military personnel and 2800 Civil Service employees would have been reduced by almost 90-percent under the original Presidio of San Bernardino Closure and Realignment Study. In the case of the Presidio Post, most of the military personnel and Civil Service employees to include the Headquarters, Sixth US Army staff would have been realigned to Treasure Island with the balance going to the Fort Ord Post and other West Coast military Installations. The Letterman Army Medical Center Realignment Study would have involved closing the Medical Center in the City of San Francisco and expanding the Oakland Naval Medical Center at Oak Knoll to accommodate US Army patients. Letterman Army Institute of Research would have been closing the US Army Medical Research facilities and realigning its functions elsewhere in the US.

Findings of the Economics Research Associates

While contracting out for a study as an independent firm, Economics Research Associates worked in an advocacy role while trying to develop a report that would strongly support the retention of the Headquarters, Sixth US Army staff and the Presidio Garrison, as well as retention of the Letterman Army Medical Center at the Presidio Post. Their role was not to serve as a Management Consultant in such an advocacy role, but work within the limited time and monetary budgets available. Their work was primarily limited to developing data furnished by the Headquarters, Sixth US Army Executive Board; Presidio Garrison officials; Letterman Army Medical Center officials; City of San Francisco officials; "Save

---

[62] Message from Headquarters, Sixth US Army, Presidio of San Francisco, Subject: "Base Realignment Study." to (Commander, US Army forces Command, Atlanta, Georgia), March 16, 1979.

the Presidio" Committee; and other existing sources rather than conducting extensive primary research. It was critical for Economics Research Associates to address a series of issues rather than trying to oppose the Presidio Closure and Realignment Study based on one or two socioeconomic arguments. The Economics Research Associates worked very closely with the City of San Francisco officials and the Headquarters, Sixth US Army Executive Board to collect data, analyze facts, and prepare advocacy arguments.[63]

Findings of Touche Ross & Company

The principal rationale for the Headquarters, Sixth US Army staff realignment, Presidio Garrison discontinuance, and the transfer of the Presidio Garrison's operations, repair, and maintenance activities to the US National Park Service was to reduce total expenditures by the DA and not National Defense. In the City of San Francisco's independent review of the Headquarters, Sixth US Army proposed realignment, Touche Ross & Company estimated that the period required for the annual projected savings to pay back the initial costs of realignment would be in excess of 10-years and possibly as high as 20-years.[64]

Findings of the Management Consultant

The Management Consultant used the theory that underline laboratory training to improve organization functioning and effectiveness. The goal and objectives were to effect a change in values of the Headquarters, Sixth US Army Executive Board so that human factors and feelings would be considered as legitimate; to assist in developing skills among managers and supervisors; and to increase inter-personal competence. The models that implement laboratory training for organization improvement could be viewed along two dimensions. For example, internal and external, and legitimate power versus expert power. If the choice of the change strategy was internal, then legitimate or expert power could be utilized. If the choice of the change strategy was external, then only one power alternative of expert power was open as legitimate power must be drawn from sources internal to the target system.

The Management Consultant found the Headquarters, Sixth US Army staff was a viable organization that had dynamic systems where procedural and structural changes frequently took place. Modifications took place in tasks accomplished; in the way that military personnel and Civil Service employee positions were

[63] Letter from Mr. J. Richard McElyea and Mr. Daniel Stephan, Economics Research Associates, San Francisco, to (Mr. William D. Evers, President, Economics Development Advisory Council, Office of the Mayor, City of San Francisco), January 22, 1979.

[64] Letter from Mayor Dianne Feinstein, City of San Francisco, to (the Honorable Clifford L. Alexander, Jr., Secretary of the Army, Washington, DC), March 16, 1979.

grouped together; in the areas of responsibility for decision making held by various managers and supervisors; in the patterning of communications; and so forth. Modifications could be triggered by environmental changes; changes in inputs utilized; outputs produced; and transformational methods employed. The possibility of organizational change could come from the analysis of day-to-day operations, periodic analysis, and from monitoring environmental factors having a bearing on operations. Both changes in the management system and in the operational structure could have resulted from a decision that organizational changes were required. The effectiveness of rapid technological changes or organizational changes, or both, required careful planning of adjustments in a network of systems within the organization. In addition, careful preparation and maintenance of a psychological environment conducive to change was essential. Important ingredients included effective communications; relating desired changes to the employee's needs and goals; legitimate and relevant participation of subordinates in planning for change; and personnel policies designed to motivate behavior in the appropriate directions while minimizing defensive behavior.

The Management Consultant needed to succeed in achieving some changes by finding conditions of dis-satisfactions with current operations; support of higher level management for the change effort; and existence of a prestigious proponent of the change as proposed changes could have been a lengthy process. A successful attempt appeared to have been characterized by the sharing of influence to make alterations with the individuals directly affected by the changes, and a clarification of the problems by a statement by the Management Consultant as to the specific overall goal and objectives of the changes. The Executive Board, managers, and supervisors had to ensure that the existence of a number of conditions necessary to facilitate rapid changes such as the repair and maintenance of communications among Sub-units; top level support and reassurance; encouragement of legitimate and relevant participation; reorganization of reward and appraisal systems; and the development and implementation of appropriate management policies such as personnel transfers and separations.

The Management Consultant needed to provide guidance in analyzing the minimum steps required to justify the changes prior to the planning and implementation of organizational changes, and to establish the necessity for changes. The criteria established by the Management Consultant would provide criteria for participants and not for observers. That is, criteria that gave a model that could assess the effectiveness of the proposed changes in terms of positive or negative values while planning the changes. Change is a natural and sometimes a rather informal process that can accurately be described as organization learning; a combination of efforts at individual learning; and general improvement efforts. Major changes, in contrast, are conscious efforts to alter aspects of a system or Sub-system functioning. The change process was complex that consisted of a series of distinctly different kinds of activities being undertaken. If changes were to be successful, the goal and objectives would have to be specified at the lowest levels of organization; social ties would have to be altered; individual self-esteem levels would have to increase; and internalization of change, goal, objectives, and new behavior would have to take place.

The Management Consultant would have to alter the steps in the change process, or would fail to achieve changes in these Sub-components of changes. It would have introduced serious doubt that overall goal and objectives of the changes could be implemented. The most familiar variety of such change would be technological innovation. But if change became a permanent and accelerating factor in life, then adaptability to changes would have become increasingly the most important single determination of survival. The profit, efficiency, savings, and the morale of the moment would become secondary to keeping the door open for a rapid readjustment to changing conditions.

The Management Consultant did propose the goal and objectives for the Headquarters, Sixth US Army Executive Board and Presidio Garrison officials that would provide the basis for generating other types of plans. Logically, following the setting the goal and objectives was a form of strategic planning. An organizational strategy would consist of interrelated decisions setting forth the major methods the Executive Board would follow to achieve its planned organizational goal and objectives. Strategic plans formed patterns to identify the types of decisions the Executive Board would engage with the general approaches the organization would employ to obtain its goal and objectives. The strategic plans would provide the operating boundaries where the Executive Board human resources and equipment could be employed.

The Management Consultant processed planned changes, and assisted in a client-system that referred to the target of change. The Management Consultant, in collaboration with a client system, applied valid knowledge to the Executive Board's problems. These four elements in combination-consultant, client-system, valid knowledge, and a deliberate and collaborative relationship circumscribed the class of activities referred to as planned organizational change. These four elements also helped to distinguish planned organizational change (collaborative) from other forms of change (non-collaborative). That is, planned organization changes differ from technocratic changes in that they attempt to implement research results and relied more heavily on the relationships between the Management Consultant and the Executive Board. Planned organization changes differed from coercive change programs where the Management Consultant had no formal power over the Executive Board. Planned organizational changes differ from spontaneous and secondary innovations in that it was a conscious and deliberate induction process.

The Management Consultant relied on Operations Research (OR) and planned organizational changes that were both problem-centered; emphasized concepts or methods; and emphasized improvement and optimization of organizational performance. To that extent, the Management Consultant was normative in his approach to problems in that he attempted to maximize the organizational goal and objectives under certain conditions.

The Management Consultant relied heavily on empirical science as the main means of influence, and relied on a relationship with his clients based on confidence and valid communications.

The Management Consultant emphasized a systems approach to problem solving, meaning essentially an awareness of the interdependence with the internal parts of the system as well as boundary maintenance within its environment.

Finally, the Management Consultant worked with systems that were complex, rapidly changing, and somewhat science-based.

Findings about the Organizational Goal and Objectives

The questionnaire contained several questions designed to explore the attitudes and perceptions regarding the fundamental management goal of the organization of which the respondents were members (See Appendixes, Appendix G). The answers to Question A-1 identified that a large majority of the managers, supervisors, technicians, and administrative employees considered the primary goal of the Headquarters, Sixth US Army staff to be one of achieving maximum results and effectiveness. Some managers and supervisors placed a heavy emphasis on achieving a satisfactory level of results and effectiveness or to give a satisfactory service. However, the difference was not significant since most of the managers and supervisors defined a "satisfactory" level of results and effectiveness as the "best possible" level of results and effectiveness under the circumstances that would be in effect simply another form of maximization.

There was a distinct emphasis on results and effectiveness·and the perceived relationship between results and effectiveness, and the perceived relationship between results and effectiveness and competitive costs. The answers to Question A-1 suggested that management policies were viewed as primarily a device for enhancing the performance of employees, a necessary and important aspect of organization activity in terms of achieving maximum results and effectiveness. The nature of these replies, as well as the forcefulness with that they were given, indicated that, at best in this sample, both management and employee views of the organizational goal was closely related to the "traditional" model of behavior.

The answers to Question C-16 inquired into the possibility of management policies creating goal conflicts between behaviors that were in the best interest of the organization. Most replies indicated that such goal conflicts could and sometimes do appear. These responses demonstrated that managers, supervisors, military personnel, and Civil Service employees in practice were aware of goal congruence problems and realized that what was perceived as good (as in goal accomplishment) for the employee and the organization may not have been best for the organization. However, the usual analysis of this problem by employees was that such conflict was not very common and that the solution to it was in recruiting or training better managers and supervisors and not in changing management policies. It appeared; therefore, that although military personnel and Civil Service employees may have recognized the possibility that employees and activity Sub-goals were not always compatible, they nevertheless tended to follow management policies as if they were.

Findings about the Behavior of Employees

Several questions were designed to obtain the views those supervisors and managers, military personnel, and Civil Service employees held about the behavior of organization participants. The most general inquiry about the behavior of participants concerned the perceived necessity of controlling costs. Approximately half of the employees who answered Question B-3 indicated their belief was that management policies were necessary because employees tended to be, at worst, deliberately wasteful and lazy and, at best, indifferent to any cost saving efforts. These respondents usually made the point that such behavior was "human nature." The remaining half of the responses to Question B-2 suggested that management policies were necessary because, even though managers might attempt to reduce costs on their own, they could not effectively do so without the information provided by management policies.

Nearly all of the Civil Service employees who answered Question B-3 reflected a view of the employees that paralleled almost exactly the view of the behavior of employees associated with the "traditional" model of behavior. In other words, employees were considered to be motivated largely by economic forces, interested in doing as little work as possible, and ordinarily inefficient and wasteful. It should be emphasized that although there were differences of degrees, few responses deviated very far from this general view of the behavior of employees. For example, in the case of the perceived behavior of supervisors and managers, two different views were expressed about equally. One group considered most managers to be in the same class as professionals. The other group who answered Question C-11 tended to believe that promotion to a supervisory position required a certain amount of demonstrated loyalty and devotion to duty to the organization.

According to this view, managers and supervisors could be depended on to at least make an effort to control costs. The respondents were asked to indicate their opinions about the probable effects on their organization if management policies were discontinued as a control mechanism. In general, managers, supervisors, technicians, and Civil Service employees who answered Question C-8 predicted that material and labor costs would be unfavorably affected. The reason given for anticipating these unfavorable effects were primarily related to the view of behavior discussed below. It was interesting to observe that while managers and supervisors tended to take the same position as employees on these matters, the answers of the managers and supervisors were less unanimous. Of the answers to this set of questions, managers and supervisors predicted a high percentage of unfavorable effects than employees. This appeared to indicate that as a group, employees were somewhat more convinced of the importance of management policies than managers and supervisors.

In view of the foregoing, it might have been expected that the Civil Service employees would prefer not to be controlled by management policies, procedures, and standards. Therefore, it is difficult to understand why only a small amount of the answers to this set of questions indicated that they believed employees would have a more favorable attitude toward management and their positions if the controls under consideration were eliminated. In fact, the large amount of the answers to Question C-14 to this set of questions expressed the belief that those employees were actually in favor of the use of management policies as control devices. Apparently, they preferred to be associated with an organization where there was a relatively high-level of control and where they could "respect" management.

Further, a number of employees expressed their opinions on the answers to Question C-15 that they enjoyed the challenge of having to meet "properly determined" work standards. It was possible that some of the inconsistencies observed in the answers to these questions were actually a reflection of similar inconsistencies in the overall logic of contemporary management. In any event, there appeared to be little doubt that management views of behavior of organizational participants that was most commonly suggested by the questionnaire was a concept that came rather close to the "traditional" model of behavior. Further, while there were some variations in the answers of the group to the questions just discussed, the responses from managers and supervisors tended to coincide with the answers and views of the employees.

Findings about the Behavior of Managers

An indication of attitudes and perceptions about the role of managers and supervisors held by military personnel and Civil Service employees who answered Question C-1 can be found in the term "management authority." It should be noted that most respondents had difficulty in verbalizing such a definition. Despite the difficulty, most managers, supervisors, and employees did express definite opinions as to the source of management authority. Most of the managers, supervisors, technicians, and Civil Service employees identified the source of authority in such "traditional" terms as the formal Job Description title and Organizational Chart. The "traditional" concept of authority was nearly always related to the necessity of achieving a balance between authority and responsibility. The remaining managers, supervisors, technicians, and Civil Service employees suggested a view of authority that was closer to the "modern" organization theory

208

idea of "acceptance from below." While no questions were concerned directly with the primary function of management, it was reasonable to assume that the managers, supervisors, technicians, and Civil Service employees who answered the questionnaire would have related that function to the accomplishment of the previously designated goal of maximum results and effectiveness. The responses to those questions concerning the attitudes and behavior of Civil Service employees implied that management must somehow attempt to cope with and control the essentially negative behavior of Civil Service employees. The role of management appeared to be viewed as that of applying traditional management principles to the solution of problems associated with the traditional view of Civil Service employees.

Findings about the Role of Management Policies

The respondents did not explicitly indicate the extent of the existence of the traditional view of the role of management policies. In a sense, the major difficulty was one of semantics. It's possible that the same words. For example, "maximum results and effectiveness" connoted several meanings depending on the context in which they were used. It became necessary, therefore, to evaluate many of the responses in terms of what was implied as well as what was actually expressed. With this in mind, the following observations might be noted concerning the perceived role of management. In virtually every questionnaire managers, supervisors, technicians, and Civil Service employees tended to relate the role of management to the idea of maximum results and effectiveness, and there was a strong emphasis on the use of management policies as instruments in the process of reducing and controlling costs. The replies to questions that were concerned with the objectives of management policies suggested that many of those Civil Service employees who answered the questionnaire considered the role of management policies to be primarily one of cost minimization.

Conversely, another group seemed to recognize a broader view and tended to emphasize the "information system" approach to management policies. An important insight into the attitudes and perceptions of managers, supervisors, technicians, and Civil Service employees who answered the questionnaire can be gained from the fact that most managers, supervisors, technicians, and Civil Service employees who answered Question C-9 believed the activity should be "less lenient" in analyzing variances and enforcing management policies, procedures, and standards. In addition, the Civil Service employees who answered Question C-10 supported the use of unfavorable rather than favorable variances as motivational devices. They believed that standards should be set high enough so that they could not ordinarily be met, and performance could be expected to result in unfavorable variances. The response to these questions seemed to confirm the subjective appraisal that some of the managers, supervisors, technicians, and Civil Service employees who at first glance appeared to have moved away from the "traditional" view had not, in fact, moved very far at all.

Findings about the transfer to the
US National Park Service

During 1993, what happened to the breath-taking beauty of the Presidio of San Francisco since this author left his position as an Advisor and Consultant to the Commanding General? It remained a mystery until a feature article appeared in the New York Times on March 30, 2000 entitled <u>A Force in Film Meets a Force of Nature</u>, by Patricia Leigh Brown. An appropriate insight to this Case Study became apparent; the theme of this article would become an additional finding to compliment a narrative history requiring a befitting epilogue. Ms. Brown had inquired into the usage and maintenance of the historical land and buildings made possible by the sweat and toil of officers and enlisted men stationed at the Presidio of San Francisco. For those soldiers, the Presidio Post was their home and they took great efforts to improve its appearance. For some of us who served in or out of uniform at the Presidio Post, the land and historical buildings were considered to be an American treasure. Appreciation, therefore, goes to members of the US Congress who had the wisdom to ensure the proper continuance of a National treasure even in its self-sufficient mode.

During 1776 through 1994, the 1480-acre Presidio of San Francisco, adjacent to the Golden Gate Bridge, was a military Installation. The Presidio Post is now a National Park featuring historical forest; rare plants; and outdoor museum of American architecture. During 2013, the Presidio's 470 historical buildings that house a community of organizations and businesses that should make the Presidio Park self-sufficient. Many sunrises and sunsets have occurred since this author drove over the Golden Gate Bridge to and from his work Site, and walked between the Presidio Post buildings as the coordinator of the Presidio Post closure proposal as an honest broker for Personnel with the Headquarters, Sixth US Army staff. Many improvements have been accomplished to date historical buildings that once accommodated the Headquarters, Sixth US Army staff and Presidio Garrison officials. This Case Study then is an ongoing story that hopefully will continue to grow until the next millennium with the assistance of the US National Park Service and American entrepreneurs.

The sound of bugles is no longer heard. The roar of a cannon heard during retreat ceremony is now quiet. The parade ground is void of smartly dressed, marching officers and enlisted men with Commanders shouting cadence and commands. The Presidio of San Francisco sentries of long past are silent, buried beneath rows of eucalyptus trees. The Headquarters, Sixth US Army staff and Presidio Garrison no longer display its honored colors and combat streamers. The Officer's Club no longer has dining-in ceremonies to honor our Country and Officers and Enlisted Men of the US Army. The Presidio of San Francisco is no longer a proud US Army military Post steeped in military traditions. The Presidio Post has joined with the rank and file of the US National Park Service and American entrepreneurs, subjugated to the modern era of Congressional budget decisions.

In secluded groves of eucalyptus and along a once dusty parade ground lined with red-brick Victorians, history still stands watch over the Presidio of San Francisco; the windswept 1480-acre former Presidio of San Francisco wrapped by the headlands of the Golden Gate Bridge. Since 1994, when this National Historic Landmark about twice the size of New York's Central Park became a National Park, a novel and much-debated experiment in preservation and Presidio Park planning has been under way at the 200-year old Presidio Post. Once the Northern most point of the Spanish empire, it's a place that, though part of the City of San Francisco, still feels like the edge of the American world. Home to some 470 historic structures and now approximately 2000 people, the Presidio Post as one resident put it, an "oddball" National Park and the only one that is required by the US Congress to be self-sufficient. The 1917 Fire Station was sensitively updated during 1997. The National Military Cemetery dates from 1884. The 1932 Spanish colonial-style Post Chapel has a beautiful WPA mural visible from the outside. The 1.5-mile Golden Gate Promenade offers spectacular views of the City of San Francisco and Bay Area. It led to the Crissy Marsh Restoration, a stretch of restored beach, tidal marsh and native plant-covered dunes that replaced 70-acres of asphalt from a 1921 Airfield. The $32 million restoration has been a decade in the making; it even has a private Golf Course overlooking the Pacific Ocean that the US Army wanted to keep for itself after the transfer to the US National Park Service.

The Montgomery Street Barracks Visitor Center in the 1890s brick barracks facing the parade ground is the best place to start exploring the Presidio Park. The mile-long, self-guided walk circling the heart of the Presidio of San Francisco spans 200-years of military history and American architecture. Most of this vast and wild urban terrain of wildflower-covered sea cliffs and extraordinary architecture, Officer's homes, cavalry stables, airline hangers, and a psychiatric ward is preserved over by the Presidio Trust, a Corporation created by the US Congress that assumed control over 80-percent of the Presidio Park two-years ago (the US National Park Service controls the rest). The Presidio Post is a delicate piece of property in progress, and the Trust a controversial landlord. Born during a cost cutting Republican Congress that had seriously considered selling off this verdant jewel, the Trust had a dual and, some critics say, impossible mission. For example, to preserve and protect the Presidio of San Francisco that made the Presidio Park economically self-sufficient during 2013.

To create an "economic engine" generating $5 million a year toward the $36 million the Trust estimated it would cost annually to maintain the Presidio Park, the filmmaker Mr. George Lucas, after heated competition, won preliminary approval to build a 23-acre Digital Arts Center on the site of a dilapidated 1960s hospital. He envisioned a "Lincoln Center West," a corporate campus, stylistically drawing on Presidio of San Francisco architecture that would house five Lucas enterprises to include Industrial Light and Magic, special effects, and animation. Development has long been planned for this Site. However, the Lucas proposal, along with the rental of some houses for upward of $5 thousand a month, may signify the intrusion of a business culture into a National Park. Some charge that the need to generate income may irrevocably change the nature of the place, recasting the Presidio Post as an elite City-within-a-City for wealthy individuals and corporations. Mr. Brian Huse, Pacific Regional Director of the National Parks Conservation Association that is a private watchdog group stated: "Is it possible to preserve the Presidio Post's natural and historic treasures unimpaired with a mandate to raise money off the very resources we are trying to protect?" At the Presidio Post, the US Congress looked at one thing and one thing only: "Just how much would it cost?" Where Enlisted Men once exchanged war stories in the Mess Hall, there is now talk about "synergy" and wireless Internet.

Following the turnover of the Presidio of San Francisco to the US National Park Service, approximately 80 historic structures were rehabilitated. Among the new tenants, a quirky array of businesses and not-for-profit, are Febber Futures (dedicated to tree-free paper); the Pachamama Alliance (protects indigenous Amazon cultures); Trash Talk (a waste prevention radio show); the San Francisco Film Center;, and a group of 14 film related businesses and organizations that spent $6 million to restore a sprawling Barracks built in the Mission style by WPA. The Sundance Institute reviewed the Presidio Post's Mission Revival Theater as a potential cinema for independent films. Mr. Mark Linder, unofficial "Mayor" of his neighborhood, called Simon's Loop, and President of Food, Land and People, an environmental organization stated: "You cannot help but be inspired here." The juxtaposition of dot-coms like WebMD with the still operating Post Exchange, the Sustainability Art Show with Burger King, not to mention a nudist beach beside a string of bunkers with retractable cannons gives the latter-day Presidio Post a sort of loopy charm. It has always been a place of secret corners awaiting discovery, like the tombstone in the pet cemetery that read: "Skipper: Best Damn Dog We Ever Had." Having been the Country's longest continuously operating military Post until 1994; the Presidio Post parallels the growth of the Country as a World power. Established during 1776 as El Presidio de San Francisco, an isolated Garrison (a fragment of the original adobe foundation can be seen inside the Officer's Club), the Presidio Post was briefly controlled by Mexico prior to 1847. A visiting military officer stated it was not a place of beauty. The view of the Bay is fine from the high hills, but everything looked dirty and sandy; you cannot void the impression that it was a mean Country."

During the Civil War era, the Nation's most important military complex added a central parade ground surrounded by rows of Enlisted Men's barracks and Officer's Row, and a Civil War street essentially unchanged. The Presidio of San Francisco was the central deployment point for the Indian campaigns; the Spanish-American War; and Pacific operations. It's winding, thickly forested landscape was highly unusual for a military Installation, and where roads and terrain are usually flat and straight was strongly influenced by the late 19th Century City Beautiful Movement. A foresighted US Army engineer, Major William A. Jones, planted the forests of eucalyptus, cypress, and pine in orderly rows, like soldiers in formation. A role model for the rest of the Presidio Post is the Thoreau Center for sustainability, where some 50 organizations have taken over a dilapidated hospital complex and restored it according to green principles. At its heart is a three story white clapboard hospital (1899), where pressed tin ceilings and Victorian banisters now commune with a glass canopied entryway with photo voltaic panels.

The biggest success story so far may have been at Crissy Field, a 1921 Airfield from where US Army aviators and DeHavilland biplanes once patrolled the skies. After decades of environmental abuse, this mile and a half stretch of waterfront beside the Golden Gate Bridge has been reborn as one of the Country's most ambitious public spaces under the aegis of the US National Park Service, that still oversees the Presidio of San Francisco's perimeters, and the Golden Gate National Park Association, that raised $32 million in private funds to reclaim the Site. It opened in 2000, replacing 70-acres of asphalt with a recreational tidal marsh and native grasses. But this is not Yellowstone or Yosemite. The Presidio Post was situated on prime real estate located on one of the Worlds' most desirable Cities. The Lucas proposal, and the decision to rent historic buildings at fair market prices, has tenants like Doris Heeren, 49, who is married to a Park Service Ranger, was frankly worried. Ms. Heeren stated: "This is no longer going to be a National Park. My feeling is that this will be a gated community."

The Trust, overseen by a seven member presidentially appointed board, was obliged to follow Federal Government environmental and historic preservation guidelines. It was created based on the US Congress' view that the scope and complexity of the Presidio of San Francisco required professional real estate expertise that was beyond the US National Park Service. Board members included Mr. Donald Fisher, founder and Chairman of the GAP, and Mr. William K. Reilly, a former administrator of the Environmental Protection Agency. But tensions have come to light recently around the question of who gets to live in the Presidio of San Francisco's 1100 housing units. At this moment, the full time Presidio Post community is a hodgepodge of Presidio Park employees; Office Workers; Students; Park Police; Firefighters; about 150 remaining military families (who will be phased out over a five year period); and members of the public who can afford the rents, which range from $450 for a single student to $6000 a month for an Officer's mansion. The goal, said Mr. Jim Meadows, the Trust's Executive Director, is a community of people who live and work at the Presidio Post, from low earners to CEOs, people like Ms. Leanne Headley, 32, who lives in a complex mostly for students. Ms. Headley stated: "I live in an ugly apartment. But I'm looking over the Pacific Ocean ten-minutes from Robin William's house."

Some say that the Presidio Trust has not established a strong connection with the community or the US National Park Service. Mr. Ed Blakely, a former board member who is now Dean of the School of Management and Urban Policy at the New School in New York stated: "There's an insularity that is unfortunate. The Trust is hunkering down rather than opening up." The grand test case may be the Letterman Digital Center, as the Lucas complex would be known, where local

213

environmentalists and others have raised concerns about traffic, water quality, and the appropriate scale and density for the Presidio Park. During February 2000, speaking at the University of California at Berkeley, Mr Lucas stated: "I think the Presidio Park should stay a Park." But he also observed: "One of the prominent issues is: What is the Presidio Park? There's no Old Faithful, there's no Half Dome, there's no Grand Canyon there." Mr. Gordon Radley, President of Lucas Film Ltd. described a Corporate Campus with underground parking for 1500 cars; various public space for cafes and coffee bars; a tuition free Digital Training Institute; and a special effects visual archive open by appointment. Mr. Radley also stated: "No one wants to create Universal Studios at the Presidio Post." But in a private film making campus some foresee a waning of the soul and spirit of American's National Parks.

Mr. Drummond Pike, President of the Tides Foundation in the Thoreau Center stated: "The Presidio of San Francisco is a significant departure for a National Park. I do not believe the public interest is served by having Lucas as a tenant, though it will be nicer to have Lucas than a bunch of venture capitalists." Ms. Amy Meyer, a board member and Bay Area environmentalist, argued that the Lucas plan must pass various environmental design reviews and create a financial entity that would keep the rest of the Presidio of San Francisco intact as a National Park. Ms. Meyer agreed with Mr. Meadows of the Trust who stated: "Preservation and self-sufficiency are not mutually exclusive if we do our job right. The Presidio of San Francisco will look a great deal like it does today, with 20-percent more open space and historic buildings all renovated to Code."

Mr. Roger Kennedy, a former Director of the US National Park Service, noted: "that other National Parks are not expected to pay for themselves and that the Trust concept, born of political compromise, must be watched zealously." The question Mr. Kennedy asked was: "How many transactions do you consummate during the course of this process toward self-sufficiency that you will regret later?" Like any huge real estate business venture, the US National Park Service will be making contracts that they will have to live with, as well as contracts needed for making a profit or just breaking even on the upkeep of this military facility. The US National Park Service now has the task of making money to be self-sufficient and not just managing the facility and spending an unlimited supply of taxpayer's money.

The US National Park Service will be largely responsible for interpreting the National Park to visitors brought in a team from the Smithsonian Institution to assist in establishing new exhibits for the site. For all the future-thinking, wireless or otherwise, it's still the past that will anchor this place, where soldiers' tombs peek through eucalyptus trees. Sensitive reshaping is not for the meek, but it appears well worth the fight to Mr. Rinehart Moe, President of the National Trust for the Historic Preservation, who optimistically stated: "It's not trouble free and there are and will be inevitable tensions in the formula." The good news Mr. Moe stated: "Nobody is talking about tearing down historic buildings, but rather, preserving them in innovative ways." At best, the Presidio of San Francisco contained the architecture of possibility. Ms. Marcia Smith-White, Head of the Neighborhood Association stated: "There are so many empty buildings here. You find yourself thinking: 'Why not'?"[65] "This is probably best illustrated by the conversion of the Presidio of San Francisco into a National Park operated by the US National Park Service. With the 1996 creation of a Trust Fund that will support the operation of the National Park, there is an opportunity to keep it open and in the 'black' financially. But it is unlikely that the activities there can match the employment offered by the US Army during the Presidio Post's long history as a military Installation."[66]

Concluding Comments

What happened to the Base closure emphasis since the Presidio of San Francisco, the Fort Ord Post, George AFB, Norton AFB, Beale AFB, Castle AFB, and Mather AFB closures during 1993? It has remained a mystery until a featured article appeared in the US Navy Times on March 31, 2003, entitled <u>Lawmakers warn of closing too many Bases</u>, by Ms. Karen Jowers. Another appropriate insight became apparent and the theme of this article would become the final finding to compliment a narrative history that required a befitting epilogue. Ms. Jowers had inquired into the usage and maintenance of the historical land and buildings made possible by many military Post and Base closures, together with the closure of overseas military Posts and Bases that would require transferring military personnel and Civil Service employees back to stateside military Posts and Bases. Before Defense officials decided to close many more stateside military Posts and Bases, they needed to ascertain that they would not need the physical space after closing down overseas military Posts and Bases. At a March 18th hearing, Senator Kay Bailey Hutchison, Republican from Texas, noted that Defense officials considered closing down or moving overseas military Posts and Bases; many military personnel and Civil Service employees would be sent to stateside Posts and Bases. Senator Hutchison, who chaired the Senator Appropriations Sub-Committee on military construction stated: "The last thing you want to do is close a military Post or Base and then find you need to reopen it. How are you going to ensure that during 2005 when you are making the final round of Post and Base closures, that you have totally in hand the information you need about closing foreign military Posts and Bases?"

Mr. Raymond DuBois, Deputy Undersecretary of Defense for Installations and Environment agreed that: "decisions on closing domestic military Posts and Bases cannot be done intelligently unless there is a rationalization of the

---

[65] Editorial, New York Times, New York, New York, "<u>A Force in Film Meets a Force of Nature,</u>" March 30, 2000, pp. F-1 and F-6.

[66] David S. Sorenson, "<u>Shutting Down The Cold War: The Politics of Military Base Closure,</u>" (St. Martin's Press, New York, July 1998), p.234.

overseas infrastructure." Mr. DuBois stated senior Defense officials discussed an "integrated global basing strategy and approach." Although the domestic Post and Base Realignment and Closure analysis had already started, information submitted by overseas Commanders would help inform the framework of that analysis. Mr. DuBois stated: "The overseas infrastructure did need reconfiguring," The immediate question was whether combatant Commanders felt the need to reprogram or change overseas construction projects during the 2003 through 2004 budget season. Defense officials had asked for input from the Commanders. In the meantime, military overseas construction projects funded during the 2003 Congressional budget were frozen.

Mr. DuBois stated: "Army General Leon LaPorte, Commander of US Forces Korea, had identified military Posts and Bases he believes were 'enduring' and those that were not. US Army officials were reviewing the list." Mr. DuBois had planned to ask the US Congress for authority to reprogram some funds and shifts them among projects. Mr. DuBois expected to have input for both the 2003 and 2004 budget soon. Mr. LaPorte stated: "he might recommend that a scheduled new barracks project be moved to a different location, where it would be built for the same amount of money." Mr. DuBois stated: "Since 1990, the US military had scaled back or closed 1000 overseas Sites, a 60-percent cut in infrastructure." In the US, prior rounds of military Post and Base closings had shut 97 major military Installations and realigned another 55 military Installations. Mr. DuBois stated: "All told, BRAC actions have saved the DOD about $17 billion, with annual recurring savings totaling about $7 billion." Mr. Du Bois stated: "Defense Secretary Donald Rumsfeld emphasized his desire to have a stronger process for evaluating military Posts and Bases, and their functions across the military services during the incoming round of military Post and Base closings." For example, in previous rounds the US Navy looked only at US Navy Bases when considering where it could move a function from a military Post or Base programmed for closure. This time, however, some functions would be considered as joint functions along with service specific reviews. In sum, as a result of previous BRAC rounds, the services have transferred about 271,769-acres to neighboring communities.[67] In the case of the Presidio of San Francisco; however, the Headquarters, Sixth US Army staff did not proceed to find a solution that would have more fully utilized vacant office space and other physical assets at the Presidio Post. This logic if applied particularly relating to the joint use of the Presidio Post by other Federal Government agencies in the City of San Francisco and Bay Area, had a largely unexplored set of possibilities. Such a solution would have definitely reduced operations, repair, and maintenance costs, and may have justified maintaining the Presidio Post an operational US Army Installation.

---

[67] Editorial, US Navy Times, Washington, DC, "Lawmakers warn of closing too many bases," March 31, 2003, p. 27.

CHAPTER XII

The Impact on Civil Service Employees

The Presidio of San Francisco Closure and Realignment Study presented a detailed schedule and description of personnel actions related to the realignment of the Headquarters, Sixth US Army staff along with the discontinuance of the Presidio Garrison; the transfer of Reserve organizations and mission functions to the US Army Reserve Command; and the transfer of the Presidio of San Francisco operations, repair, and maintenance mission and functions to the US National Park Service. The Headquarters, Sixth US Army's Personnel Action Plan was predicated on the planning and preparation for a major RIF with an effective date of September 30, 1992. It was planned to issue RIF notices to all Civil Service employees of the Presidio Post on August 1, 1992. The administrative preparation for these actions had already begun to include review and validation of personnel records for further employment qualifications, and review of competitive levels for RIF purposes. The Presidio Post employed 2619 Civil Service employees. All possible placement efforts were made to assist displaced Civil Service employees to find new positions. The DOD Priority Placement Program (PPP) was available for Civil Service employees willing to relocate to other military Installations. The PPP provided the principal mechanism for placing the affected employees elsewhere in the DOD. Through PPP, the knowledge, skills, and abilities of displaced employees were matched with vacant positions as they occur at other Federal Government activities throughout the DOD where the employees were willing to relocate.

The position match was accomplished through a computerized referral system operated by the Defense Data Support Center. If the new position involved a move to another physical location, the costs of moving the employee and his household would be borne by the Federal Government. If the new position was at a lower grade level, the employee's pay was saved to the maximum extent permitted by law. The OPM provided the Displaced Employee Program for referral to other Federal Government agencies. All Civil Service employees under RIF were registered in OPM's Displaced Employee Program. Through this avenue, the Civil Service employees were given priority consideration for vacancies in other Federal Government agencies. The State Employment Services provided placement assistance for displaced Civil Service employees desiring positions in private industry. And local placement programs existed to assist the Civil Service employees to find positions with State, County, City, and private employers within the community. These actions were expected to save the DOD an estimated $4 million.

The two conditions that contributed most surely to the best utilization of talent of human resources at the Presidio of San Francisco were the openness of the service and its facilitation of mobility. A static service is a stagnant service. Nothing more energizing has been found than occasional new blood in an organization and the stimulation of a new assignment for a Federal Civil Service employee. Monolithic careers that were commonplace with Civil Service positions were giving way to interchange and movement. This mobility was extending to industry, education, and international scene. Where selection processes, retirement systems, or other elements of Personnel policy inhibited such movement, modification should have been encouraged. Obviously, for mobility to mean anything, the concept of "closed" careers should have disappeared in Civil Service employee careers. The essential characteristics of such Personnel systems are non-adaptive and are incompatible with the dynamic, ever-changing imperatives of the modern Federal Government. There were 172 Civil Service employees assigned to the Headquarters, Sixth US Army staff against an authorization of 199. Effective September 30, 1992, the Headquarters, Sixth US Army staff lost 127 Civil Service authorizations. Personnel projections indicated 55 Civil Service employees on permanent appointments would be involuntarily separated as a result of these actions. In addition, all temporary Civil Service employees would be terminated. Notices were to be delivered to affected permanent employees on August 1, 1992 with an effective date no later than September 30, 1992, and to temporary employees on August 31, 1992 with an effective date no later than September 30, 1992. The remaining Civil Service employees would stay in positions authorized in the downsized Headquarters, Sixth US Army staff, the Presidio Garrison, or other tenant military organizations at the Presidio Post.

Individual Position Descriptions that contained organizational controls and major duties were reviewed, and appropriate titles, series, and grades were determined and certified by the Classification Review Process. Existing personnel assignments, their grade levels, functional duties, experiences, and educational backgrounds were reviewed. An evaluation of a revised organizational entity along with Position Descriptions that were matched to the new organizational structure was also included. Pertinent changes to Position Descriptions and the preparation and transmittal of reassignment papers were necessary to inform individual employees officially of anticipated and planned management actions. It was anticipated that the shift of major organizational elements would require a group transfer action that would be accomplished to reduce the Human Resource Office workload. To support the overall shift of Civil Service employees and the necessary Position Description evaluations, continued effort of experienced personnel from the Human Resource Office, organizational elements, and staff offices would be required. Preparation of new or revised Position Descriptions and Evaluation Reports, development of position factors, advertisement of vacant positions, formulation of rating panels, and management selection would also be required.

The estimated number of Civil Service positions eliminated would have increased if the budget proposal was changed, or if civilian personnel departures through retirement, transfer, or RIF did not occur as projected. The Letterman Army

Medical Center at the Presidio of San Francesco would be closed by 1994 as a result of the Base Closure and Realignment Act of 1988. As a result of the Letterman Army Medical Center closure, 554 permanent and 98 temporary Civil Service positions would be abolished over a three to four-year period. All career Civil Service employees affected by the reduction in authorized strength were given maximum assistance to continue their careers as employees of the DOD through reassignments within the DOD and other Federal Government agencies. In addition, in cooperation with the Department of Labor and State Employment Services, assistance was given to employees in locating positions in private industry. Employees whose positions were eliminated were given priority placement rights to other vacant positions in DOD and other Federal Government agencies. The employees were also given assistance in locating positions in private industry if they so desired.

Previously, the Headquarters, Sixth US Army staff and the Presidio Garrison officials had been fortunate inasmuch as very few Civil Service employees had been separated involuntarily. The Letterman Army Medical Center had been under a RIF since March 1990 because of the Base Closure and Realignment Act of 1988. During March 1990, it was announced that 652 Civil Service positions would be abolished and the Center closed by Fiscal Year 1995. The number of involuntarily separated Civil Service employees had eventually shrunk to 19 because of PPP, VERA, Job Fair, voluntary retirements, and Civil Service employees seeking other employment. On June 12, 1992, the DA had announced approval of a plan to close the 18-year old Letterman Army Institute of Research and relocate its three research programs as early as October 1992.[68] Under this plan, the Institute would be closed by the end of 1993. The closure was part of a medical research and development realignment directed by the DOD. Among the departments scheduled to be relocated were the Military Trauma Research Program to be transferred and consolidated with the US Army Institute of Surgical Research at Fort Sam Houston at San Antonio in Texas. The Laser Bio-effects Research Program would be relocated to the Walter Reed Institute of Research at the Armstrong Laboratory at Brooks AFB in Texas. The Blood Research Program would be relocated to the Walter Reed Institute of Research at the Naval Medical Research Institute at Bethesda in Maryland.

The closure of the Institute was one of many actions called for under the Base Closure and Realignment Act of 1991, and was a change from the 1988 Act of the same name that mandated relocation of the Institute to Fort Detrick in Maryland. Approval of the plan was good news for Colonel George J. Brown, Commander, Letterman Army Institute of Research. Colonel Brown stated: "We have all worked very diligently to formulate a solid, workable plan for transitioning our research programs and closing the Institute. We can now begin implementing the plan." The plan supported President Bush's objective of strengthening defense

---

[68] Star Presidian (San Francisco), "DA announces 1993 institute disestablishment." June 18, 1992, p. 1, col 1.

science and technology while implementing cost saving measures. Total estimated savings would amount to $6.6 million between Fiscal Years 1992 through 1997 according to DOD statistics. The closure would result in the elimination of 56 military personnel and 53 Civil Service employee administrative support positions. An estimated 57 military personnel and 54 Civil Service employees would be automatically transferred with the research programs.

Changes to the Headquarters, Sixth US Army Force Structure and Budget restrictions were the primary consideration in "running" a RIF. The Headquarters, Sixth US Army staff and the Presidio Garrison officials were responsible for determining what manpower "spaces" would be abolished. The socioeconomic and environmental impacts were excluded by definition from the first analysis as they did not constitute a significant effect with regard to the RIF of 127 permanent Civil Service employees with a $4 million payroll on the Headquarters, Sixth US Army staff. During 1995, the socioeconomic and environmental impacts would have to be submitted to the DOD with the discontinuance of the Headquarters, Sixth US Army staff and the Presidio Garrison, and the transfer of the Presidio of San Francisco's repair and maintenance mission and functions to the US National Park Service.

In actuality, it was every Civil Service employee's obligation to fulfill the requirements of the position once transferred or hired. The Position Description was not created to provide an employee with an income, but meticulously designed to render a service to the public and military service. It is the obligation of the employee who accepts the conditions of employment in the position to give it the full measure of his capacity and, if necessary, to move with the position or face termination. One of the most trying circumstances faced by harassed managers and supervisors at the Presidio of San Francisco was employees who considered it an imposition to be reassigned to another location when the needs of the military service and his own career development and aspirations clearly called for such a transfer.

Likewise, employee organizations had some obligations, not merely privileges. The tendency of Civil Service Unions to resist recognition of human differences; to fight the effect to discipline poor employees; to display little regard for quality performance; and to press for seniority as the main criterion for advancement and retention did nothing to facilitate the wholehearted acceptance as partners in setting the tone of the Headquarters, Sixth US Army staff. As an aside, a dichotomy did exist when all military officers are automatically promoted by date-of-rank unless passed over for inefficiency or other causes. So I respectfully ask the never-ending military argument: Why shouldn't enlisted military personnel and Civil Service employees be promoted in the same manner instead of world-wide competition or strictly biased in-house selection? And why should military enlished personnel lose stripes and Civil Service employees lose grades when military officers get a letter of reprimand or a slap on the wrist as a disciplinary action for the identical offense?

There could have been greater unification or coordination among the Federal Union at the Presidio of San Francisco. Until there was a more progressive and responsible leadership in some of them, the full possibilities of constructive consultation and negotiation would never be realized. Militancy, work stoppages, defense of mediocre employees, and submission to the selfish interests of their members did not build the kind of trust that was needed to develop a participative relationship with management in determining the terms and conditions of employment. The voice of employees was one that should have been heard. Its clarity and effectiveness should not have been compromised; however, by transmission through leadership that was still living in the industrial revolution, and that portrayed management as some kind of Scrooge or Simon Legree. Insistence on outmoded work methods and work relationships would only serve to weaken Federal Union influence. The innate conservation of the Federal Union and its resistance to technological, social, and organizational change was the most serious deterrent to Federal Union/management relations in the public service. In the case of the Presidio of San Francisco Closure and Realignment Study; however, there was little to negotiate about with the Federal Union.

Employment with the Federal Government (with minor exceptions) provided employees with position security; a prevailing wage rate; advancement potential; medical benefits; a safe and comfortable working environment; paid vacations; and a retirement plan. These were the very reasons people aspired to find Federal Government employment. History has shown that the Federal Government had at times exercised unlimited authority over its employees, and this authority had been based on its sovereignty. This related to the idea that Federal Government employees have only the rights that the Federal Government permitted them to have. The idea of Federal Government sovereignty was in accordance with the concepts that the King can do no wrong and that the Federal Government can only be sued with its consent. Employee resistance in the Federal Government then might be viewed as an application of the Magna Charta against the King. However; the Headquarters, Sixth US Army staff did allow Civil Service employee to have some control over their destiny and their rights as employees were not jeopardized under the guise of Federal Government sovereignty.

The Impact on Military Employees

General Forrester was directed to address only operational mission implications. However, General Forrester brought other areas to the attention of the US Army Forces Command. The Headquarters, Sixth US Army staff was deeply concerned and alarmed over the loss of enlisted military personnel services as documented and accepted as basic study parameters. The loss of the Post Exchange; Commissary; Morale, Welfare, and Recreational facilities servicing military personnel and retired service members was considered a serious mistake. The provisions for operation of these facilities should have been added to the Presidio of San Francisco Closure and Realignment Study. Even with the

221

Headquarters, Sixth US Army staff consolidation with the Presidio Garrison, there would be no significant loss in population at the Presidio of San Francisco. All of the 1286 sets of housing (Presidio Post, Fort Mason, West Fort Baker, Fort Cronkite, and Fort Barry) would be filled. The Headquarters, Sixth US Army staff expected a military and dependent population of at least 5000 personnel. The Headquarters, Sixth US Army staff was obligated to provide soldiers and their families the foregoing services within a reasonable distance of their homes. A round trip commute of over 15-miles through congested downtown City of San Francisco just to shop and use the limited recreational facilities at Treasure Island would not support the policy of the Chief of Staff of the US Army to protect and enhance the life styles of members of the US Army and their dependents. The latest Commissary Customer Composition Survey showed the average daily use of the Presidio Post Commissary was1194 patrons. Of this number, 17-percent were active duty, 33-percent were active duty dependents, and the remaining 50-percent were retired military personnel and their dependents.

A similar survey of the Post Exchange revealed a daily average of 975 patrons. Of this number, 19-percent were active duty, 36-percent were active duty dependents, 44-percent were retired members and their dependents, and the remaining 1-percent were Reserve personnel. Of equal importance to the remaining residents of the Presidio of San Francisco was the Morale, Welfare, and Recreational facilities. The loss of the Library; Bowling Alley; Officers' Club; Non-commissioned Officers' Club; Army Community Services; and Craft Shops were morally wrong. Those facilities, and the personnel and funds to operate them should have been placed back in the Study. Since the "Establishment" had put their stamp of approval on this ill-considered action, the Headquarters, Sixth US Army staff was obligated to carry it out. The decision was irreversible and sounded like the proverbial adage of "locking the barn door after the horse was out."

The loss of the Presidio Yacht Club (PYC) if the Fort Baker Post closure alternative was selected was also a big issue with military personnel. There was little rationale to justify the loss of this recreational facility, particularly when established procedures and precedence provided for retention of recreational facilities for the US Army under permit from the US National Park Service. The Yacht Club was completely self-sustaining to include the cost of utilities. Almost all repair and maintenance worload was performed by club members with the cost of materials coming from club revenue. The ongoing membership boasted over 300 members with 65 boats berthed at the docking facilities. Berthing at civilian facilities required a wait of two or more years with costs averaging four times that of the PYC rates. The increased expense would force military members to dispose of their privately owned boats.

The Impact on Retired Personnel

The City of San Francisco and Bay Area had a large retired military contingent, with heavy populations in Marin County and the City of San Francisco. If the Commissary and Post Exchange facilities were to be moved to Treasure Island, the service connected traffic traversing both the Golden Gate and the Bay Bridges would further congest San Francisco's already congested streets and wastefully increase the use of fossil fuels. Moreover, the Presidio of San Francisco was far more accessible by public transit than was Treasure Island.

General Forrester stated: "he was persuaded that there was sound operational and economic justification for the Headquarters, Sixth US Army staff and the Presidio Garrison officials to remain at the Presidio of San Francisco. General Forrester concluded by stating he could make the justification even stronger by using efficiently all available resources; for example, space, personnel, and services."[69] The primary question remains unanswered; Why General Forrester was not authorized or did not take steps to make an offer to Federal Government agencies in the City of San Francisco and Bay Area for the transfer to the Presidio Post made possibility?

Months of hard work by the Headquarters, Sixth US Army staff, Presidio Garrison officials, "Save the Presidio Committee," several outstanding Legislators, City Mayors, City Councils, County Supervisors, the media, and a lot of other dedicated public citizens had tried to culminate in an unprecedented reversal of an alleged policy decision to realign the Presidio of San Francisco, and contract out operating service and support functions that were provided by Civil Service employees. Both houses of the US Congress agreed that the Presidio Post plan was an unveracious concoction that would benefit only big business; would do nothing to improve conditions of the Reserve forces; and would result in making the US taxpayer pay an annual repair and maintenance budget several million dollars more than the present cost of Civil Service employee participation. In addition, it would cost the taxpayer several million dollars more just to transfer the Presidio Post to the US National Park Service and get the Presidio Post ready for a private contractor to walk in and take over operations, repair, and maintenance activities. The Administration ordered plan should go down in history as one of the most impertinent deceptions ever attempted. The Civil Service employees at the Presidio of San Francisco would have liked to believe that the Presidio Post contract conversion was dead and buried but they realized that the ideas of OMB Director Roy Ash would not give up that easily. Look at OMB's proposal that 185,000 US Air Force military personnel and Civil Service employees be turned over to big business. Look at Mr. Ash's drive to sell 33-percent of the San Diego

---

[69] Message from Headquarters, Sixth US Army, Presidio of San Francisco, Subject: "Base Realignment Study," to (Commander, US Army Forces Command, Atlanta, Georgia), March 16, 1979.

area Civil Service employee authorizations to the lowest bidder. Look at the other 42,000 Civil Service positions in California that were going on the auction block.

In addition, Representative Holifield, who was the Chairman of the House Legislation and Military Operations Sub-committee, who hailed from Downey in California, had introduced four bills in the US Congress that would have meant more trouble for Civil Service employees at the Presidio of San Francisco. HR-9059 and the Nixon Administration sponsored HR-9060, HR-9061, and HR-9062 for the purpose of establishing the Federal Office for Procurement under the Executive Branch of the Federal Government. HR-9059 for example originally contained language that could have placed this new Federal agency directly under the control of Mr. Roy Ash. However, the wording was changed in such a way that the new Federal Office of Procurement would be an independent agency.

All the President would have to do was appoint Mr. Roy Ash or one of his political cronies to supervise the Federal Office of Procurement and that would have been the demise of Civil Service employees in this Country. Section 16 of HR-9061 contained a blank check type of provision in that the Federal Office of Procurement could contract anything and everything it wanted unless specifically prohibited by the US Congress. Since most reactions from the US Congress would be too little and too late, the Federal Office of Procurement could have easily eliminated the entire Civil Service employee work force before anything or anybody could do to stop it.

One thing was for sure on the immediate status of Civil Service employees working at the Presidio of San Francisco. The Presidio Closure and Realignment Study would be ineffective insofar as the US Army and US Congress was concerned. There would be either a merger between the Headquarters, Sixth US Army staff and the Presidio Garrison; realignment of the Headquarters, Sixth US Army staff to Treasure Island or Fort Carson in Colorado; or the transfer of the Presidio Post to the US National Park Service. Efforts would continue, by a limited staff, to terminate actions underway to preserve an accurate record of programmed documentation, correspondence, and reports so that the workload that had been accomplished could be utilized to improve the management and execution of the mission and functions to be transferred.

The Impact on California

During May 2006, the DOD announced what military Posts and Bases should be closed. Expected to dwarf prior closure cycles, the BRAC 05 round came 10-years after a series of closures that targeted the State of California for far more reductions than any other State. Despite those reductions, the military services in California remained a significant economic force, and California's military Post and Base communities were girding for a potentially difficult year. In that context, this Case Study provides some background regarding past actions, current status, and future processes. It intends to complement and support an upcoming report prepared by the California Council on Base Support and Retention, appointed by the Governor, to oversee preparation for the upcoming BRAC round. This Case Study includes supporting material and other military Post, Base, and Department of Defense information.

On May 16, 2005, a list of military Posts and Bases recommended for closure and realignment was released by the DOD. The BRAC 05 Base Realignment and Closure round, sought by the DOD and authorized by the US Congress, would reduce the military Installation capacity by as much as one forth and in the process, deciding the fate of hundreds of thousands of DOD's military personnel and Civil Service employees throughout the US and around the World.

Citing a need to reduce unnecessary spending and to better distribute Defense assets, the DOD used the BRAC process to close purportedly less effective military Installations; and to realign forces, capital, weaponry, funds, and other limited resources to maximize the military's effectiveness. A GAO report estimated that the four previous rounds of military Post and Base closures conducted during 1988, 1991, 1993, and 1995 had saved the Defense budget more than $35 billion.

Despite the military and budgetary benefits BRAC may have yielded, the military Post and Base closure process stirred enormous concern and consternation at the community level. Entire communities risked losing an important, if not essential, source of economic, cultural, and social support. Politicians worried about the potential harm to their regions' constituents, businesses, and tax base. Military contractors wondered how the closure of military Posts and Bases might affect their employees and Shareholders. The unknown information exacerbated the angst surrounding the BRAC nature of the process. For the most part, closure and realignment decisions were made internally at the DOD with little input from outside sources. If a military Post or Base appeared on the Secretary's list for Post or Base closure, it would have been extremely difficult to alter its fate.

The State of California, more than any other State, had an intimate understanding of the pain that military Post or Base closures could cause and how unevenly that pain could be distributed. In the four previous BRAC rounds, the State of California absorbed 54-percent of the nation's overall personnel lose losing 93,000 military personnel and Civil Service employees, and nearly 30 major military Posts and Bases. Many communities in California have still not recovered from military Posts and Bases closures. Analysts estimated that base closures would cost the State of California close to $9.6 billion in revenue.

Despite disproportionate reductions, the State of California still hosted more military Posts and Bases, military personnel, and Civil Service employees than any other State in the nation. California's 424 military locations, to include 26 large and medium military Installations, supported nearly 200,000 military personnel and Civil Service employees. The DOD directly spends more than $40 billion annually in California yielding considerable more in overall benefits to California's economy. Even though California experienced severe losses in the first four BRAC rounds of Post and Base closures, the military services still played a very important role in California.

The first four rounds of Post and Base closures during 1988, 1991, 1993, and 1995 comprised a distressing chapter in California's military, political, and economic history. California suffered disproportionate reductions in each of the four rounds. Once the dust settled, the military presence in California was sharply reduced from pre-BRAC levels. Before BRAC 88, California had by far the largest military presence of any State housing 335,979 (14.7-percent) of the 2,275,264 DOD military personnel and Civil Service employees and 91 (18.3-percent) of the 495 military Posts and Bases in the US. After the first four BRAC rounds, California lost 93,546 military personnel and Civil Service employees within the DOD, a staggering 53.8-percent of the 173,919 military personnel and Civil Service employees that net the DOD reductions for the entire US. California shouldered the loss of nearly 100,000 military personnel and Civil Service employees, whereas the other 49 States combined absorbed just 80,383 reductions. While California lost 27.8-percent of its personnel between 1988 and 1995, the rest of the nation saw military personnel reduced by just 3.6-percent.

Comparing the number of Posts and Bases rather than military personnel and Civil Service employees, California fared slightly better. According to the 1995 Defense Base Closure and Realignment Commission Report to the President, the four BRAC rounds closed 98 major military Installations throughout the US. Of those, 24 (25-percent) military Installations were in California. The BRAC rounds also led to the realignment of 65 major military Installations where eight (11-percent) were in California. If Post and Base closures were examined with a focus on the military Installation size that have closed, the magnitude of California's losses would become more apparent. California absorbed 30-percent of the closures at military Installations with more than 1000 military personnel and Civil Service employees, 59-percent of the closures at military Installations with more than 5000 military personnel and Civil Service employees, and 100-percent of the closures at military Installations with more than 10,000 military personnel and Civil Service employees. The BRAC processes disproportionate treatment of California was surprising, particularly to California's elected officials. Some charged that California's lopsided reductions were at least partly due to a lack of preparation for the Post or Base closure process and to political disunity at the National, State, and local levels. Instead of cooperating to consolidate and strengthen California's preeminent position as a home for the military, some communities within California fought against one another over the dwindling number of Post and Bases. Although some collaboration with California may have proven effective, when they are compared with campaigns waged by some other States, lawmakers neither organized a broad State-wide effort to protect the State of California's military interests nor used their strength to protect California. In fact, some observers had speculated that decision makers within the DOD relied on disunity within California in targeting the State of California for drastic reductions, convinced that rivalries would prevent California from mounting an effective organized defense of its military Posts and Bases, and of military personnel and Civil Service employees.

Throughout California, military Post and Base closures had a dramatic ripple effect on the economy. In particular, the aerospace industry, most heavily concentrated in Los Angeles County but significant to many other regions, experienced a severe recession that negatively impacted the economic health of California for a decade. The City of San Francisco to San Diego communities were forced to undergo the slow, often painful process of designing and implementing Transition and Re-Use Plans for closed military Posts and Bases. A number of closed military facilities in California are still not fully transitioned to non-military use. Each of the first four BRAC rounds was similarly harsh on California. Unlike other States, where one round hit hard while others had no effect at all, California's share of reductions was grossly disproportionate. The cumulative effect of the BRAC 88, 91, 93, and 95 rounds of military Post and Base closures were nothing less than disastrous. Analysts estimated that California would experience approximately $9.6 billion in annual economic loss from the BRAC process.

During the BRAC 88 round, the State of California had four major military Installations closed to include the Presidio of California, the Fort Ord Post, George AFB, Norton AFB, Beale AFB, Castle AFB, and Mather AFB as mentioned above. There were, 16 other major Posts and Bases; zero realigned; and the lost of 17,252 military personnel and Civil Service employees. Nationally, this round of closures eliminated a net total of 20,607 military personnel and Civil Service employees, and 16 major military Posts and Bases. California sustained 84-percent of the nation's net personnel reductions and 25-percent of military Post and Base closures in California. In addition, the Naval Station Hunter Point that was classified as major by the DOD lost more than 4000 military personnel and Civil Service employees.

During the BRAC 91 round, the State of California had eight major military Installations closed; three realigned; and lost a total of 31,452 military personnel and Civil Service employees. Nationally, this BRAC round closed 26 major military Posts and Bases; realigned 19 other military Posts or Bases, and eliminated a total of 59,466 military personnel and Civil Service employees. California sustained 31-percent of major military Post and Base closures, 16-percent of major realignments, and 53-percent of the nation's personnel reductions. In California, BRAC 91 Post or Base closures included the Fort Ord Post; Castle AFB; Hunters Point Annex; Long Beach Naval Station; Marine Corps Air Station Tustin; Naval Air Station Moffett Field; Sacramento Army Depot; and the Naval Electronics Systems Engineering Center San Diego. Beale AFB; Naval Weapons Center China Lake; and the Pacific Missile Test Center at Point Mugu were realigned. Some observers have opined that the lessons of the Mather AFB stutter-step re-use were learned by the time the Sacramento Army Depot was closed at high speed. The day the US Army flag came down, the City leased the facility to Packard Bell that transferred 5000 employees from its former headquarters in Southern California. Unfortunately, the technology company's fortunes faltered, and by the close of 2000, all of the employees had been laid off. Sacramento Army Depot serves as a reminder that the economic recovery of a military Post depended on controllable factors such as transfer speeds, usability of land, uncontrollable factors strength of the local economy, and the success of individual businesses.

During the BRAC 93 round, the State of California had several military Installations closed and two military Installations realigned, leading to the loss of 29,683 military personnel and Civil Service employees. Nationally, this round closed 28 major military Posts and Bases, realigned 13 major military Installations, and eliminated 62,426 military personnel and Civil Service employees meaning California sustained 25-percent of military Post or Base closures, 15-percent realignments, and 48-percent of the nation's personnel reductions. For the BRAC 93 round, the DOD closures included El Toro Marine Corps Air Station, Mare Island Naval Shipyard, Alameda Naval Air Station and Depot, Naval Hospital Oakland, Naval Training Center San Diego, and Treasure Island Naval Station all in California. Marine Corps Logistics Base Barstow and Naval Weapons Center Seal Beach both in California were realigned. In addition, the Naval Public Works Center at Oakland in California was discontinued, and March AFB at Riverside in California was significantly realigned.

The BRAC 93 round also decimated the Oakland/Alameda Naval operations. The Naval Air Station Alameda and Depot, the Oakland Naval Hospital, and the Navy Public Works Center were eliminated complementing the City of San Francisco and Bay Area. The Mare Island facility was initially christened as a Shipyard at the North end of the San Francisco Bay during 1853. The Mare Island Naval Shipyard served as a major Refueling and Renovation facility for ships to include those powered by nuclear energy. The Mare Island facility also built more than 500 new vessels, from a Paddle wheel Gunboat during 1959, to a Nuclear Submarine during 1970. During 1996, the Mare Island facility closed with a relatively swift de-commissioning. However, not surprisingly given the diversity and age of the facility, Mare Island remained heavily contaminated with myriad toxins, to include PCBs, asbestos, solvents, oil and petroleum products, aging ordinances, and the by-products of several decades conducting work on Nuclear Submarines.

During 1997, the Mare Island Naval Shipyard Base and Treasure Island once employing 18,000 military personnel and Civil Service employees; and the NAS Alameda was transferred to the City of Alameda; and the City's initial tenant included the Federal Government's Maritime Administration (MARAD) and a local Re-Use Authority. The facility was built by diking off muddy flats and filling it in with dredging material with a mixture of tidewater, submerged land, and dry land. Environmental issues were also raised by the sites past use as an Oil

Refinery and a Borax Processing Plant. Some sites have been successfully re-used by non-profit organizations.

During the BRAC 95 round, the State California had five major military Installations closed and three realigned, leading to the loss of 15,058 military personnel and Civil Service employees. Nationally, this round closed 28 major Posts and Bases, realigned 22 major military Installations, and reduced 31,420 military personnel and Civil Service employees meaning that California sustained 18-percent of major military Post and Base closures 14-percent of major realignments, and 48-percent of the nation's personnel reductions. Closed Posts and Bases included: Long Beach Naval Shipyard, McClellan AFB, Oakland Army Base, Ontario International Airport Air Guard Station, and Defense Distribution Depot McClellan. Onizuka AFB, Fort Hunter Liggett, and Sierra Army Depot were realigned.

Well before it was slated for closure during 1995, the Long Beach Naval Shipyard was assigned elsewhere when the Base went on the BRAC 91 closure list, taking with them an estimated 17,000 military personnel and Civil Service employees when it was ultimately closed during 1994. The nearby shipyard, built on Terminal Island largely during World War II and highly respected for its workmanship, was slated for closure one-year later. During September 1997, its military gates were closed and more than two-thirds of the acreage was transferred to other entities in various parcels. The City of Long Beach assumed most of the land and dry docks, with other parcels transferred to the US Army, US Air Force, profit organizations, and to a housing developer for a College and Preparatory School. Final transfer was expected during September 2005.

Once a major DOD Technology Repair Center employing 13,500 Civil Service employees before 1995, McClellan AFB North of Sacramento became battlefield regarding political influence over the BRAC process. McClellan and a second Base outside of San Antonio in Texas were on the BRAC list proposed by the US Air Force. However, the Nixon Administration pledged to retain military and Civil Service employees as long as possible and to privatize many of those positions thereby raising the eyebrows and ire of many BRAC proponents. The facility later returned to the more traditional military Post and Base closure pipeline and was shuttered during 2001, but not until after widespread criticism that the Clinton Administration tampered with a supposedly political military Post and Base closure process in order to better his and other Democrat's 1996 election prospects in two key States. Many believe that lingering resentment among Republicans over the President's breaking of rules by choosing favorites of the McClellan AFB in California and the Kelly AFB in Texas that were responsible for the 10-year hiatus in the Post and Base closure process.

As evident by these details, the State of California found no refuge from the bad news throughout four rounds of Post and Base downsizing. More than half of the nation's net personnel reductions were taken from California military

Installations. Each BRAC round battered California's military Post and Base communities, but the results were far from uniform across the State. The military presence in the San Francisco Bay Area has been nearly eliminated by military Post and Base closures, with the bulk of the reductions affected by the BRAC 93 military Post and Base closure round. Once the dust had settled, the City of San Francisco and Bay Area had experienced a reduction of more than 44,000 military personnel and Civil Service employees. A mere 2617 in military personnel and Civil Service employee gains offset gross personnel reductions. In addition, most of the 17,306 reductions from the Central Coast region came from the Fort Ord Post that is often associated with the Presidio of San Francisco and the City of San Francisco and Bay Area.

In contrast, the San Diego Area became a net receiver. The military Post and Base closures at the Presidio of San Francisco and the City of San Francisco and Bay Area resulted in the elimination of more than 24,000 military personnel and Civil Service employees; however, the DOD elected to relocate more than 30,000 military personnel and Civil Service employees to San Diego military Installations by the time the BRAC process had closed yielding a net increase of 6099 military personnel and Civil Service employees for the San Diego area. Two other California areas had vast reductions in military personnel and Civil Service employees. The greater Los Angeles region declined by nearly 24,000 military personnel and Civil Serviced employees, and the Central Valley military Installations declined by more than 17,000 military personnel and Civil Service employees.

It's not a coincidence that the States of California, Virginia, and Texas ranked first, second, and third in terms of both prime contract awards, and military personnel and Civil Service employees. Furthermore, as discussed above, California's disproportionate decline in Defense spending over the past 20-years is at least partly due to past military Post and Base closures. If California were to lose a significant number of military Posts and Bases during the upcoming closure round, the State would expect to lose some portion of the DOD contract spending. For industries of any type impact California's economy more than the military combined, the DOD payroll and prime contract awards in California accounted for $42 billion of Federal Government spending for Fiscal Year 2003. During Fiscal Year 2003 or comparison, according to the California Department of Food and Agriculture, the agriculture industry, sometimes viewed as California's largest industry, had an aggregate economic impact of $27.8 billion.

At the same time that the State of California was experiencing disproportionate decreases in military personnel and Civil Service employees, and in the numbers of military Posts and Bases, California suffered the parallel blow of a steep decline in Federal Defense procurement expenditures. During 1994, according to the US Census Bureau, California's share of contract procurement spending for National Defense was once as high as 23-percent; the DOD spent $29 billion on contracts in California; and $141 billion in all States. During 2003, after a slow but steady decline, California received just 14.2-percent of Defense contract expenditures; $26 billion of the $201 billion total distributed nation-wide. In the aftermath of Post and Base closures, contract spending in all States had risen by $60 billion (42-percent). Whereas spending in California was now roughly half of its inflation adjusted 1984 levels.

When the DOD contracts were considered alongside salary and other Defense spending, California experienced a similar and starker decline. During 1984 through 1986, total Defense spending in California hovered near the $40 billion mark, accounting for more than 20-percent of the nation's $197 billion in total 1984 Defense spending in all States. Nearly two decades later, California's share of total 2003 Defense spending Nationwide, including salaries, contracts, and other categories, was just 13-percent or $39 billion of the nation's $320 billion total spending in all States. Thus, 2003 Defense spending in California remained at $2 billion; five-percent less than during 1984 (even before adjusting inflation), whereas spending in all States had grown by $$89 billion (38-percent) during the same period.

Military Post and Base closures and concomitant decline in Federal Defense spending in California had much to do with the changing post-World War II era. Many officials argue the fall of the Soviet Union was hastened by the US Defense decline spending on military personnel and Civil Service employees, military Posts and Bases, and California procurement. After all, maintaining a force strength and Defense spending at Cold War levels after the end of the Cold War conflict made little sense. After essentially spending itself to WW II victory, it was not surprising that the US pared back on military spending by terminating weapons programs; downscaling recruitment; and closing military Installations. While California had a particularly negative experience with military Post and Base closures, the DOD viewed the first four BRAC rounds as a collective success, effectively reducing excess force capacity and cutting costs. A January 2005 GAO report to the US Congress measured net savings from the four prior BRAC rounds through fiscal year 2003 at $28.9 billion. The DOD estimated approximately $7 billion in savings for Fiscal Year 2004 and every year thereafter, generated mostly from reduced operating expenses. As of September 30, 2004, the DOD data shows that 72-percent of 504,000 acres of closed military Post and Base land had been transferred to Federal Government or non-Federal Government entities.

The same GAO report examined how individual military Posts and Bases and their surrounding communities have recovered from the closure process. While the data was not comprehensive or incisive enough to paint a full picture of these community experiences, the report concluded that most communities had recovered or are recovering from the impact of military Post and Base closures. During 2002, nearly 70-percent of the 62 BRAC communities reviewed by the GAO had unemployment rates lower than the national average, and 48-percent had annual real per capita income growth rates above the US average. On October 31, 2003, 92,921 (72-percent) of the 129,649 Civil Service employees lost on 73 military Posts and Bases as a result of military Post and Base closures have been replaced at these locations.

The State of California's overall recovery, measured by Civil Service employees replaced, had been worse by the national average. The 18 California military Posts and Bases examined in the GAO report lost approximately 42,800 Civil Service employees from the DOD payroll. On October 31, 2003, these military Posts and Bases had only regained 24,179 jobs (57-percent). The remainder of the closed military Posts and Bases in the US considered by the GAO report regained approximately 68,742 of 86,849 eliminated positions, a 79-percent recovery rate. California had four of the 18 BRAC locations (22-percent) with unemployment rates higher than the US average, including two of the three communities with the highest unemployment rates (Merced, 16-percent, and Salinas, 11-percent). In terms of average annual real per capita growth rates for BRAC communities, California fared better, housing only five of 33 BRAC locations with growth rates below the US average (15-percent).

The Cities of San Francisco and San Jose had the two highest average annual real per capita income growths rates of any of the 62 communities included in the report. The Federal Government data painted a mixed picture of California's recovery, certainly not as optimistic as the overall GAO report. The speed of a military Post or Base recovery from closure also depended on factors beyond economics. Most closed and closing military Posts and Bases required some environmental remediation work to render them suitable for alternative uses. The cost of clean-up activities at military Posts and Bases previously slated for closure far exceeded Federal Government resources that have been committed to them to date, and the backlog of unpaid costs will continue rising with any new closure. Federal Government clean-up resources have barely scratched the surface of an environmental remediation problem where total costs may not be fully appreciated for decades. Through the Defense Environmental Restoration Program (DERP), the DOD worked to ameliorate environmental problems at open, closing, and closed military Posts and Bases. The DERP spending on active clean-up activities at all types of military Posts and Bases through Fiscal Year 2003 totaled $21.7 billion, of which $5 billion was spent in California. Of the California amount, $3 billion was spent at military Installations slated for closure in one of the four BRAC rounds

In addition, the DERP estimated total clean-up expenditures that would still be required between 2004 and the clean-up completion (which is some cases may be many decades away). Although notoriously difficult to predict, the DERP estimated spending still required at all open, closed, and closing military Posts and Bases nationwide at $33 billion, with $6.6 billion required in California. The DERP estimated ongoing clean-up (from 2004 through completion) at California military Posts and Bases closed the BRAC 88-95 at $1.8 billion. Liability for clean-up costs and in some situations including damage from environmentally focused tort lawsuits were a major bone of contention among the major transactional players.

For example, the DOD, State of California, local Governments, previous property owners, and new tenants. Other environmental and structural issues make former military Posts and Bases less desirable than private sector alternatives, and often military facilities were not constructed in compliance with local building codes. Because of the complexity of the re-use process, the transformation of closed military Posts and Bases could take decades. There still remained more than 130 thousand acres of land on previously closed military Posts and Bases that have not yet transitioned to non-military use.

With the BRAC 05 process underway, it was important that the State of California not overlook the lessons of the four previous military Post and Base closure rounds. While it has produced a more favorable outcome, it's certain that California suffered disproportionately from the DOD decisions. During 1988, California bore 54-percent of personnel reductions in the DOD, despite having housed only 15-percent of the DOD personnel. From 1988 through 1995, California lost nearly 28-percent of its DOD military personnel and Civil Service employees; military Post and Base closures; where the nation's total net reduction was just 3.6-percent. By the time the four BRAC rounds came to an end, California had lost more than 93 thousand military personnel and Civil Service employees, and California's economic activity had been dialed back by nearly $10 billion per year. Despite devastating Defense reductions, California still had much more to lose. Nationally, California was much more closely identified with Hollywood, Silicon Valley, beaches, agriculture, military and National security industry that have enormous presence in California, and much of California's development came thanks to the financial intellectual resources associated with Defense expenditures. Despite the reduction of military personnel and Civil Service employees, and large Military Post and Base Installations, the State of California experienced during the first four rounds of military Post and Base closures, California still housed the most military Installations and personnel of any State in the Country. According to the DOD's Fiscal Year 2004 Base Structure Report, the military had 3727 locations in the US, 93 large military Installations, 99 medium military Installations, and 3535 small military Installations and locations. California had the most total locations of any State with 424, accounting for 11.3-percent of all locations, 175 more than the State of Montana that was second with 249. California's military strength became even more apparent when its large and medium military Installations were compared to the rest of the Country. California had 15 large and 11 medium military Installations within its borders, 13.5-percent of the military Post and Bases in those two categories. No other State had more than six large military Installations, and only the State of Virginia, with 11, had more than six medium military Installations.

California's military Posts and Bases are most heavily concentrated in Southern California, particularly in the San Diego area and other areas South of Los Angeles County. The center of the US Navy's Pacific operations was located in San Diego, with at least six important military Posts and Bases in the area. There are; however, Posts and Bases in nearly every region of California, ranging from the

Sierra Army Depot in the Northern sector of the State, to the Naval Air Weapons Station China Lake in Ridgecrest to the Naval Air Facility in El Centro.

The State of California was also home to more military personnel and Civil Service employees than any other State in the Country. The DOD's Directorate for Information Operations and Reports (DIOR) that compiles annual statistics for the DOD, showed 188,104 active duty military personnel and Civil Service employees were located in California. That total represented 11.1-percent of all military personnel and Civil Service employees in the US. Only North Carolina (113,302), Texas (152,214), and Virginia (170,508) had more than 100,000 in military Posts and Bases within their States.

The US Navy and the Marine Corps had 74,779 military personnel and 59,636 Civil Service employees in California respectively. The Marine Corps' Camp Pendleton, located north of San Diego, is by far the largest military Base in the State supporting a total of 37,262-military personnel and Civil Service employees. Various San Diego military Bases and Twenty-Nine Palms also function as home to more than 10,000 military personnel and Civil Service employees. Among other active military personnel in California were 20,658 in the US Air Force and 8145 in the US Army. The Civil Service employees working directly for the DOD comprised another important component of California's employment base. According to DIOR data for September 30, 2003, associated with the US Navy or Marine Corps, 10,213 with the US Air Force, 7139 with the US Army, and 7534 with other DOD agencies. During 2003, California housed 130,473 military personnel and 57,631 Civil Service employees.

During Fiscal Year 2003, the DOD spent $13.3 billion for payrolls in California, to include $6.0 billion for active duty military pay, $3.4 billion for Civil Service employee pay, $427 million for Reserve and National Guard pay, and $2.5 billion for retired military pay. The DOD remained one of the largest employers in California. The DOD affects California in important ways beyond military Posts and Bases, military personnel and Civil Service employees. Every year, the DOD distributes hundreds of billions of dollars for contracts with private Companies, Universities, and other organizations to do everything from disposal of waste on military Posts and Bases to manufacture aircraft carriers, missiles, planes, and satellite technologies. According to the DIOR, that calculated contracts slightly different than the Census Bureau during Fiscal Year 2004, the DOD awarded $203 billion in prime contract awards. Of those awards, California Companies and other recipients won $27.9 billion, (13.7-percent) of all contracts. Other States with large total awards included Virginia, with $23.5 billion, (11-percent) and Texas with $21 billion (10-percent). On a per capita basis, however, California ranked 16th out of the States and District of Columbia, with $786 in spending per person; the District of Columbia $6,212 per person, Virginia $3,181 per person, and Connecticut $2,583 per person are the three States with the highest per capita prime contract awards.

Among the military services, procurement spending by the US Air Force is the most California centric. During 2003, the US Air Force contract spending of $12.8 billion was nearly 24-percent of the $53.3 billion total spent nation-wide. On a per capita basis, US Air Force contracts provided California $183 for every man, woman, and child in the State was exactly twice the national per capita amount of $91. Nation-wide, total procurement spending by the US Navy was slightly higher, at $54.1 billion, but California's $7.3 billion represented a much smaller share (13.6-percent) of total US Navy contracts. Historically, California's share of US Army contracts had been smaller; the State received $3.7 billion (7.8-percent) of the nation's $48 billion.

The Counties of Los Angeles, San Diego, and Santa Clara led the way during 2004 as recipients of prime contract awards, receiving $9.7 billion, $5.1 billion, and $3.8 billion respectively. During Fiscal Year 2003, (Sub-County contract data were not yet available for Fiscal Year 2004), the five corporations receiving more than $1 billion in Federal Government contracts in California were the Boeing Company ($5.3 billion), Lockheed Martin Corporation ($4.3 billion), Northrop Grumman Corporation ($3.3 billion), Health Net Inc. ($1.8 billion), and Science Applications International Corporation ($1.0 billion). Because expenditures for some programs were classified; it was difficult to determine an exact figure for how many positions these prime contract awards directly supported. Some estimated the number of positions outside of the DOD payroll supported by the DOD spending in California at considerably more than $100 thousand. Prime contract awards were not necessarily related to the presence of military Posts and Bases in a given area. However, the relative concentration of contract awards in California was at least in some part linked to a large military presence in California.

As with most industries, the effect of the DOD spending in California reached well beyond payrolls and prime contract award totals. Military personnel use their wages to purchase goods at non-military stores throughout California. The Civil Service employees bought goods, services, and homes near the military Installation where they worked. Employees working for the corporations that won DOD contracts also re-circulated their earnings through California's economy with that multiplier effect in mind; it's likely that DOD spending in California had an annual impact on the State that exceeded $100 thousand.

During 2001, the birth of the BRAC 05 round occurred with the passing of the National Defense Reauthorization Act of Fiscal Year 2002. On December 28,2001, in this bill, President Bush signed into law the US Congress gave the Secretary of Defense the authority to implement a new round of military Post and Base closures during 2005, the first in more than a decade. The authorized language required that the DOD "consider all military Installations within the US equally without regard to whether the military Installation had been previously considered for closure or realignment by DOD." By December 22, 2005, the Bill initiated the procedural steps that would ultimately culminate in a final list of military Posts and Bases designated for closure or realignment.

The push for another round of military Post and Base closures began almost as soon as President Bush and Defense Secretary Rumsfeld assumed office. Since the start of the first Bush Administration, the DOD has been working to reshape the Force Structure of the military services by making them smaller, sleeker, and more agile. Secretary Rumsfeld had pointed to Post and Base closures as an opportunity to trim ineffective and wasteful military Installations while simultaneously realigning the current Force Structure into a more effective and efficient organization. During March 2004, in an analysis required by the BRAC process and submitted to the US Congress, the DOD estimated that it was currently supporting 24-percent excess military Installation capacity. The DOD found that "recent events have exacerbated the need to rapidly accomplish transformation and reshaping. Excessive infrastructure did exist and was available for reshaping or needed to be eliminated."

On March 29, 2005, Secretary Rumsfeld indicated that the upcoming round of military Post and Base closures may not reduce as deeply as 24-percent. During comments to Reporters at the DOD, Secretary Rumsfeld stated: "The reductions may be less than 20-percent, as opposed to the previously established 24-percent." Even with the lower estimate, the BRAC 05 round would be enormous; larger than at previous rounds. During 2003, the DOD had a world-wide workforce of 2,098,901 active duty military personnel and Civil Service employees; a 24-percent cutback in military personnel and Civil Service employees would result in the reduction of over 500 thousand positions. The same reductions would result in more than 45 thousand positions in Caliifornia. In retrospect, the four previous rounds of Post and Base closures eliminated a total of 173,919 military personnel and Civil Service employees, a mere 8-percent reduction in DOD's personnel.

The DOD had implied that the domestic pain of this round of closures might be eased by closuring overseas military Posts and Bases. As many as 77 thousand overseas military personnel and Civil Service employees may return to domestic military Posts and Bases officials noted. However, closer analysis of the DOD data regarding overseas personnel suggested that a reduction of 77 thousand overseas positions would not necessarily lessen the pressure to downsize domestic military Posts and Bases and might in fact increase it. In any case, the round of Post and Base closures was expected to be massive, affecting hundreds of Posts and Bases, communities, and hundreds of thousands of DOD Civil Service positions.

The DOD had already submitted Force Structure projections that extended through 2004, and the US Congress had approved the DOD's Final Criteria for determining the status of existing military Posts and Bases and deciding what military Posts and Bases to close and realign. During mid-March 2005, after the White House announced the preliminary BRAC nominations-recommended by

Congressional party leaders and the Administration itself, President Bush on April 1st used his recess-appointment power to confirm the nine Commissioners.

The Commission would wait until May 16, 2005 for the official release by the Secretary of Defense of the military Posts and Bases identified for closure or realignment (although it could have been released before that date). Once the so called "hit" list had been announced, the Commission had until September 8, 2005 to review, analyze, and modify the Secretary of Defense's recommendations. During this time period, the Commission would have had held public sessions at all military Posts and Bases recommended for closure. In an important change from the past BRAC rounds, seven of nine votes on the Commission were required to add a military Post or Base to the closure list. Now a simple majority (five out of nine votes), could remove a military Installation from the so called "hit" list.

By September 23, 2005, the President would have to approve the Commission's so called "hit" list of military Post and Base closures and realignments, or disapprove the list and send it back to the Commission for further modification. If the President disapproved the Commission's "hit" list, they had until October 20, 2005 to revise it. By November 7, 2005, the President had to transmit the military Post and Base closure and realignment "hit" list to the US Congress or the BRAC process would become null and void. By December 22, 2005, the US Congress had to approve or disapprove the "hit" list transmitted to them by the President. If the US Congress disapproved the "hit" list, the BRAC process again would become null and void. If Congress approved the "hit" list, the closures and realignments assumed the power of law, and military Posts and Bases would begin to close. During February 2004, criteria were published to determine military Post and Base closures and realignments focused primarily on military value. Of the eight published criteria, the factors that form the core of the criteria addressed military value. They were:

- The current and future mission requirements and the impact on operational readiness of the total DOD force, to include the impact on joint "war fighting;" training; readiness; research; development; test; and evaluation of weapons systems and equipment;

- The availability and condition of land, facilities, infrastructure, and associated air and water spa at both existing and potential receiving locations;

- The ability to accommodate contingency, mobilization, and future force requirements at both existing and potential receiving locations to support operations, training, repair, and maintenance;

- Preservation of land, air, water space, facilities, and infrastructure necessary to support training and operations of military forces determined to be surge requirements by the DOD;

- The final criteria addressed "other considerations" and could generally be used as tiebreakers between military Posts and Bases that are considered equal under the military value criteria;

- The extent and timing of potential costs and savings of military Post and Base realignments and closure actions on the entire Federal Government budget as well as the DOD. Those costs would include items related to potential environmental restoration, waste management, and environmental compliance activities;

- The economic impact on existing communities in the vicinity of military Installations;

- The ability of the infrastructure of both existing and potential receiving of living standards for members of the armed forces and their dependents;

- The environmental impact on receiving locations.

Two important points separated the criteria for the BRAC 05 round from criteria for earlier rounds. First, the DOD included joint "war fighting" as a consideration that referred to the shared use of resources by the various branches of the armed services. Developing joint capabilities among services had been a long-term goal of the current Administration. As such, the DOD had explicitly stated that it would use the BRAC round to reshape the military service, placing an emphasis on increasing efficiency through joint "war fighting" capabilities. Second, the DOD had made a statutory change to the criteria, requiring that military value be the primary consideration as opposed to one of the primary considerations, in determining what military Posts or Bases are to be closed. This relegates socioeconomic impact on surrounding communities to a secondary criterion.

In the interest of avoiding political battles over military Post and Base closures, the BRAC process was relatively insular, and consequently, quite difficult to influence. The DOD in conjunction with the four branches of the military services received significant freedom to determine what military Posts and Bases were to be selected for closure and realignment. For more than a year, the DOD had been collecting and assessing information from all of its military Posts and Bases. Using that data, the DOD had constructed a variety of scenarios that simultaneously accomplished its long term military goal of reshaping the armed services and its military Post and Base closing objectives. All of these decisions occurred outside of public citizen view, with no opportunity for public citizen comment or criticism before the list was released. Over the past two-years, a number of purported military Post and Base closure lists have surfaced on the Internet or in newspapers. The DOD had consistently stated that any such list was not valid.

Despite the insulating nature of the BRAC process, military Post and Base closures were not beyond the influence of politics. In general, there were three ways to affect the final list of military Post and Base closures and realignments. First, before the DOD published the list of closures and realignments, politicians, lobbyists, and community activists could use connections at the DOD and in the Executive Board to attempt to prevent a military Post or Base from appearing on the May 16th list submitted by the Secretary of Defense. Second, the political party leaders in the US Congress influenced the make-up of the BRAC Commission to ensure that his or her State or constituents' concerns were represented. Finally, once the DOD's list had been released, politicians, retired military personnel, and community activists could argue the merits of their military Installation to the BRAC Commission at public hearings in the hope of convincing the Commissioners to remove it from the list.

The State of California (at the Federal Government, State, and local levels) had already been active in attempting to protect its military Posts and Bases before the list was published. California's Bipartisan Congressional Delegation had been unified and extremely vocal, emphasizing California's disproportionate losses from previous military Post and Base closures and promoting California as an ideal home for the military services. During November 2004, Governor Arnold Schwarzenegger created the California Council on military Post and Base Support and Retention. The Council chaired jointly by Leon Panetta, President Bill Clinton's former Chief of Administration, was charged with organizing a state-wide effort to minimize the negative impact of the upcoming BRAC round to California.

During January 2005, the Council held a series of public sessions throughout the State to hear concerns from communities potentially affected by BRAC, and submitted a report to the Governor during April 2005. During February 2005, Governor Swarzenegger and leaders of the State Legislature had been visible in Washington devoting a portion of their time during a delegation to address the military Post and Base closure issues and strategizing with the Bipartisan California Congressional Delegation and other decision makers. Locally, a number of communities throughout California put together their own efforts to prepare for BRAC. These included, among others, Los Angeles Air Force Base Regional Alliance, San Diego Regional Economic Development Corporation, Beale Regional Alliance Committee, and the Travis Community Consortium that has raised more than $1 million to lobby on behalf of California's military Posts and Bases.

During January 2005, the League of California Cities, California Chamber of Commerce, California State Association of Counties (CSAC), and the California State Space Authority (CSA) initiated a non-aggressive compact "in an effort to unite local Government officials and community based organizations in support of military Post and Base retention and closure preparedness." One military Base, the Concord Naval Weapons Station had even offered itself up for Base closure, preferring to commercially develop the military Base's land that was valued at approximately $1 billion. Before the release of the list of Base and Post closures and realignments, California preparation for the upcoming BRAC round was significantly more robust than for any of the previous rounds.

These pro-California, pre-emptive BRAC campaigns served several purposes. First and foremost, they represented genuine efforts to alert BRAC decision makers about California's BRAC history and the virtues of keeping California military Posts and Bases open. Because of the private nature of the BRAC process; however, it was very difficult to gauge the effectiveness of these pleas. Second, with the BRAC process largely out of State and in local hands, elected officials could use such pre-BRAC efforts to encourage public citizen support and demonstrate their public commitment to the military Posts and Bases in their communities.

On March 15, 2005, the naming of nominees for the BRAC Commission and the subsequent recess appointment of the Commissioners by the President on April 1, 2005, presented the first quasi-public opportunity to affect the BRAC process. Because the BRAC Commission had the power to add, remove, or modify the fate of any military Post or Base, on or off the list, having a person on the Commission with knowledge of a particular State and its concerns could provide significant power. Congressional leaders suggested individuals to serve on the Commission, who then must receive White House approval and Senate confirmation. The Senate Majority Leader, Senator Bill Frist of Tennessee, and the Speaker of the House, Representative J. Dennis Hastert of Illinois, were each entitled to recommend two individuals for the Commission, while Senate Minority Leader, Senator Harry Reid of Nevada, and House Minority Leader, Representative Nancy Pelosi of California suggested one name each. The President named the final three Commissioners.

On February 17, 2005, President Bush used one of his recommendations to name former Veterans Affairs Secretary and current San Diego resident, Mr. Anthony J. Principi to Chair the Commission. Mr. Principi's close ties to and understanding of California military Posts and Bases could prove very valuable to the State of California during the Commission's work. Senator Frist proposed Harold W. Gehman, Jr. of Virginia, a retired US Navy Admiral and former NATO Supreme Allied Commander, and John G. Coburn, former Commanding General of Army Material Command, and the military services Deputy Chief of Staff of Logistics. Representative Hastert recommended Mr. James Hansen of Utah, a US Navy veteran and former Congressman who served on the Armed Services Committee, and Mr. Samuel Knox Skinner of Illinois, a former US Army reservist and one-time Chief of Staff of Secretary of Transportation under President George H.W. Bush.

Senator Reid proposed Mr. James H. Bibray of Nevada, a former US Army reservist and a former Congressman who served on International Relations, Armed Services and Intelligence Committees. Representative Pelosi recommended

Mr. Philip Coyle of Los Angeles, California, a senior adviser to the Center for Defense Information and a former Assistant Defense Secretary. The White House accepted all of the recommendations with the exception of Mr. Colburn. Mr. Lloyd Warren Newton of Connecticut, a retired US Air Force General, was named in Mr. Coburn's place.

For his final two recommendations, the President named Mr. James T. Hill of Florida, a retired US Army General and former combatant Commander of the US Southern Command, and Ms. Sue Turner from Texas, a retired US Air Force Brigadier General who was a member of the American Battle Monuments Commission. From a California perspective, the Commission's make-up appeared favorable. With the naming of Mr. Principi as the Chairman of the Commission and Mr. Coyle as a Commissioner, there would be at least two individuals familiar with the State of California's unique strengths when the Commission reviewed and revised the DOD's closure and realignment list. Additionally, four of the nine Commissioners hailed from the Western Region of the US, meaning that the West Coast concerns were unlikely to be ignored.

On May 16, 2005, once the DOD released the closure and realignment list the Commission began to review the Secretary's recommendations, pouring over records and analysis provided by the DOD, and holding hearings across the Country at military Posts and Bases suggested for closure or realignment. This component of the process was fully public, and provided organizations outside of the Federal Government with an opportunity to argue the merits of a military Post or Base. As mentioned, the Federal Government, California Congressional Delegation, California Council on Post and Base Support and Retention, and local military Post and Base support organizations would present arguments why the State of California should not realign or close more military Posts and Bases.

The fate of military Posts and Bases could change during the review period. For example, a rough count showed that in the BRAC 95 closure round, 18 of the approximately 140 military Posts and Bases scheduled for closure or realignment in the Secretary's list were saved and removed from the list by the Commission. The Commission also added nine military Posts and Bases not named by the Secretary to their final recommendations for closure. For most military Posts and Bases, however, selection for the list was close to a "death sentence," as the vast majority of the recommendations passed to the President and the US Congress remained unchanged. The modifications to the Commission's voting rules made it more difficult than in previous BRAC rounds. Ultimately, after hundreds of visits to military Posts and Bases around the Country, the BRAC Commission submitted a final list of military Post and Base closures and realignments that required Presidential and Congressional approval. The President or the US Congress had never rejected their final recommendations.

Once the list was finalized, the DOD began the actual closure process that could be long and complicated. The DOD produced an inventory of real and other assets at each of the military Posts and Bases designated for closure and conducted an environmental analysis of a closed military Post's or Base's suitability for transfer. The DOD would then organize the transfer of the property. Following the GAO outlines, the DOD first offered the property to other Federal Government agencies. Any closed military Post or Base that were not taken by other Federal Government agencies were considered "surplus" and were then to be "disposed of through a variety of means to State and local Governments, local redevelopment authorities, or private parties."

When a surplus facility was deemed ready for the military's final departure, or more often well before then, the DOD, public and private successors entered into protracted negotiations over transfer. Frequently closed military Posts and Bases were handed over to economic development agencies consisting of decision makers from the affected community. The development agency then became responsible for the implementation of a Re-Use Plan. In other instances, the DOD would sell land on closed military Posts and Bases to private developers. Throughout the transfer and re-use process, the DOD's Office of Economic Adjustment functioned as the primary contact and source of support and supplemental funding for communities for military Posts and Base closures. As demonstrated by the brief examples on the history of military Post and Base closures in California, the transfer and re-use of closed military Posts and Bases could proceed in a variety of ways that yielded results with varying levels of success.[70]

The Impact on Local Economies

No other military Post or Base closure clean-up has received as much public and political scrutiny as accomplished by the Presidio of San Francisco. Located in the Northwest section of San Francisco, and containing both a Western and Northern shore, the Presidio Post was one of the most valuable real estate parcels in the World. It was also located in one of the most politically active communities in the nation. The Presidio Post was not a military Post closure but a transfer to the Department of the Interior with the US Army retaining responsibility for the clean-up needed for transfer by deed.

During the late 1980s, investigations began. The Presidio of San Francisco was divided into three Operable Units (OUs): the Public Health Service Hospital, a small area near the Golden Gate Bridge, and the main Presidio Post that constitutes the bulk of the military Installation. Only four-removal actions had been undertaken. Approximately $50 million was expended on the clean-up at the Presidio Post. The Presidio Post was not on the National Priorities List (NPL) that made the State of California the lead regulator. Typically this would imply governance by a Federal Government Facility Site Remediable Agreement (FFSRA); however, the US Army did not agree to schedules and milestones. The

---

[70]   Past Base Closure Experiences and the 2005 BRAC Round, April 2000.com

State of California expected the Remedial Investigation and Feasibility Study (RI/FS) to be completed by the Summer of 2003. As with other military Posts and Bases, the clean-up had taken a Post-wide focus with an emphasis on studies and analysis. Oddly enough, the US Army reluctance to agree to an FFSRA resulted in some flexibility where there was decisions to focus on clean-up efforts.

As the time an FFSRA would normally have been negotiated, it would have been reasonable to expect adequate funding for a Post-wide clean-up approach. One option for focusing on the clean-up efforts was to concentrate activities on the roughly 1000-foot wide strip of land the run several miles parallel to the Northern shore and North of US Highway 101. Here there was already extensive public use, and the area was widely recognized as desirable for more expanded civilian use. Those responsible for assembling the Department of Interior's General Management Plan had continually viewed the area as a high priority. However, the use of aggressive removal actions, as was accomplished at March AFB, would come under intense Federal Government and public scrutiny. Although Restoration Advisory Boards (RABs), BRAC Clean-Up Teams (BCTs), and Re-Use Authorities ((RUAs) had simplified the complex climate in many situations, the intense interest in the Presidio of San Francisco was overwhelming because of the long-term usage by the US Army. Instead, it may have been more desirable to have negotiated an FFSRA that allowed focus on this parcel or on whatever may have represented the clean-up tasks of highest priority.

Would communities or States that were impacted by past military Post and Base closures are protected in future base closure rounds? The DOD would consider all military Installations equally, without regard to whether the military Installation was previously considered or proposed for closure or realignment. Additionally, the DOD would adhere to the statutory requirements regarding the selection criteria that would be used in the BRAC process where military value was the primary consideration. Would their past losses be calculated in determining any "cumulative socioeconomic impact?" In doing so, the DOD would consider "the economic impact on existing communities in the vicinity of military Installations." Application and evaluation of economic impacts would be consistently and fairly applied.

Some military Post and Base closures and realignments could conceivably cause near-term social and economic disruption. However, there were many success stories from previous closures. For example, at Charleston Naval Base in South Carolina, the local community, assisted by the DOD, was able to create approximately 4500 new positions. Approximately 90 Federal Government, State, and private entities were currently re-using the Naval Base. Since the closure of Mather AFB in California, more than 54 leases were generated at the Mather Field complex. Its prime location and one of the Country's longest runways had made it an active Air Cargo Hub for California's Central Valley and the Sacramento Region. Additionally, the facility now employs nearly 3700-personnel with its high-technical businesses, manufacturing, operations, Educational

Centers, Federal Government agencies, and Recreational facilities. At Fort Devens in Massachutes, more than three thousand new positions were generated and 2.7-million square feet of new construction has occurred with 68 different employers on site, and redevelopment ranges from small business incubators to the Gillette Corporation that occupies a large Warehouse and Distribution Center and Manufacturing Plant. Therefore, a military Post and Base closure could actually have an economic opportunity especially when all elements of a community worked together.

By 2003, the DOD reduced its total active duty military personnel end strength by 32-percent, and that figure would grow to 36-percent as a result of the 1997 Quadrennial Defense Review [QDR] from 1989 to 1997. After four military Post and Base closing rounds, only 21-percent of the military Installations in the continental US had been reduced. By 1997, the DOD had already reduced its overseas military Post and Base Force Structure by almost 60-percent. Before the first Post and Base closure round, there were approximately 500 military Posts and Bases. When all of the military Posts and Bases from the first four-BRAC rounds were closed, there would be 400 military Posts and Bases remaining. Accordingly, 97 major military Posts and Bases had already been closed in the US.

The overseas military Post and Base Force Structure had been further reduced ceasing operations at over 960 military facilities. The US Army in Europe had already closed the equivalent of 12 major maneuvers military Posts and Bases. President George W. Bush had proposed the realignment and closure of military Posts and Bases in Europe and Asia. During 2004, Bush's Administration believed that the cost of shutting overseas military Posts and Bases, and transferring military personnel and Civil Service employees, was worth the result of having military strength and defense closer to the realities of World situations rather than keeping military Posts and Bases developed and enhanced during the "Cold War Era." However, today's military organizations are highly mobile and can be moved in hours and days rather than months.

It will be debated in the US Congress as to whether faster response was possible due to new technologies and war-time strategies as if actual moving, closing, and rebuilding military Posts and Bases elsewhere overseas. The 1997 QDR concluded that additional infrastructure savings were required to reduce the share of the Defense budget devoted to infrastructure. Retaining excessive infrastructure would be unnecessary with a smaller military force, and would waste scarce Defense resources that were essential to future military modernization. The military Post and Base closings were an integral part of the plan. During 1993 through 1995, the QDR found that the DOD has enough excess military Post and Base structures to warrant two additional BRAC rounds similar in scale. It was estimated that two-additional military Post and Base closure rounds would result in a saving of approximately $2.7 billion annually.

Altering the existing BRAC process requiring an exclusion list would seriously by undermining the DOD's ability to reconfigure its current infrastructure into one where operational capacity would maximize both "war fighting" capability and efficiency. This is one reason why the DOD did not support an "Early-Out or Exclusion List" for BRAC. Developing an "Early-Out Exclusion List" or excluding an arbitrary number of military Installations from closure or realignment consideration would have destroyed the DOD's ability to conduct a comprehensive rationalization of its infrastructure to its Force Structure, thereby undermining its efforts to continue transformation of the Forces required to meet the security challenges of the 21ˢ Century. The BRAC 05 round would not be merely a military Installation capacity reduction exercise.

The DOD emphasized analysis of joint functions and joint use of facilities more so than in previous rounds to enhance the transformation effort. Excluding military Installations up front would preclude options that would become apparent as a result of conducting a comprehensive analysis covering all military Installations. In order to truly reshape infrastructure to match Force Structure, realignment options under BRAC 05 would be critically important; that is, exclusionary lists would restrict realignments and preclude options.

DOD-BRAC Intervention

On May 3, 1988, in accordance with the provisions of the Federal Advisory Committee Act, as amended (5 U.S.C. App. I), Mr. Frank Carlucci, Secretary of Defense, established a Commission for military Post and Base Realignment and Closure. The BRAC mission was to close and realign military Installations and transfer Federal Government property as quickly, cheaply, and safely as possible was composed of 12 members. The Commission was to be appointed or designated by the Secretary of Defense. The composition would include persons with broad experience in the Federal Government and National Defense agencies. The Secretary would designate two Chairmen from members of the Commission.

By November 15, 1988, the functions of the Commission would study the issues surrounding military Post and Base realignments and closures within the US, its commonwealths, territories, and possessions. The purpose of the Commission would be determined the best process to include necessary administrative changes for identifying military Posts and Bases to be closed or realigned; how to improve and the best use Federal Government incentive programs to overcome the negative impact of military Post and Base closure or realignment; and establish criteria for realigning and closing military Posts and Bases to include at least current and future mission requirements and the impact on operational readiness of the military Departments concerned:

- The availability and condition of land and facilities at both the existing and potential receiving locations;

- The potential to accommodate contingency, mobilization, and future Force Structure requirements at receiving locations;

- The cost and manpower implications;

- The extent and timing of potential cost savings to include whether the total cost savings realized from the closure or realignment of military Posts and Bases would, by the end of the six-year period beginning with the date of the completion of the closure or realignment of the military Post or Base, exceed the amount expended to close or realign the military Post or Base;

- The socioeconomic impact on the community where the military Post or Base to be closed or realigned was located;

- The community support at receiving locations;

- The environmental impact;

- The implementation process involved;

- Review the current and planned military Post or Base Force Structure in light of Force Structure assumptions, the process and criteria developed pursuant to Sub-paragraph A, and to identify those military Posts or Bases that should be closed or realigned;

- Report findings and recommendations to the Secretary of Defense;

- By December 31, 1988, re-think how RABs are supposed to represent the community.

Members of the Commission served without compensation for their work on the Commission. However, members appointed from among private citizens would be allowed travel expenses to include per diem in lieu of subsistence as authorized by law for persons serving intermittently in the Federal Government service (5 US Code 5701-5707) to the full extent funds were available. The Secretary of Defense would provide the Commission with such administrative services, facilities, staff, and other support services as were necessary. Any expenses of the Commission would be paid from such funds as may be available to the Secretary of Defense. The Commission would be in place and operational as soon as possible. Thereafter, the Commission would brief the Secretary of Defense on the Commission's plan of action. The Commission's final report would include recommendations to realign and close military Posts and Bases only upon a vote of a majority of the members of the Commission. By December 31, 1988, the Commission would complete recommendations to realign or close military Posts and Bases.

To sustain military readiness and improve the Defense mission during changing times and requirements, the DOD recognized the need to close some of the military Installations and realign DOD missions at others. During the late 1980s and early 1990s, the DOD worked with the US Congress to identify military Installations that could be closed or realigned. The result was four rounds of military Post and Base realignment and closure (BRAC) during 1988, 1991, 1993, and 1995. While the DOD was realigning missions or transferring property within the Department at some BRAC identified military Installations, a large portion of BRAC property was intended for transfer to another Federal Government agency or non-Federal Government entity. There were 206 of the almost four hundred military Installations on the BRAC list that required some type of activity under the DERP before the property was ready for transfer.

In addition to environmental restoration, the DOD also considered the possible socioeconomic effects of military Installation closure at the local community level. When a military Installation was closed or realigned, the DOD understood that the local community would want to return the available property to productive use as soon as possible. To facilitate transfer and economic re-use to the local community, the DOD endeavored to conduct environmental restoration activities that were the responsibility of the DOD's Office of Economic Adjustment (OEA). To work together with OEA, the Clean-Up Office created DERP management tools such as BRAC Clean-Up Teams and Local Redevelopment Authorities (LRAs) to engage the community in the clean-up and transfer processes. As is the case at active military Installations, the DOD also worked with surrounding military Installations under BRAC through Restoration Advisory Boards (RABs); however, RABs focused solely on environmental restoration issues. BRAC documents included policies, guidance, and Fact Sheets on issues relevant to environmental remediation and property transfer at closing and realigning military Installations.

During 1977 through 1995, during the last 10-years of the 20th Century, the DOD had been eliminating military Posts and Bases or downsizing military Installation structures during the congressionally mandated rounds of military Post and Base closures and realignments. After the first four rounds of military Post and Base closures and realignments, the DOD has closed 97 military Installations to include 23 military Posts that belonged to the US Army. Many other minor military Installations were closed or realigned but not counted. Nevertheless, many officials believed those excessive military Installations still remained during the first 10-years of the 21st Century. As a result, more military Post and Base closures and realignments under BRAC would be forthcoming.

The DOD's position that there was a need for another BRAC round was that significant excessive capacity remained in the Defense infrastructure and was supported by independent agencies. The specific level of excessiveness was very dependent on the assumptions used in the analysis. Past experience indicated that a more extensive study of joint basing use and cross-service functional analysis could further increase the level of excessiveness through better utilization of the remaining infrastructure, the DOD estimated that a future BRAC round based on costs and savings experiences of BRAC' 93 and 95 rounds, and a reduction in military Installation infrastructure of approximately 20-percent, would generate approximately $7 billion of annual recurring savings in today's dollars.

Resources currently spent on excessive military Installation infrastructure could be allocated to higher priority requirements such as efforts to modernize weapons, enhance quality of life, and improve operational readiness. Additionally, another BRAC round would afford the DOD a significant transformation opportunity. On September 11, 2001, the imperative to convert an excess capacity into "war fighting" ability was reinforced. The performance of our Force Structure in Iraq underscored the benefit of transformational "war fighting." The DOD could reconfigure the infrastructure to best support the transformation of their "war fighting" capability. The DOD could use the opportunity to assess its military Installation infrastructure to ensure it was best sized and placed to support emerging mission requirements for our National Security.

The DOD developed a long-term, comprehensive and integrated overseas strategy based on the Secretary's Memorandum, March 20, 2003, "Integrated Global Presence and Basing Strategy." The DOD anticipated that decisions regarding the closure of overseas military Installations would be developed after a thorough review of this strategy later that year. During May 2005, this effort would inform the BRAC process as the statutory requirement for publishing BRAC recommendations and would accommodate decisions regarding overseas basing generated by efforts currently underway.

Following President Clinton's action, lawmakers did not agree until 2001 to schedule another round of military Post and Base closings. Before it was resolved, the dispute held up a conference agreement on the Fiscal Year 2002 Defense Authorization Bill (Public Law 107-107) and led President Bush to threaten to veto the bill if it did not allow a new round during 2005. During July 2001, Defense Secretary Donald H. Rumsfeld and Army General Henry H. Shelton, Chairman of the Joint Chiefs of Staff, told the House Armed Services Committee that the DOD maintained 25-percent more facilities than it needed, even after four rounds of military Post and Base closings during the 1990s. By some accounts, the excessive military Posts and Bases cost taxpayers an estimated $3.5 billion annually.

On December 13, 2001, the 107th US Congress authorized a round of military Post and Base Realignments and Closures (BRAC 05). This policy decision was preceded by years of political dispute and dialogue between the US Congress and the Executive Board. Much of this debate centered on the Clinton Administration's privatization-in-place of two military Posts and Bases scheduled for closure by the BRAC 95 Commission and the dispute over estimated BRAC costs and savings. After painstaking compromise and a National Security crisis, reformed BRAC legislation was passed balancing political leadership and National Strategy with position loss and disruption to local communities.

A comprehensive analysis of journal articles, books, relevant congressional records, Federal Government reports, and legislation identified the variables that explained the US Congress' decision to amend the Defense Base Closure and Realignment Act of 1990 and authorize a BRAC 03 round. The US Congress eventually approved BRAC 05 because: (1) a new Administration concurred with the DOD's argument regarding excessive infrastructure and anticipated savings from BRAC; (2) national economic conditions could not support both spending for excessive infrastructure and the war on terrorism; (3) studies confirmed that most Posts and Bases were economically sound after Post or Base closures; and (4) the improved law purportedly reduced the parochial politics of military Post and Base closings.

During July 2001, the DOD announced an Efficient Facilities Initiative (EFI)). This consolidation was projected to save an estimated $3.5 billion annually. The EFI would enable the DOD to match Facilities to Forces. The EFI would ensure the primacy of military value in making decisions on facilities and harness the strength and creativity of the private sector by creating partnerships with local communities. All military Installations would be reviewed, and recommendations would be based on the military value of the facilities and the Force Structure. The EFI would encourage a cooperative effort between the President, US Congress, military services, and local communities to achieve the most effective and efficient military Post or Base structure for America's Armed Forces.

It would give local communities a significant role in determining the future use of facilities in their area by transferring closed military Installations to local redevelopers at no cost provided that proceeds were reinvested, and by creating partnerships with local communities to own, operate, or maintain the Installations that remained. During mid-December 2001, House and Senate negotiators authorized a new round of military Post and Base closures but delayed any action until 2005. During 2003, while the Bush Administration and the US Senate had wanted the military Post and Base closure process to start the House of Representatives had shown its opposition.

Under a compromise plan, the Secretary of Defense would submit a Force Structure Plan and Facility Inventory with a certification that proposed closings were justified by the Force Structure Plan and that they would produce net savings. The closings would also consider environmental costs and community impact. Seven of the nine Commission members could vote to add military Posts or Bases to DOD's proposed closure list, but a simple majority would suffice to drop Posts and Bases from the Closure Plan.

The Bush Administration estimated 20-percent to 25-percent of military Posts and Bases were surplus, and that the DOD could save $3 billion a year by eliminating surplus military facilities. During 2005, the Fiscal Year 2002 Defense Authorization Act included the authorization to conduct an additional round of military Post and Base closure and realignment actions. As a result, Mr. Donald

H. Rumsfeld, Secretary of Defense, stated on November 15, 2002: "Congress authorized a military Post and Base closure and realignment round during 2005. At the minimum, BRAC 05 would eliminate excessive physical capacity; the operation, sustainment, and re-capitalization that diverted scarce resources from the military Defense capability. However, BRAC 05 would make an even more profound contribution to transforming the Department by rationalizing our infrastructure with defense strategy. BRAC 05 would be the means that the DOD would reconfigure the infrastructure into one where the operational capacity maximized both the 'war fighting' capability and efficiency."

In addition to statutory changes, there were BRAC process changes that the Secretary directed in his November 15, 2002 kick-off Memorandum: "Transformation through Base Realignment and Closure." Based on recommendations from the Infrastructure Steering Group to the Infrastructure Executive Council, specific common or business oriented support functions that received analysis by Joint Cross-Service Groups (JCSG) rather than with military Departments. The JCSGs were empowered to make military Post or Base closure and realignment recommendations for review and approval by the Secretary. During previous BRAC rounds, the JCSGs developed alternatives for consideration by military Departments. Also at the outset of the process, the JCSGs identified a broad series of options for stationing and supporting Force Structures and functions to increase efficiency and effectiveness of the military services. Reference to these options was identified as analytical frameworks.

What was transformation? According to the DOD's April 2003 Transformation Planning Guidance document, transformation was: "A process that shaped the changing nature of military competition and cooperation through new combinations of concepts, capabilities, people and organizations that exploit the Nation's advantages and protect against our asymmetric vulnerabilities to sustain our strategic position, that help underpin peace and stability in the World."

Why was the DOD transforming? Over time, the DOD strategy called for the transformation of the US Defense establishment. To transform, the DOD would need to change its culture in many important areas. The DOD's budgeting; acquisition, military personnel; Civil Service employees; and management systems were to be able to operate in a World that changed rapidly. Without change, the current Defense Program would only become more expensive in the future, and the DOD would forfeit many of the opportunities available today.

How was BRAC transformational? BRAC provided a singular opportunity to reshape Defense infrastructure to optimize military readiness. The BRAC 05 process helped find innovative ways to consolidate, realign, or find alternative uses for current facilities to ensure that the US continued to field the best prepared and best equipped military service in the World. BRAC would also enable the military services to better match Facilities to Forces, meet the threats and challenges of a new Century, and make the well-advised use of limited Defense dollars. Undersecretary of Defense for Installations and the Environment estimated the next round of military Post and Base closures during 2005 would save $6 billion a year, even if it cut only 12-percent of the DOD's military infrastructure. One 1998 study suggested that 20 to 25-percent of the military infrastructure could be considered surplus. During 2004, Mr. Goren indicated that an analysis to "shed excess capacity" could be completed before the DOD decided how many military Posts or Bases must be closed during the BRAC 05 round.

On January 6, 2004, the DOD announced that it had requested military Installation Commanders in the US, territories, and possessions to gather information about their military Installations as part of the BRAC 05 round. All military Installations were to participate. While none of the questions or data associated with the questions would be released to the public prior to DOD's recommendations being forwarded to the Defense Base Closure and Realignment Commission that would be named by March 2005, and with all questions and data to be publicly available once the Commission receives them. In a related action, the DOD also published Draft Selection Criteria in the December 23, 2003 Federal Register for public comments that would be used as part of the evaluation process. On November 15, 2002, Secretary of Defense Donald H. Rumsfeld stated: "Congress authorized a military Post and Base realignment and closure round during 2005. At a minimum, BRAC 05 would eliminate excess physical capacity; the operation, sustainment, and re-capitalization that diverts scarce resources from Defense capability. However, BRAC 05 could make an even more profound contribution to transforming the Department by rationalizing the infrastructure with Defense strategy. BRAC 05 would be the means that the US Army could reconfigure the current infrastructure into one that the operational capacity maximized both 'war fighting' capability and efficiency."

The major elements of the BRAC 05 process would be to govern by law; specifically, the Defense Base Closure and Realignment Act of 1990. The process would begin with a threat assessment of the future National Security environment, followed by the development of a Force Structure Plan and basing requirements to meet those threats. The DOD would apply selection criteria to determine what military Installations to recommend realignment and closure. The Secretary of Defense would publish a report containing realignment and closure recommendations, forwarding supporting documentation to an independent Commission appointed by the President in consultation with congressional leadership.

The Commission had the authority to change the DOD's recommendations if it was determined that the Secretary deviated substantially from the Force Structure Plan and selection criteria. The Commission would hold regional meetings to solicit public input prior to making its recommendations. History has shown that the use of an independent Commission and public meetings would make the process as open and fair as possible. The Commission would forward its recommendations to the President for review and approval, who would forward recommendations to the US Congress.

The US Congress would then have 45 legislative days to act on the Commission report on an all-or none basis. After that time, the Commission's realignment and closure recommendations would become binding on the DOD. Implementation would start within two-years, and actions would be completed within six-years. The BRAC 05 process outlined in the BRAC Act of 1990, Public Law 101-510, as amended, would remain primarily the same as used in the three previous rounds. This process had served DOD well during previous rounds and was designed to be as fair as possible. However, there were some changes. Military value would continue to be an element of the published selection criteria. In previous rounds, as DOD policy, the military value criteria had priority over the other criteria. However, during BRAC 05, there would be a statutory requirement that military value was to be the primary consideration for military Post or Base closure.

The BRAC 05 process would require a separate report prior to the Secretary's recommendations on closures and realignments. In this report, that was due to the US Congress along with the budget for Fiscal Year 2005 (February 2004), the Secretary would include, among other things, the 20-year Force Structure Plan of Probable Threats, a comprehensive inventory of military Installations, a discussion of categories of excess capacity, and a certification from the Secretary that a BRAC round during 2005 was necessary. The BRAC 05 round would have the following milestones:

- That the DOD would publish proposed selection criteria for a 30-day comment period by December 31, 2003;

- That the DOD would publish final selection criteria by February 16, 2004.

The DOD would submit a report to the US Congress during the 2005 Budget justification cycle that included:

- A Force Structure Plan based on an assessment of probable threats to the National Security over the next 20-years, the probable end strength levels and military force units needed to meet those threats, and the anticipated levels of available funding;

- A comprehensive inventory of military Installations worldwide;

- A description of infrastructure necessary to support the Force Structure;

- A discussion of categories of excess capacity;

- A socioeconomic analysis of the effect of realignments and closures to reduce excess infrastructure;

- Secretary of Defense Certification of the need for BRAC, and that annual net savings would result by 2011.

The Secretary of Defense would forward recommendations for realignments and closures to the BRAC Commission prior to May 16, 2005; and the BRAC Commission would forward its report on the recommendations to the President prior to September 8, 2005. The President had until September 23, 2005 to accept or reject the recommendations in the entirety. The US Congress had 45 legislative days to reject the recommendations in their entirety or they became binding on the DOD. From 1988 through 2001, the four previous BRAC rounds eliminated approximately 20-percent of DOD's capacity that existed produced a net savings of approximately $16.7 billion that included the cost of environmental clean-up. Recurring savings beyond 2001 were approximately $7 billion annually. In independent studies conducted over previous years, both the General Accounting Office and the Congressional Budget Office have consistently supported the DOD's view that closing and realigning unneeded military Installations produced savings that far exceed costs.

The DOD selection criteria for Closing and Realigning Military Installations inside the US Federal Register: February 12, 2004 (Volume 69, Number 29); indicated military value would be the focus for the final selection criteria to be used in the BRAC 05 round of military Posts and Base realignment and closures. That value would represent the ability of the military Installation to contribute to the DOD future mission capabilities and operational readiness. The final selection criteria were also based on factors such as potential costs and savings, community support, and environmental considerations.

The BRAC 95 Commission recommended that the US Congress authorize another military Base Closure Commission during 2001, giving military Departments time to complete the current closures in an orderly fashion. Implementing the BRAC actions in the first four rounds would result in $23 billion in one-time implementation costs, offset by savings of $36.5 billion, for a total net savings of $13.5 billion between 1990 and 2001 when the implementation of the first four rounds were to be concluded. However, the DOD had not included the total cost of environmental clean-up beyond 2001 in the net savings figures.

Approximately half the savings that the DOD assumed would come from BRAC during the implementation were due to assumed savings in repair and maintenance costs. Much of those assumed savings were due to reductions in Civil Service employees. Under the BRAC process, the Secretary of Defense made recommendations to a Commission, nominated by the President, and confirmed by the US Senate. The Commission, after being confirmed by the Senate, would review these recommendations and make their own recommendations to the President. The President would review the recommendations, either send them back to the Commission for additional work, or forwarded them without changes to the US Congress. Finally, recommendations of the Commission would go into effect unless disapproved by a joint resolution of the US Congress.

During 1995, the BRAC Commission recommended closing two Maintenance Depots at McClellan Air Logistics Center near Sacramento in California, and Kelly Air Logistics Center at San Antonio in Texas. As an alternative to realigning the Depots in the two politically powerful States, President Bill Clinton proposed having private contractors take over repair and maintenance work at the Sites. The 1995 Base Closure Commission did not recommend or authorize "privatization-in-place" at Kelly AFB in Texas or McClellan AFB in California. Concern was raised about the integrity of the BRAC process in light of this attempt to privatize-in-place the work at the Air Logistics Centers at Kelly AFB in Texas and McClellan AFB in California. Republicans charged that President Clinton could not be trusted to respect the political nature of the process.

US Army-BRAC Intervention

During 1991, 1993, and 1995, the US Army's selection processes have remained fairly constant during these three rounds. During the BRAC 95 round, the US Army's policies, procedures, and implementing instructions used to identify military Post and Base closures followed the two previous rounds of 1991 and 1993. Of the three military services, the US Army has received the most praise. However, Mr. William Hix wrote that the US Army's selection criteria was lacking in certain attributes. The US Army's selection processes entailed categorizing each military Installation according to its current principal functions. For example, ranking each military Installation according to a weighted score of about two dozen attributes, the number varying by category of the military Installation. This ranking was synthesized with a stationing strategy for each category. Each strategy describes future requirements for military Installations of the particular category, based on National Security requirements and programmed Force Structure. The next step was repositions military Installations was based on the synthesis, assigning a future military value to each military Installation, and then selecting the lower ranking ones for future study. From this step, specific closure and realignment options were developed and assessed against four criteria. For example, cost, economic impact on communities, infrastructure, and environmental impact.[71]

The US Army provided the selection process to Installation Commanders that would serve as design standards for proposed future processes. Along these lines, the US Army's selection process provided a basis for assessing the strengths and weaknesses of the US Army's past processes. Mr. Hix proposed a number of desirable options to improve the US Army's decision process of selecting BRAC

---

[71]   William H. Hix, "Taking Stock of the Army's Base Realignment and Closure Selection Process," (RAND Corporation, 2001), p. xiv.

candidates. Mr. Hix suggested 10 criteria that group into three larger categories that addressed essential internal characteristics, the breadth of the process and the outcome:

- Could be audited and reproduced: A process can be audited and reproduced if a qualified person who was not part of the process could take the data used in the process and independently produce the same results. This implies a process based on defined quantitative measures and explicit qualitative assessment;

- Maximizes objectivity and internal consistency: An ideal process would contain no hidden or explicit bias toward change or toward the status quo. Instead, it would generate and assess options according

- to an objectively determined set of goals. Its various steps would rest on assumptions used consistently in all parts of the process;

- Uses separate and independent assessment criteria: Criteria should be considered singly and not embedded in multiple criteria. For example, cost should not both be considered explicitly and be embedded in other criteria such as condition of buildings;

- Considers externalities: Externalities consisted of effects on people or activities outside the US Army. Solutions that ignore externalities are unlikely to survive the political process. Four classes of externalities were important socioeconomic impact on communities, local infrastructure environment, and politics;

- Provides a complete option set: A process whose design or rule limit the range of options stands to miss creative and beneficial changes. It's easier for decision makers to discuss options that for whatever reason, are later considered un-attractive than trying to generate those options at the end of the process;

- Considers current and future needs: While satisfying today's requirements is straightforward, this criterion presents difficulties with respect to the future. The effects of BRAC decisions last for decades and some are irreversible. Yet National Security Strategies change from Administration to Administration and sometimes even during the Administration. Such changes drive force structure changes and resulting military Installation requirements. Hence, BRAC decisions need to serve not only the current National Security Strategy but also future strategies. The time horizon of the analysis was critically important. The 1990 law that authorized the last three BRAC rounds restricted the DOD to considering only the Force Structure programmed out to a six-year horizon. Longer term trends and events could not be considered. For example, the trend toward faster vehicles and longer rang weapons has long term implications for the utility of today's maneuver and training military Installations, but the US Army was not allowed to address such considerations;

- Hedges against important uncertainties: Because the future was cloudy and ideal BRAC process would produce closure and realignment options that hedged against likely changes in future demands and against less likely but potentially devastating changes. A BRAC can err in two directions. First, it can realign and close too few military Installations, permitting unneeded ones to persist thereby wasting limited resources. Second, a BRAC can also err in other directions by permanently divesting military Installations not needed but may be needed in the future;

- Leads to efficient use of assets: At one level, this is an obvious criterion. However it also has less obvious implications. For example, it implies considering the cost effectiveness of using each military Installation for as many functions as it can support so that the maximum number of small, ineffective, single function military Installations can be closed;

- Leads to lower long term costs: High initial costs may be required to achieve substantial long term savings. Options that required substantial up-front construction or other transitional costs should not be dismissed out of hand before considering the net present value of the long term stream of costs and savings;

- Leads to improved operations: Certain realignments or closures could have had synergistic effects on the activities that occupy the military Installations. While these operational improvements may be difficult or impossible to quantify, they may be real and potentially significant. For example, the co-location of individual training schools and maneuver units could enhance the export of doctrine to the field and better capitalize on field experience in schools. Such considerations should be brought into the qualitative portion of the assessment."[72]

The process presented an assessment of how well the US Army's BRAC 95 process satisfied each of the 10 criteria. The BRAC 95 process fully satisfied only one criterion, i.e., consideration of externalities. It largely satisfied three and was judged as somewhat deficient in six of the criteria. In no case did the process fail completely. A critical review of the US Army's initial military Posts and Bases closure selection list that described the decision process the US Army used against the above 10 selection criteria was made. The 10 criteria were sequenced with the first three concerned with internal features of the process, the next four concerned with the breadth of inquiry, and the last three concerned organizational outcomes.

---

[72] William M. Hix, "Taking Stock of the Army's Base Realignment and Closure Selection Process," (RAND Corporation, 2001), pp. xv-xvii.

One of those organizational outcomes reduced long term costs that were central to any BRAC. Therefore, that criterion was assessed in-depth.

Assessing the extent where the US Army's process satisfied or did not satisfy the 10 criteria mentioned above would have resulted in developing an improved decision process for any future rounds in the US Army's list of military Post and Base closures. This action would have addressed the deficiencies of the US Army's methodology mentioned above by proposing alternatives that would eliminate deficiencies and embrace broader, systematic closures and realignments using available human resources and military Installations more efficiently and effectively.

The proposed process should improve all six properties to a fully satisfactory extent. Most deficient during the BRAC 95 process were the narrowness of the range of options and the consideration of future requirements and hedging; efficient use of assets; reduction of long term costs; and improved operations. Because the proposed process took an integrated, systemic approach in the analysis, it would inherently produce a broader range of options developed explicitly with hedging; reduced long term cost; and the improved operations. The principal benefits in terms of audit ability and reproducibility came from the elimination of highly subjective and un-documented assignment of weights to the attributes of military Installations. With reduction in long term costs as the central criterion, the proposed process completely avoided the complex and detailed military Installation assessment that, despite its quantitative basis, relied on the subjective assignment of weights that were entirely dependent on the pre-assignment of a military Installation to a principal function. Reliance on cost as a criterion also enhanced the objectivity and internal consistency of the selection process and eliminated the hidden inclusion of costs in the many criteria of the military Installation assessment. Both selection processes properly considered externalities.

The Presidio of San Francisco Closure

The US Army had several major reorganization actions programmed and ongoing under the Base Closure and Realignment Act that included the Presidio of San Francisco. The Presidio Post became a battleground; however, even though the Presidio Post could only win on the one issue that it could affect economy of operations and monetary savings by relocating DOD agencies and Federal organizations located in the City of San Francisco and Bay Area to the Presidio Post. However, the Presidio Post was on the "hit" list for military Post closure because it was an administrative headquarters without a combat ready training capability. That is, the Presidio Post had no combat organizations or was not a military Post for combat training.

Over several years, General Forrester and the Mayor of San Francisco resisted a Presidio of San Francisco closure based on anticipated economy of operations and the financial impact on the City of San Francisco. Correspondence from higher headquarters was concerned with Presidio Post transfers and the Presidio Post closure with the idea that the Presidio Post could possibly be saved by a reorganization of the Headquarters, Six US Army staff and the Presidio Garrison. The announcement; however, was a facade to camouflage the intent of "discontinuing" in lieu of "reorganizing" the Headquarters, Sixth US Army, discontinuing the Presidio Garrison, and transferring the Presidio of San Francisco to the US National Park Service.

Senator Alan Cranston stated: "Thank you for contacting me about the US Navy's announced Base closure and realignment. I believe it's an outrage that Civil Service employees will lose their positions as a result of this transfer while the Federal Government continues to maintain a vast network of overseas military Posts and Bases employing over 166 thousand foreign nationals. More upsetting than this, however, it was the manner where the decision to discontinue the military Base appeared to have been made."[73] To understand the political reasons for this decision, it may be imagined that brain storming sessions were held days after the decision to discontinue the Presidio of San Francisco was called in an attempt to justify the previously announced transfer. In other words, the decision seemed to have been made backwards. Those responsible for studying the cost effectiveness of the Presidio Post transfer were apparently told what conclusions their study would reach, and then proceeded to substantiate those conclusions.

Representative Charles Teague wrote a similar letter to Mr. Elmer B. Staats, Comptroller General of the US, requesting a review of the DOD decision to realign the Headquarters, Sixth US Army to Treasure Island and then at Fort Carson in Colorado. Representative Teague stated: "As the stated reason for this action was to reduce military personnel and Civil Service employees in consonance with the Federal Government's policy of relying on private enterprise systems to supply its needs and does provide for considerable savings over the long term."[74]

Representative Teague was primarily interested in two areas of inquiry. First, was the policy fully in keeping with the letter and spirit of Civil Service Commission regulations and law with regard to termination of Federal Government employees? Second, was the DOD economic analysis upon which savings were made based upon sound economic and statistical data, and was it conducted in a thorough and vigorous manner? Third, could the GAO substantiate the announced savings based on an independent feasibility analysis? Second, were underlying assumptions of the DOD analysis open to question, and if so, on what basis? Apparently, the GAO

---

[73] Letter from Alan Cranston, US Senator, Washington, DC, to (1st Vice President, NFFE, Local #1374, Point Mugu, California), July 25, 1973.

[74] Letter from Charles M. Teague, House of Representatives, Washington, DC, to (the Comptroller General of the US, Washington, DC), May 24, 1973.

had already started its own top-priority Presidio of San Francisco investigation because the GAO investigators were already at the Presidio Post interviewing members of the Presidio of San Francisco task force.

In the interim, the Headquarters, Sixth US Army staff submitted a report detailing the requirements for implementing the Presidio of San Francisco Closure and Realignment Study. The report identified a detailed plan to provide for realignment implementation for a consolidated command to include transferring ten DOD organizations located in the City of San Francisco and Bay Area to the Presidio of San Francisco. The Under Secretary of the Navy statement to the Senate Armed Services Committee in compliance with governing procedures specified in OMB Circular A-76, a cost analysis would be completed in advance of, and in addition to, the cost analysis performed in connection with the evaluation of contractor proposals in response to the RFP.

If it turned out that the contract operations did not hold promise for cost savings, appropriate recommendations to change the current plan would be initiated. The effective date for completion of the RIF resulting from the Presidio of San Francisco Closure and Realignment Study was established as September 30, 1992. On August 1, 1992, t was planned to issue RIF notices and to issue specific, individual notices on August 31, 1992. One time realignment costs, to include severance pay costs for Civil Service employees, contract preparation costs, contractor overlap and start-up costs, and military personnel realignment to other military Installations was estimated in the millions of dollars.

At the same time, NASA announced that it would launch an all-out propaganda campaign at Venture County in California that contracting out was going to be a beautiful event. At least US Civil Service employees now knew the competition with its 25 Aerospace Corporations all of that were big, wealthy, and anxious to get bigger and wealthier. The Presidio Post was referred to as one of the contract plums in the Pentagon's Post and Base Realignment Plan. Mr. Robert E. Lee, NASA's President, stated: "It's new, it's big, and industry wants it."

The Federal Government's philosophy appeared to be that the elimination of all Federal Government in-house activities that were obtainable from industry or private contractors offered a greater potential for reducing the size of the Federal Government and achieving economy and efficiency. The issue at large demanded a clear definition of Federal Government law so that there would be no further "misinterpretation" and that it was perfectly "legal" to transfer Federal Government facilities to the US National Park Service or to sell Federal Government activities to the lowest bidder through contracting out procedures.

The Indian Intervention

The final outcome of this saga was reported in a San Francisco Chronicle article adding to the dilemma, the "Bay Area Tribe Staked Its Claim to the Presidio," Tuesday, June 16, 1992. The article stated: "A group of native Americans who stated they were descendants of the original inhabitants of San Francisco were laying claim to the Presidio of San Francisco."[75] During 1994, the Muwekma Ohlone Tribe that had 175 members based in San Jose said they were the original San Franciscans and had the right of first refusal when the US Army withdrew from the Presidio of San Francisco. Their claim could have thrown a monkey wrench into plans to transform the Presidio Post into a spectacular new National Park. The Tribe's claim goes back to the dim past of the San Francisco Bay Area, a time before European settlement of the Pacific Coast, and raised a number of questions about California's nearly forgotten native people to include their rights and their very identify.

A statement issued by the Muwekma Tribe stated: "From time immemorial this land has been Ohlone. Therefore, the original indigenous Ohlone Muwekma Tribe now lay claim to first right of use to the Presidio of San Francisco." Ms. Norma Sanchez Tribal Administrator stated: "We will exercise the right of first refusal. We want the land to be placed in trust for the Tribe." This would be the first time native Americans have claimed what would be Federal Government parkland since Indians occupied Alcatraz Island more than 20-years ago, and who were eventually evicted by Federal Marshals. The US National Park Service had been soliciting ideas for use of the Presidio of San Francisco was pleased that the Indians responded to their call for proposals but was astonished when the Ohlone Tribe claimed the whole Presidio Post. Mr. Howard Levitt, Chief of Interpretation for the Golden Gate National Recreational Area stated: "We are looking forward to a continuing discussion. However, it was a decision for the Secretary of the Interior."

Mr. Bob Walker, a spokesman for the Department of the Interior in Washington, DC stated: "the Department did not so understand. Anybody can lay claim for anything if they want to. We will proceed under Federal Government law with plans for the National Park Service to take charge of the property." Mr. Walker stated: "he did not know who had the right of first refusal to Federal Government land, and he also stated the Federal Government is not giving up ownership of the Presidio of San Francisco, only transferring it to another Federal Government agency." Mr. Walker further stated: "I don't know if this group of people claiming to be an Indian Tribe has this right."

Mr. Walker's response touched on one of the principal difficulties of the Muwekma claim to Indian Tribe land. The Ohlone Tribe is not officially recognized as an

---

[75] San Francisco Chronicle (San Francisco), "Bay Area Tribe Stakes Its Claim to the Presidio," June 16, 1992, p. A11 and A13.

Indian Tribe by the Federal Government. Official recognition implies that the Tribe existed in years past, lived in a specific territory, and had certain rights that may or may not include rights to land, such as the Presidio of San Francisco. Although many California Tribes, such as the Hoopa in the far Northern California were recognized by the Federal Government, many were not to include the Chattahoochee who was the original inhabitants of Yosemite Valley. Many other Indian groups in the Central Sierra and the Ohlone people, who were descendants of the first San Francisco Bay Area residents, are not recognized. Ms. Sanchez stated: "the Muwekma Ohlone is among 32 California Tribes that were seeking recognition by the Federal Government." Ms. Sanchez stated: "several steps are necessary and that the Muwekma Tribe was working on the case." Ms. Sanchez stated: "A Bill to recognize the 32 Tribes had been introduced in the US Congress. The other question was that although there could be no doubt that the San Francisco Peninsula was inhabited by native peoples, and there could be no doubt that the Muwekma Ohlone was their descendants."

The University gathered evidence of Indian occupation of the Presidio of California Anthropologists in the 19th Century indicating that the area had been settled for several thousand years. According to Mr. Richard S. Levy of American Archaeological Consultants, at least 14 hundred people lived in San Francisco and San Mateo counties when Europeans "discovered" California. An additional 12 hundred lived in the Santa Clara Valley, and about two thousand lived in the East Bay Area. These were people now called Ohlone, who inhabited an area from the Carquinez Strait to San Benito County. The Spanish arrived in 1769 and established a Mission they named San Francisco during June 1776, and they established the Presidio of San Francisco during the same year. A number of local Indians were converted to Christianity by the Franciscan padres, but many more died of diseases carried by Europeans. During 1816, the Padres also impressed the Indians into work gangs; a lithograph exists showing Spanish soldiers with Indian workers on the Presidio of San Francisco.

When the Mexican Government took over the area, the Missions were disbanded and the Indians were told they were free to leave. Many of the San Francisco Indians, who were Mexican citizens and Christian, went to the East Bay where they still have relatives. Levy believed that their descendants are still there. Mr. Levy stated: "Sure, there are people who are descendants of the San Francisco people. I know for a fact there are descendants of the Mission San Jose Indians, Mission Santa Clara, and Carmel Mission people." San Francisco Bay Area Indians have kept a low profile for a number of years. After the US occupied California, many of them claimed to be Mexicans, rather than Indians because the US policy toward Indians was much harsher than Mexican policy.

The Muwekma Ohlone Tribe had a number of proposals for the Presidio of San Francisco to include health facilities for all California Tribal people, a native housing village, a social service center, a California Indian museum, and a Tribal Government economic center. They had not submitted detailed plans for any of these activities. Instead, they had asserted a claim to the whole Presidio Post. Ms. Sanchez stated: "We would have jurisdiction over the whole Presidio of San Francisco," stated Tribal Administrator Sanchez. Mr. Levitt stated: "that one previous example of Indian claims to Federal Government land came during the 1970s when the Chumash Tribe that lived in Santa Barbara County claimed Anacapa Island that became part of the Channels Islands National Park. Their claim was denied by the Secretary of the Interior and later was also turned down by the Courts."

The Locus of the Presidio Closure

The locus of the Presidio of San Francisco closure tries to illuminate and explain some of the political and socioeconomic reasons of military Post and Base closures and realignments, as opposed to justifying National Defense issues and the build-up of military Posts and Bases. Those politics expressed themselves in a somewhat chaotic way with unique circumstances surrounding most military Post and Base closures. In essence, no two military Post or Base closures were exactly alike, nor did politicians react in similar ways when they fought to protect military Post and Base closures in their geographic areas of consideration. This study has considered the military Post and Base closure process in the larger context of American politics. At what may have become a success story, at the same time the outcome was less than what "optimal analysis" might have produced. Concurrently, BRAC did not take politics out of the military Post and Base closure process; however, this is a tribute to the nature of the American political system.[76]

The US has been closing and realigning military Posts and Bases as part of its efforts to downsize and restructure its Forces Structure, and to reduce Defense spending. To ensure that the process was consistent, the US Congress enacted the Defense Base Closure and Realignment Act of 1990 (PL 101-510). The Act established an independent Commission (the Defense Base Closure and Realignment Commission), and specified procedures that the President, the DOD, the GAO, and the Commission had to follow through 1995 to close and realign military Posts and Bases.

On March 12, 1993, under these procedures, the Secretary of Defense recommended 165-Post and Base closures or realignments affecting military Posts and Bases within the US. By April 15, 1993, the Act, as amended by Public Law 102-484, required the GAO to provide the Commission and the US Congress with a detailed analysis of the Secretary of Defense's recommendations and selection process.

---

[76] David S. Sorenson, "Shutting Down The Cold War: The Politics of Military Base Closure." (St. Martin's Press, New York, July 1998), pp. 242-243.

The BRAC 93 round of Post and Base closures and realignments was the second of three rounds required by the Act. During 1991, the DOD recommended the closure of 43 Posts and Bases and the realignment of 28 military Posts and Bases. The Commission made several adjustments to the DOD's list and proposed 34 military Post and Base closures and 48 realignments. The President and the US Congress accepted Commission recommendations. The final round of military Post and Base closures was scheduled for 1999.

For the current round, the US Congress retained basically the same requirements and procedures as during 1991. As before, the Secretary's recommendations were to be based on selection criteria established by the DOD and on a six-year Force Structure Plan. However, the US Congress added a new requirement that the DOD would certify and validate the data to ensure its accuracy. The eight selection criteria remained unchanged from 1991 to include four that related to the military value of military Installations and four that addressed the number of years needed to recover the costs of military Post and Base closures and realignments; the economic impact on communities; the ability of both the existing and potential receiving communities; infrastructure to support Force Structures, missions, military personnel and Civil Service employees; and the environmental impact. Concurrently, the DOD guidance to the military services and Defense agencies directed that they give priority to the four military value criteria.

The Force Structure Plan was the "base force" for Fiscal Years 1994 through 1999 developed under the Bush Administration. Major elements of the Plan included 12 active US Army Divisions, 12 US Navy Carriers, and 1098 US Air Force aircraft. The Office of the Secretary of Defense (OSD) relied on the military services and Defense agencies to select military Posts and Bases for possible closure or realignment and established guidance concerning the selection processes. During February 1993, the components submitted their proposed military Post and Base closures and realignments to the OSD and the Secretary of Defense made some revisions to these before transmitting recommendations to the Commission.[77]

During the course of this investigation, additional information concerning the nature and consequences of management policies for the Headquarters, Sixth US Army staff was provided. Most of the managers displayed personal attitudes toward management policies that ranged from mildly cautious to totally distrustful and hostile. These attitudes were not difficult to understand. In the subject of motivation, any discussion of MBO would have included the observation that military personnel and Civil Service employees tended to work harder to achieve goals and objectives when they had participated in the process of establishing these goals and objectives. The same point is often made in management literature

---

[77] Charles A. Bowsher, Comptroller General of the US, "Military Bases, Analysis of DOD's Recommendations and Selection Process for Closures and Realignments." (GAO, Washington, DC, April 15, 1993), pp. 2-3.

where it's emphasized that supervisors and managers should have been involved in the setting of performance standards.

Along these lines, it appeared that a good deal of lip service was paid to the importance of viewing management policies as an aid to management rather than as a punitive tool to coerce military personnel and Civil Service employee performance. There was little evidence; however, to indicate that such admonitions were being heeded. In some instances, no effort at all was made to consult with managers and supervisors or permit them to participate in setting standards; rather, the standards were viewed as something that was given to managers and supervisors. Even in those cases where managers and supervisors had the right to approve or propose standards before they were fully implemented, the approval appeared to be more a question of political bargaining than of legitimate analytical discussion between General Forrester and intermediate managers and supervisors. It was also evident that when Human Resource Office reports indicated some weakness in overall performance, the most common responses were the attempt to assign blame and a highly critical attitude toward military personnel and Civil Service employees who appeared to be responsible for the deficiency.

Under such circumstances, it would have been surprising to find many managers and supervisors who viewed management policies with such fondness. Some of the managers and supervisors were not completely aware of the manner of how standards were engineered or the manner in which management policies functioned. In this regard, there were significant differences between what was said and what actually took place. Since managers and supervisors were supposed to understand these matters, some managers and supervisors were reluctant to admit that they did not. For example, most of the personnel who answered Question C-2 in the questionnaire indicated that they understood the details of management policies that were in use. During the course of this study, it became clear from the nature of the questions asked, that management officials who had indicated that they fully understood management policies did not understand them at all.

Virtually all managers, supervisors, military personnel, Civil Service employees who answered the questionnaire demonstrated a good understanding of how management policies were to be re-implemented. In addition, there was universal agreement among them that the system was not punitive but designed to assist managers, supervisors, military personnel, and Civil Service employees to accomplish a better job. In fact, managers, supervisors, military personnel, and Civil Service employees had nothing negative to say about management policies until the level of Civil Service employees were reached. This investigation included such interviews because of the significantly more positive attitudes expressed about management policies. Their reaction to performance standards where their performances were judged was quite different from that of managers and supervisors.

In the Civil Service employee's view, performance standards were tight and could only be achieved if everything went according to plan. Any mistake would immediately drop employees below their standard performance quota. If the employees tried to hurry to catch up, they tended to make mistakes and fall even further behind. As a result, the employees believed that their efficiency would be increased if they did not know what their quota was, or worked under an "implicit" program. What is important here is that those managers and supervisors had never taken the trouble to ascertain how employees felt about management policies. Yet it was these employees who actually performed the tasks that determined the success or failure of the assigned program. As indicated above, management policies appeared to represent a significant improvement over the more "traditional" systems.

Thus, the design of this Case Study contemplated management policies used by the Headquarters, Sixth US Army staff would tend to be both modern and innovative. It was therefore interesting that the Headquarters, Sixth US Army staff exhibited a relatively "traditional" view of behavior, and that those management policies were being used in a punitive and coercive fashion. This seeming paradox was not difficult to reconcile. Management policies had the potential for being used either to encourage goal congruence in the modern sense described above, or for achieving even higher levels of authoritarian control that could be realized with "traditional" management policies. Most military Officers and Civil Service managers and supervisors involved in this Case Study were using management policies in the latter manner. Thus, a return to the proposition that it was not management policies that determined the behavioral consequences of its operations; rather, it was the attitudes of the managers, supervisors, military personnel, and Civil Service employees who assisted in the design and implementation of management policies.

The Headquarters, Sixth US Army history at the Presidio of San Francisco was steeped in military tradition. The Spanish originally established the Presidio Post more than two centuries ago, and occupied approximately 1400-acres of the City's Northwest quadrant. The Sixth US Army, one of five Armies in the Continental US, was headquartered at the Presidio of San Francisco. The Presidio Post was last commanded by General Forrester who was the Commanding General of the Sixth US Army. The Presidio Post's area of responsibility covered 12 Western States-1.2-million square miles, and comprised 40-percent of the landmass of the Continental US. Military personnel and Civil Service employees under the command or training supervision of the Headquarters, Sixth US Army staff totaled approximately 100,000 active military personnel consisting of approximately 800 Officers and Enlisted Men, 130 Civil Service employees, 64 thousand Army National Guard Officers and Enlisted Men in 512 military organizations located at 500 communities, and 35,000 Army Reserve Officers and Enlisted Men in 612 military organizations located at 150 communities.

Under the last reorganization of the Sixth US Army geographic area, the individual State Adjutant General and major US Army Reserve Command (MUSARC) Post Commanders performed many of the functions and had many of the responsibilities formerly held by the Army Readiness and Mobilization Regions. The Headquarters, Sixth US Army staff performed its mission from the Presidio Post, and was assisted by five Readiness Groups strategically located throughout the area. The Reserve Groups provided specialized teams to support training and mobilization preparedness requirements of Reserve Component units.

The primary responsibility of the Headquarters, Sixth US Army staff was to ensure a high state of readiness of its Guard and Reserve units. However, the Command relationship of the Headquarters, Sixth US Army staff to the Guard and Reserve differed. While the Sixth US Army commanded the Army Reserve, Army Guard organizations were under the command of their respective State Governors, unless mobilized by the President of the US. Other responsibilities of the Headquarters, Sixth US Army staff included preparing and implementing plans for mobilization of Reserve Component units and for emergency support of civilian communities in the event of civil disturbances or natural disaster in the Sixth US army area of responsibility.

Historically, the Headquarters Sixth US Army was initially activated on January 25, 1943, at Fort Sam Houston in Texas, with the mission of recapturing the vast chain of islands seized by Japan during the months of World War II in the Pacific Theater. In helping to fulfill General MacArthur's vow, "I shall return," the Sixth US Army fought its way across 3600-miles of ocean and jungle land. These battles were highlighted by engagements at New Britain, the Admiralties, New Guinea, Leyte, and finally Luzon and the capture of the Philippine Islands. During September 1945, following Japan's surrender, the Sixth US Army served as an occupation force until inactivated during January, 1946. On March 1, 1946, the Headquarters, Sixth US Army was reactivated at the Presidio of San Francisco and assumed its vital role of training active duty and Reserve forces. During mid-1950, the Sixth US Army again sent its units into combat with the 2nd Division bearing the brunt of early fighting in Korea. The California National Guard's 40th Division later joined them; one of only two Army National Guard Divisions to serve in the Korean War.

During the Vietnam War, the call for combat troops was again met by the Sixth US Army's 4th Division and various Army National Guard and Army Reserve units. As it has done since its inception, the Sixth US Army continued to stand as the "Guardian of the West." Though "Born of War" and raised to maturity and glory during periods of hostility, the Sixth US Army was, in peace, dedicating itself to helping produce US Army Reserve and National Guard forces to a high state of readiness, and to assist civilian communities in the area in times of earthquake or disaster. With the transfer of the Headquarters, Sixth US Army staff along with the discontinuance of Garrison, the Headquarters, Sixth US Army's mission and functions were transferred to the Fifth US Army at San Antonio in Texas.

CHAPTER XIII

Concluding Comments

The future viability of the realignment of the Headquarters, Sixth US Army staff to Treasure Island and then to Fort Carson in Colorado along with the discontinuance of the Presidio Garrison; the transfer of Reserve mission and functions from the Headquarters, Sixth US Army to the US Army Reserve Command; and the transfer of the Presidio of San Francisco to the US National Park Service had many dimensions to include the degree where the efforts accurately reflected perceptions, concerns, and aspirations of the participating members. Other dimensions included the degree to which participants were innovative and successful in helping bring about congruence with other military Post and Base closure programs. The final decision affecting the possible realignment of the Headquarters, Sixth US Army staff, and the final fate of the Presidio Post closure were still unknown at that time.

The Presidio of San Francisco Closure and Realignment Study had addressed the proposed merger with the Headquarters, Sixth US Army staff with the Presidio Garrison rather than a Presidio of San Francisco closure. The final revision to the Presidio of San Francisco Closure and Realignment Study was submitted to General Shoemaker for approval or disapproval. The plan presented a proposed organizational structure for the Headquarters, Sixth US Army staff merger with the Presidio Garrison, and an analysis of various organizational alternatives for the reorganization and inter-relationships among US Army activities based at the Presidio of San Francisco. The basic management model adopted was a hybrid matrix structure embodying the Program Manager concept. The hybrid feature provided flexibility in the organizational location of a Program Manager. For the Headquarters, Sixth US Army staff workload, the Program Manager was responsible for conceptualizing the project in terms of basic technical objectives, scope, and nature of technical output. The process usually involved direction of a planning team assembled from participating functional organizations. The Program Manager was authorized to determine the degree of participation by the various functional activities, and to make in-house versus out-of-house choices, such as realigning to Treasure Island and then to Fort Carson in Colorado. The participating Functional Manager and the Program Manager entered into a task agreement that specified desired output, established schedules, and specified effort levels in terms of socioeconomic resource allocations.

The conclusions reached in the Presidio of San Francisco Closure and Realignment Study was considered sound. The first proposal to combine the Headquarters, Sixth US Army staff with the Presidio Garrison was considered the most attractive organizational alternative, and was also considered the most socioeconomic, feasible, and prudent. As a result of this Study, the following recommendations were made to General Shoemaker:

- Under the current organization, Command and supervision relationships and among the Commanding General, Sixth US Army and the Commander, Presidio Garrison, presented no identified deviations from governing US Army regulations and Base Closure and Realignment Act instructions;

- Many of the troublesome issues identified during the assessment of Command and support relationships would be resolved with the implementation of a single Command;

- A consolidated Command option that would merge the Headquarters, Sixth US Army and the Presidio Garrison into a single organization was the most attractive organizational alternative in that it provided consistency in Command and support relationships as well as the greatest potential for consolidation and tangible savings;

- The consolidated organization prototypes embodied the feature most likely to satisfy the requirements of an organization oriented to Command and support;

- Through the use of a financial system utilizing the US Army industrial accounting procedures, an integrated command organization could account for its activities through the use of both the US Army industrial fund and institutional funding;

- The Headquarters, Sixth US Army's unity of purpose would be optimized with one, and only one, Command level with all functional organizations and activities reporting to the Commanding General, Sixth US Army. Such a consolidation of organizations and the use of single Program Managers for each major program would improve responsiveness from and to outside customers and organizational entities;

- The alternative structure would provide for the implementation of the Base Closure and Realignment Act in a cost effective manner while ensuring the responsiveness of Command and support effort;

- The alternative organizational structure was oriented toward Command and support with a Reserve support emphasis, and

- presented an organization oriented toward evaluation with more emphasis on an integral development capability;

- The internal reorganization of the Headquarters, Sixth US Army staff to include the Presidio Garrison organization would provide major advantages over the organization with respect to effectiveness and the implementation of the Base Closure and Realignment Act. However, the fully combined Headquarters, Sixth US Army staff would be significantly more attractive, particularly with respect to responsiveness to Command and support requirements of the future. A saving in military personnel and Civil Service employee positions would be achieved through implementation of a consolidated organization, while a similar billet reduction was estimated through implementation of an internal Presidio Post reorganized structure. This was separate from any reduction in positions due to implementation of the Base Closure and Realignment Act of 1988;

- The responsibility for performing critical US Army management functions related to major contracts as well as for the performance of common service staff support functions was properly vested to the Headquarters, Sixth US Army as the host;

- Further development and refinement of organization detail and contracting out area selection were needed before implementation of the Base Closure and Realignment Act;

- The influence of external developments during the planning and implementation period could be expected to require changes in the estimates presented in the study;

Historically, the Presidio of San Francisco Post closure emerged from two interrelated origins:

- Innovations stemming from economic and financial difficulties;

- Innovations centering on the effective feedback of attitudes.

Successful military Post and Base closure efforts would require skill in intervention, a systems view to management support and involvement, an open and shared technology and value system, and a long-range perspective. In addition to being sustained, changes stemming from the military Post and Base closure and realignment should have been linked to changes in organization Sub-systems. The Headquarters, Sixth US Army was reviewed as consisting of goals, objectives, tasks, technological, human-social, structural, and external interface Sub-systems existing in a state of dynamic inter-dependence. Such concepts as interface, entropy, feedback, and openness would have useful to understand the organization and in raising issues relating to improving strategies.

As they say "in the old ball game," the Presidio Post closure would not be over until the last pitch and the last out in the bottom of the ninth inning. However, the US National Park Service was going to be there to throw the last pitch. Where else could the National Park Service obtain free land, buildings, and equipment, free Federal Government assistance, and a fully established and going business without investing a single cent? Because of this, the DA accused military personnel and Civil Service employees at the Presidio of San Francisco of being overly emotional. When issues of the military Post and Base closure and realignment were involved, this author had never seen anyone get more emotional involved than managers and supervisors at the DA and DOD level.

The investigation of the behavioral implications of management policies suggested three major points. First, actual management policies, although important for the purpose of cost control, had little value for management control purposes. Second, the proper use of management policies, procedures, and standards fit very nicely into the overall concepts of the "decision making" model of behavior. Finally, management policies had the potential to be used one of two ways. For example, either as aids in increasing motivation and goal congruence, or as devices to achieve high levels of autocratic and coercive control. The locus concludes that management policies or at least the policies studied tended to be based on behavioral assumptions that are very closely related to the "traditional" model.

It appeared reasonably evident that the existence of the degree of hostility and distrust among participants that were observed during the course of this study could hardly have been in the best interest of the Headqauarters, Sixth US Army. While this author cannot say with complete assurance that managerial attitudes oriented toward a "modern" organization theory view of behavior would have eliminated or reduced all of these problems. However, it did appear consistent with "modern" organization theory philosophy to anticipate that managers holding such attitudes should have at least been aware of the problems, and should have attempted to work toward a solution. In any event, it was unlikely that the effort to apply behavioral theory to management policies would have generated very much additional conflict and discontent within the Headquarters, Sixth US Army; however, it was possible that such a movement might have produced favorable results.

It cost money to employ and train new managers, supervisors, and Civil Service employees. And, after Civil Service employees have been hired and trained, it takes additional time and money to build them into a loyal, well knit, and effectively functioning organization with well-established goals and objectives. The more supportive the supervision and the better the organization (in terms of loyalty; level of performance goals; communications; motivation; and so forth), the greater was its capacity for high quality performance at a lower cost. In the Headquarters, Sixth US Army hierarchy, putting pressure on this well established organization to produce yielded substantial and immediate increases in productivity.

This increase was obtained; however, at a cost to the human assets of the organization. For example, as hostilities increased in the organization, there was greater reliance upon authority, loyalties declined, and motivations to restrict production increased. In other words, the quality of the Headquarters, Sixth US Army human organization deteriorated as a functioning social system. The proposed Headquarters, Sixth US Army realignment was originally expected to bring about a more efficient, effective, and dynamic organization that would have achieved economies through the elimination of duplicate staff positions between the Headquarters, Sixth US Army staff and the Presidio Garrison. However, the proposed reorganization became more a political and administrative maneuver. Years of previous political interference in trying to reorganize or realign the Headquarters, Sixth US Army staff had made supervisors and managers indecisive in their responsibilities of fulfilling a planned management action, and finally resulted in the discontinuance of the Headquarters, Sixth US Army and the Presidio Garrison, and the transfer of the Presidio of San Francisco to the US National Park Service.

The BRAC Clean-Up Plan (BCP) described the status, management and response strategy, and action items relating to the Presidio of San Francisco's ongoing military Post-wide environmental restoration and surplus property compliance programs. These programs supported the restoration of the military Installation property that was necessary to meet the requirements for property disposal and re-use activities associated with the closure of the military Installation. The scope of the BCP considered the following regulatory mechanisms: the BRAC Act; National Environmental Policy Act (NEPA); Comprehensive Environmental Response, Compensation, and Liability Act (CERCLA) as amended, to include the Community Environmental Response Facilitation Act (CERFA); Resource Conservation and Recovery Act (RCRA); and other applicable laws.

The Presidio of San Francisco's BCP was a dynamic planning document developed by the BRAC Clean-Up Team (BCT) consisting of the US Army, US Environmental Protection Agency, and representatives of the State of California Environmental Protection Agency (EPA). It was necessary to make certain assumptions and interpretations to develop the schedule and cost estimates provided in the plan. The BCP was updated regularly to reflect the current status and strategies of remedial actions. This document was the latest in a series of updates and modifications and represented conditions and strategies as of the date of closing.

The Base Realignment and Closure (BRAC) Clean-Up Plan (BCP), Version II, summarized the status of the environmental restoration and associated environmental compliance programs, and presented a comprehensive strategy for implementing response actions necessary to protect human health and the environment. The Presidio of San Francisco was situated on hundreds of acres within the corporate limits of San Francisco and performed clearances for the Department of Defense and other Federal Government agencies. The Presidio Post was finally approved for closure under the Base Closure and Realignment Act of 1988. The official closure date was October 1, 1998.

The Headquarters, Sixth US Army staff transferred all operations to the Fifth US Army at Fort Sam Houston at San Antonio in Texas. In addition to laying out the response action approach at the military Installation in support of military Post closure, this BCP defines the status of efforts to resolve technical issues so that continued progress and implementation of scheduled activities could occur. This BCP, originally prepared as Version I, Draft Document, during September 1996 had been updated regularly to incorporate newly obtained information. Version II BCP was prepared with information available as of December 10, 1998.

In sum, the Presidio of San Francisco closure portrayed a running account of a crisis action precipitated by insensitive and irresponsible higher headquarters management decisions made by Federal Government officials who did not have valid information to make a proper decision. These administrative decisions resulted in political pressure being put on the Headquarters, Sixth US Army staff to conform to its initial evaluation to close the Presidio Post. The final decision; however, would cost the US Army one of the most beautiful US Army military Posts in the Country, and cost the City of San Francisco a reduced tax base through the elimination of military personnel and Civil Service employees, and mainly the immediate protection of the US Army during a civil emergency or earthquake.

The end of a heroic era for the Headquarters, Sixth US Army at the Presidio of San Francisco was becoming evident to the Headquarters, Sixth US Army staff. Nobody knew; however, that the final coup de grace for the Headquarters, Sixth US Army would be in its eventual disestablishment and not in its realignment. The demise of the Headquarters, Sixth US Army; however, could now be seen coming over the near horizon. Lieutenant General Forrester, Commanding General, Sixth US Army on May 24, 1992 published an open letter to the citizens of the Presidio of San Francisco.[78]

General Forrester stated: "The US Army was very proud of its long stewardship of this great old military Post. During 1846, the US Army inherited the Preside of San Francisco to the people of the US during 1995, a thickly, forested, emerald jewel considered by many to be the most beautiful military Installation in the World. The planting, cultivation, preservation, and maintenance of this priceless legacy were made possible through the conscientious efforts of the US Army and those associated with it over the years. As Presidians, you and I have a great deal of which to be proud because of what the US Army and all of us have done to preserve and to make the Presidio Post a 'Very Special Place.' Were it not for the US Army's creation and care of this beautiful sit, soon to become one of America's most beautiful scenic parks, this parcel of land would likely, long ago, have been dissected, zoned, and developed commercially and residentially. Again, thanks to the US Army, that never happened.

---

[78] Editorial, <u>Star Presidian</u> (San Francisco), "<u>Open letter to the citizens of the Presidio of San Francisco,</u>" May 24, 1990, p.3.

The Headquarters, Sixth US Army was committed and turned over to the Department of the Interior acres and acres of historical buildings and lush greenery in as fine a state as was humanly possible, and in a condition, better beyond expectations than that which the US Army inherited 144-years ago. The history of the Presidio of San Francisco closure and transfer to the US National Park Service was steeped in contributions of Federal Government, State, local and private sector officials, and the contributions of many volunteers in the Mayor's "Save the Presidio" Committee, many of whom are very well known. Even if the author was aware of all the significant events and contributors, which the author is not, the author could not add to the summary of this history. Therefore, all the author could do was document the central themes of that history and hope that the many significant events and persons involved who are not mentioned would not be offended by its incompleteness.

The Presidio of San Francisco is hardly a success story despite the value and beauty of its land. The prolonged fight to keep the Presidio of San Francisco in operation, followed by the necessity to turn it over to the US National Park Service only delayed what may still be successful conversion. Sometime must pass before the conversion of the Presidio Post to a self-sustaining enterprise is deemed successful or not. Should it fail, the oldest US Army Post may be sold to commercial interests and the oldest military Post in the Country may finally disappear despite the often heroic and (unusual) efforts made to preserve it. BRAC 93 procedure made changes from 1991, particularly in the terms of "openness."

The Commissioners did realize that the 1991 closure process had left the taint of politics in the process and the one way to purge the taint was to open public access to the process. Nothing illustrated that more than the fight over the Presidio of San Francisco that among other things showed that military Post and Base closure politics during an election year was particularly contentious given the stakes at hand. In the Presidio Post's case, as in the Fort Ord Post, George AFB, Norton AFB, Beale AFB, Castle AFB, and Mather AFB, the original closure decisions during 1988 carried over again and again, and produced just as much 'heat' in 1996 as it had during 1988."[79]

But what remained unanswered was the question why the Headquarters, Sixth US Army staff did not take positive action to invite Federal Government agencies in the City of San Francisco and Bay Area to physically move onto the Presidio of San Francisco. Especially since the Headquarters, Sixth US Army staff considered it to be the only possibility solution and justification for the Presidio Post to remain operational as a US Army Installation. Research has revealed; however, that the Headquarters, Sixth US Army staff never requested formal authority from the US Army Forces Command to propose or implement such a decision. Nor did research provide any information that suggested mutual benefit realignment was

---

[79] David S. Sorenson, "Shutting Down The Cold War: The Politics of Military Base Closure," (St. Martin's Press, New York, July 1998), pp. 152-158.

even discussed with several Federal Government agencies located in the City of San Francisco and Bay Area. Therefore, the history of events that occurred would suggest that it was a result of inertia or lethargy by the Headquarters, Sixth US Army staff. That is, the Headquarters, Sixth US Army staff took little or no action to satisfy the goals and objectives of keeping the Presidio Post operational as a military Installation. It appeared the final decision to close the Presidio Post, and to discontinue the Headquarters, Sixth US Army and the Presidio Garrison was made to avoid further embarrassment to the US Army.

This haphazard decision; however, was made even though it would remove the Headquarters, Sixth US Army staff, together with its Earthquake Response Center farther away from the 12 Western States it serviced during an actual emergency. The Headquarters, Fifth US Army staff located at San Antonio in Texas would not be able to respond to any future emergency in the 12 Western States as quickly and effectively as did the Headquarters, Sixth US Army staff closely located on the Presidio of San Francisco. The conclusion to the above question; therefore, was believed to follow contemporary thinking that Federal Government agencies do not talk to each other trying to protect their "mission" and their "turf." The bureaucratic military organization is just not compatible with or comfortable co-existing with other Federal Government agencies managed by high-ranking Civil Service employees. Simply stated, the US Army did not desire to have other Federal Government agencies interfering in their military mission and daily operations by demanding available support services that would affect or interfere with the military bureaucracy, management, training, or workload. For practical purposes, the BRAC process in California is well underway as all of the military Posts and Bases have been reviewed for closure or realignment. At this point, the avenues for effecting meaningful change for military Posts and Bases in California are limited. However, it's more than certain that California will loss additional military Posts and Bases, military personnel, and Civil Service employees. California is now better prepared for the next BRAC process than it was for the earlier rounds of military Post and Base closures. With the release of the DOD's new closure and realignment list and BRAC Commission hearings on the horizon, military Post and Base proponents are preparing strong arguments that could be presented to the BRAC Commission, touting California military value as the "Gibraltar of the Pacific." Complaining about the State's past inequities would likely be less effective than explaining the detrimental implications for national security of an inadequate Pacific Coast Defense infrastructure. Assuming that all goes well, such preparation may avert California's experiencing anything near the gross disproportionate military Post and Base closures and realignments it has already experienced.

Preventing military Post and Base closures and realignments may be California's first and most important priority. It is also important to look past the initial trauma of military Post and Base closures and realignments and work toward minimizing the initial impact. Delays and poor planning for re-use of closed military Posts and Bases exacerbated California's bad fortune. In the event more military Posts and Bases are targeted for Post or Base closures, smart investment and quick, careful planning could make the re-use process less damaging to local economies and may ultimately lead to long-term economic growth. Federal Government and State financial support during the transformation stage could make a significant difference in the outcome for closed military Posts and Bases. Re-use planning organizations should examine the transitions at the Presidio of San Francisco, the Fort Ord Post, George AFB, Norton AFB, Beale AFB, Castle AFB, and Mather AFB to see how to approach transition after an announcement of a military Post or Base closure.

The most effective inoculation against the myriad ills of inevitable future Post and Base closures and realignments of military organizations is to make California the best and most hospitable home to the military services. Although the current deficits in California and Federal Government budgets limit the ability to invest in the infrastructure that supports the military services, military Post and Base proponents can continually plan, organize, collaborate, and act. California could make land use and encroachment regulations friendlier for existing military Posts and Bases. California and community leaders could promote affordable housing near military Posts and Bases. Coordination of infrastructure improvements could raise California's value as a facility host in the eyes of the DOD. Ultimately, California could put itself in a position to receive, rather than in a position to lose, military personnel and Civil Service employees in future military Post or Base closures but only if California would take proactive steps to be a friendlier home to military Posts and Bases, military personnel, and Civil Service employees.

California's military communities were battered by five BRAC rounds. The lessons learned from California's past military Post and Base closures and realignments of military components should influence the State's future course of action while addressing anticipated BRAC closures. In addition, a united front and strategic outlook should assist defense oriented communities to survive and thrive regardless of what the next BRAC round may yield

What happened to the Base closure emphasis since the Presidio of San Francisco closure during 1993? It remained a mystery to me until a featured article appeared in the November-December 2004 issue of the magazine "via," The AAA Traveler's Companion, entitled The Presidio Secret of the City, by Ms. Deborah Franklin. Another appropriate insight became apparent and the theme of this article would become the final closure to compliment a narrative history that required a befitting epilogue. Ms. Franklin had investigated into the operation, repair, and maintenance of the historical land and buildings at the Presidio of San Francisco. The Presidio of San Francisco had served the Country for over 200-years as a military outpost. The Presidio of San Francisco is now a US National Recreational Park like no other Park in the Country. The Presidio Post's 1491-acre expanse of brick and forest is a blend of urban and rural, spread across the City's Northern waterfront. The Presidio is home to a think tank; a gallery; deep woods; a meadow; and a small town. The Presidio Post has a beach; a day camp; and two cemeteries—a vast one for veterans and family members and a small one for military pets. The Presidio Post has a movie studio; a fortress; a bowling alley; and an archaeological dig. The Presidio Post boasts a web of hiking and biking trails and is a windsurfer's dream. Approximately 2400 people currently reside at the Presidio Post as do parrots; gray foxes; and coyotes.

Since 2001, when the former military airstrip was torn up and converted to wetlands, dunes, and a bayside promenade, some four million people a year have come to San Francisco to revel in the big sky vista. You can pick up Presidio maps and schedules of ranger-led walks and seasonal programs—and get cappuccino, sandwiches, guide books, and Eco themed gifts—at the popular Warming Hut, between Crissy Field and Torpedo Wharf at the former Garrison's Northern edge. Every day anglers haul in crab or bass from the pier, and foghorns trade basso profundo calls with passing ships. Ambling couples pull each other closer as blustery tufts of fog drift through the Golden Gate Bridge toward a glittering down-town San Francisco. This is San Francisco where visitors leave their hearts. And it almost did not happen. When the US Army turned over the Presidio of San Francisco to the US National Park Service during 1994, the gift carried an unprecedented catch. The US Congress insisted that the new National Park become financially self-sufficient by 2013 or risk being sold at auction. Since this period, the Presidio Trust, the Presidio National Park's governing Board, has had to walk a tricky line, trying to get the natural resources to pay for itself without destroying itself.

Much of the new funding has come from residential and commercial leases. The Presidio's splashiest tenant—movie mogul George Lucas's special effects group would be housed in the Letterman Digital Arts Center—was set to open shop during 2005. The Presidio Trust now has another big named client on deck. The Disney Family Foundation has confirmed that it hoped to rent space in the 1890s brick barracks of the Main Post for a museum dedicated to Walt Disney. But the future of this private-public National Park was still far from certain. To assist in navigating this unique and unusual National Park, the Presidio's diversions are split into several categories—one for history lovers and others for those drawn to the San Francisco Bay, the woods, and the wildlife. But feel free to mix-and-match your diversional activities. To discover the Presidio, you have plenty of diversions to choose from.

Ms. Barbara Voss of Stanford University is just one of several archaeologists who are searching for clues to San Francisco's past in the Presidio of San Francisco. A lot of people tend to think of this area's history as starting with the Gold Rush. Ms. Voss stated: "The Presidio dig has allowed us to look into the period before that, to document some of the diversity of the early San Franciscans." The Visitor Center located in the former Officer's Club (Building 50 on Moraga Avenue) is the information hub for all things historical. You will find books, free maps, and brochures to include pamphlets for a self-guided walking tour around the Main

Post that covers 200-years of history and architecture. A posted schedule lists ranger-and—docent led talks and walks (and shuttle tours) that vary daily.

Artifacts sifted from the sand around the Main Post and displayed in the Mesa Lounge of the former Officer's Club suggests the ups and downs of an early soldier's life: a Spanish crucifix, leather holsters, home dominoes, and a comb for lice. Archaeologists have pried up floorboards and peeled away plaster to permit a glimpse of the walls and green serpentine rock foundation of the early 19th Century adobe structure hidden beneath and within the building. Around the corner, black-and-white photographs hanging in the hallway and period uniforms under glass conjure still other eras. The Exhibition Hall was displaying a collection of contemporary Maya textiles on loan from the Mexican National Museum of Anthropology and History.

Though 469 of the Presidio's buildings—more than half—have been designated as "historic," relatively few are open to the public, and many of these may be seen on US National Park Service tours. The guided walks offer a peek at fascinating but obscure chapters in San Francisco history. On one tour you will explore refugee cottages that were among the thousands built on the Presidio to house some of the 250,000 San Franciscans left homeless by the 1906 quake. On a walk through the National Cemetery you can hear the story of Pauline Cushman Fryer, a Southern actress who successfully spied for the Union on movements of the Army of Tennessee. Also buried there are nearly 300 buffalo soldiers from African-American regiments (the Ninth and 10th Cavalry and 24th and 25th Infantry) that spent time at the Presidio in the 19th and early 20th Centuries on their way to various wars. Another little known historical fact: Some members of the Ninth Cavalry who had been garrisoned at the Presidio were among the first National Park Rangers. They patrolled Yosemite and Sequoia by horse. Take an aviation tour and discover why Crissy Field was considered the last work in airfields when it was completed during 1921 by future WW II US Army Air Corps hero General Hap Arnold. Have a look at the barracks where Japanese American code breakers worked to foil enemy plans—even as their families lived in internment camps.

From Friday through Sunday, you can enter Fort Point, the cavernous Gold Rush era outpost at the foot of the Golden Gate Bridge. A couple of informational films recount the history of the Fort and the building of the San Francisco Bay Bridge. The ranger-led tour provides interesting details about Fort life during the 1860s for the 500 soldiers garrisoned there—they slept head to toe, two to a bunk and 24 to a room, taking precious few baths. Rushed to completion on the eve of the Civil War to help keep Southern sympathizers from nabbing California's gold. Fort Point was obsolete almost before it opened. Newly developed rifled cannons could easily blast holes through the masonry. But it never came under enemy fire, and the artillery soldiers, along with 102 cannons, were all withdrawn by 1900, though the Fort was again briefly unmanned during WW II to protect a submarine net strung across the entrance to the San Francisco Nay.

Look for a list of guided nature and other special activities each day on a board in front of the Warming Hut on Torpedo Wharf. In the early Fall, Rangers loan crab traps and teach children of all ages how to catch the clawed critters from the pier. Or you can bring your own gear throughout the year. (Note: only 35-crabs per crabber, and no Dungeness—the Bay is their nursery.) To learn more about the rich diversity of marine life offshore and to get friendly with sea stars and anemones in a touch tank, stop in at the Visitor Center Faralllones National Marine Sanctuary at the water's edge. Do not fret if a winter storm descends; the Crissy Field Center on Mason Street overlooking the Bay brings the outdoors in, with environment themed workshops, readings, displays, and activities. Programs are diverse and change seasonally. Listen to a lecture on urban wildlife (where do those City-bred skunks and raccoons sleep?), learn how to grow mushrooms in your garden, or paint a landscape. Programs are inexpensive or, in some cases, free.

San Francisco citizens prize the peaceful, rosy glow of dawn at Chrissy Field when the winds are still, and the San Francisco Bay is a reflecting pond of lavender and pink. For a nature trek beyond compare, park your car at the East Beach lot on Mason Street near the Palace of Fine Arts and head West along the gray-City promenade, past the tidewater lagoon, marsh, and dunes—excavated, restored, and replanted during 2001 thanks to thousands of volunteers and $35 million in mostly private funds. Squads of Pelicans roam the heavens above the marsh—the same skies where name-sake Major Dana Crissy and crewmen of the US Army Air Corps flew in their De Havilland biplanes. Take your dog for a walk along the beach (leash required) or stroll on to where the ocean meets the Bay at Fort Point and watch humans and sea lions surf the breakers under the Golden Gate Bridge.

Many of the sheltered paths winding through the Presidio's forested hills remain dry and warm even on the foggiest, windiest days. The Ecology Trail that runs South from just behind the old Officer's Club loops a little more than a mile through groves of redwood, eucalyptus, and cypress. Look carefully to see pockets of the endangered wild-flowered Presidio clarkia (four lavender pedals with red center). It's a rare prim-rose cousin that was discovered at the Presidio. A free children's guide to activities along the Ecology Trail, is available in English and Spanish at the various visitor centers and include a picture of the flower. During fine weather, take the short spur trail of the loop to Inspiration Point for a panoramic view of the woods; the San Francisco Bay; Marin County; and beyond.

But do not stop there. From the point, ambitious walkers are well-placed to hike to several more of the Presidio's best Sites. A 10-minute walk South from Inspiration Point will take you to a dirt trail that parallels West Pacific Avenue, bordering the wealthy residental neighborhood of Pacific Heights. Turen East and you will soon stumble upon Julius Kahn Playground surrounded by what looks like Winnie-the-Pooh's hundred-acre Wood. Neighborhood children say the playground, that was overhauled several years ago to include futuristic equipment that not only swings but also bounces and spins, is the best in San Francisco. The 100-year-old forest is gradually being sown with younger trees to prevent a sudden, catastrophic decline as the original trees all grow old at the same time.

You wander behind the playground where you will find a trail back down the hill through Tennessee Hollow to El Polin Spring, a natural water source and bird haven where foxes or even coyotes can also be spotted on quiet mornings. Or double back up the hill along West Pacific Avenue to the public Pacific Golf Course. Cruise pass the 18-hole, cypress-studded fairways another mile and a half to find Mountain Lake. Conte on to Lobos Dunes and a pretty half-mile natural trail with a boardwalk that skirts one of the Park's with a free-flowing creeks. You have nearly reached the continents edge. Cross Lincoln Boulevard and take the dirt path through the trees that will soon part to reveal the sands and long stretch of surf of Baker Beach. You can sit down at this location and absorb the peace and quiet. Spanish colonial Captain Juan Bautista de Anza is thought to have done just that during 1776 when his weary band of Spanish soldiers and mestizo emigrants rested here after a long walk from Sonora in Mexico—an expedition that led to the founding of the Presidio of San Francisco. [80]

---

[80] Deborah Franklin, "The Presidio Secret of the City," via, The AAA Traveler's Companion, San Francusci Presidio, November-December 2004, pp. 28-34 .

BIBLIOGRAPHY

Primary Sources

House of Representatives. Official correspondence between Representative Charles M. Teague and Comptroller General of the US. May 24, 1973.

United States Senate, Official correspondence between Senator Allan Cranston and Vice President, NFFE, Local 1374. July 25, 1973.

Cramer, John, Reporter from Washington Star, (Washington, DC), "Judge Strikes a Blow Against Contracting Out Jobs." December 5, 1973.

Moscone, Mayor George R. Letter to Mr. Howard Freeman. July 12, 1978.

Headquarters, US Army Forces Command. Official correspondence between Colonels Patrick D. Chisolm, Jr., Chief of Public Affairs and the Department of the Army Chief of Public Affairs. September 6, 1978.

Headquarters, US Army Forces Command. Proposed News Release. September 6, 1978.

National Park Service, Department of the Interior. Personal correspondence between Mr. William J. Whalen, Director and Mr. George Dean, President, Fort Point and Army Museum Association. November 1, 1978.

United States Department of the Interior, US National Park Service. Personal Correspondence between Mr. William J. Whalen, Director and Mr. George M. Dean, President, Fort Point and Army Museum. November 1, 1978.

City of San Francisco. Personal correspondence between Mayor Dianne Feinstein and The Honorable Harold Brown, Chairman, President's Economic Adjustment Committee. December 5, 1978.

United States Senate. Personal correspondence between Senator Alan Cranston and Mr. Benjamin H. Swig, Co-chairman, "Save the Presidio" Committee. December 13, 1978.

San Francisco Planning and Urban Research Association (SPUR). Personal Correspondence between Mr. John H. Jacobs, Executive Director and Dr. Jan F. Sassaman, Ph. D. December 15, 1978.

Headquarters, Sixth US Army. Official correspondence between Lieutenant General Eugene P. Forrester, Commanding General and Commander, Headquarters, US Army Forces Command. December 19, 1978.

Headquarters, Sixth US Army. Official correspondence between Lieutenant General Eugene Forrester, Commanding General and the Honorable Dianne Feinstein, Mayor of San Francisco. December 21, 1978.

Headquarters, Sixth US Army. Official correspondence between Colonel H. Gordon Waite, Chief, Public Affairs and Colonel Patrick D. Chisolm, Jr., Chief, Public Affairs, Headquarters, US Army Forces Command. December 27, 1978.

Fact Sheet. Subject: Construction at Presidio of San Francisco; H.R. 12536, 95th Congress, 2d Section. December 27, 1978.

Geological Survey, US Department of the Interior. Official correspondence between Mr. David P. Hill, Chief, Seismology Branch and Colonel John Kern, Chief Engineering Division, Headquarters, Sixth US Army. December 29, 1973.

Headquarters, US Army Forces Command. Official message to the US Navy and US Army Corps of Engineers, Subject: Presidio of San Francisco Realignment. December 29, 1978.

The Secretary of Defense. Official correspondence between Deputy Secretary and the Honorable Dianne Feinstein, Mayor of San Francisco. December 30, 1978.

Headquarters, US Army Forces Command. Official correspondence between General R. M. Shoemaker, Commanding General and Commander, Sixth US Army. January 9, 1979.

Headquarters, Sixth US Army. Official correspondence between Lieutenant General Eugene P. Forrester, Commanding General and Commander, US Army Forces Command. January 10, 1979.

Economics Research Associates. Personal correspondence between Mr. J. Richard McElyea, Senior Vice President and Mr. Daniel Stephan, Senior Associate to Mr. William D. Evers, President, Economic Development Advisory Council, Office of the Mayor, San Francisco. January 22, 1979.

Touche Ross & Company. Personal correspondence between Touche Ross & Company and Mr. William D. Evers, President, "Save the Presidio" Committee. January 23, 1979

Headquarters, US Army Forces Command. Official correspondence between General R. M. Shoemaker, Commanding General and Commander, Sixth US Army. January 23, 1979.

Headquarters, Sixth US Army. Official correspondence between Brigadier General Michael N. Bakarich, Chief of Staff and Commander, Presidio of San Francisco. January 29, 1979.

Touche Ross & Company. Personal correspondence between Touche Ross & Company and Mr. William D. Evers, President, "Save the Presidio" Committee. February 7, 1979.

Headquarters, Sixth US Army. Official correspondence between Lieutenant General Eugene P. Forrester, Commanding General and General Robert M. Shoemaker, Commander, US Army Forces Command. March 2, 1979.

Headquarters, Sixth US Army. Routing and Disposition Form from Colonel H. Gordon Waite, Chief Public Affairs, Headquarters, Sixth US Army. March 7, 1979.

Headquarters, Sixth US Army. Memorandum for Commander from Colonel H. Gordon Waite, Chief, Public Affairs, Subject: Summary of Mayor's "Save the Presidio" Committee Meeting. March 9, 1979.

Headquarters, Sixth US Army. Official message to Headquarters, US Army Forces Command, Subject: Base Realignment Study. March 15, 1979.

City of San Francisco. Personal correspondence between Mayor Dianne Feinstein and The Honorable Clifford L. Alexander, Jr., Secretary of the Army. March 16, 1979.

City of Oakland. Personal correspondence between Mayor Lionel J. Wilson and Lieutenant General Eugene P. Forrester, Commanding General, Sixth US Army. March 19, 1979.

Headquarters, US Army Forces Command. Official correspondence between General R. M. Shoemaker, Commanding General and Chief of Staff, Department of the Army. March 21, 1979.

City of San Francisco. Personal correspondence between Mr. Melvin Swig and Mr. J. Edward Fleishell, Co-chairmen, Mayor's "Save the Presidio" Committee and Mr. Howard Freeman. March 21, 1979.

Headquarters, Sixth US Army. Memorandum for Record from Colonel H. Gordon Waite, Chief, Public Affairs, Subject: Mayor's "Save the Presidio" Committee. April 10, 1979.

Touche Ross & Company. Personal correspondence between Touche Ross & Company and Colonel Bazaney, Health Services Command. April 11, 1979.

Headquarters, Sixth US Army. Official correspondence between Colonel F. M. Crocetti, DCS/Personnel and US Total Army Personnel Command. September 5, 1991.

Headquarters, Sixth US Army. Official correspondence between Colonel F. Crocetti, DCS/Personnel and Commander, US Army Forces Command October 9, 1991.

San Francisco Chronicle, (City of San Francisco), "Bay Area Tribe Stakes Its Claim to the Presidio Post." June 16, 1992, pp. A11 and A13.

www.Fort Ord History and Closure.com.

www.Castle AFB History and Closure.com.

www.Mather AFB History and Closure.com.

www.California Institute Special Report: California's Past Base Closure Experiences and the 2005 BRAC Round, April 2000.com.

Secondary Sources

John E. Lynch, "Local Economic Development after Military Base Closures," (Praeger, New York, 1970).

Editorial. "Closure: LAMC CG discusses plans," (Star Presidian. San Francisco, California, March 15, 1990).

Editorial. "Commander addresses closure issues," (Star Presidian. San Francisco, California, May 3, 1990).

Editorial. "Budget forces worker cutbacks," (Star Presidian. San Francisco, California, May 10, 1990

Editorial. "Presidio's future? National Park Service holds public hearing-citizens speak out," (Star Presidian. San Francisco, California, May 24, 1990).

Editorial. "Open letter to citizens of the Presidio of San Francisco," (Star Presidian. San Francisco, California, May 24, 1990).

Editorial. "Base closure-An in depth interview with BRACO chief," (Star Presidian. San Francisco, California, June 7, 1990).

Editorial. "CPO works for employees, mission," (Star Presidian. San Francisco, California, June 14, 1990).

Editorial. "News to Use-No sweeping early retirements," (Star Presidian. San Francisco, California, June 21, 1990).

Editorial. "Lawmakers looking to "soften" cuts," (Star Presidian. San Francisco, California, July 6, 1990).

Editorial. "Harrison-Army to be better, smaller," (Star Presidian. San Francisco, California, July 12, 1990).

Editorial. "BRAC releases movement plans," (Star Presidian. San Francisco, California, July 26, 1990).

Editorial. "Closure may hurt homeowners-Affected soldiers to get Federal $," (Star Presidian. San Francisco, California, August 16, 1990).

Editorial. "Post gets final closure plan," (Star Presidian. San Francisco, California, August 16, 1990).

Editorial. "Public meeting to be held on Presidio closure," (Star Presidian. San Francisco, California, September 6, 1990).

Editorial. "New HQ for Sixth US Army," (Star Presidian. San Francisco, California, September 27, 1990).

Editorial. "Army and Interior develop land use plan for Presidio," (Star Presidian. San Francisco, California, October 11, 1990).

Editorial. "What lies ahead for the Presidio," (Star Presidian. San Francisco, California, February 7, 1991).

Editorial. "LAMC begins downsizing," (Star Presidian. San Francisco, California, February 14, 1991).

Editorial. "Civilian personnel closure concerns addressed," (Star Presidian. San Francisco, California, February 21, 1991).

Editorial. "LAMC CG discusses plans for closure," (Star Presidian. San Francisco, California, February 28, 1991).

Editorial. "Civilian RIP regulations outlined," (Star Presidian. San Francisco, California, February 28, 1991).

Editorial. "Base realignments and closures, Selection criteria-second major round," (Star Presidian. San Francisco, California, March 7, 1991).

Editorial. "Coping with closure, Questions and answers: RIFs, Rights, and Transfers." (Star Presidian. San Francisco, California, March 7, 1991).

Editorial. "Questions and answers: RIFs, rights, transfers," (Star Presidian. San Francisco, California, March 14, 1991).

Editorial. "Future use of Letterman facilities studied," (Star Presidian. San Francisco, California, March 14, 1991).

Editorial. "Coping with closure, Civilian health care is a reality as retirees prepare for LAMC closure," (Star Presidian. San Francisco, California, March 21, 1991).

Editorial. "Military medical forum for all military and families," (Star Presidian. San Francisco, California, March 21, 1991).

Editorial. "Senator Roth's 'Early Out' Bill," (Star Presidian. San Francisco, California, March 21, 1991).

Editorial. "USAR C coming on line, (Star Presidian. San Francisco, California, March 28, 1991).

Editorial. "RIP facts: Placement assistance programs," (Star Presidian. San Francisco, California, March 28, 1991).

Editorial. "Coping with Closure-Grade and pay retention after a RIP," (Star Presidian. San Francisco, California, March 28, 1991).

Editorial. "RIP facts: Leaves and severance pay under RIFS," (Star Presidian. San Francisco, California, April 4, 1991).

Editorial. "RIP facts: Health and life insurance," (Star Presidian. San Francisco, California, April 11, 1991).

Editorial. "RIP facts: Retirement issues discussed," (Star Presidian. San Francisco, California, April 18, 1991).

Editorial. "Chaney recommends closures," (Star Presidian. San Francisco, California, April 18, 1991).

Editorial. "Closure Questions-More answers to closure questions," (Star Presidian. San Francisco, California, May 2, 1991).

Editorial. "RIFed employees and unemployment compensation," (Star Presidian. San Francisco, California, May 9, 1991).

Editorial. "Boxer introduces new early-out bill," (Star Presidian. San Francisco, California, May 23, 1991).

Editorial. "Base closure issues—Reader responds to editor's letter," (Star Presidian. San Francisco, California, May 23, 1991).

Editorial. "Job tips," (Star Presidian. San Francisco, California, May 29, 1991).

Editorial. "RIFed Take charge of your future: It's in your hands," (Star Presidian. San Francisco, California, May 30, 1991).

Editorial. "News-More on staffing at USARC," (Star Presidian. San Francisco, California, June 13, 1991).

Editorial. "Sixth Army briefed on downsizing," (Star Presidian. San Francisco, California, June 20, 1991).

Editorial. "Commentary-Severance pay, discontinued service, placement program registration," (Star Presidian. San Francisco. California, June 20, 1991).

Editorial. "LAMC cuts services July 1," (Star Presidian. San Francisco, California, June 27, 1991).

Editorial. "40 Plus Job Searchers," (Star Presidian. San Francisco, California, June 27, 1991).

Editorial. "Commander addresses Army departure confusion," (Star Presidian. San Francisco, California, July 4, 1991).

Editorial. "What to do when expecting a RIP," (Star Presidian. San Francisco, California, July 4, 1991).

Editorial. "Lump Sum Option-To take or take not," (Star Persidian. San Francisco, California, July 18, 1991).

Editorial. "Editorial comment on the LAMC RIP," (Star Presidian. San Francisco, California, July 18, 1991).

Editorial. "RIP hits LAMC," (Star Presidian. San Francisco, California, July 18, 1991).

Editorial. "Retirement 'Catch 62', Beware ye civilians with prior military Service," (Star Presidian. San Francisco, California, August 8, 1991).

Editorial. "DOD proposal for early out incentive pay sent to Congress," (Star Presidian. San Francisco, California, August 15, 1991).

Editorial. "More Catch 62," Your Social Security benefits," (Star Presidian. San Francisco, California, August 15, 1991).

Editorial. "Momentum increasing for early outs," (Star Presidian. San Francisco, California, August 29, 1991).

Editorial. "Congress, DOD debate draw down plan," (Star Presidian. San Francisco, California, August 29, 1991).

Editorial. "RIP actions for HQ, Sixth Army underway," (Star Presidian. San Francisco, California. September 12, 1991).

Editorial. "Military retirees may get greater protection under RIP," (Star Presidian. San Francisco, California, September 19, 1991).

Editorial. "Staffing USARC positions," (Star Presidian. San Francisco, California, September 26, 1991).

Editorial. "Sixth Army RIP briefings underway," (Star Presidian. San Francisco, California, October 3, 1991).

Editorial. "Deactivations signal start of BRAC execution," (Star Presidian. San Francisco, California, November 27, 1991).

Editorial. "Base Closure Hot line established," (Star Presidian. San Francisco, California, November 27, 1991).

Editorial. "Placement assistance under a RIP," (Star Presidian. San Francisco, California, December 19, 1991).

Editorial. "Sixth Army mock RIF's results released," (Star Presidian. San Francisco, California, December 19, 1991).

Zachary Z. Kinney and Bill Roller (Ed), "Bug out Diary: MT. Pinatubo and the Destruction of Clark Air Base," (Creative Designs, Inc., January 1992).

Editorial. "1991 issues-a review and status report," (Star Presidian. San Francisco, California, January 9, 1992).

Editorial. "Commentary: Of cutbacks and closures," (Star Presidian. San Francisco, California, January 16, 1992).

Editorial. "DA announces 1993 institute disestablishment," (Star Presidian. San Francisco, California, June 18, 1992).

Charlene Wear Simmons, Roger Dunstan, and Ken Umbach, "California Military Base Closures," (California Research Bureau, April 1993).

Charles A. Bowsher, Comptroller General of the US, "Military Bases: Analysis of DOD's Recommendations, Selection Process for Closures and Realignments," (GAO, April 15, 1993).

Publishing Company Diane (Ed), "Base Closures: Long and Costly Process of Reducing the Local National Work Force in Germany," (Diane Publishing Company, July 1993).

Raymond W. Cox III, Susan J. Buck, and Betty M. Morgan, "Public Administration in Theory and Practice," (Prentice-Hall, Inc. 1994).

Alan W. Norrie (Ed), "Closure or Critique: New Directions in Legal Theory," (Edinburgh University Press, February 1994).

Publishing Company Diane (Ed), "Defense Base Closure and Realignment Commission: Report to the President (1995)," (Diane Publishing Company, May 1994).

David Rubenson and John R. Anderson, "California Base Closure, Lessons for DOD's Cleanup Program," (The RAND Corporation, January 1995).

Press, Limited Rector (Ed), "Philippine Business and U.S. Base Closures," (Rector Press, Limited, July 1995).

BPI Publishing Services (Ed), "Defense Base Closure and Realignment Commission: 1995 Report to the President," (Diane Publishing Company, July 1995).

Publishing Company Diane (Ed), "Defense Base Closure and Realignment Commission: Report to the President (1995)," (Diane Publishing Company, October 1995).

Michael Dardia, Kevin F. McCarthy, Georges Vernez, and Robert F. Schoeni, "Defense Cutbacks," (The RAND Corporation, March 1996).

Michael Dardia, Georges Vernez, Jesse Malkin, and Kevin F. McCarthy, "Effects of Military Base Closures on Local Communities: A Short-Term Perspective," (The RAND Corporation, March 1996).

Michael Dardia, Kevin F. McCarthy, George Vernez, and Robert F. Schoeni, "Defense Cutback." (The RAND Corporation, March 1996).

Renae F. Broderick (Ed) and National Research Council (Ed), "Issues in Civilian Outplacement Strategies: Proceeding of a Workshop," (National Academy Press, August 1996).

James F. Wiggins and John J. Klotz, "Military Bases: Update on the Status of Bases Closed in 1988, 1991, and 1993," (Diane Publishing Co., November 1996).

Harry E. Taylor (Ed), David A. Schmidt (Ed), and George O. Morse (Ed), "Military Bases: Analysis of DOD's Recommendations and Selection Process for Closures and Realignments," (US General Accounting Office, February 1997).

Diane Publishing Company (Ed), "Military Bases: Letters and Requests Received on Proposed Closures and Realignments," (Diane Publishing Company, February 1997).

Shirley A. Gilley, "Closing Down the American Base at Adak, Alaska: The Social and Psychological Trauma of Relocating Military Families," (Edwin Mellen, Jr., June 1997).

David R. Warren, Barry W. Holman, H. Harvey, and Kay D. Kuhlman, "Military Bases: Lessons Learned from Prior Base Closure Rounds," (Diane Publishing Company, 1998).

Jeffrey A. Drezner and Frank Camm, "Using Process Redesign to Improve DOD's Environmental Security Program: Remediation Program Management," (The RAND Corporation, January 1998).

David S. Sorenson, "Shutting Down the Cold War: The Politics of Military Base Closure," (Martin's Press, Inc., May 1998).

David R. Warren, Barry W. Holman, Marian H. Harvey, and Kay D. Kuhlman, "Military Bases: Lessons Learned from Prior Base Closure Rounds," (Diane Publishing Co., December 1998).

Barry W. Holman, Military Bases: "Review of Sod's 1998 Report on Base Realignment and Closure," (Diane Publishing Company, April 1999).

Editorial. "A Force in Film Meets a Force of Nature," (New York Times. New York, New York, March 30, 2000).

William M. Hix, "Taking Stock of the Army's Base Realignment and Closure Selection Process," (The RAND Corporation, June 2001).

Editorial. "Lawmakers warn of closing too many bases." (US Navy Times Washington, DC, March 31, 2003).

APPENDIX A

Emergency Operations Center Special Mission
Considerations-Presidio of San Francisco Realignment Study

1. References:

   a. Federal Disaster Assistance Administration, Region 9, Final Draft, Federal Earthquake Response Plan, February 1, 1974.

   b. US Army Forces Command Military Assistance to Civil Authorities Plan (MACAP), April 28, 1978.

   c. Public Law 95-124, Earthquake Hazards Reduction Act of 1977, October 7, 1977.

2. The Headquarters, Sixth US Army was responsible in the event of a major earthquake in San Francisco and Bay Area to provide emergency support for all Federal, State, local and volunteer relief agencies with primary responsibility for vital emergency functions as requested by the Disaster Field Office (DFO). Also, the Headquarters, Sixth US Army maintained the capability of providing the primary DFO site for San Francisco County. This site was selected based on the following criteria:

   a. Capacity to accommodate 125 personnel.

   b. Minimum essential communications with expansion capability.

   c. Adequate parking.

   d. Accessibility by land, air (rotary and fixed wing), and water.

   e. Additional facilities nearby.

3. The Headquarters, Sixth US Army was tasked to coordinate and control unilateral and multi-service disaster relief operations throughout the 15-Western States.

4. With the Headquarters, Sixth US Army, the Emergency Operations Center (EOC) was the focal point for the previously mentioned disaster relief operations and for contingencies and exercises outlined in land defense, general war, and mobilization plans.

5. In the event of a presidentially declared or threatened natural disaster or domestic emergency, the Headquarters, Sixth US Army would respond to requests for military support from Federal Agencies having statutory responsibilities for disaster relief by coordinating all DOD resources. The Agencies included:

   a. Federal Disaster Assistance Administration.

   b. Boise Inter agency Fire Center.

   c. US Army Corps of Engineers.

   d. American National Red Cross.

   e. Environmental Protection Agency.

   f. US Coast Guard.

6. Within the natural disaster role, one of the major responsibilities of the Headquarters, Sixth US Army was the coordination and control of all DOD support following an earthquake in San Francisco and Bay Area. Additionally, the FDAA and other Federal Agencies would physically report to the Sixth US Army EOC as the initial location for communicating with the "outside" world and establishing a Federal base of operations.

7. To accomplish the Headquarters, Sixth US Army mission, the EOC was designed and constructed to current requirements to survive the anticipated intensity of and be provided with the following facilities:

   a. General Criteria:

   (1) Hardened location.

   (2) High potential for structural survival.

   (3) Emergency power (60kw generator) with fuel storage.

   (4) Close proximity to radio room and Command Group

   (5) Fresh water.

   (6) Immediate accessibility by land, sea, and air.

   (7) Parking facility.

   (8) Nearby housing for critical EOC personnel.

b. Briefing Room (for 50 personnel; 1000 square feet).

   (1) Suitable for Secret briefings.

   (2) Concrete walls.

   (3) Ventilation system that cannot be monitored.

   (4) Three projection screens and six map boards.

   (5) No windows.

   (6) Three projection booths.

   (7) Acoustic tile.

   (8) Vault type door.

c. Emergency Operations Coordination Center (work area for 20 personnel; 1200 square feet).

   (1) Three map boards.

   (2) Twenty station communication, 1 each Class A and Class C lines.

   (3) Secure for Secret.

   (4) Acoustic tile.

   (5) Must be adjacent to the Emergency Action Office.

d. Emergency Action Office (work area for 3 personnel; 400 square feet).

   (1) One map board.

   (2) Call director phones.

   (3) Close proximity to Emergency Action Console.

   (4) AUTOSEVOCOM.

e. Radio Room (for 2 personnel; 375 square feet)

   (1) Ten each-110 volt AC electrical outlets.

(2) Antenna for FDAA radio which is a Log Periodic Directional Antenna with a 20foot roof mount mast, weight 700 pounds, Main boom length 40 feet. Must have had adequate anchor and turning space.

f. WEST Terminal: Must be constructed as a TOP SECRET facility:

(1) Air conditioned.

(2) Class V vault door.

(3) Concrete walls.

(4) No windows.

(5) Filtered telephone and power lines.

8. Construction of new facilities must have been completed and the structure operational prior to vacating existing facilities to provide the necessary continuity of operation of this vital emergency role.

9. To satisfy the minimum special structural requirements, consideration for movement of the EOC and Command headquarters to Treasure Island must have included the following:

a. Treasure Island, the largest man-made island in the world, was constructed on shoals varying in depth from 2 feet to 27 feet. 19 million cubic yards of sand, silt and clay were placed on the shoals to form a 402-acre island at an elevation of 13 feet above sea level. Subsidence and soil consolidation have reduced the surface fret board to less than 4 feet at mean higher high water (MHHW).

b. Granular soils located beneath the free water surface had a high potential for liquefaction during moderate earthquake conditions (magnitude 6.5). Ground failures are common consequences of liquefaction. Porosity of partially or unconsolidated sub-soils surrounded by water renders the entire soil base in a supersaturated condition. Surface stability was aggravated by the capillary attraction of the subsurface soils.

c. San Francisco and Bay Area, located between the San Andreas and Hayward faults, was likely to experience large earthquakes in the future on the order of the 1906 San Francisco earthquake (8.2 on the Richter scale).

d. A magnitude of this kind would in turn cause ground failure through liquefaction and probably cause structural failure of the proposed EOC and any connecting utilities such as water, electricity, telephone, etc.

e. National Oceanographic and Aviation Administration Study of Seismic threats in the San Francisco Bay Area suggests a moderate quake would cause total or partial failure of the freeway approach routes to San Francisco-Oakland Bay Bridge, that would probably preclude vehicular use.

f. The truss supported side hill road on Yerba Buena Island (leading to Treasure Island) was not expected to survive a moderate intensity quake. The stability of the side hill cut to accommodate this structure suggested excessive rock fall and soil slippage if disturbed by seismic action.

g. An in-depth seismic study was initiated to determine the extent of threat posed to the existing family dwellings, dependent school, and administrative structures now existing on Treasure Island. No additional structures would be planned or constructed until this study was completed. Following this, the provision of Public Law 95-124 (91 Stat 1098) had to be complied with for planned structures. Also, the provisions of California Seismic Construction Codes had to be used as a guide for minimal standards.

h. California highway regulations did not permit transport of explosive devices or hazardous cargo across the San Francisco Bay Bridge. Oversize vehicles would be severely restricted to non-peak hours or totally prohibited.

10. Without the benefit of detailed construction requirements and analyses of existing US Navy facilities, it was premature to draw final conclusions. Based upon the preliminary analysis, the potential relocation to Treasure Island would require extensive new construction, refurbishment of all offered permanent structures, extensive repair or replacement of utilities systems and an exorbitant expenditure of funds. All this effort would still be placed on an island that would probably fail or become inaccessible without boats or helicopter transport. All electrical power and water now enter the island via the Oakland Bay Bridge. In view of its doubtful survival of a seismic occurrence, emergency backup systems would be required for the emergency centers and personnel who survive a major disaster.

11. Because of its doubtful survivability and inaccessibility should an earthquake of moderate to major proportions occur, it appeared inadvisable to construct a structure of such importance on Treasure Island.

APPENDIX B

Questionnaire
Realignment Impact

Q1. What impact would the realignment have on the civilian work force transfers, grade reductions, reductions-in-force, and job eliminations?

A.

Q2. What will be the one-time costs for the US Army to relocate to Treasure Island?

A.

Q3. What will be the savings by operating at Treasure Island? Compare San Francisco operating costs with Treasure Island?

A.

Q4. What would it cost Department of the Interior to maintain the Presidio of San Francisco?

A.

Q5. How would the Headquarters, Sixth US Army operate from Treasure Island if there was an earthquake?

A.

Q6. Was the Oakland Army Base going to be affected by the Presidio of San Francisco realignment?

A.

Q7. How many military and civilian personnel would remain at the Presidio of San Francisco to include the Letterman Army Medical Center and the Letterman Army Institute of Research?

A.

Q8. Why was the US Army keeping the Presidio of San Francisco family housing?

A.

Q9. What has been done to comply with NEPA regarding this realignment?

A.

Q10. With the Presidio of San Francisco closure, how much revenue would be lost to the San Francisco Bay Area?

A.

Q11. Would there be any political considerations in this decision?

A.

Q12. Who would make the final decision to take this action?

A.

Q13. What were NPS plans for the Presidio of San Francisco?

A.

Q14. Where will US Army activities at Fort Baker go?

A.

Q15. What would happen to the US Army Yacht Club?

A.

Q16. What would happen to the golf course on the Presidio of San Francisco?

A.

APPENDIX C

Questionnaire
Position and Personnel Impact

Q1. Number of permanent positions prior to this action?

A. 126 Military and 199 Civilian.

Q2. Number of positions to be eliminated as a result of this action?

A. 21 Military and 127 Civilian.

Q3. Number of position to be transferred from the Headquarters, Sixth US Army during the period of this action?

A. None.

Q4. Number of positions to be transferred to Headquarters, Sixth US Army during the period of this action?

A. None.

Q5. Number of permanent positions remaining at the Headquarters, Sixth US Army after completion of this action?

A. 105 Military and 72 Civilian.

Q6. Number of permanent personnel on board prior to this action?

A. 128 Military and 172 Civilian.

Q7. Estimated normal retirements during the period of this action?

A. 24 Military and 12 Civilian.

Q8. Estimated other retirements (VERA) during the period of this action?

A. Military Not Applicable and 15 Civilian.

Q9. Estimated number of personnel to be placed with other US Army or Federal activities within the commuting area?

A.   Military Not Applicable and 5 Civilian.

Q10. Estimated number of personnel to be placed within other US Army or federal activities outside the commuting area?

A.   Military and Civilian Not Applicable.

Q11. Estimated other attrition during the period of this action?

A.   21 Military and 5 Civilian.

Q12. Estimated number of temporaries to be terminated and/or released as a result of this action?

A.   Military Not Applicable and 4 Civilian.

Q13. Estimated number of employees to be transferred (TOF) to other activities?

A.   8 Military and Civilian Not Applicable.

Q14. Estimated number of employees to be transferred (TOF) to this activity?

A.   30 Military and Civilian Not Applicable.

Q15. Estimated number of employees to be separated by reduction-in-force?

A.   Military Not Applicable and 59 Civilian.

Q16. Estimated number of permanent employees on-board after completion of this action?

A.   105 Military and 72 Civilian.

Q17. Estimated civilian cost reduction?

A. $4 million dollars.

APPENDIX D

Questionnaire
Reduction-in-Force (RIF)

Q Why is the reduction-in-force (RIF) going to take place?

A. The Headquarters, Sixth US Army at the Presidio of San Francisco is losing 127 civilian authorizations effective September 30, 1992.

Q2. How many civilian employees would be involuntarily separated as a result of this action?

A. Current projections indicate that 55 civilians on permanent appointments may be involuntarily separated. In addition, the appointment of four temporary employees is expected to be terminated.

Q3. When would the affected employees be notified that their jobs have been eliminated?

A. Notices would be delivered to affected permanent employees on August 1, 1992 with an effective date no later than September 30, 1992, and to affected temporary employees on August 31, 1992 with an effective date no later than September 30, 1992.

Q4. What would happen to the remaining employees?

A. The remaining employees would stay in positions authorized in the downsized Headquarters, Sixth US Army, n positions at other organizations at the Presidio of San Francisco, at other Federal Agencies, or retirement.

Q5. What would be done for employees who actually lose their jobs?

A. Career employees affected by the reduction-in-force would be given maximum assistance to continue their careers as employees of the Department of Defense or other Federal Agencies. In addition, in cooperation with the Department of Labor and State Unemployment Services, assistance would be given to civilian employees in locating positions in private industry.

Q6.   How does this compare with previous reductions-in-force?

A.   In the past, the Presidio of San Francisco has been fortunate inasmuch as very few civilian employees have been separated involuntarily. The Letterman Army Medical Center and the Letterman Institute of Research have been under a reduction-in-force since March 1990 because of the Base Closure and Realignment Act of 1988. During March 1980, it was announced that 652 civilian positions would be abolished and the center closed by Fiscal Year 1992/95. Since this announcement, the number of involuntarily separated employees had shrunk to 19 because of the Department of Defense Priority Placement Program (PPP), Voluntary Early Retirement Authority (VERA), Job Fairs, Voluntary Retirements, and employees seeking other employment within the US government and private industry.

Q7.   Who decided what positions were to be abolished and/or eliminated?

A.   Changes to the Headquarters, Sixth US Army force structure and budget restrictions were the primary consideration. Management officials of the installation were responsible for identifying manpower spaces to be abolished.

Q8.   What would be done to comply with the potential socioeconomic and environmental impact with regard to this reduction-in-force?

A.   The socioeconomic and environmental impacts were excluded by definition from this analysis as they did not constitute a significant effect with regard to the reduction-in-force of 127 permanent employees with a $4 million dollar payroll and was therefore supported by a Record of Environmental Consideration.

Q9.   Do other installations have to make such cutbacks?

A.   Budget constraints are affecting every US Government Agency.

Q10.   Would there be more reductions-in-force?

A.   The Headquarters, Sixth US Army reduction-in-force was based on projected force structure changes, cuts in programs, projected funded workload, and the President's Fiscal Year 1992 (Fiscal Year 1992 92) budget. If further budget reductions were made, additional personnel reductions would be experienced.

APPENDIX E

Questionnaire
Request for Voluntary Early Retirement Authority (VERA)

Q1. Organization?

A. Headquarters, Sixth US Army.

Q2. Geographic location?

A. Presidio of San Francisco, California.

Q3. Occupational series and/or grade levels?

A. All series and grades represented in the competitive area to include those with special salary rates. Voluntary Early Retirement Authority (VERA) requested for all employees, to include special salary rate employees because these employees occupy positions with occupational series to be affected during the reduction-in-force (RIF). With early retirement, employees with seniority and relatively high retention standings were targeted. Allowing these employees to take advantage of early retirement would provide placement opportunities for less senior employees in the same affected occupational series and minimize the adverse impact of the reduction-in-force.

Q4. Effective date of reductions-in-force?

A. September 3, 1992.

Q5. Time period covered by requested authority?

A. Primary Window: January 1, 1992-January 31, 1992.
Alternative Window: February 1, 1992-February 29, 1992.

Q6. Number of non-temporary employees in the organization covered by requested authority?

A. 168.

Q7. Number of temporary employees covered by requested authority to be terminated prior to the effective date of the reduction-in-force?

Q8. Estimated number of permanent employees who would after attrition be separated by reductions-in-force if early retirement is not approve?

A. 88.

Q9. Estimated number of permanent employees who would be demoted?

A. 5 (7% of remaining permanent authorizations).

Q10. Estimated number of permanent employees who would be transferred to a different local commuting area?

A. None.

Q11. Estimated number of permanent employees who would be eligible for early retirement?

A. 23.

Q12. Estimated number of permanent employees who would accept early retirement?

A. 15.

Q13. Estimated number of permanent employees who would not be separated, demoted, and/or transferred because of the projected early retirements?

A. 7.

Q14. Estimated number of permanent employees who would leave the organization voluntarily before planned effective date of reduction-in-force?

A. 8 (5% of current permanent work force).

Q15. Estimated number of new hires to replace employees who accept early retirement?

A. None.

APPENDIX F

Rights and Benefits of Civilian Employees

All career employees would be given maximum assistance in continuing their careers as employees of the US Government through reassignment to other positions in the Department of Defense (DOD) of other Federal Agencies. In addition, in cooperation with the Department of Labor and State Employment Services, assistance would be given to employees in locating positions in private industry.

Employees whose jobs are eliminated would be given priority rights to other vacant positions in the Department of Defense and other Federal Agencies. They also would be given assistance in locating jobs in private industry if they so desired.

The Department of Defense Priority Placement Program (PPP) provides the principal mechanism for placing affected employees elsewhere within the DOD. Through the Priority Placement Program, the skills of displaced employees were matched with vacant positions as they occur at other activities throughout the DOD and that the employees were willing to work. The job match was accomplished through a computerized referral system operated by the Defense Data Support Center. If the new job involved a move to another location, the costs of moving the employee and household were borne by the US government. If the new job is at a lower grade level, the employee's pay was saved to the maximum extent permitted by law.

Employees were also registered in the Office of Personnel Management's Displaced Employee Program and through this means were given priority consideration for vacancies in other Federal agencies. The State Employment Services provided placement assistance for employees desiring jobs in private industry.

a. Benefits of Employees Who Are Separated: A career employee who was separated by a reduction-in-force (RIF) in most circumstances was entitled by law to either an immediate retirement annuity or severance pay (but not both). The amount of annuity or severance pay was determined by age and length of service.

b. Severance Pay: A career employee who was not eligible for immediate annuity and was separated by RIF was generally entitled to severance pay unless the employee was already drawing a US government annuity from some other service, such as a military service retirement. The maximum severance pay allowance is one year's pay. Severance payments would cease when the employee receiving them was re-employed by the US government. Severance pay was based upon age and length of service. An employee would receive a week's salary for each year of the first 10 years of service; 2 weeks' salary for each year of service after 10 years; and an age adjustment allowance of 10-percent of the total basic severance allowance for each year by which the employee's age exceeds 40:

(1) Retirement: Optional Retirement Annuities-Civil Service Retirement System (CSRS). Employees meeting any of the following combinations of age and length of service could retire on immediate annuities without any reduction to age.

AGE	YEARS OF SERVICE
62	5
60	30
55	32
*Any	5

* If totally disabled for service in the position occupied.

(2) Retirement: Intermediate Retirement Annuities-Federal Employees Retirement System (FERS). Employees who were covered under FERS were eligible to retire at any time if the following conditions were met:

AGE	YEARS OF SERVICE
Any	30
60	20
*	10+

* Minimum Retirement Age (MRA): Unlike the CSRS that has fixed retirement ages, the FERS requires that the employee reach a certain age before receiving reduced voluntary retirement benefits with thirty years of service. The MRA varies from age 55 to 59 and would be determined based on the year of birth. Under FERS the employee could elect voluntary retirement with a reduced annuity that was available at the MRA with at least 10 years of service. The benefits were reduced 5-percent per year for each year payment begins before age 62. This reduction would continue throughout the annuitant's life.

Discontinued Service Retirement Annuities. Employees separated involuntarily were entitled to an immediate discontinued service annuity if they had 25 years of service (at any age), or if they had 20 years of service and are 50 years of age. The annuity of a CSRS employee who retired under age 55 were permanently reduced 2-percent for each year they were under age 55. The annuity of a FERS employee who retired under age 55 was not reduced; however, they were ineligible to receive the Special Retirement Supplement until they reached the MRA. This benefit approximated the proportion of a full career social security benefit earned while employed under FERS and it continued until age 62.

c. Other benefits:

(1) Life Insurance. Employees who were under 65 years of age, and separated on an immediate annuity may have elected to retain their basic life insurance coverage (that equals their current salary plus $2,000). This insurance was free of charge to employees and retirees over age 65. The basic life insurance coverage continued at its present level until age 65 when it starts reducing at the rate of 2-percent a month until it reaches 25-percent of the original value. Employees may have elected to have coverage of 50-percent or 100-percent of the basic insurance amount. In such cases, the full cost of the additional protection was deducted from the employee's annuity, beginning at retirement and continuing for life or until the election was canceled. Employees who were not retiring on an immediate annuity had the option, within 31 days, to convert to another life insurance plan, without medical examination, for which they pay the full cost.

(2) Health Insurance. Most employees separated on an immediate annuity met the eligibility requirements to continue in the same health insurance plan by which they were covered as active employees with no change in benefits or US government contributions. The cost may have been deducted from the annuity payments. Employees separated who are not eligible for an immediate annuity or who did not meet the minimum service requirements for continuation of their health insurance program received a 31 day temporary extension of coverage during which time they could convert to a non-group contract without evidence of insurability by the carrier of the plan in which they were enrolled. Employees converting to such plans pay the full cost plus an administrative charge equal to 2-percent of the total cost.

d. Leave. Employees separated received a lump sum payment for their accumulated annual leave. Unused leave generally could accumulate up to a total of 30 days. For those CSRS employees who retired on an immediate annuity, the number of days of sick leave accumulated was credited toward the computation of their years of service for a retirement annuity. If an employee was physically incapacitated at the time of proposed separation, the separation date was extended until the employees recover or sick leave was exhausted, whichever came first.

e. Deferred Annuities and Retirement Contribution Refunds. If an employee was separated before attaining eligibility for an immediate annuity, the employee could have elected to have deductions refunded or leave the money in the retirement fund. If the money was left in the retirement fund, and the employee has a minimum of 5 years of creditable service, the employee would be entitled to a deferred annuity at age 62.

f. Homeowners Assistance. Under the Homeowners Assistance Program, career employees separated at bases being closed (in whole or in part) in situations where the real estate market was determined to be severely affected by a base closure may receive assistance in one of three ways:

- By cash payment from the US government to cover part of the loss resulting from a private sale of the home.

- By sale of the house to the US government.

- By reimbursement of losses incurred as a result of foreclosure of a mortgage.

APPENDIX G

Questionnaire
Interpretation of Organizational and Management
Goals and Management Practices

The questionnaire format was modified from another management survey to provide information concerning organizational and management goals and practices in the Headquarters, Sixth US Army. It was given to managers, professionals, technicians, and administrative employees for statistical accuracy. A total of 100 out of 172 employees in the Headquarters, Sixth US Army were chosen for the survey. Most of the 72 that were not considered were military officers who most probably would not answer correctly because of a conflict of interest or fear of career reprisal that would bias the questionnaire. Of the 100 workers that were asked, 69 responded. Their answers formed a statistical array with parity between technical and administrative personnel. There were no right or wrong answers, and there were no questions designed to trick or deceive respondents. The author only asked that respondents give, to the best of their ability, their personal opinions and attitudes. Under no circumstances was any employee identified in reporting the results of the survey.

PART A - ORGANIZATIONAL GOALS	MGR	PROF	TECH/ ADMIN
A-1 What in your opinion was the principal (i.e., single most important) goal or objective of your activity?			
• To achieve maximum results and effectiveness.	1	1	23
• To achieve a satisfactory level of results and effectiveness	3	2	3
• To give a satisfactory service or produce a high quality product at a competitive cost.	1	4	5
• To be a leader in the field.	1	0	0
• To stay in existence.	0	2	2
TOTAL RESPONSES:	6	30	33

A-2. Who (i.e., what person or group) established this principal goal?

• Department of Defense.	0	0	0
• Department of the Army.	0	0	0
• US Army Forces Command.	1	2	6
• Headquarters, Sixth US Army.	5	28	27
• Presidio Garrison.	0	0	0
TOTAL RESPONSES:	6	30	33

A-3. Do you agree with the choice of a principal goal or do you believe that some other objective would be more realistic?

• Agree.	6	27	31
• Other.	0	3	2
TOTAL RESPONSES:	6	30	33

PART B - MANAGEMENT GOALS

B-1. From the standpoint of established policies, what do you believe is the single most important purpose of the Headquarters, Sixth US Army and the Presidio Garrison?

• The use of management primarily for the purpose of reducing of controlling cost.	1	11	4
• The use of management primarily to establish and/or implement policies.	2	11	15
• Overlapping the two categories indicated above.	1	4	5
• Planning activities.	1	3	5
• Other.	0	1	2
• Don't know.	1	0	2
TOTAL RESPONSES:	6	30	33

B-2. Do you personally agree with this purpose, or do you believe some other purpose should be considered?

•	Agree.	5	28	27
•	Should be less emphasis on cost reduction.	1	2	5
•	Other.	0	0	1

TOTAL RESPONSES: 6   30   33

B-3. Do you believe that it is necessary to "control" costs in your activity? Why? (Wouldn't employees and managers try to reduce costs as a normal practice even without "controls?")

•	Yes, it is necessary to "control" costs because employees will either be deliberately wasteful, or lazy, or will at best, make no real effort to reduce costs on their own.	4	10	8
•	Yes, it is necessary to "control" costs because management (but not employees) might try to reduce costs on their own but would not have the necessary information to do so.	12	14	8
•	No, it is not necessary to "control" costs-employees would do better without such controls."	0	0	7

TOTAL RESPONSES: 6   30   33

PART C -MANAGEMENT POLICIES

C-1. Please give your definition of the term management authority?"

•	Strictly "traditional" definition (i.e., authority goes with the position and is delegated from above.)	4	23	21

313

• Some awareness of the modern organizational theory view of authority as that which others accept.	1	7	5
• Don't know.	1	0	7
TOTAL RESPONSES:	6	30	33

C-2. Do you believe that you understand established policies-both in general and particular as they relate to your job?

• Yes.	5	0	28
• No	1	29	5
TOTAL RESPONSES:	6	30	33

C-3. In your activity, what is the major objective or policy?

• To control costs.	3	12	9
• To measure performance.	1	8	11
• To provide data to management.	1	8	10
• For planning purposes.	1	2	3
• Other.	0	0	0
TOTAL RESPONSES:	6	30	33

C-4. How would you rate the importance of policies in use at the Presidio of San Francisco in terms of their contributions to the accomplishment of organizational goals discussed in Question A-1?

• Extremely important-makes a substantial contribution to mission accomplishment.	3	25	21
• Important-make a fairly substantial contribution to mission accomplishment.	2	3	7
• Not too important-makes some contribution to mission accomplishment.	1	1	2

• Unimportant-makes very little contribution to mission accomplishment.	0	1	3

TOTAL RESPONSES: 6 30 33

C-5   Please indicate in what ways you believe policies make the contribution discussed in Question C-3?

• Emphasize the idea of control.	1	10	9
• Emphasize the idea of management and/or providing a "tool" for management.	5	20	23
• Other.	0	0	1

TOTAL RESPONSES: 6 30 33

C-6.   Do you believe policies in use in your activity contribute to the accomplishment of the "other goals" discussed in Part A?

• Yes.	5	30	26
• No.	1	0	7

TOTAL RESPONSES: 6 30 33

C-7.   Do you believe that your activity would be better off if it discontinued the use of policies?

• Yes.	5	30	27
• No.	1	0	6

TOTAL RESPONSES: 6 30 33

C-8.   If policies were discontinued by your activity, do you believe that it would have a favorable or unfavorable effect on each of the following:

(a)   Attitudes of Professionals toward Managers?

• Favorable effect.	2	7	4

•	Unfavorable effect.	3	20	26
•	No particular effect.	1	3	3

TOTAL RESPONSES:	6	30	33

(b)   Attitudes of Technicians towards Managers?

•	Favorable effect.	1	9	7
•	Unfavorable effect.	2	14	22
•	No particular effect.	3	7	4

TOTAL RESPONSES:	6	30	33

(c)   Attitudes of Managers toward Professionals, Technicians, and Administrative Employees?

•	Favorable effect.	2	0	3
•	Unfavorable effect.	2	14	19
•	No Particular effect.	2	16	11

TOTAL RESPONSES:	6	30	33

(d)   Attitudes of Supervisors toward their own job?

•	Favorable effect.	2	3	4
•	Unfavorable effect.	4	22	23
•	No particular effect.	5	6	6

TOTAL RESPONSES:	6	30	33

(e)   Attitudes of Professionals, Technicians, and Administrative Employees toward Managers?

•	Favorable effect.	3	17	23
•	No particular effect.	1	5	3

TOTAL RESPONSES:	6	30	33

C-9.   In terms of accomplishing the major goals and objectives of the activity, do you believe that it would be better for management to become more or less lenient in analyzing and enforcing policies?

•	More lenient.	1	0	0
•	Less lenient.	4	25	27
•	About right as it is.	1	0	3
•	Don't know.	0	5	3

TOTAL RESPONSES: 6   30   33

C-10. Since policies represent different work processes, some variances are bound to appear. Which of the following do you believe is a better method in establishing policies?

•	When in doubt, establish policies above what is expected and expect some unfavorable variances as normal.	3	24	25
•	When in doubt, establish policies below what is expected and expect some favorable variances as normal.	2	4	5
•	When in doubt, establish policies on what is expected and expect some favorable and unfavorable variances as normal.	1	2	3

TOTAL RESPONSES: 6   30   33

C-11. In your activity, does a supervisor's performance depend on complying with policies? Does it affect promotion and salary progress?

•	Quite important.	2	2	3
•	Important to an extent--but only one of a number of factors considered.	2	6	8
•	Not important.	1	0	2
•	Don't know.	1	22	20

TOTAL RESPONSES: 6   30   33

C-12. Who is primarily responsible for establishing policies in your activity?

- Department of Defense.   0   0   0
- Department of the Army.   0   0   0
- US Army Forces Command.   2   9   10
- Headquarters, Sixth US Army   4   21   20
- Presidio Garrison.   0   0   0
- Don't know.   0   0   3

TOTAL RESPONSES: 6   30   33

C-13. Do you believe that policies in use in your Agency tend to strengthen or weaken management authority?

- Strengthen.   4   24   27
- Weaken.   0   0   0
- No particular effect.   2   6   6

TOTAL RESPONSES   6   30   33

C-14. What do you believe is the general attitude of managers, professionals, technicians, and administrative employees as to the use of policies as a "control" technique in your activity?

(a)   Managers:

- In favor.   5   30   33
- Not in favor.   1   0   0

TOTAL RESPONSES: 6   30   33

(b)   Professionals:

- In favor.   5   27   27
- Not in for   1   3   6

TOTAL RESPONSES: 6   30   33

318

(c)   Technicians/Administrative Employee:

•	In favor.	4	18	17
•	Not in favor.	1	9	12
•	Not aware of the system or indifferent.	1	3	4

TOTAL RESPONSES:	6	30	33

C-15. If your answer to Question 14 indicated a generally favorable attitude, please indicate why you believe this attitude prevails. If your answer indicates a generally unfavorable attitude, please indicate why you believe this attitude exists and what steps might be taken to improve it.

(a) Reasons why managers are in favor of policies.

•	Realize that policies are a "tool" that helps them reduce uncertainty and do a better job.	3	24	26
•	Prefer to work for an office where there is discipline.	1	3	4

TOTAL RESPONSES:	4	27	30

(b)   Reasons why managers are not in favor of policies.

•	Have no respect for policies because they have found too many errors in the past.	1	0	0
•	Don't like to be "controlled." Without policies there would be less pressure and more satisfaction.	1	3	3

TOTAL RESPONSES:	2	3	3
TOTAL (a) and (b)	6	30	33

(c)   Reasons why professionals, technicians, and administrative employees
       are in favor of policies.

•	Prefer to work for an office that controls production and/or behavior in some way.	1	7	10
•	Like to know how they are doing. Policies provide a goal and a challenge.	2	10	11

TOTAL RESPONSES:	3	17	21

(d)   Reasons why professionals, technicians, and administrative employees
       are not in favor of policies.

•	Don't like to be "controlled." Without policies there would be less pressure and more satisfaction.	1	8	9
•	Workers distrust the system.	1	2	3
•	Employees are indifferent to (or unaware of) the system.	0	3	0

TOTAL RESPONSES:	3	13	12

TOTAL (c) AND (d)	6	30	33

C-16. Do you believe those policies in use in your activity sometimes
       encourage employees to take action that they perceive to be in their
       own best interest, but that is not in the best interest of the activity?

•	Yes.	6	30	19
•	No.	0	0	8
•	Don't know.	0	0	6

TOTAL RESPONSES:	6	30	33